ALL LIGHTS ON
IN THE
MASTER'S HOUSE

By Jason C.N. Jordan

The above painting is called the *Baptism of Christ* and
was done in 1710 by Flemish artist Aert de Gelder.

Jason C. N. Jordan
ALL LIGHTS ON IN THE MASTER'S HOUSE / Jordan

National Library of Australia Cataloguing-in-Publication data:

Jordan, Jason C. N.
All lights on in the Master's house.

ISBN 1 921019 67 0.

1. Bible - Criticism, interpretation, etc. 2. Religion - History. I. Title.

220.6

Printed on demand and distributed by:
Booksurge Publishing
143-149 Abbotsford Street,
North Melbourne 3051
http://www.booksurgepublishing.com.au

Layout by Michael Hanrahan
http://www.mhps.com.au

Cover Art and Design by Jason Jordan

Address all inquires about this book to:

Flying Chariot Ministries

58 Heather Rd,
Winmalee 2777
NSW AUST

Contents

Foreword

FOR HUNDREDS OF YEARS the Bible has been interpreted by scholars who have had a particular way of understanding the text. This interpretation has been passed down from scholar to student without the student ever considering a different interpretation of the Biblical text and to do so would be considered theological mutiny.

But, many times these interpretations conflict with physical evidence and unexplained mysteries found around the world. In my years of research into the Ancient Hebrew language of the Bible I have come to realize that the "sanitized" translations and interpretations of the Biblical text are frequently inadequate in their portrayal of the Biblical text.

If the Bible contains images of advanced technology, either of the ancients or in their prophetic view of the future, we would not easily recognize them in the text as the authors were writing the account from the perspective of their own limited knowledge of these "creatures."

It is time for a revolution in Biblical interpretation and *All lights on in the Master's house* is a unique work that opens the door to a new approach to how we read and understand the Bible.

While I cannot say that I agree with all of the conclusions of this book I can say that it has caused me to question my own method of interpretation of the Biblical text. Mr. Jordan has done a remarkable job of providing us with a glimpse into the world of the future through the eyes of those who lived in the past.

Jeff A. Benner
Ancient Hebrew Research Center

Acknowledgements

Without the encouragement, advice and invaluable assistance from the following people this work would not have been possible. I would like to thank Clinton Boreham for his many questions and challenges, Julius Timmerman for his meticulous proof-reading, Stan Deyo for his much welcomed correspondence and his surprising accessibility, Jude Brown who introduced me to the Sacred Name, Patrick Cooke for his kind words, John and Matthew Trotter for their encouragement after reading a flimsy early draft of this work.

Thanks to Glenda and Morrie Hollman and Dallas and Warren Wichman for their loving guidance in Torah and helping my wife and I remove our Greco-Roman spectacles. Thank you all for introducing me to Rabbi Robert Miller, whose extensive teachings have helped maintain the Scriptural thrust of this work.

Respect and acknowledgement must also go out to authors, Ann Madden Jones, Lew White and Jeff A. Benner whose works unveiled so much astonishing truth.

I praise YHWH for my beautiful wife, Shabnam. Her endearing patience and tireless support kept me going when I had doubts about releasing this work. She has comfortably stood by my side when in the company of alienating stares and hostile objection and for that I am grateful.

Warning

Some of the information contained within this work is confronting and consequently should be approached with extreme caution. Though some ideas and opinions presented are based on careful research and independent literary investigation, this author discourages a reader to be completely convinced of a subject without subsequently seeking additional verification.

To get the most out of this work it is suggested that the reader have access to a good encyclopedic dictionary, a study Bible and a Bible Concordance. Neither the author nor the publisher can be held responsible for the misuse of any information contained herein.

The author of this work is not affiliated with any church denomination. He is a Nazarene / Notsri Israelite (offshoot branch watchman) who serves YHWH (God) through the redeemed finished work of the resurrected Messiah Yahushua (Jesus).

Use of the New King James Version

Unless otherwise noted I have used the NKJV despite its many errors. I have done this to prove that a modern translation can be useful. I recommend the following Scriptures to the discerning student:

The Restoration Scriptures – Sacred Name Edition (RSNE)
Compiled by Rabbi Moshe Yoseph Koniuchowsky

The Hebrew Roots Version Scriptures (HRV)
Compiled by James S. Trimm

The Scriptures
Published by the Institute of Scripture Research (South Africa)

As most Christians do not commonly use the above versions I recommend retaining and using popular Bibles such as the NIV, KJV, NASB and NKJV for initial sharing as an unfamiliar book may distance a potential individual or audience.

"My people are destroyed from lack of knowledge. Because you have rejected knowledge, I also reject you as my priests; because you have ignored the law (Torah) of your God (Elohim), I also will ignore your children." – **Hosea 4:6**

"How can you say, we are wise, for we have the law (Torah) of the LORD (YHWH), when actually the lying pen of the scribes has handled it falsely?" – **Jeremiah 8:8**

Introduction

It has been my observation that many aspects of the Scriptures appear to be overlooked by mainstream church organisations that claim they are 100% Bible based. These same churches cling to many concepts that have no biblical basis beyond that of man-made tradition. My initial suspicions, aroused from boredom and the unshakable feeling of receiving a watered-down version of the Scriptures, turned to genuine concern after I began digging through the Bible myself. I decided to look further into the issue by firstly finding a congregation that at least adhered to basic Bible principles. Secondly I began studying the protocols of accepted religious colleges and churches alike and cross-referenced them with the revived congregation in the New Testament. What you will read in this book are some of my findings. It is a culmination of biblical information that is either seldom dealt with, ignored outright or deliberately misinterpreted by the church.

It is not my intention in writing this book to point the finger at anyone, but rather show what has happened and is still happening, and to shine lights on parts of the Scripture that are usually kept in the dark. I have attempted to reveal these things in a fresh non-religious way, with the ultimate goal being to glorify the Creator and bring people to know His Son. In the pursuit of these findings I have developed the definite opinion (though it sounds cliché) that truth is stranger than fiction. The events in our true history are so rich, wondrous, and spectacular, that the details of their unfolding over time pale the visual grandeur of the *Lord of the Rings* imagery into insignificance. It is almost as if the current interpretations of stories and events in the Bible (while not necessarily being drastically wrong) are foremost designed to steer people away from the truth and bore them to tears in the process.

Let me take you on a journey to places in the Scripture that Christians seldom go, as we look at forgotten technologies, super-human beings, suppressed history and the end result of current trends revealed centuries before. Hold on to your faith as I switch on all the lights in the Master's house.

Chapter One

Part One
Sifting Through the Rubble

THERE ARE LITERALLY thousands of different religions and philosophies scattered throughout the world today. There can be little blame placed on a person who is bewildered and disinterested by the concept of religion when there are so many religions whose ideals conflict with each other and even those that are broadly similar are broken down into hundreds of denominations that focus and observe specific concepts. Which one is right? Are a few of them right? Are they all wrong? Does religion help us know God? Is it all just a big business? Are we going to an eternal fiery lake if we don't choose the right one and commit to it? Which ones if any stand out from the rest, and if so, for what reason? Before I answer any of these questions it is important to lay the foundation of the reality of people's mindsets in this current age.

First of all you have my sympathies if you have come to a point where you've drawn the conclusion that there must be more to life than earning money to maintain a comfortable lifestyle while entertaining yourself by whatever means possible. You might have been generally happy, but realised that your happiness was based on circumstance or you might have had a shake up in your life that led you to start thinking about new issues. Whoever you are and whatever stage you're at, there is not a human being alive who, at one time or another, has not wondered about the cosmos, its origins and one's place in the universe. But for the majority of people, these thoughts often evolve into baseless emotionally driven opinion or are conveniently washed away in a sea of diversion.

Society today is driven by the distractions of entertainment and consumerism. Massive environmentally sealed shopping malls are the churches of the future. People wander through miles of marble flooring self-administering retail therapy. Buying stuff gives them a temporary high and makes them feel good, but this sensation is short lived. Looking around at people today, I think that a vast majority of the first world population feel that life should be like a theme park. They pay their hard earned money at the gates expecting to be treated to thrills and rides, exotic foods, live performances and daring spectacles, all culminating in an elaborate fireworks display at the end of the day. If a ride is closed or there is a disruption in the day's proceedings, tempers can reach boiling point. Nobody is willing to have their time of fun shortened or cancelled after they paid such an exorbitant price to get in. There is that sense of "entertain me" in people's attitudes today. We have this awareness that extends little further than ourselves with little or no time for other people. If you don't believe me, just put this book down, head outside and go out of your way to help someone and watch (though they will be grateful) how perplexed and confused they will be as they struggle to pinpoint the motives of your action.

One evening, at the local pub, a frail old man confronted me. After initially wanting him to leave me alone, I managed to listen long enough to work out this guy needed someone to seriously talk to. During our conversation it became apparent that he could barely stand up, let alone walk. I knew there were no taxis running at such a late hour and I became concerned as to how this guy was going to get home. So I offered to drive him to his house, have a coffee and meet his dog. It was one of the most moving experiences I ever had as I listened to this man, struggling through painful tears, tell me his life story. It woke me up. Earlier that evening I heard him verbally wrestling with the concept of this young fellow helping him. He kept asking me, "Why are you helping me? Why are you helping me?" He eventually accused me of being an angel. I'd been accused of many things before, but never an angel. I spent some time convincing him otherwise.

There is a self-centeredness that permeates the air these days. People are looking out for number one. I can't help you with your problem; I have enough of my own. The fact is we all have our fears and doubts, losses and let downs, disappointments and grief in our lives and we labour under a misconception that money or success will cure it all. The fact is nothing you can do will ensure a life devoid of trouble. Distractions are the antidote for life's hurdles, which morph into addictions that intensify the illusion of escape. The most commonly visible distractions are sport and work. Work can engulf a person's life to an extreme degree. A friend told me the following piece of information that illustrates this perfectly. He said contrary to popular belief the highest number of fatalities in an office building fire does not result from people who are oblivious of the crisis or trapped etc. It actually results from people staying at their desks and literally ignoring the alarms so they can back up all the information on their computers before they leave. Victims are sometimes found on their knees, shriveled and looking up, with their hands melted to their keyboards.

The other most common distraction came to my attention one night when I was with two friends. Both of them were avid football fans so our conversation gravitated to their favourite subject. My small interest in and little knowledge of the topic meant I drifted to the avid listener position. I began to see an enthusiasm and energy in their words as they commented on tactics and new rulings. I could see the passion they had for the sport. They displayed the same level of excitement that I have seen in some Christians when they talk about God. In fact if you were to change a few critical words in their exchange they would have sounded a bit like two learned theologians in deep discussion.

No doubt you've heard the phrase "society's to blame," and while that maybe true, there are countless factors that have been gently administered into us over the years that are responsible for the confusion and disinterest we have for religion, church or God. Life is so fast paced now with the Internet, mobile phones, and the vanishing weekend. There is an emphasis on us to buy now, pay later, eat fast food, bank from home, claim instant rewards, you need this, and you need that. To function comfortably families need both parents to be working fulltime. I remember always being looked after by my mum and having her there after school. The word childcare was rarely used when I was growing up. Those days are gone. Now it's a fully-fledged industry with armies of trained nannies knowing whether little Jessie likes to eat chicken or not when her real parents haven't got a clue. People's values have shifted and you don't have to be Einstein to work out that it is for the worst. Certain changes and rulings have spiralled so far out of control in the education and law system that they have fostered a generation with little or no regard for anything beyond that which they can already see, potentially own, or gain immediate benefit from.

When I was at school I was a fairly disruptive kid, but whenever I was threatened with the cane or the metre ruler I would usually settle down. Now with any form of physical punishment withdrawn from schools it is virtually impossible to teach discipline. I can remember often quitting whatever I was up to when the teacher simply mentioned the word "cane." Now without that tool available and no form of physical contact permissible, teachers' hands are literally tied. I have even heard that some kindergartens do not allow teachers to hug children at all now, and the worst an uncontrollable child or student can expect is being sent out of class or sent home. Pick up a newspaper and pay attention to the more domestic articles and you'll see an interesting regularity of stories about parents in trouble with the law for whacking their kids. Articles about parents being charged over smacking their children are becoming more frequent as are reports of children taking their parents to court. Belting a child for being disobedient was the order of the day when I was a kid and now not only are teacher's hands tied, but the parents of the child as well. In effect the government's role has crept into the very lounge room of the modern-day family and withdrawn a basic tool of parenting that without it, is seeing a growing number of children receiving unnecessary medication. Granted, the physical disciplining of children was being abused by some parents, probably recipients of the same treatment, but a standard rule of measure such as not putting a hand to a child at all stands in stark contrast to **Proverbs 23:13-14; "Do not withhold** *correction from a child, for if you beat him with a rod, he will not die. You shall beat him with a rod, and deliver his soul from hell."*

Another observation worth making is at your local park. The odds are it will be a barren wasteland, which will probably have more to do with parents not having enough time to spend with their kids or public liability than because of crime. Where are all the kids? On their Play Stations, watching movies, or on the Internet, all perched before these things in stony silence, which help perpetuate the declining rate of social and physical skills in young adults.

And amidst all this we are supposed to gain comfort in the thought that we are a technologically advanced society that does not have to deal with half the issues our ancestors faced as the frontier of sciences moves us steadily toward a better tomorrow. The truth is that technological advancement and science is used whenever possible to erode and diminish the existence of God and in so doing erode a base value system that is never meant to change. Though necessary in their functionality, technology and science are often portrayed in a way that can confuse people when they try to approach the question of an interventionist God. Put simply, technological advancement changes us only in the same way that cannibals, who might have formerly eaten with their hands, later eat the same thing with a knife and fork. We still have the same drives and needs as people who lived thousands of years ago. Apparatus that make life more efficient or convenient cannot and will not ever change the core of our being. Science is a fascinating subject and extensive research and experimentation has yielded much understanding in many areas, but while science may tell us HOW things work it will never answer the question WHY things work; as in what initiates the divine spark that sets the ball rolling.

There is a god alive in all these things today; he is called "the god of confusion," and he's working overtime. Endless hours can be spent in intellectual debate over all the levels of society that have become entangled in his tentacles, inevitably followed with the appropriate suggestions and solutions to remove them. This god, though not specifically named, relates to an age-old subject. It forms the type of talk that inhabits the conversation of a group of friends who stand around a BBQ on a Sunday afternoon solving the world's problems. In the end someone usually trots out the hapless question, "what's the world coming to?" This work will attempt to answer this question and in the process investigate some critical issues that are avoided or deliberately misinterpreted by both church and government institutions.

In an ancient Greek story, the god Theseus enters a complex underground maze to vanquish a vicious Minotaur. Before his descent, the goddess Aphrodite fastens one end of a ball of wool to the entrance and the other to his waist. After slaying the beast Theseus is able to retrace his steps with the help of the wool and make his way out of the labyrinth. Today human technology has overcome the Minotaur, but man having abandoned the ball of wool, still wanders about the complex labyrinth of life looking in vain for its meaning. Amazingly the wool is still attached to mankind's waist, but few bother to let it be their guide. By simply tracing back to its origin we can find the true answer to all things and be free of this network of misinformation and confusion. Until the orthodox academic world accepts the fact that our ancient ancestors knew things about the cosmos that are only now beginning to be rediscovered, the truth will continue to elude us. Making an honest attempt to trace one's belief back to a point of origin can often determine if that belief is worth defending.

Years ago, when I was at a job, I observed an interesting incident. A staff member produced an electronic toy that sang, danced and played music. The first question that a curious onlooker asked was, "where did you get that?" The person wanted to know its origin. If we see something interesting it is inevitably followed by this question in our minds: "where was it from?"

Many Perspectives – One Truth

It has been widely accepted that all the world's diverse cultures and beliefs originated from the same initial source. One binding similarity appears in the creation stories of almost every ancient society. Take for example Noah's flood.

∞   In Greek mythology Zeus flooded the planet.

∞   In Roman mythology Jupiter flooded the planet.

8

∞ In Scandinavian mythology Oden flooded the planet from the blood of a defeated god's wound.

∞ In Celtic mythology Heaven was a giant who was cut into many pieces, which caused the planet to be flooded with blood.

∞ In Lithuanian mythology the god Pramzimas sent two giants to flood the planet.

∞ In Welsh mythology a lake burst that flooded all the lands.

∞ In Mayan mythology the gods Gucumatz and Hurricane flooded the land after they became displeased with early human prototypes.

∞ In Egyptian mythology, the *Book of the Dead* records that the world was flooded because of ongoing hostilities, mass slaughter and oppression.

∞ In Indian Vedic mythology a man named Manu was instructed by the fish god Vishnu to prepare a sea-vessel before a great flood.

∞ In Sumerian mythology the god Enlil flooded the planet after being angered by the persistent noise of overpopulated human cities.

Interestingly the word "myth" at one time simply meant "ancient story" or "story of unclear origin." *The Oxford Dictionary of English Folklore* states: "Myths are stories about divine beings, generally arranged in a coherent system; they are revered as true and sacred; they are endorsed by rulers and priests; and closely linked to religion."

The Athenian philosopher Plato originally coined the word "mythologia," to distinguish between the accounts of gods and the accounts of men. This word later developed into a term that carried a distinction between imaginative accounts and factual accounts. While these fantastic stories may have evolved over the centuries they should never be dismissed as tales that originated completely from an individual's imagination. The gods of myth did exist and the Scriptures do make clear mention of such mighty beings. Genesis 6 clearly establishes a period where disobedient angels procreated with the "daughters of men," giving rise to a race of beings that spread much influence on the face of the earth. The myths and legends that the average Christian has been conditioned to dismiss as fiction are, however loosely knit together, records of these "mighty men of renown."

The ancient Hebrews had the strictest regime of accurately preserving written documents. It is perhaps for this reason that the book we now call the Bible, while still containing many translational flaws, represents the most distinguished authority on the beginnings of mankind. Even the act of creation itself is unapologetically recorded with a level of complexity that elevate it clearly above any other books that make the same or similar claims. Beyond that, the Creator of which it speaks distinguishes Himself above any other god by physically appearing to His entire nation to disseminate His eternal law[1]. *Exodus 19:9-11; "And the Lord said to Moses, 'Behold, I come to you in the thick cloud, that the people may hear when I speak with you, and believe you forever.' So Moses told the words of the people to the Lord. Then the Lord said to Moses, 'Go to the people and consecrate them today and tomorrow, and let them wash their clothes. And let them be ready for the third day. For on the third day the <u>Lord will come down upon Mount Sinai in the sight of ALL the people.</u>"* This account was a national revelation and surprisingly is acknowledged in some capacity by three of the most conflicting religions in the world today. They are Christianity, Islam and Judaism.

Interestingly these three major religions recognise and revere the earliest biblical character to be blessed by God – Abraham. They share many similar foundations, but at certain points depart from or adhere to subsequent teachings. Nonetheless an expectation of a deliverer, whether having already arrived or yet to arrive, is shared as a central theme. Islam departs drastically from many biblical principles at the teachings of Muhammad. Christianity departs drastically from many biblical principles at the influence of Emperor Constantine and Orthodox Judaism refuses to accept the credentials of Jesus who is accepted in a greater or lesser capacity by the former two.

---

1   In this context I refer to the Torah, which is God's eternal revelation, teaching and counsel.

All other recognised religions (whose origins can be clearly traced) are based on one individual's perspective of God's requirements. This statement includes all other known offshoot sects from the above three faiths. To arrange a fully comprehensive list to support this observation would require several volumes. Here are just a handful of religions (as they are practiced today) that were based off the philosophies (whether whole or in part) of a single founder that have not, to date, been subsequently corroborated by a public appearance of their god to all current members:

Religion		**Founder (or Chief Founder)**
Christianity	–	Emperor Constantine
Islam	–	Muhammad
Sikhism	–	Guru Nanak
Mormonism	–	Joseph Smith
Buddhism	–	Siddhartha Gautama (Buddha)
Jehovah's Witness	–	Charles Taze Russell
Seventh Day Adventism	–	William Miller
Zoroastrianism	–	Zoroaster
Confucianism	–	Chiu King (Confucious)
Taoism	–	Lao-tzu
Hare Krishna	–	Chaitanya Mahaprabhu
Shi'ites	–	Abdullah bin Saba'a

Jesus Christ does not qualify as a founding father or as a nationally witnessed deity because he never implemented any additional rulings by his own will *(John 6:38)* and nothing that he said was subsequently corroborated by an appearance of his Father to every follower in one sitting. Contrary to popular theological teaching, Jesus did not come to bring about a new religion, but restore men to the one true faith of old (Though it was certainly new to the people of his day). Shintoism and Hinduism are not included in the above list because they represent an amalgamation of many ancient religions whose specific origins merge into obscurity.

The New Testament of the Christian Bible relates the already arrived hypothesis. That is that God sent His Son, and in effect Himself, to not only appear among His created subjects in their

11

lesser mortal forms, but also had him undergo ridicule, torture, and execution. His ultimate sacrifice and resurrection was to reconcile mankind with the same God that appeared to the Hebrews.

Though I endorse the accuracy of both the Old and New Testament Scriptures, I do not necessarily endorse the popular Christian teaching that professes to expound from them or the common translations used within such circles. Throughout the course of this work I will explain this stance.

Slightly less emphasised, but no less significant is the fact that this New Covenant act *fulfilled* the law and the writings of the Old Testament prophets *(Matthew 5:17)*. The word "fulfill" is significant because woven throughout these sacred texts are glimpses of specific actions and events that point to the Messiah. Scripture is the only trustworthy gauge that allows us to measure the authenticity of any contender who would claim to be the Saviour of the world. This last point is crucial to understand, because according to the oldest written records, the concept of a dieing and resurrecting god-man was not exclusive to Christianity.

Evidence of Sacrifice and Resurrections in Many Mythologies

Over the last two centuries some historians, teachers and authors have stepped forward on seemingly strong grounds to question the existence of the Christian Messiah. This observation is based on the evidence of an array of writings that predate Christianity, which portray pagan gods with characteristics that parallel the resurrected Son of God.

Below, I have arranged a list of dieing and resurrecting gods, predominantly compiled from two sources, Kersey Graves', *Sixteen Crucified Saviours* and a work by Acharya S called, *Suns of God – Krishna Budda and Christ Unveiled*.

Not all gods listed were specifically crucified and even fewer are recorded as resurrecting. Some accounts are among several conflicting mythological stories that surround a particular god, which appear to have later picked up elements of the Gospel accounts. Aspects of gods and religions were sometimes merged together or taken completely or partially from other faiths. Christianity was not exempt from this practice, when examined against the former pagan[2] religion of Mithraism[3].

Here is a brief summary:

∞ **Tammuz (Dumuzi),** the **Mesopotamian** god of Assyria, Babylonia and Sumeria was a god who died and rose again.

∞ The god **Iao of Nepal** survived crucifixion, but bore the evidence in his hands and feet.

∞ **Hesus** of the **Celtic** Druids was crucified between a lamb and an elephant. The lamb represented innocence, while the elephant represented sin.

∞ **Quezalcoatl,** the Plumed Serpent god of **Mexico**, is said to have incinerated himself and ascended to the sky. Before he left he promised to return and bring about peace and harmony to the earth.

∞ The **Roman** war god **Quirinius** was born of a virgin. A reigning king called Amulius sought his life. When he was put to death the day became as night.

∞ **Prometheus,** the god of **Caucasus** had his crucifixion, burial and resurrection performed in pantomime five hundred years before the Messiah.

∞ Sculptures discovered in **Egypt** reveal the story of the god Thulis, who came to earth to save mankind. He eventually suffered a violent death, but resurrected and became the judge of the dead.

∞ The **Tibetan** god **Indra** was born of a virgin. He walked upon water and was crucified and resurrected. He existed as an eternal spirit and his followers were called Heavenly Teachers.

∞ The female god **Alcestos** of **Euripides** was part of a trinity. She was crucified for the sins of the world.

---

2   Originally the term pagan meant "fixed stake," then later became associated with "country dweller." I use the term to represent all other religions except Judaism, Christianity, and Mohammedanism.

3   Mithraism was also an amalgamation of Persian and Babylonian religions, which was adopted by Rome before Christianity.

∞ The god **Attis** of **Phrygia** was crucified, buried and resurrected.

∞ The **Chaldaean** god **Crite** was called the "ever blessed son of god," "the saviour," and after he was crucified he was seen as the "atonement offering for an angry god."

∞ **Bali** of **Orissa** went by several names, all of which signified "lord second," as in the second person of a trinity. He was crucified as a sin offering.

∞ The **Persian** god **Mithras** was born on the 25th of December and crucified on a tree to atone for mankind.

∞ **Devatat,** the god of **Siam** died on a cross.

∞ **Ixion** of **Rome** was crucified on a rotating wheel.

∞ **Apollonius** of **Tyana** in Cappadocia died on a cross. There are long lists of miracles attributed to Apollonius in Christian writings yet they are allegedly silent on the manner of his death.

∞ **Inanna** (also known as Ishtar), a **Sumerian** goddess was crucified and descended into the underworld from which she subsequently escaped after defeating a great enemy.

∞ **Indian** god **Krishna** was pierced by an arrow under a tree, which he was later hung from. His followers came to let him down but his body had vanished.

∞ The **Nordic** god **Odin** hung from a tree and was resurrected.

∞ **Perseus** of **Greece** was conceived of a virgin and grew up among fishermen. He chose to rule over a lesser kingdom and ascended to the sky.

∞ **Buddha** of **India** was born on December 25th of a virgin. A king threatened his life, he was baptised in water and he performed miracles. He died and rose to Nirvana.

Relevant Christian groups boastfully exhibit the flood comparison in ancient cultures to endorse the authenticity of the Genesis account, but unfortunately shy away from exhibiting the above list of died and risen gods through fear of exposing the ingredients of a fabricated New Testament Messiah.

The concept of death and resurrection among the gods appears irrefutable. Though archaeological evidence of these accounts predating the Messiah's death and resurrection is scarce, there are notable exceptions that must be addressed. But before we do, let's delve deeper into the debate.

Reference books relate that Rome eventually accepted Christianity, but they fail to specify that this came about by commandeering a sect of Messianic Judaism and absorbing it into existing pagan practices. This product became known as Christianity, which is largely a Gentile centered faith completely apposed to the nation to which was originally entrusted with God's oracles. As a result Christianity today ultimately sees itself as something separate to Old Testament Israel. Despite the warning in *Isaiah 56:3; "Do not let the son of the foreigner who has joined himself to the Lord speak saying, 'The Lord has utterly separated me from his people (Israel).'"* This act of separation, now known as "fourth century replacement theology" or "supersessionism," was implemented to appeal to a pagan populace. Any Jewish elements contained in the practices of the first apostles and their converts were eroded through gradual legal restrictions, until the only alternative was to follow a style of faith that was totally devoid of Semitic traditions. The only way for followers of the true faith to survive was to convert to a Greco-Roman alternative or to go underground. As a result the religion we now call Christianity is littered with a number of non-biblical practices and observances that stemmed from this period. Naturally if this were the case, which it is, many find this to be further evidence to support the belief that Jesus Christ was borrowed from the gods of pagan religions. Many stop here and draw this inevitable conclusion. But if one continues to delve deeper more enlightening information comes to hand.

As briefly pointed out earlier, Mithraism was the previous pagan religion observed by Rome and holds many key similarities to Christianity. But by continuing to trace to a point of origin we soon find that this former belief was also an amalgamation of two previous religions that were practiced by two competing ancient civilisations. Interestingly Abraham hailed from one of these areas, which was called Sumer (In southern Iraq). This area contains the world's earliest written pagan records. These writings parallel later scriptural themes, as do ancient Egyptian hieroglyphs, which contain records of pharaohs with comparable lives to major biblical characters. Sadly many stop here and draw their inevitable conclusion that Christianity had pagan roots. But again, if one continues to delve deeper more enlightening information becomes evident.

Early civilisations functioned without written language for a considerable time. In fact there is much evidence to show that complex structures and sizable ancient civilizations functioned quite happily without writing. During this period the first teaching, that of the "Oral Torah" of the Semitic tribes existed from the first humans. During this time massive amounts of information were completely committed to memory. This guarded against corruption, as knowledge would only be transmitted from a conscious delivery from a teacher to a trusted student. The concept of visual records was seen as vulnerable as they could be damaged, lost, misinterpreted or altered. *In the Handbook of Jewish Thought* (1979) by Rabbi Aryeh Kaplan, he relates: "The Oral Torah was originally meant to be transmitted by word of mouth. It was transmitted from master to student in such a manner that if the student had any questions, he would be able to ask, and thus avoid ambiguity. A written text, on the other hand, no matter how perfect, is always subject to misinterpretation."

"Further, the Oral Torah was meant to cover the infinitude of cases, which could arise in the course of time. It could never have been written in its entirety. It is thus written *(Ecclesiastes 12:12), "Of making many books there is no end."* God therefore gave Moses a set of rules through which the Torah could be applied to every possible case."

The prophecies of Enoch, referred to in *Jude 14-15*, explicitly state that a fallen angel introduced written language. The motive for this past action is clear when we see the present repercussions of influencing a pagan tribe to conceive the written word. Modern day opponents to the Scriptures successfully take the bait as they parade earlier records of these counterfeit gods and religions to support the premise that they were the source of the one true faith.

Author William Crossman in his book, *Last Writes: Previewing the Reasons Why Written Language Will Become Obsolete by 2050*, clearly illustrates that mankind is moving back to a previous existence that no longer relies on the written word. Though I disagree with his hypothesis that early men turned to writing because they needed a way to transcend their memory limits, he does accurately describe the process and evolution of man's relationship to writing. On the contrary, writing promoted a gradual decline on the reliance of one's memory, which gradually spread throughout the ancient world. As a consequence the true faith had to enter into the written arena if it was going to survive.

The only solid guideline to discern the true faith and the true Messiah should be through examination of the prophetic assignments that are contained within the books that are based off the Oral Torah and the early sayings of Torah observant prophets. Choosing the earliest pictographic or cuneiform record to ascertain the true Messiah or faith without checking all the Messianic prophecies kept by the strictest record keeping nation in all history is folly. *Acts 18:28* describe the Apostle Paul exclusively using the Scriptures to reason with the Jews about the credentials of Messiah. *"For he vigorously refuted the Jews publicly, showing from the Scriptures that Jesus is the Christ."*

Other Gods Under The Microscope

The "crucified saviours" deception is multifaceted. Opponents also add to the illusion by omitting and adding variations to the descriptions of others gods. When seeking authoritative references to a crucifixion of Buddha, Krishna, and Dionysus prepare to be let down. When delving into the footnotes of several authors that parade much of the above list in their works, I was immediately struck with the feeling that the term "crucified" was used when a god happened to meet his or her demise by an impaling weapon within a twenty-mile vicinity of a single shrub. When certain details are omitted and slight variations on existing records are made, almost any god can appear to fit a crucified saviour pattern. I deliberately kept my list brief and ambiguous to hopefully illustrate this point. Because, like the authors who have compiled similar lists, the addition of more specific information reduces their shock value. Take for example the Greek god Perseus. In his entry I added that he ascended to the sky from references that simply say he had a constellation named after him toward the end of his career, inferring his eternal place in the heavens.

Most of the gods in the above mythological stories did not die to atone for man's sin and absolutely NONE fulfilled the New or rather the Renewed Covenant, which first appeared in the Torah. *Deuteronomy 30:6; "And the Lord your God will circumcize your heart and the heart of your descendants, to love the Lord your God with all your heart and with all your soul, that you may live."*

According to *The Encyclopedia of Modern Mythology*, The Roman god Ixion was not crucified for anything more than giving into his own lustful desires. He was condemned for all eternity in the prison underworld Tartarus chained to a rolling wheel after raping a copy of Zeus's wife Hera.

In the *Myths of the Norsemen* by Roger Lancelyn Green, the mighty god Odin was not crucified for the sins of men. His quest was for wisdom and after seeking it from the living, "He sought also after the wisdom of the dead, and hung for nine nights and days as if on the gallows <u>sacrificed to himself</u>. For he caused himself to be hanged from the branches of Yggdrasill the World Tree, and gave command to the Aesir that none of them should give him bread or wine during that time. And thus the mysteries of death were borne up to him from the depths below the Nid Hog's den, before he came down from the tree."

The Babylonian god, Tammuz met his death after marrying the goddess Ishtar who descended into the underworld to retrieve him. In an effort to make comparisons with the Messiah, relevant authors conveniently portray both gods independently dying and rising again.

Messiah or Naughty Boy?

Throughout history all manner of men have endured public beatings before being led staggering to an execution stake for supporting causes that threatened political and religious powers of their day. Many men also laid claim to a range of miracles, which were later performed by Jesus. They knew, as did the fallen angels they worshipped, that these were signs of his ministry and absolute victory over death was seen as an eternal mark of divine authority. Satan could never present himself to men as a viable alternative to God. Witchcraft and outwardly occult practices have formed a convenient smoke screen for Satan's gradual strategy of assimilation to the original faith. This is why Satan chooses to appear as an angel of light *(2 Corinthians 11:14)* and has his most effective followers pose as ministers of righteousness *(2 Corinthians 11:15)* who will perform great wonders at key times *(Revelation 13:13)*.

Pre-written word reliant humans who fell from the original faith still retained the memory of its ways and remodeled it to suit their rebellious sects at the coaxing of fallen angels. These angels having the ability to foresee the future, within the limits of God's divine plan, could see how a Messiah doctrine could be used as a vehicle to introduce a "counterfeit saviour" at a latter date.

This raises the question; can fallen angels see into the future? Throughout history, seers (people with the gift of foretelling) have been commonplace in all cultures. It is widely accepted that Nostradamus was in contact with spirits that, to a limited degree, revealed to him glimpses of the future. The Scriptures are rampant with the concept of men, both good and bad, enquiring and receiving insight in such a manner. King Saul sought out the witch of En Dor to gain foreknowledge to avoid his fate. The summoned spirit of his former comrade, Samuel, obliged by revealing exactly what awaited him *(1 Samuel 28:19)*. It would be naive to assume that Satan would not try to simulate a crucifixion and resurrection event. Such methods are certainly not foreign to him, as was the case with the Sumerian "creator god" Enki, who according to ancient cuneiform writings was the true architect of men. The Book of Revelation portrays the second beast as arriving before Jesus and having the appearance of a lamb *(Revelation 13:11)*, which also supports a preference Satan has to preempt and imitate key events by impersonating his enemy. The Scriptures clearly indicate that Satan knows its contents as he freely quotes from it time and again *(Matthew 4:6)*.

The Old Testament constantly points to a coming Messiah and all Israel expectantly awaited his arrival. Sadly the Orthodox Jew still waits. Even the New Testament warns of false Christs still to come. To believe that ancient history was devoid of multiple hijack attempts of the true faith is to believe that Satan would not exercise an obvious opportunity to instill confusion and plant seeds of misinformation. Early church father, Justin Martyr[4] combated this very issue in his *Dialogue with Trypho the Jew*:

"Be well assured, then, Trypho, that I am established in the knowledge of the faith in the Scriptures by those counterfeits which he who is called the devil is said to have performed among the Greeks; just as some were wrought by the Magi in Egypt, and others by the false prophets in Elijah's days. For when they tell that Bacchus, son of Jupiter, was begotten by (Jupiter's) intercourse with Semele, and that he was the discoverer of the vine; and when they introduce wine into his mysteries, do I not perceive that (the devil) has imitated the prophecy announced by the patriarch Jacob, and recorded by Moses?"

I'm the Messiah! No I'm the Messiah!

If an emphasised aspect of a popular religion becomes a common characteristic in many, this can cause what I call the "Spartacus effect." In the classic gladiator film with *Kirk Douglas*, Roman armies eventually round up all the rebel gladiators that had risen against them. When a general enquires as to the whereabouts of their ringleader Spartacus, he is immediately confronted with the warrior as he obediently gets to his feet. When he declares that he is the man, all his comrades begin standing up one at a time to make the same claim. Unable to identify the ringleader the General departs the scene denied his prize. Could this have been Satan's motive in attempting to decorate other religions with a similar defining event? The war between heaven and hell is not restricted to a linier timeframe. Prophecy is God's gift to His people and clairvoyance is Satan's seductive counterfeit. Scripture clearly shows that both abilities exist and can help in anticipating a future event. But only one costs a price too high to pay. If both parties can

---

4   It must be noted that I do not side with a great majority of views held by the early church fathers nor am I in full disagreement with the Jewish mindset. My personal theological identity is founded in the Messiah alone who displayed many characteristics that were contrary to the both the Orthodox Jewish and Gentile Christian mind.

bestow prophecy and clairvoyance to men, it would stand to reason that they could also call on these disciplines themselves with little difficulty.

The Mimicry of Mother Worship and its Origin in the Nimrod Dynasty

There is an avenue that reveals the origin of another theme practiced in religions throughout the world. The worship of a mother goddess was and is still a common element in pagan religions. Many ancient carvings from across the globe carry a similar depiction of a cradled infant in the arms of a maternal deity. While many authors have acknowledged this in demonstrating the origin of the Catholic Church's Mary doctrine, they often fail to examine the reason for its prior conception and its widespread popularity among different religions. Here are some examples of this type of deity in various cultural settings:

∞ The Chinese had a mother goddess called Shingmoo

∞ The Germans had a mother goddess called Hertha

∞ The Scandinavians had a mother goddess called Disa

∞ The Etruscans had a mother goddess called Nutria

∞ The Druids had a mother goddess called Virgo-Patitura

∞ In India the mother goddess was called Indrani

∞ The Greek's had a mother goddess called Aphrodite

∞ The Sumerians had a mother goddess called Nana

∞ The Romans had a mother goddess who went by the names Venus or Fortuna

∞ In Asia the mother goddess was called Cybele

∞ In Ephesus the mother goddess was known as Diana

∞ In Egypt the mother goddess was called Isis and her child was Horus

Why did so many cultures feel the need to carry a mother and infant theme in their religious customs?" The answer lies at the heart of a great dispersal of civilisation at a time when men strove to be like gods.

Not long after Noah's flood men began to multiply upon the face of the earth. They eventually journeyed in an easterly direction until they came upon a great plain in the land of Shinar. There they settled and built a city, which was called Babylon and later Mesopotamia *(Genesis 11:2)*.

Though the land was prosperous, residents faced the ongoing threat of wild animals *(Exodus 23:29-30)*. At about that time a great warrior called Nimrod began to make a name for himself by slaughtering many of these native beasts. It was in this manner that he earned the title "mighty hunter before the Lord" *(Genesis 10:8-9)*. Though the term "mighty" carries a hostile connotation in Hebrew, because "before" is used in the context of "against." The name Nimrod is also translated as, "he rebelled." Eventually he became a powerful leader by providing protection to the local population from the beasts of the field. He then devised great-fortified kingdoms, one of which was called Babel *(Genesis 10:10)*. From here sprang a great rectangular shaped tower called a "ziggurat", which was built by men who no longer feared God, but were instead driven by Nimrod's rebellious determination of seeking self worth *(Genesis 11:4)*.

Nimrod took his own mother, Semiramis, as his wife, but was soon killed by his uncle Shem who had become enraged by his idolatry. His mother/wife told the people that Nimrod had ascended to the sky and become the sun. A prophecy of a Messiah being born of a woman was known in these days *(Genesis 3:15)* and was the obvious motivation of Semiramis' declaration that her only son Tammuz was Nimrod reborn. The people then began to worship the sun as the father, Semiramis as the earth mother, and the child as a manifestation of the father.

From here the foundation of Babylonian religion had taken root and at God's confusion of languages *(Genesis 11:7)* the people and events of this period emerged with different names and slightly varying interpretations.

There Can Be Only One

At the end of the day, one has to weigh up which religious account to believe. The Messiah sent by the God of the Hebrews displays an exclusive set of characteristics in that he fulfills, down to the last detail, all the prophecies that were laid down in the Old Testament Scriptures. He appears without fanfare or grandeur in a humble shelter and emerges thirty years later to expose himself to the scrutiny and judgment of his Father's creations. This was very much a lead by example scenario where a standard was set and people that spent any amount of time with this Son of God became inspired and compelled to follow him. His character is consistently portrayed as committed, compassionate and uncompromising. In my opinion, the most accurate portrayal of this type of character was not found in the film, *The Passion*, which served as little more than a feature length depiction of someone being beaten, battered and executed. I believe a glimpse of Jesus' true nature is more accurately portrayed in an earlier film by the same director. At the close of Mel Gibson's film *Braveheart*[5], it becomes very apparent that the character of William Wallace has a conviction that not only extends to risking his life in fighting the English, but also holds firm in the face of severe torture and death. Rather than succumb to the request of his enemies in crying out "mercy" he saves his final breath for the defiant word "freedom." His men fought so bravely with him because they could sense his passion and even some of his enemies showed signs of admiration in his qualities. Even his archenemy, Edward the Long Shanks curiously enquires of the queen after her meeting with the Scotsman, "What kind of man is he?"

---

5   I reference this film not to endorse its historical accuracy, but to highlight Mel Gibson's driven portrayal of William Wallace and in so doing, point out its similarity to the single minded nature of the Messiah's no compromise disposition.

Part Two
People of the Way

Dr. C. Truman Davis wrote a revealing article (inspired by Jim Bishop's book, *The Day Christ Died*) on the testimony of the crucifixion from the perspective of a physician, that leaves no doubt as to the level of suffering this God was and is willing to go through so that His people might come to know Him. The account shows the various methods and details of crucifixion at that time, the beatings, the judicial system, the physical and anatomical impacts to Jesus' body during his ordeal, and examines in detail the final seven statements that he uttered. Along the way it manages to effortlessly shatter a few fables, such as the exact location of the nails that pierced the Messiah's hands, his prayer that induced the sweating of blood, and the visual depiction of the cross itself. In fact whenever "the cross" is mentioned throughout all modern Bible translations, it is usually translated from the Greek word "stauros" meaning "upright pale," "stake," "tree," "beam" or "staff." The problem is that a cross denotes a specific shape of something and these root meanings describe objects of varying form. This being so and having an innate desire to remain as accurate as possible to the Scriptures, I have inserted more neutral terminology in favour of Dr. Truman's preference for this term. I hope advocates of his wonderful essay will not feel that I have defaced his work by doing this.

The symbol of the cross most Christians are familiar with today originated in ancient Chalda, where it was the symbol of the god Tammuz. The much-loved image of the cross was a pagan symbol, which was a latter attributed to represent the Nazarene sect of Judaism. Until the middle of the 3rd century A.D. the concept of a cross, particularly with the crossbar lowered was foreign to all believers. Subjects relating to the introduction of this and other pagan concepts to Christianity are dealt with in finer detail in Chapter Five of this work. I have therefore seen it imperative to include at least 80% of Dr. Davis' article, as it originally appeared in a medical journal back in the late 60's. I found that culling it any more meant losing valuable information and therefore have left it otherwise intact. It states:

"Apparently, the first known practice of crucifixion was by the Persians. Alexander and his generals brought it back to the Mediterranean world to Egypt and to Carthage. The Romans apparently learned the practice from the Carthaginians and rapidly developed a very high degree of efficiency and skill at it. A number of Roman authors comment on crucifixion, and several innovations, modifications, and variations are described in ancient literature...The most common form used in our Lord's day, was the *Tau* (formation), shaped like a T. In this (version) the *patiblum* (crossbeam) was placed in a notch at the top of the *stipes* (upright portion of the stake)...Without any historical or biblical proof, Medieval and Renaissance painters have given us our picture of Christ carrying (an) entire cross. But the upright post, or *stipes*, was generally fixed permanently in the ground at the site of the execution and the condemned man was forced to carry the *patibulum*, weighing about 110 pounds, from the prison to the place of execution. Many of the painters and most of the sculptors of the crucifixion, also show the nails through the palms. Historical Roman accounts and experimental work have established that the nails were driven between the small bones of the wrists (*radial and ulna*) and not through the palms. Nails driven through the palms will strip out between the fingers when made to support the weight of the human body. The misconception may have come about through a misunderstanding of Jesus' words to Thomas, 'Observe my hands.' Anatomists, both modern and ancient, have always considered the wrist as a part of the hand."

"A titulus, or small sign, stating the victim's crime was usually placed on a staff, carried at the front of the procession from the prison, and later nailed to the (upright post) so that it extended above the head."

"…Of the many aspects of this initial suffering, the one of greatest physiological interest is the bloody sweat. It is interesting that St Luke, the physician, is the only one to mention this. He says, 'And being in agony, He prayed the longer. And His sweat became as drops of blood, trickling down upon the ground.'"

"…A great deal of effort could have been saved had the doubters (skeptics of this occurrence) consulted the medical literature. Though very rare, the phenomenon of Hematidrosis, or bloody sweat, is well documented. Under great emotional stress of the kind our Lord suffered, tiny capillaries in the sweat glands can break, thus mixing with blood and sweat…"

"…After the arrest in the middle of the night, Jesus was brought before the Sanhedrin and Caiphus, the High Priest; it is here that the first physical trauma was inflicted. A soldier struck Jesus across the face for remaining silent when questioned by Caiphus. The palace guards then blindfolded Him and mockingly taunted Him to identify them as they each passed by, spat upon Him, and struck Him in the face."

"In the early morning, battered and bruised, dehydrated, and exhausted from a sleepless night, Jesus is taken across the Praetorium of the Fortress Antonia, the seat of government of the Procurator of Judea, Pontius Pilate. You are, of course, familiar with Pilate's action in attempting to pass responsibility to Herod Antipas, the Tetrarch of Judea. Jesus apparently suffered no physical mistreatment at the hands of Herod and was returned to Pilate. It was in response to the cries of the mob, that Pilate ordered Barabbas released and condemned Jesus to scourging and crucifixion."

"…Preparations for the scourging were carried out when the prisoner was stripped of his clothing and his hands tied to a post above his head. It is doubtful the Romans would have made any attempt to follow the Jewish law in this matter, but the Jews had an ancient law prohibiting more than forty lashes."

"The Roman legionnaire steps forward with the flagrum (or flagellum) in his hand. This is a short whip consisting of several heavy, leather thongs with two small balls of lead attached near the ends of each. The heavy whip is brought down with full force again and again across Jesus' shoulders, back and legs. At first the thongs cut through the skin only. Then, as the blows continue, they cut deeper into the subcutaneous tissues, producing first an oozing of blood from the capillaries and veins of the skin, and finally spurting arterial bleeding from vessels in the underlying muscles."

"The small balls of lead first produce large, deep bruises, which are broken open by subsequent blows. Finally the skin of the back is hanging in long ribbons and the entire area is an unrecognisable mass of torn, bleeding tissue. When it is determined by the centurion in charge that the prisoner is near death, the beating is finally stopped."

"The half-fainting Jesus is then untied and allowed to slump to the stone pavement, wet with His own blood. The Roman soldiers see a great joke in this provincial Jew claiming to be king. They throw a robe across His shoulders and place a stick in His hand for a scepter. They still need a crown to make their travesty complete. Flexible branches covered with long thorns (commonly used in bundles for firewood) are plaited into the shape of a crown and this is pressed into his scalp. Again there is copious bleeding, the scalp being one of the most vascular areas of the body."

"After mocking Him and striking Him across the face, the soldiers take the stick from His hand and strike Him across the head, driving the thorns deeper into His scalp. Finally, they tire of their sadistic sport and the robe is torn from his back. Already having adhered to the clots of blood and serum in the wounds, its removal causes excruciating pain just as in the careless removal of a surgical bandage, and almost as though He were again being whipped the wounds once more begin to bleed."

"...The heavy patibulum...is tied across His shoulders, and the procession of the condemned Christ, two thieves, and the execution detail of the Roman soldiers headed by a centurion begins its slow journey along the Via Dolorosa. In spite of His efforts to walk erect, the weight of the heavy wooden beam, together with the shock produced by copious amounts of blood loss, is too much. He stumbles and falls. The rough wood of the beam gouges into the lacerated skin and muscles of the shoulders. He tries to rise, but human muscles have been pushed beyond their endurance."

"The centurion...selects (an onlooker)...Simon of Cyrene, to carry the (beam). Jesus follows...until the 650-yard journey from the fortress Antonia to Golgotha is finally complete."

"Jesus is offered wine mixed with myrrh…He refuses…Simon is ordered (away)…and Jesus (is) quickly thrown backward with His shoulders against the wood. The legionnaire feels for the depression at the front of the wrist. He drives a heavy, square, wrought-iron nail through the wrist and deep into the wood….he moves to the other side and repeats the action…The patibulum is then lifted in place at the top of the stipes and the titulus reading "Jesus of Nazareth, King of the Jews" is nailed in place."

"The left foot is now pressed backward against the right foot, and with both feet extended, toes down, a nail is driven through the arch of each, leaving the knees moderately flexed. The victim is now crucified. As He slowly sags down with more weight on the nails in the wrists excruciating pain shoots along the fingers and up the arms to explode in the brain – the nails in the wrists are putting pressure on the median nerves. As He pushes Himself upward to avoid this stretching torment, He places His full weight on the nail through His feet. Again there is the searing agony of the nail tearing through the nerves between the metatarsal bones of the feet."

"At this point, as the arms fatigue, great waves of cramps sweep over the muscles, knotting them in deep, relentless, throbbing pain. With these cramps comes the inability to push himself upward. Hanging by the arms, the pectoral muscles are paralyzed and the intercostal muscles are unable to act. Air can be drawn into the lungs, but cannot be exhaled. Jesus fights to raise Himself in order to get even one short breath. Finally, carbon dioxide builds up in the lungs and in the blood stream and the cramps partially subside. Spasmodically, he is able to push Himself upward to exhale and bring in the life-giving oxygen. It was undoubtedly during these periods that He uttered the seven short sentences recorded."

"The first, looking down at the Roman soldiers throwing dice for His seamless garment, 'Father, forgive them for they know not what they do.'"

"The second, to the penitent thief, '(I tell you) today thou shalt be with me in Paradise.'"

"The third, looking down at the terrified, grief-stricken adolescent John – the beloved Apostle – he said, 'behold thy mother.' Then, looking at His mother Mary, 'Woman behold thy son.'"

"The forth cry is from the beginning of the 22nd Psalm, 'My God, my God, why has thou forsaken me?'"

"Hours of limitless pain, cycles of twisting, joint-rending cramps, intermittent partial asphyxiation, searing pain where tissue is torn from His lacerated back as He moves up and down against the rough timber. Then another agony begins…A terrible crushing pain deep in the chest as the pericardium slowly fills with serum and begins to compress the heart."

"One remembers again the 22nd Psalm, the 14th verse: 'I am poured out like water, and all my bones are out of joint; my heart is like wax; it is melted in the midst of my bowls.'"

"It is now almost over. The loss of tissue fluids has reached a critical level; the compressed heart is struggling to pump heavy, thick sluggish blood into the tissue; the tortured lungs are making a frantic effort to grasp in small gulps of air. The markedly dehydrated tissues send their flood of stimuli to the brain."

"Jesus gasps His fifth cry, 'I thirst.'"

"One remembers another verse from the prophetic 22nd Psalm: 'My strength is dried up like a potsherd; and my tongue cleaveth to my jaws; and thou has brought me into the dust of death.'"

"A sponge soaked in Posca…is lifted to His lips. He apparently doesn't take any of the liquid. The body of Jesus is now in extremes, and He can feel the chill of death creeping through His tissues. This realisation brings out His sixth words, possibly little more than a tortured whisper, 'It is finished.'"

"His mission of atonement has completed. Finally He can allow his body to die."

"With one last surge of strength, he once again presses His torn feet against the nails, straightens His legs, takes a deeper breath, and utters His seventh and last cry, 'Father! Into thy hands I commit my spirit.'"

"…The common method of ending a crucifixion was by crurifracture, the breaking of the bones of the legs. This prevented the victim from pushing himself upward; thus the tension could not be relieved from the muscles of the chest and rapid suffocation occurred. The legs of the two thieves were broken, but when the soldiers came to Jesus they saw that this was unnecessary."

"Apparently to make doubly sure of death, the legionnaire drove his lance through the fifth interspace between the ribs, upward through the pericardium and into the heart. The 34th verse of the 19th chapter of the Gospel according to St John reports: 'And immediately there came out blood and water.' That is, there was an escape of water fluid from the sac surrounding the heart, giving postmortem evidence that our Lord died not the usual crucifixion death by suffocation, but of heart failure (a broken heart) due to shock and constriction of the heart by fluid in the pericardium."

This essay gives such a unique perspective of one of the most well known executions in the history of mankind. What greater love could a supreme being show his people than to lead with the above example? This God means business enough to offer His Son in human form to be among us for a time to make clear the way to everlasting life. This was done devoid of noble position, wealth or elegant stature and in a manner that induced mental, verbal, and physical abuse, which ultimately led to an excruciating exit. Do any of us who would stand to be counted with this man know the true immensity of this bitter cup? Do Christians realise the folly of their words when they say to anyone that salvation was a free gift?

The very cornerstone of this faith, lies at the heart of the actions of this Nazarene man who was born of a virgin. The Old Testament contains over 3 hundred and 30 references to his ministry and as we have seen already Jesus' quote of the 22nd Psalm, seen by the ill-informed as a moment of spiritual weakness, in actuality is a verbal direction to Scripture that confirms specific events to be suffered by the coming Saviour that finally unfolded to the letter on that day. Old Testament Scripture tells us for example that his bones would not be broken *(Psalms 34:20)* and though he was crucified with two others who received such injuries, which was the normal procedure in that type of execution, he did not.

Below is a sequentially arranged extract from an extensive list of Old Testament prophecies that outline keys events in the Messiah's life:

∞ Malachi 3:1 & Isaiah 40:3 – Preceded by a forerunner (John the Baptist)

∞ Psalms 2:7 – Declared the Son of God

∞ Isaiah 9:1-2 – Galilean Ministry

∞ Malachi 3:1, Daniel 9:26 – Messiah to appear in Temple

∞ Deuteronomy 18:15 – A prophet of men like Moses

∞ Isaiah 53:3 – Rejected by his own people

∞ Isaiah 53:2 – Possessed no outward beauty

∞ Psalm 110:4 – A priest after the order of Melchizedek

∞ Zechariah 9:9 & Exodus 12:3 – Entry on a donkey and plot to kill him formulated

∞ Psalms 41:9 – Betrayed by a friend (Judas)

∞ Zechariah 11:12-13 – 30 pieces of silver thrown down on Temple floor

∞ Psalms 109:2-3 & Isaiah 53:7 – Accused by false witnesses but remains silent

A mathematician by the name of Peter Stoner calculated the odds of an individual fulfilling just 8 of 300 Old Testament prophecies. "We find that the chance that any man might have lived down to the present time and fulfilled all eight prophecies is one in ten (to the seventeenth power). That would be one in 100,000,000,000,000,000."

Now, centuries later, if we come to believe that this is truth, how should we respond? If this man was who he said he was and did what he said he was going to do, what is it that is really expected of us when or if we finally believe? And if we do finally believe do we bolt to the nearest church on our block and leap at the first opportunity to tell everyone we're Christian?

Christians, Cretins, Anointed Ones or Israelites?

The religion that Christianity purports to be based on had many of its foundations revealed to men in the days of Moses. These foundations were set by the hand, voice and movement of God. Followers of this original faith were known as His chosen people and called, "Israelites" (Yisraelites), meaning "those who struggle with

EL (Mighty One)" or "El rules these men." This name "Israel" was originally given to a forefather called Jacob whose offspring multiplied and emerged into twelve tribes. One of these tribes was called Judah (Yahudah), which means, "Belonging to YHWH." Gradually the term "Jew" (Yahudi) came to be used as the general name for Israelites and by the time of the New Testament the title of Jew held national significance. This was because they were the only tribe among the whole nation who retained the oracles or law (Torah) of God. *Genesis 49:10; "The scepter shall not depart from Judah, nor a lawgiver from between his feet."* This is why Paul says in *Romans 3:1-2; "What advantage then has the Jew, or what is the profit of circumcision? Much in every way! Chiefly because to them were committed the oracles of God."* The term Jew could refer to a native Judaen or a direct descendant of the Israelite forefathers, Abraham, Isaac and Jacob. All the other tribes, having forsaken the Torah, lost their identity and became absorbed into pagan nations. Though various splinter groups began to spring up, two major groups that retained the Torah and recognised Messiah emerged. These were the Nazarenes (Ha-Notsarim) and Ebionites. Christianity, though the term "Christian" pops up in modern translations, did not commence until many centuries after the events in Scripture took place. The term was popularised by translators and later adopted as the name for God's people. Though the word "Christian" appears several times in the New Testament it replaces the original word "Notsri" or "Notsarim" (plural) which is transliterated as "Nazarene." The term Nazarene comes from the Hebrew word "Netser," meaning "branch," and forms a Hebrew word play with "Natsar" which means, "to watch." This marriage of words signifies a member of an offshoot faith that watches diligently. The Hebrew word Notsarim is preserved in both the Aramaic and Greek texts. Therefore the term Christianity has nothing whatsoever to do with Scripture and because its meaning is not related to this original word, it cannot be considered a legal transliteration by any means.

In an effort to remain objective I suspended the premise that the original words were "Notsri" or "Notsarim" and decided to see if there was any truth into the widely accepted claim that the original term was a slur. This led to one of the most perplexing observations that I have noted in my studies. It concerns scholars' admittance that the name "Christian" was originally a derogatory term in its three appearances in the New Testament. ***Acts 11:26*** being the first instance, *"And the disciples were first called **Christians** in Antioch"* and so on in ***Acts 26:28*** and ***1 Peter 4:16***. Generally the same scholars that make this claim also say that Christian is taken from Christ, which means "anointed." The act of anointing was a sacred consecration partaken by both pagan and Judaic faiths alike and is therefore difficult to view from either perspective as an insult. The only association I have found that links Christian with a slur meaning is the word "cretin."

The Webster New World Medical Dictionary states: "The word 'cretin' is said to have come from the old French 'Chretien' meaning 'Christian' because heretical Christians, to escape persecution, fled into iodine-deficient valleys in the Pyrenees in southwest France and had children with congenital iodine-deficient hypothyoidism. However, the original term "cretin" is conjectural and could come from 'creature' (creature) or 'creta' (chalk, pale) or some other root."

And the *1911 encyclopedia* adds: "The word is usually explained as derived from chritien (Christian) in the sense of innocent. But Christianus...is probably a translation of the older cretin, and the latter is probably connected with creta (era ie) a sallow or yellow-earthy complexion being a common mark of cretinism."

The word "cretin" does not appear to have been in use before the 1700's yet it is the only reference I can find that has a slur connotation to the word "Christian." Furthermore its French origin could be linked to Antioch as the French did occupy settlements there, but my understanding is that this was some considerable time after the events recorded in the Book of Acts. If cretin was not its original slur meaning, then what was it? And why is this all maintained anyway if the original word, "Notsri" was replaced by the word "Christian," which means something completely different?

Other sources state that "Christ" is the Greek word for "anointed," meaning "the application of oil for consecration" and the addition of the "ian" came from the Latin suffix "ianus," which means "associated with." Therefore the name "Christian" is born out of the Greek rendering of this sacred act (Christos). Still other sources claim that the origin of the word Christ is related to the Hindu god, "Krishna," which I will discuss further in the languages

33

chapter of this book. One thing is certain about the word "Christian." Its exact meaning is conjectural.

Amazingly the "Greco-Roman" term "Christianity" was not used in this complete English form until the year 1526. The religion this word represents had its principle foundations planted some time earlier by a powerful Roman Emperor who convened a counsel at Nicaea. Most churches still openly support this religion while others who outwardly oppose it, still knowingly or unknowingly follow a great majority of its doctrines. The Scriptures speak of only one people that will be saved *(Romans 11:26)* and it is these followers who still observe a particular walk with God that I wish to single out as I make the following statement.

Unlike many other religions, observers of this faith have had a long and bloody history of persecution through the ages, as many nations have been offended enough by its people to be driven to make war, cause genocide and institute slavery upon them. At this point one might be forgiven for thinking that I am talking about Christians. But I am certainly not. Surprisingly, a great many of these attacks have been launched under the very banner of Christianity. The people I refer to are "Israelites," both before and after the resurrection of Messiah. The Church wrongly maintains that it has replaced the old Israel, but Paul makes it exceedingly clear that Israel will never be replaced. *Romans 11:1; "I say then, has God cast away His people? Certainly not!"* and verse *2; "God has not cast away His people that He foreknew."* These people, who the world calls "Jews," have been blinded for a time. But according to *Romans 11:25*, Israel will awaken when a preordained number of foreigners, who graft in, have been reached. *"...that blindness has happened in part to Israel until the fullness of the Gentiles has come in."*

The Survival of a Resilient and Peculiar People

Many New Testament era Israelites carried a loving allegiance to the risen Messiah by happily upholding the Torah *(Acts 21:17-27)*. This sect multiplied and grew into thousands of Jews *(Acts 2:41,47; 4:4, 6:7; 9:31)*. Later, many grafted-in former Gentiles were added to their numbers, which led to a dispute between Paul and Peter as to how they should be instructed *(Galatians 2)*. This demographic were persecuted by both fellow Israelites *(Thessalonians 2:14-16)* and wider Gentile oppositions. Mass persecutions of those who observed a Notsarim (off-shoot) walk cannot be clearly ascertained from the records of early (Gentile) church fathers. This is because the eye of the Gentile saw little distinction between the Notsarim and the "blinded Israelite." This view led to a general reference that later evolved into the term, "Christian." Paul, who was formerly opposed to the Notsarim or "Followers of the Way," spoke directly to those of them who had suffered persecution by their own people in *Romans 11:28-29; "Concerning the gospel they are enemies for your sake, but concerning the election they are beloved for the sake of the fathers. For the gifts and the calling of God are irrevocable."*

The Ongoing Struggle for Jerusalem

In 168BC the Syrian General Antiochus IV Epiphanes marched his army upon the Israelite nation. He invaded their temple at Jerusalem (Yahrushalayim), massacred 40,000 men, women and children, and forced those that remained to "Hellenise" by outlawing their sacred Torah. This led to the victorious Maccabean revolt in 166BC in which the temple was reclaimed. This important event of extreme persecution and triumph is contained within the works of the Apocrypha, which are at best discouraged within the Christian community, despite Jesus attending a festival that commemorated this insurgence in *John 10:22*. Incidentally, unless one is willing to concede that the Book of the Maccabees is Scripture, Jesus is recorded as observing a custom that is not biblical!

By 63AD Roman General Pompey had a turn and took Jerusalem by storm, establishing control over the land. 66AD saw another revolt ensue that inevitably led to a second assault and another victory for Rome in 70AD. Then by 132AD yet another Jewish revolt erupted, this time resulting in the city's total demise by the conqueror Hadrian, who banished any survivors for 100 years, rebuilt a temple to Jupiter on the site of the old temple and renamed the city "Aelia Capitolina." Interestingly Washington DC's "Capitol Hill" shares the same spelling. The origin of its name can be confirmed in any good encyclopedia.

The Scriptures sum up the fate of the Israelite people in a single verse: *Luke 21:24; "And they will fall by the edge of the sword, and be led away captive into all nations. And Jerusalem will be trampled by Gentiles until the times of the Gentiles are fulfilled."*

While many great and powerful nations have come and gone, amazingly Israel still stands today, a tiny piece of land nestled in between seventeen Muslim nations who hunger for its complete and utter obliteration. Its existence defies logic, but it is there because YHWH, the God of Israel made a promise.

No Compromise and No Generalities

Much of the contempt against these followers throughout history concerns the unique claim that they followed "The Way," while many other religions claim to be "A Way," as in a way to achieve enlightenment among others. These followers adhered to what observers must have seen as a narrow and uncompromising path. This observation of a "specific" is plainly visible when we read Jesus' very own words in *John 14:6 "I am THE WAY, the truth, and the life..."* The assertion of this view immediately assaulted and continues to assault the credibility of any other religion and has thus for this reason made it a target for elimination in the past, present and future.

The Existence of the Remnant

As pointed out earlier, not all Jews rejected Jesus. Paul clearly established this fact in *Romans 11:2-5; "God did not cast away his people whom He foreknew. Or do you not know what the Scriptures says of Elijah, how he pleads with God against Israel, saying, "Lord, they have killed Your prophets and torn down Your altars, and I alone am left, and they seek my life? But what does the divine response say to Him? I have reserved for Myself seven thousand men who have not bowed a knee to Baal. Even so then, at this present time there is a remnant according to the election of grace."* Paul was obviously combating the same replacement theology that permeates the church today. That is that the church has replaced Israel. Today, as the time of the Gentiles draws to a close, some Orthodox Jewish Rabbis are secretly studying the Gospels and gradually coming out in support of the Messiah. This is not a new phenomenon because even in Jesus' day some teachers of the Law followed him in secret *(John 19:38)*. A remnant has always known he was the fulfillment of the New Covenant and anyone who says they follow the truth and say they are something other than this people have either not come to this knowledge yet or have rejected it. I will discuss the topic of the remnant near the close of this chapter.

It is of great importance to understand that the concept of a New Covenant is used in context of a reaffirming of a plan that was established before creation and by its very nature cannot be subtracted from, added to or superseded. *Jeremiah 31:31 Behold, the days are coming, says the Lord, when I will make a <u>new covenant with the house of Israel</u> and with the house of Judah."*

The Origin of the Born Again Christian

The question arises, "where do Christians fit into this equation?" Not only did the word "Christian" appear some time after as an appropriated term, its link to the word "Christ," is also suspect. *The Oxford Companion to the Bible 1993 edition* admits that, "The origin of the term Christian is *uncertain.*" Therefore to stringently use this name to profess the faith of one who follows Jesus has no biblical foundation whatsoever. Christians invariably respond to this observation with the statement, "names don't matter." Yet to them the term "Christian" seems to matter enough to be used as a marker to immediately pigeonhole someone's allegiance of faith. As a consequence unnecessary pressure is continually brought to bear on newly converted members of the faith to use this term exclusively to profess who they are. This attitude convinces a new believer that they are going against biblical doctrine if they don't assume this title, when in actual fact it is merely a requirement of man-made tradition. Though many Christian evangelists and ministers would agree that the term was never used in Jesus Christ's day as indeed was this rendering of his name, they support nonetheless that the prevailing attitude to anyone not professing to be a "born again Christian," should be one of suspicion. Their biblical support of this view is found in *Acts 11:26, 26:28* and *1 Peter 4:16*, which all exhibit the word "Christian." Yet as pointed out previously, the term "Christian" does not share the same meaning as the original word "Notsarim." As for the "born again" reference, this is used in Jesus' exchange with Nicodemus in *John 3:1-8.* The second birth concept in John is an isolated take on the very foundation of the Torah, which is used by the Messiah. This term has been simply favoured and later adopted as a mass generic prefix in the title of all modern-day followers. Evangelist Billy Graham principally ignited this trend.

You'll Never Learn This in Church

The concept of being "born again" was not a new teaching as is evident in Jesus' exchange with Nicodemus, the head Pharisee of the Jews. *John 3:10* states; *"... Are you the teacher of Israel, and you do not know these things?"* The Messiah is clearly surprised at Nicodemus' unfamiliarity with the concept of a "new birth" because this was the foundation of the whole Torah. That is, it was and is by faith that one is saved, and not by works. This is seen in *Deuteronomy 10:16; "Therefore circumcize the foreskin of your heart <u>and be stiff-necked no longer."</u>* (Meaning: Proceed by faith and be dead in your transgressions no longer) And in *30:6; "And the Lord your God will circumcize your heart and the heart of your descendants, to love the Lord your God with all your heart and with all your soul, <u>that you may live."</u>* When one accepts God by faith they die to their carnal self, but are "reborn" or "live again" with a new spirit of faith. This teaching is what Jesus was talking about.

The preference for the name Christian is also supported by the fact that it is the current universally understood name for people who follow Jesus. To be hesitant in the use of it in most evangelistic circles is looked upon as a sure sign of a questionable acceptance of the Saviour. While hesitancy in calling oneself a Christian may usually stem from unbelief, to assume that it is always the case is dangerous. History has indeed put forward an unlikely array of men who also professed an allegiance to this name that modern history lecturers have managed to avoid mentioning. We can see why when we read this section of a speech by Adolf Hitler: "...My feeling as a Christian leads me to be a fighter for my Lord and Saviour. It leads me to the man who, at one time lonely and with only a few followers, recognised the Jews for what they were, and called on men to fight against them...As a Christian, I owe something to my people." In the book called, *I Became a Jew*, *Shira Sorko-Ram* writes: "The culmination of all persecutions was masterminded by Hitler. Since Hitler was neither a Jew nor a Moslem, he was, in the eyes of the Jews, a Christian. (He had a Catholic background.) If a questioning Christian Gentile strongly resisted the idea that Hitler was a Christian, the Jew will answer that Hitler did not destroy these millions of Jews by himself. Thousands of Germans, Poles and others who called themselves Christians herded Jews onto trains or met them at sites of destruction. If you should have the opportunity to look through old World War II pictures, notice the Crusader's Cross pinned to the Nazi uniform. The cross is the symbol of Christianity to the Jews."

Prior to this universal use of the term Christian, members of this faith were known by many names. "Followers of the Way" is the second most widely known reference as found in ***Acts 9:2;*** "*... and asked letters from him to the synagogues of Damascus, so that if he found any <u>who were of the Way</u>, whether men or women, he might bring them bound to Jerusalem.*" A considerably lesser-known reference appears in ***Acts 24:5;*** "*For we have found this man a plague, a creator of dissension among all the Jews throughout the world, and <u>a ringleader of the sect of Nazarenes</u>.*" The Scriptures also portray followers referring to each other as "brothers," "saints" or "disciples."

At the end of the day if anyone prefers to go by any of the above names *exclusively* they are taking a name given by men over a name that has been exclusively given by God. Within any church environment, the taking on of the title "Christian" is seen as an extremely important step for a new believer. The result of this type of conditioning presented itself when I invited a woman to attend a Messianic meeting. She insisted on knowing if the people at this meeting were Christian to gauge whether she would attend or not.

I am not promoting that followers of Jesus should immediately drop the use of the term Christian because of reading anything contained solely within this work. My desire is that Christians might be inspired to investigate the issue and make a calculated decision based on information gathering and research rather than the hearsay of a guy with a back-to-front collar.

One of the main characteristics of this Eternal Creator is that He is "unchanging," and suitably so should our actions be toward Him. While an almost unnoticeable aspect of our walk, such as a change in a name or a slight deviation in a style of worship may appear to be unimportant or of no consequence, over time a thousand changes of equal value, could one day see God's chosen people practicing a completely foreign faith. Contrary to popular belief the Israelites did not abandoned their God when Moses went up into Mount Sinai. They simply chose to worship Him in a manner that they assumed would be acceptable *(Exodus 32:4-5)*. This assumption proved catastrophic. There is a fundamental practicality and simplicity in remaining securely anchored to the teachings of Scripture.

Over the centuries men of influence have caused the masses to deviate away from many God ordained Commandments, despite Scripture warning believers to retain the traditions of God. *Thessalonians 2:15; "Therefore brethren, <u>stand fast and hold the traditions</u>, which you were taught, whether by word or our epistle."*

Today, there is no shortage of sermons that focus on carrying out and sharing God's word in a loving manner. But there are few that emphasise "guarding" or "holding fast" to it *(Deuteronomy 11:22, Isaiah 56:6)*. Because this raises the question, "hold fast to what?" Popular Christian theology unravels in this area because it is forced to explain an adherence to subsequent man-made traditions over former rulings set down by God. *Leviticus 22:9* and *31* emphasizes guarding His commandments, because people *"seek* (the) *truth from the lips of* (His) *priests" (Malachi 2:7)* and if they do not hold onto His former knowledge (or teachings) His commands will become corrupted. Then these men will be held "contemptible" *(Malachi 2:9)* and receive a stricter judgment. *James 3:1; "Let not many of you become teachers, <u>knowing that we shall receive a stricter judgment</u>."*

Paradoxically Christians are taught to avoid man-made traditions. As they do this they unwittingly let go of many of God's traditions as well. The result is a vague teaching, which subconsciously promotes tradition as "legalism." Such a climate has given birth to a people who have claimed a foreign name, which has subsequently given birth to a foreign identity. Through His Son, God always leads by example and does not change. *Malachi 3:6-7; "For I am the Lord, I do not change; Therefore you are not consumed, O sons of Jacob, Yet from the days of your fathers You have gone away from My ordinances and have not kept them. Return to Me, and I will return to you."* And *Hebrews 13:8; "Jesus Christ is the same yesterday, today and forever."* If we find ourselves at a point in history where we've inherited lies from our ancestors, we should return to the truth.

Reclaiming a True Name Reclaims a True Identity

While it may be enlightening to reveal a truth and in doing so hint at taking something away, in this case the use of the name "Christian," it is important to attempt to fill the potential vacuum that this revelation might create. Calling into question a comforting and familiar term, that represents a person's belief, and walking away can be a bit like turning up to their house, telling them that it is poorly built, demolishing it and leaving them with no house at all. What name then should a people who profess to follow the same God as the Hebrews go by? The answer is found in *Genesis 32:28; "And He said, "Your name shall no longer be called Jacob, BUT ISRAEL; for you have struggled with God and with men, and have prevailed."* This verse reveals the name of God's chosen people and its meaning displays their character; in that they will "struggle" with Him. The Scriptures are overwhelmingly clear on who these people were and what their name was. There are no other people that God is ever mentioned as being sovereign over throughout the whole of the Old or New Testament. The frequent appearance within Scripture of "all nations" being under God contextually describes foreign nations joining into one commonwealth, as is evident in *Zechariah 2:11-12; "Many nations shall be joined to the Lord, in that day, and they shall become My people. And I will dwell in your midst. Then you will know that the Lord of hosts has sent Me to you. And the Lord will take possession of Judah as His inheritance in the Holy Land, and will again choose Jerusalem."* The Christian mindset is that the Jew strayed from God and Jesus came to bring about a new faith based in the Gentile camp into which the Jew must adhere. But the truth is that there was never initially a division between Jew and Gentile. The Jews lost their way by adding to God's law and observing it as a means of salvation in itself. The Gentiles were lost because they abandoned His law altogether.

The Jews were originally just one of the twelve tribes that made up Israel and they, like the rest of their dispersed brethren, have to return to the living Torah, whom the world calls Jesus. This realisation has been (in part) made all the more difficult because the church has hidden the Messiah's true identity under a foreign Greco-Roman name and a law destroying persona. The reason Jews are singled out in the New Testament is because they were the only tribe left who, however legalistically, still kept the Torah in the Messiah's day. The Gentile is under the same requirement as the legalistic Torah keeping Jew to get to the same place. But the Gentile Christian comes from a lawless or Torah-less background. *John 10:66 "And other sheep I have which are not of this fold; them also I must bring, and they will hear My voice; and there will be one flock and one shepherd."* Ultimately both peoples must reunite under the one banner of Israel. This is not to say that salvation is any more easily acquired on the grounds of one's ethnicity. *Galatians 6:16* reveals that though Israel is God's chosen nation, anyone who walks in loving obedience as they once did will be accepted as a member of this commonwealth *(And as many as walked according to his rule, peace and mercy be upon them, AND UPON ISRAEL OF GOD).* The question then arises, how does one become a member of Israel? Moving to Israel and applying for citizenship is certainly not the answer. This walk is defined by maintaining an obedient love of God's Commandments as portrayed in the character of Jesus. No matter what physical state, race, or profession, all are eligible to join the commonwealth of Israel. *Exodus 12:49 "One law shall be for the native-born and for the stranger who dwells among them."* Both Jew and Gentile shall love the same law and have the same Commandments written on their hearts and minds. The Scriptures speak of only two denominations of people in God's eyes. They are His people (Israel) and *"outside are dogs,"* sorcerers, sexually immoral, murderers, idolaters and liars *(Revelation 22:15)*.

Loving God Through Open Obedience to His Law (Torah)

Churches today teach us to love grace. But the Bible teaches us to love God by maintaining loving obedience to His law. King David, a man after God's own heart, wrote shamelessly about loving the law (Torah) in the Psalms, despite this concept being in direct conflict to Christian theology *(Psalms 119: 47, 113, 127, 163 & 165)*.

Those that love and profess to know Him are to have the law on their hearts and minds *(Hebrews 10:16)* and speak of it persistently *(Deuteronomy 11:19)*. According to *Romans 7:22* the law (Torah) should be a believer's "delight!"

The Christian mindset views any deliberate emphasis on keeping God's law as legalism. This is despite Jesus himself saying that this act is the very key to walking in his fullness. *John 14:15; "If you love Me, keep My commandments."* Contrary to popular opinion, no commandments or laws were ever permanently cancelled. The following verse is often misinterpreted to support the notion that the law was nailed to the cross. *Colossians 2:14; "...having wiped out the handwriting of requirements that was against us, which was contrary to us. And He has taken it out of the way, having nailed it to the cross."* To surmise that this verse confirms the removal of the law is a bold view because it leaves one wondering why the commandments are put on our hearts and what commandments are to be kept if one wants to love the Creator *(1 John 2:3)*? Nowhere are there any specific laws cancelled in the New Testament. When I ask Christians to tell me what laws were nailed to the cross they will usually say the ceremonial laws, food laws and sacrificial laws, despite the above reference containing no such specifications. This array is subconsciously picked out because they don't appear to affect Jesus' motivational commandment of loving one another. A Christian's unfamiliarity with these laws also forces them to be the ones that are naturally discarded.

Keeping the law lovingly <u>is not</u> legalism, but keeping it in a begrudging, self-righteous manner or as a means of attaining Salvation is another story. In the following verse Jesus states the manner in which the law should be kept. *Matthew 22:37-40; "Jesus said to him, 'You shall love the Lord your God with all your heart, with all your soul, and with all your mind, This is the first and great commandment. And the second is like it: You shall love your neighbour as yourself. <u>On these two commandments hang all the Law</u> and the Prophets.'"* These two commandments carry the motive and manner in which all other commandments are to be observed. In no way is there any hint of them being a replacement or consolidation of the other eight or even the other six hundred and thirteen laws.

To advocate that the law or any aspect of it has been done away with based on *Colossians 2:14* is to be an advocate of lawlessness. We cannot keep some of the commandments and discard others because they sound irrelevant or obscure *(James 2:10-12)*. What then does this verse in Colossians refer to? This verse clearly points to the curses of the adulterous woman mentioned in *Numbers 5:23; "Then the priest shall write these curses in a book, and he shall scrape them off into the bitter water."* This handwriting consisted of lists of broken Torah ordinances that the adulterous woman (Israel) had committed, which are now "blotted out."

The Messiah never came to nullify the old law. *Mathew 5:17; "Do not think that I come to destroy the Law or the prophets. <u>I did not come to destroy but to fulfill</u>."* His fulfillment is the hook, which the law (before and after his sacrifice) hangs for all eternity.

The Restoration of the Altar of Sacrifice

The following topic is politically incorrect and must be read through and studied carefully.

The big question that arises in the mind of the Christian, when all aspects of the law are alleged to remain intact, is the issue of animal sacrifices. Christian theology teaches that Jesus' crucifixion and resurrection put an end to animal sacrifice for all time. Therefore any law pertaining to such an act is now destroyed and replaced by the precious blood of Jesus. However, any aspect of the law being done away with must be filtered through Jesus' statement in *Luke 16:17; "And it is easier for heaven and earth to pass away <u>than for one tittle of the law to fail</u>."* According to him, heaven and earth will cease to exist before even the smallest Hebrew marking (tittle) on a Torah scroll is removed.

A skim of the Scriptures does appear to uphold the notion that animal sacrifices have been done away with. This is compounded by the false view that the "abomination of desolation" (Anti-Christ) resumes animal sacrifices in *Daniel 12:11*, which are then stopped by God. In actual fact the sacrifices are *"taken away"* by the abomination of desolation and not the other way round. *"And From the time that the daily sacrifice is taken away, and the abomination of desolation is set up there shall be one thousand two hundred and ninety days."*

Atoning sacrifices in the tabernacle DID NOT, of themselves, take away sins. *Hebrews 10:4; "For it is not possible that the blood of bulls and goats could take away sins."* To believe that the atoning sacrifice took away sin is to believe that there were two ways of salvation. The former way, by the blood of an animal and the later way, in the finished work of Messiah. The sacrificial offering was only accepted if the one bringing it saw it as a foreshadowing of Messiah (i.e. faith in a future promise). But curiously *Hebrews 10:3* speaks of them as being a "REMINDER" and further on in *verse 32* as an act that recalls "FORMER DAYS." Then in *13:10* it says, *"we have an altar..."* as opposed to saying, "we had an altar," to which the bodies of animals are to be brought. The accepted view, according to *Hebrews 13:15,* is that these offerings are now a *"sacrifice of praise...that is the fruit of our lips."* But *Hosea 14:2,* written when the atoning sacrifices were still in effect also states, *"Take words with you, and return to the Lord. Say to Him. 'Take away all iniquity; receive us graciously, for we will offer the sacrifices of our lips.'"* The physical sacrifice or the flowing of an innocent animal's blood will cause people to praise with their lips. Praise of the lips alone is not meant to replace physical sacrifices.

Future animal sacrifices will resume in the millennial reign, but they will be done based on the faith of an individual in the Messiah's past work. There is evidence of sacrifices in the New Testament after the crucifixion. *Acts 21:26* portrays Paul entering the Temple, under the instruction of James and the elect, with several Nazarite men to bring forward offerings. This incident is interrupted, but the intention is nonetheless recorded. The reality of seeing the shed blood of an innocent animal is to jolt the one seeking atonement into the stark reality of the Messiah's selfless act. The atonement offering is and has always been an object lesson for generations to meditate on, whether before or after the crucifixion.

While there is no Temple in Jerusalem only 271 of the 613 laws can be fulfilled. Upon the restoration of the Temple at the commencement of the millennial reign of Jesus on earth *(Ezekiel 37:28)* all 613 laws will resume. Jesus will work together with the priests to worship the Father. *Ezekiel 45:17; "Then it shall be the (P)rince's[6] (Sar's / Messiah's) part to give burnt offerings, grain offerings, and drink offerings, at the feasts, the New Moons, the Sabbaths, and at all the appointed seasons of the house of Israel. He shall prepare the sin offering, the grain offering, the burnt offering, and the peace offerings to make atonement for the house of Israel."*

The Food Laws are Cancelled Lie

Man's failure to adhere to the food or Kosher[7] laws that were set down in the Scriptures has given rise to some of the most severe illnesses and ecological imbalances sweeping the globe today. Capitalist greed has driven Food Companies to feed animals their faeces, the remains of their own dead and cocktails of chemical enhancements that accelerate growth to increase productivity.

This generation is now reaping the consequences of these long-term practices in the form of mad cow disease, bird flue, Alzheimer's and a host of cancers. The environment is under extreme threat because seemingly insignificant animals that performed critical roles in stabilising ecological harmony are now disappearing.

In the beginning of creation animals were separated by the creator as clean and unclean. This was done not only for the physical well being of the earth's inhabitants but also for the stability of the environment as well.

The food laws didn't just extend to a list of animals that man could and couldn't eat. They included things like not eating a clean

---

6 Modern translations hide the fact that this section of Ezekiel is talking about the "Prince of Peace," Jesus (Yahushua) the Messiah by substituting the word "Prince" with a lower case "p."

7 The Hebrew word "Kosher" means fit.

animal if it died of natural causes, correct slaughter techniques and letting the land (where crops were grown) have a period of rest. The majority of these laws were primarily laid down in *Leviticus 11* and *Deuteronomy 14* of the Scriptures.

But how are these current claims and foundational teachings to be reconciled when Christian theology apparently teaches quite convincingly from Scripture that Jesus did away with food laws?

Let's look carefully at their argument by examining key Biblical verses that are commonly sited as cancelling the food or Jewish Kosher laws (Each verse is followed by a clear contextual explanation). They are as follows:

Mark 7:15, 18; "__There is nothing that enters a man from outside which can defile him__; but the things which come out of him, these are the things which defile a man...And he said to them, 'Are you thus without understanding also. Do you not perceive that whatever enters a man from outside cannot defile him.'" This teaching is in response to the Pharisees objection to Jesus and his disciples eating with unwashed hands. The man-made tradition of washing hands in a certain ritualistic manner (even when the Pharisees had no intention of eating) became a doctrine, while more important God ordained observances had been disregarded. Jesus bluntly reminds them that ingested bacteria can't defile a person in the same way that departing from the law (Torah) can. This incident has nothing whatsoever to do with clean or unclean foods. Be warned, the New International Version (NIV) Bible adds a sentence to *Verse 19* that IS NOT SCRIPTURE which says, "In saying this, Jesus declared all foods clean."

Luke 11:41; "But rather give alms of such things as you have; __then indeed all things are clean to you__." This verse sits on the end of a teaching that emphases the need to be clean inwardly as well as outwardly. In context it has nothing whatsoever to do with the consumption of food, let alone as a passage that endorses a drastic amendment to the food laws.

Acts 10:12; "__In it were all kinds of four-footed animals of the earth, wild beasts, creeping things and birds of the air__...And a voice came to him, 'Rise Peter, __Kill and eat.__'" The "all kinds..." reference refers to all kinds of clean animals. *Leviticus 11* exhibits the range of animals that may have been set before Peter. See *Genesis 9:2:3* for a similar proclamation given to Noah. God never changes or alters any aspect of his own Covenant.

Acts 10:14-15; "But Peter said, 'Not so, Lord! For I have never eaten anything common or unclean.' And the voice spoke to him again the second time, 'What God has cleansed you must not call common.'" God is showing Peter that exiled Israelites, who were once clean, will soon return in an unclean condition. Peter's reaction shows that he no longer recognises his formerly clean brothers and sisters. Interestingly Peter argues that he has never eaten unclean foods (in roughly ten years since Jesus' death). Surely if Jesus cancelled the food laws one of the most prominent apostles would have known and thus refrained from maintaining such a diet.

Romans 14:2 "For one believes he may eat all things, but he who is weak eats only vegetables." This verse, in context, highlights the need to avoid making disputes over believers who might avoid meats because they simply dislike their taste or cause them mild to severe illness (making them weak). "All things" means every food that is deemed clean.

Romans 14:14; "I know and am convinced by the Lord Jesus that there is nothing unclean of itself; but to him who considers anything to be unclean, to him it is unclean." This verse is not specifically talking about clean or unclean foods. It is speaking about the merit of an individual judgment on any area that is not necessarily classed as clean or otherwise.

Romans 14:20; "Do not destroy the work of God for the sake of food. All things indeed are pure, but it is evil for the man to eat with offence." This teaching was the result of a school of thought, which had arisen, that questioned the merit of certain meats and vegetables that were ordained by God to be clean. Paul is trying to set the story straight by saying that all clean food (outlined in the Torah) is pure!

1 Timothy 4:2-4; "speaking lies in hypocrisy, having their own conscience seared with a hot iron. Forbidding to marry, and commanding to abstain from foods which God created to be received with thanksgiving by those who believe and know the truth. For every creature of God is good, and nothing is to be refused if it is received with thanks giving: for it is sanctified by the word of God and prayer." These verses are rebuking those who avoid certain clean foods in the hopes of gaining a form of righteousness or spiritual reward. If every creature were good for food then bats, skunks, scorpions, lice, and countless poisonous sea-life would be acceptable (not to mention animals that can cause allergic reactions to certain individuals, which may result in death).

The Torah also prohibits the consumption of any animal's fat and blood *(Leviticus 3:17, 7:23,26,27)*.

Hebrews 13:9; "Do not be carried about with various and strange doctrines. For it is good that the heart be established by grace, <u>not with foods which have not profited those who have been occupied with them</u>." This verse is simply saying that spiritual matters are more important than diets or weight loss programs!

Translation Alert!

1 Corinthians 10:25; "<u>Eat whatever is sold in the meat market</u>, asking no questions for conscious sake." This verse is an extremely poor translation, which appears more accurately in *The Emphatic Diaglott* (Containing the Original Greek Text) as: *"Whatever is sold as food in the shambles, eat Not! But ask questions for your conscious sake[8]."* <u>Sneaky</u>!

When Adam and Eve sinned in the Garden of Eden they did so by physically eating a certain kind of fruit. Eve carefully examined this fruit and saw that it was not only edible, but also "beneficial" to her *(Genesis 3:6)*. This fruit was sanctified as a pleasant tasting nutrient that would increase one's knowledge, yet (for whatever reason) it was forbidden as food for the Adamic pair. All things are sanctified and should not be rejected, but not all things are sanctified as food!

Clearly none of the above verses provide any solid ground at adhering to a nullification of any or all of the foundational statutes that where laid down in the Torah regarding food. It is vague understanding mixed with pure ignorance that perpetuates the stance that all animals that are pleasant to taste and/or are of nutritional

---

8   This passage and verses 26 to 29 are more accurately rendered in The New Covenant Paleo Signature Edition Scriptures, published by The Remnant of YHWH. It is available in PDF format at their website www.REMNANTOFYHWH.com.

value are suitable for consumption in the current dispensation. This attitude mirrors the same kind of thinking that got Adam and Eve disqualified from the Garden of Eden.

The Pig – Biologically Closer to a Human Than an Ape

I remember having a conversation with a butcher about the slaughter of pigs that I will never forget. He said that he had a lot of trouble accepting the hind leg portion of pigs from his supplier because the animals had to be smashed on the back of their legs with baseball bats to get them to move into a position to be slaughtered. Invariably the rear leg portions would arrive with severely shattered bones rendering them unfit for sale. He witnessed pigs being slaughtered during his apprenticeship and noted that they were the only animals that seemed to know what was about to happen. He added that their squeals reminded him of small children.

Pork meat can carry up to 200 forms of disease and play host to as many as 18 different parasites. Among these parasites is the deadly "trichinella spiralis," which can cause an illness for which there is no known cure. These parasites cannot be detected in pork during any phase of its preparation. Food sanitation codes were first formulated in the United States due to pork. Pigs are essentially omnivorous (meaning they like to scavenge). They will eat anything – worms, carcasses, excrement and garbage. A pig's value is its own excrement. It is used to great effect for agricultural purposes.

Biologically a swine is the closest animal to a human. This is why people receive pig organ transplants, which incidentally is also a violation[9] of God's law (Torah). If evolutionists are right in claiming that apes are our closest ancestors why aren't we using their organs over a pig's?

Unclean animals are a last resort, but easy refuge for demons. This is why in *Luke 8:33* they plead with Jesus to send them into a herd of pigs. Ingesting a steady diet of unclean food can open doorways that may lead to increased susceptibility to demonic attack.

---

9   The phrase, "According to its own kind," found several times in the creation account of Genesis 1 signifies an emphasis of maintaining pure genetic lines. Each generation of species is to remain uninterrupted by the introduction of any organism that is not after its own kind.

Dr E. A Widmer says in this article entitled, "'Pork, Man & Disease' – Pork although one of the most common articles of diet, is one of the most injurious. God did not prohibit the Hebrews from eating swine's flesh merely to show His authority, but because it was not a proper article of food."

No New Religion, But a Return to the One From Which We Strayed

The Gospels contain the fulfillment of major events that were originally set down in the Torah and prophetic writings. The Old Testament makes up the majority of the Bible and is the foundation, which gives validity and clarity to all the books of the New Testament. Today Christians see the Old Testament as a book of old teachings that no longer apply. The truth is that the Gospels can never be completely understood without a sturdy grasp of the Torah. Therefore it should be encouraged as a good investment of one's time to learn the eternal aspect of the covenants found there before charging out and preaching a Gospel message.

Many Churches teach that Christianity was a new religion that was started by Jesus, which replaced Judaism and yet nowhere in Scripture is there any notion of this doctrine. God starts with Israel and finishes with Israel. Christianity as I hope to illustrate throughout the course of this work, is not the renewed Israel. Does this mean that only descendants of Israel will be saved? No, even true-blooded law keeping descendants of Israel, who have lost the motivation of loving obedience, will also share the same fate as Godless Gentiles. Again, it must be made clear that salvation is not based solely on one's ethnicity. This concept is neatly illustrated in *Romans 11:21-24; "For if God did not spare the natural branches, He may not spare you either. Therefore consider the goodness and severity of God: on these who fell, severity; but toward you, goodness if you continue in His goodness. Otherwise you also will be cut off. And they also, if they do not continue in unbelief, will be grafted in, for God is able to graft them in again. For if you were cut out of the olive tree which is wild by nature, and were grafted contrary to nature into a cultivated olive tree, how much more will these, who are natural branches, be grafted into their own olive tree?"* Though much of Israel is presently dispersed *(Hosea 8:8)*, they are now re-emerging to meet their husband (God) *(Revelations 21:2)*. It is my belief that it would be time well spent if the average Christian and Orthodox Jew spent some serious time studying this issue, rather than continuing to sit proudly in either camp.

Enemies of Jesus and his apostles never saw them as founders of a completely new radical religion, unlike today's worldly perspective. They were seen by them as a "Nazarene (Natzeret) sect." *Matthew 2:23; And he came and dwelt in a city called Nazareth, that it might be fulfilled which was spoken by the prophets, "He shall be called a Nazarene."* The term "sect" means a "breakaway movement" or "cult." A friend of mine became distressed when he read an article that referred to Sabbath keepers as being a sect and I had to remind him that our Saviour was also considered a member of a sect and if it was good enough for him it should be good enough for us. From the perspective of witnesses in biblical times, Jesus and his followers were seen as founders of a breakaway movement of "Judaism." In reality, they were men who came to restore a right view of the Torah to make clear the way of Salvation to all men. From a more accurate human perspective they were known as "Nazarene Israelites," because the term Nazarene signifies an offshoot faith (coming from Nazareth) who are watchful (Notsri – to watch) and is combined with the name of God's chosen people (Those who struggle with Yah [God]).

Because members of the olive tree (Israel) will also be cut away, an even more specific name for God's chosen people exists, which is spoken of through a prophet. They are called "The Remnant of Israel," *(Zephaniah 3:13)*. This refers to a body of people that are "set apart" (Holy). Therefore after careful consideration of the truth of the Scriptures, historical accounts and much reading of a wide range of material, I have grafted myself to the commonwealth of Israel, whose king is the resurrected Messiah of Nazareth. His true name and that of his Father who sent him will be discussed in a later chapter, as this subject deserves considerable space. For those reading this work that have had the veil lifted on the Saviour's name please bear with me.

Wayward Worship of a Wayward People

"You worship what you do not know; we know what we worship, for salvation is of the Jews." – (Jesus' words) *John 4:22*

For most people today religion consists of compartmentalised worship gatherings laced with motivational speaking, clique study groups and social club style interaction. Many youth coming up in the church today, wear their religion like a fashion accessory. It seasons their lives rather than becomes their lives. They pursue a trendy style of worship without receiving instruction from the Scriptures as to how this worship could best please God. The Israelites did the same thing when they built the golden calf to worship the Creator. *Exodus 32:5; "So when Aaron saw it (the Golden Calf), he built an altar before it. And Aaron made a proclamation and said, "Tomorrow is a feast to the Lord (YHWH)."* They had a sincere desire to worship God, but not according to knowledge. *Proverbs 19:2; "Desire without knowledge is not good, and to be overhasty is to sin and miss the mark.* Paul writes of Israel's misdirected longing to serve in *Romans 10:2; "For I bear them witness that they have a zeal for God, but not according to knowledge."* The result of proceeding with God without the accompanying desire to grow in knowledge is described in *Hosea 4:6; "My people are destroyed for lack of knowledge. Because you have rejected knowledge, I also will reject you from being priests for me."*

The Religion of Convenience

If a religion claims to be a way to God or enlightenment among many other options it stands to reason that the majority of people are going to gravitate to the religion that is the most convenient and requires the least amount of effort to adapt to and receive its apparent benefits. A person might assume a religion because it is the only one practiced in an immediate vicinity and everyone they associate with belongs to it. Also by definition a religion cannot be forced onto a person against their will or adopted simply on the basis of ancestral belief. This also stands with Christianity. Many people believe they are Christians simply because they are born in a Christian country or community. A person might embrace a religion because they felt it was right, which is fine, but if they don't learn that not only did it feel right, but that it could be right, they are equipped no better than any other follower of any other faith. People may enter into a religion that is already partially aligned with previous philosophies that they may have formed due to various past experiences. Surrendering of any previous opinions is a minimal requirement since the appeal usually comes in the form of a god whose form is whatever the occupant thinks he or she should be. The problem here is that the truth, whatever it is, can only be one thing. For example a person can't be both at work and off sick at the same time no matter how many ways you attempt to look at it. There is either a bottle of milk in your fridge or there isn't. This is the bottom line. Many Christian pastors unwittingly perpetuate a "many paths to enlightenment" attitude even though they claim to preach against it. This is because they cling to "a truth is relative" philosophy, when in fact the truth, by its very construct, cannot be anything else but "absolute." In actual fact it is we who are "relative" as we scoot to different vantage points to get softer and less confronting views of it, rather than park ourselves right on it. The truth cannot be many different things and depending where we're at in life, the truth may not be something that we've considered or even like when we learn it.

Chapter Two

Conspiracy is a Four-Letter Word

OVER THE LAST COUPLE of years I have observed a stigmatism slowly attaching itself to the verbal use of the word conspiracy. Mere mention of a suspicion of conspiracy behind anything from a workplace issue to a global situation is immediately met with instant pigeonholing of the user of the term into the "conspiracy nut" category. This is despite history showing us that the JFK shooting, Watergate, and even the Vietnam War had active conspirators working behind the scenes who for a time successfully concealed crucial facts. People seem to be relating to the word conspiracy as a fictitious word that is only used by crackpots and doomsday religious nuts and therefore can never be taken as a serious explanation for a given situation. Even the Bible has a verse that says: *Isaiah 8:12; "Do not say a conspiracy, concerning all that this people call a conspiracy, nor be afraid of their threats, nor be troubled."* While it is true that there are people out there who tend to think everything is a conspiracy and the tabloid media feed the fire of public paranoia by conjuring up the most bizarre and elaborate theories it should not mean that the term itself should become synonymous with an illusory situation. *Jeremiah 11:9-10a* also warns, *"And the Lord said to me, 'A conspiracy has been found among the men of Judah*

and among the inhabitants of Jerusalem. They have turned back to the iniquities of their forefathers who refused to hear My words...'"
Before I go any further it is important to read the following dictionary explanation of the word:

> "**Conspiracy** –cies. **1.** the act of conspiring **2.** a combination of persons for an evil or unlawful purpose; plot. [CONSPIR (E) + -ACY] – **conspirator, n.** – **conspiratress,** *n. fem.*"

Before I became a Christian, and subsequently a Nazarene Israelite, I watched a series of videos by the late New Zealand evangelist Barry Smith. The series was called *Eye in the Triangle* and he talked extensively about the New World Order, privatisation, and the impending cashless society. I was really intrigued and at the same time a little bit frightened by what I heard on the tapes. It challenged me and I felt there was certainly some truth in what he was saying. I wanted to find out more. Not only that, I wanted to find out more about this man called Jesus. For a short period I showed the video to a few non-Christian friends and I soon became the subject of some ridicule among them. To the extent that I still feel gentle jabs from those friends to this day. I noticed a complete disregard by them of any content in the video that spoke about God and an almost ritual suspicion of anything that was alleged to be a conspiracy, despite the speaker's clear explanations and backing up of much he had to say with countless newspaper articles, book excerpts and written testimonies. I personally believed his sincerity because he avoided speculation and delivered information straight down the line. But the attitude of my friends was disturbing. Mild accusations of brain washing were thrown about when he proceeded at one point on the video to unroll a poster that said "Welcome to the cashless society" and walked to three points of a stage and repeated the words to his audience. I felt like there was a defensive barrier that instantly went up on showing the video or at other times when I would mention anything pertaining to it. I was interested in why the subject of God or conspiracies instantly sparked such passionate objection or ridicule when just about any other topic was open for discussion.

But the most heart-breaking thing was yet to come. Some years later I tentatively showed one of the tapes to a Bible study group that I had joined and their response may have been less openly hostile, but I was immediately pegged as one of those nutty conspiracy theorist Christians and anything I offered during nightly discussions from then on was ritualistically questioned or met with silence. Any other aspect of my spiritual growth went unnoticed because a big tag of "conspiracy freak" was obscuring their vision of me.

Defuse Faith in a Word, Defuse Faith in a Concept

A conspirator's dream is to have the majority of the population instantly find no credibility in any person's allegation of a conspiracy. Whether they are right or not, anything after that word rolls off their tongue is immediately discredited. The only option is to not use the word. Interesting.

"Ridicule" – Government Policy

Author Terry Henson has stated that "The Robertson Panel," a special branch of scientists and military advisers formed by the CIA, came to the conclusion, concerning the UFO phenomena, that it would be in the best interests of the U.S. government to suppress media coverage of alleged UFO sightings. One of a number of recommended standard methods was the use of ridicule to cast subjects into disrepute. This would be done in the contexts of a training program that used the more politically correct, yet inaccurate term, "debunking."

The fact remains, no matter how small or large conspiracies are, mankind's history is riddled with them. Satan tempted Adam and Eve to eat the fruit, promising them the knowledge of both good and evil, and assured them that they would not die and would in fact become like God. This statement gives Satan the appearance of being an informative friend. But his real agenda was to make an example of their disobedience before God, in an attempt to prove a point. Judas conspired with the Pharisees to have Jesus arrested for a pathetic thirty pieces of silver, Julius Caesar was murdered by his best friend Brutus, and the Catholic Church also conspired with the Crusaders to claim back the Holy lands from the Moslems.

And so through history the same story goes, putting weight into the verse: *Ecclesiastes 1:9; There is nothing new under the sun.*

Order Out of Chaos Made Simple

Why do conspiracies exist? Generally a conspiracy arises out of a ruling or power based minority group's desire to achieve an agenda where the details have to remain anonymous to the majority. Here is an example of not only how a conspiracy works, but also the advantages it produces.

A group of thugs move to a peaceful town with an agenda to acquire money by any means. One day they drop into a convenience store and demand protection money from the owner. The owner declines the offer and asks them to leave. They do so and a month later the store is broken into and robbed by the same thugs unbeknownst to the storeowner. Some time later the thugs return with the same offer and the owner willingly gives them money and arranges a monthly fee to be paid to assure that his shop is looked after. Magically the convenience store goes back to the same peaceful state it was in before.

The thugs could have acquired money unlawfully from this owner in two different ways.

Option 1

They could have marched into the shop, held the owner at gunpoint and committed armed robbery.

Advantage:	They could have cleaned out his entire till and helped themselves to whatever items they pleased.
Disadvantage:	The storeowner may be familiar with such encounters and may have a few surprises of his own for the thugs.
	Any number of witnesses could observe the incident and pass on relevant descriptions to police.

The authorities may be in the vicinity of the scene or respond quickly to apprehend the assailants.

If successful they would not be able to acquire money from this shop on a regular basis without running the risk of facing heightened security. The risks are too high.

Option 2

They could enter the store and ask for a small fee to protect the store from harm.

Advantage: While this option may upset the storeowner it is unlikely that they will be charged for this offence. If the owner agrees they will receive regular payments as opposed to a one off amount. If the owner declines, the thugs can covertly rob and damage the store, minimising the risk of witnesses and so on.

Disadvantage: The robbery may have to be repeated several times before the storeowner takes the hint (The scale of the action does not necessarily need to be increased). The risks are minimal.

Notice that the shop ran peacefully before the thugs arrived. The thugs turn up and offer to assure future peace to the storeowner for a monthly fee. The storeowner sees no reason for this additional fee. The thugs later proceed to cause chaos for the owner by interfering with the shop. The owner then sees reason for protection and pays up. This very basic example of an invented crisis shows how it can lead to opportunity as a person or a community cries out for order and security.

The above example has happened throughout history to varying degrees. Usually a great upheaval or disorder is met with a solution that has brought with it a change of some sort that was formerly difficult to institute. During a time of chaos or crisis the victims can be more willing to accept certain changes and demands that prior to the event would not have been considered. In addition to creating a crisis for this purpose a preceding gradual relaxing of a privilege can also increase the magnitude of chaos. As the recipients take unreasonable opportunities, the inevitable outcome is a collapse in the current scheme. As the chaos is maximised so too is the solution bringing with it even more extreme rules and laws.

Terry Cook in his book *Mark of the New World Order* points out the following example. In Oklahoma City in April, 1995 a nine storey federal building containing mostly civilians collapsed under an alleged single truck-bomb outside the building. Experts familiar with the construction of the building remain sceptical to this day that the capacity of the single bomb was enough to cause such destruction. Whatever the true story, it was a tragedy of mind-blowing proportions. Fear gripped the hearts of the people and the cry arose, "Why did this happen?" Prevention becomes the top priority in their minds. Demands for justice and protection are the new focus of the surviving victims. While emotions still run high in those affected, things that they may have been reluctant to give up are now more acceptable in the light of the current climate. Ultimately people become more willing to give up certain freedoms and willingly submit to increased covert surveillance and more governmental control of their lives.

Before the September 11 attacks on the World Trade Centre a new document detailing major changes to the American Constitution had been put in circulation and was subsequently rejected on the grounds of some major increases in power to law enforcement agencies and across the board reductions of citizen's basic rights. After September 11 the document resurfaced with a new name. It was called the "Patriot Act." Cleverly titled, because if you weren't in support of it you were considered unpatriotic and ran the risk of being thrown under suspicion as the government and media started looking for terrorists behind every tree and under every rock. Finally overnight, on October 25th 2001, the USA PATRIOT Act was passed by Congress. It was hailed as the document that would "unite and strengthen" America by providing the appropriate tools necessary to intercept and obstruct terrorism. This would be the sell line in a climate that was at last overwhelmingly suitable, as the level of personal fear among people had gradually risen to an all time high and the people, like a pack of trained horses, were finally broken into the idea of losing all rights in the name of security.

Years ago I observed a badge that I was later informed was an American Air Force insignia, which I still find interesting. It depicted an eagle rising from a circle with arrows coming out of it in all-different directions. Some research revealed that the eagle was in fact a Phoenix and the circle was a chaos symbol. This Phoenix represents renewal and was originally a bird of Arabian legend that set fire to itself and was then reborn from its ashes. The chaos symbol, also of ancient origin, represents confusion or crisis.

Unpatriotic Patriot Act

It is important to note that due to the passing of an executive order by US President George W. Bush, the Department of Justice (DOJ) has now upped the ante by drafting an even more comprehensive anti-terrorism legislation as of January 9, 2003. This legislatia grants sweeping powers to the government, eliminating or further weakening the already feeble powers remaining to keep government surveillance, wiretapping, detention and criminal prosecution in check. The following is a list of some of the laws that I found the most unsettling:

1) Terrorist suspects, citizen or non-citizen face mandatory detention for indefinite periods of time without trial. To date some terrorist suspects have remained in detention for up to three years without trial.

2) Increasing power of nationwide search warrants so they do not have to meet even the broad definition of terrorism found in the USA PATRIOT Act of 2001.

3) Sampling and cataloguing of innocent person's genetic information without court order and without consent.

4) Permitting, without any formal connection to anti-terrorism matters, sensitive personal information about citizens to be shared with local and state law enforcement agencies.

5) Military Commission granted powers to now try suspected citizen and non-citizen terrorists. This format effectively strips suspects of all constitutional protections. You may remember media coverage of prisoners not coming under the Geneva Convention. You may also remember more recently, pictures taken of abuse toward Iraqi prisoners, which would have had less chance of eventuating if these prisoners were under this same rule of war. Interestingly this convention in a way not only protects the captive, but also the captor in providing a minimum guideline of humane treatment, reducing the temptation to resort to degenerating behaviour toward the enemy.

6) Alleged terrorists or citizens associated with alleged terrorists will be denied free choice of attorneys.

7) Any part of the trial, even to execution may be held in secret whether entirely, partially, or at all, and anywhere the Secretary of Defence decides. This is evident right now in the trial of Australian POW, David Hicks, who, as these words go to paper is still being held at Guantanamo Bay by the US.

8) Wiretapping of privileged communications or otherwise (with reasonable cause) will be acceptable with attorney and client exchanges.

9) Stripping even native-born Americans of all of the rights of their citizenship if they provide support to unpopular organisations labeled as terrorist by the government, EVEN IF THEY SUPPORT ONLY THE LAWFUL ACTIVITIES OF SUCH ORGANISATIONS, ALLOWING THEM TO BE INDEFINITELY IMPRISONED IN THEIR OWN COUNTRY AS UNDOCUMENTED ALIENS. (This particular law's implication is that if a known terrorist organisation partake in strict Sabbath keeping then other groups that follow this law could face imprisonment.)

10) Creation of fifteen new death penalties, including a new death penalty for "terrorism" under a definition, which could cover the simple act of protesting.

11) Complete abolition of fair hearings for lawful permanent residents of the United States convicted of even minor criminal offences. This will enable the government to be exempt from *habeas corpus* (a protection guaranteed by the Constitution). No person has been denied this form of protection since the American Civil War.

It is important to bear in mind that the word 'terrorism' or 'terrorist organisation' are broad, open-ended terms that can arbitrarily cover nearly any activity.

Michael Ratner, human rights lawyer and vice president of the Centre for Constitutional rights, concludes with this final note in an essay on the topic of current government control:

"The US Government has conceptualized the war against terrorism as a PERMANENT WAR, A WAR WITHOUT BOUNDARIES. Terrorism is frightening to all of us, but it's equally chilling to think that in the name of antiterrorism our government is willing to suspend constitutional freedoms permanently as well."

Michael Ratner has brought a number of lawsuits against the illegal use of military force by the United States Government and teaches Human Rights Litigation at Columbia Law School.

Conclusion

It is this author's humble opinion that not only do conspiracies exist, but also major government departments institute them with the same unflinching expertise as any lawful mechanism in their arsenal. If you are still not convinced, I will happily drive these points home with the ferocity of a swung sledgehammer with the following historical case. To begin, I will let someone we should all remember begin this story.

"The United States government did something that was wrong – deeply, profoundly, morally wrong. It was an outrage to our commitment to integrity and equality for all our citizens...clearly racist."

— The above statement was a public apology made by former US President Bill Clinton at the Tuskegee Syphilis Experiment to eight remaining survivors on May 16, 1997.

On July 25th, 1972 an article by Jean Heller appeared in the *Washington Star* that made the claim that since 1932 to that date the U.S. *Public Health Service* (PHS) had conducted experiments on 399 black men in which they were studied but not treated for syphilis. These men came from the poorest counties in Alabama and were initially approached with an offer of free healthcare. Many of them not having ever seen a doctor before agreed. They unknowingly became the subjects of an horrific incident in the name of medical science. Prominent news anchor Harry Reasoner described it as an experiment that "used human beings as laboratory animals in a long and inefficient study of how long it takes syphilis to kill someone."

The program started out with the men being prescribed token amounts of the syphilis remedies of the day; bismuth, neoarsphenamine, and mercury, which portrayed good public relations without interfering with the true aims of the experiment. Eventually all syphilis related treatment was reduced to the administering of pink tablets of aspirin.

James Jones, the author of the book, *Bad Blood*, identified the entire ordeal as "the longest nontherapeutic experiment on human beings in medical history."

The aim of the study was as vague as the men that perpetuated it. It had something to do with how syphilis affected blacks as opposed to whites – the theory being that the disease affected the neurological system of whites, whereas blacks were more susceptible to cardiovascular problems.

One can't help but to attribute the racist views of white government officials, who ran the experiments, as the source of fuel that was added to the fire. Yet there were numerous African Americans who also assisted – predominantly black universities assigned staff, lent their medical facilities for the study, and provided additional support from local black doctors.

A black nurse, Eunice Rivers who was involved in the experiment was obviously blinded by the possibility of recognition from prestigious government agencies to let the troubling aspects of the study stop her, while black doctors praised the educational advantages offered to their interns as well as the added standing it would give the hospital.

A closing report on the matter concluded by saying "nothing learned will prevent, find, or cure a single case of infectious syphilis or bring us closer to our basic mission of controlling venereal disease in the United States."

When the whistle finally blew on the whole operation, 128 men had died of syphilis and syphilis related illnesses, 40 of their wives were infected, and 19 babies had entered the world with congenital syphilis.

The media was quick to compare the *Tuskegee Experiment* to the appalling activities conducted by Nazi doctors on Jewish victims during World War II. The PHS responded to such allegations by claiming they were just carrying out orders and were mere cogs in the wheel of the PHS bureaucracy and therefore exempt from personal responsibility. Clearly an answer that stank with the same morally bankrupt odour that was present during the Nuremberg trials.

The above case whether you like it or not is a factual historical conspiracy. Life's too short to be spent continuously engaged in discussions on conspiracy theories that ultimately do little more than provide intellectual stimulation when there are literally truckloads of factual cases of conspiracies out there that don't ever see the light of day.

Chapter Three

The Aliens Are Coming...Again!

"What does all this stuff about flying saucers amount to? What can it mean? What is the truth?" – Sir Winston Churchill

COMBINING THE SUBJECTS of flying saucers piloted by little green men and religion are a little like eating a salad sandwich covered in warm chocolate topping. They don't go together and anyone who is able to navigate their way through both topics without compartmentalising them is considered weird or regarded with suspicion. The mainstream church has skillfully maintained a steady silence on the subject of UFO's for years, despite escalating numbers of sightings, encounters, and even abductions, reaching into the thousands worldwide. However, increased global interest in the topic has forced the issue to be retrieved from the too hard basket and acknowledged. Father Corrado Balducci, an official member of the Papal household made the following statement in regard to the issue: "It is reasonable to believe and affirm that extra-terrestrials exist. Their existence can no longer be denied, for there is too much evidence for the existence of extra-terrestrials and flying saucers."

On the 14th of December 1997, the *Sunday Times* ran a story containing details of a project run by the Vatican to confirm the existence of extra-terrestrials. An observatory in Arizona was its base of operations and was manned by Jesuits. Unbelievably the dilemma was, not whether their existence would cast doubt on the Gospels, but if contact were made, would Christian atonement be necessary for them? Despite these efforts, priests continue giving their masses without mentioning the subject, as if waiting to see which way the Vatican might swing; Are UFO's for us or against us? The current official standing of the Catholic Church on the subject, set forward by prominent Bishops, is one of demonic or manmade origin. The following two chapters will delve into this issue.

It is my observation that the subject of UFO's has for the most part been blatantly ignored by churches as a whole and when rarely broached is stumbled through with the same inept caution as sermons on The Book of Revelations or The Book of Daniel. I have watched with mounting dismay the growing public fascination with UFOs and life on other planets and by contrast a church environment devoid of the subject.

In the early eighties one could quite validly go up to the average person in the street and ask them if they believed in aliens. They would answer either yes or no. Now it seems that the more appropriate question is, "What do you think aliens look like?" What has happened in the meantime to prompt a shift in the question from belief or unbelief to an assumed belief with a query on their appearance?

The biggest player in causing the shift is the media. I believe the ball got rolling well and truly when famous author of *The Wolfen* and *The Hunger*, Whitley Streiber was abducted from his home and became the recipient of many strange experiments by humanoids. The book I'm referring to is *Communion*, which is the factual account of the author's abduction by strange beings. The book remained in the bestseller list for twenty-five weeks and was later made into a motion picture. I am not for a moment going to disbelieve this man's terrifying story and therefore proclaim him a liar. I do however stand in opposition to his theory on whom he actually encountered and why. My main concern at this stage is not so much his ordeal, but the eerie painting of the so-called alien that graced the cover of his book. And I refer to this image because it was one of the earliest major distributions of this style of "alien" that I can remember. I find it interesting that Alister Crowley, perhaps one of the most famous occultists of all time claimed that through spiritism, he met an alien from Sirius and he drew a picture of him. Crowley's painting depicts an egg headed face characterised by a vestigial nose and mouth and two eyes in narrow, elongated slits. One writer has observed that the alleged Syrian had a very similar look to Hollywood's usual portrayal of aliens and except for the eyes resembles the image on the cover of Steiber's book.

Would you an Alien, Devil or Angel be?

Another author by the name of John Keel who wrote a book in the 70's called the *Mothman Prophecy*, now also the basis of a major film, tells of his strange experiences in a town called Point Pleasant in West Virginia. He visited there as a journalist investigating an exhaustive period of heavy unexplained phenomenon in the area. Sightings, contacts and other strange oddities commenced in 1966 and continued for 13 months. He attempts in his book to put forward some theories and possibilities behind some of the strange events that took place there. At one point he makes various links with the origins of alien names, provided to contactees, to gods in Greek Mythology. For example one victim is told of receiving a handwritten letter by an alleged alien, which was signed, "A pal" or "Apal." John links this name as referring to the Greek god Apollo. Unfortunately he fails to mention this god's connection to prophetic Scripture. The name Apollo is derived from the Hebrew name "Abaddon," but in Greek is written "Apollyon." *Revelation 9:11* states: *"And they had a king over them, which is the angel of the bottomless pit, whose name in the Hebrew tongue is Abaddon, but in the Greek tongue hath his name Apollyon."* If you want to see what he looks like there's a nice big gold statue of him outside the Rockefeller Centre in New York. He's carrying a torch and held up by a circle.

Mr. Keel also refers briefly to another name that appears to have a history relating to UFO phenomena. The name is "Ashtar," which he also concludes is derived from the name of the Greek goddess "Esther," a fertility god. And here again he fails to recognise this god's biblical connection. Ashter or Esther is derived from

69

the name "Astheroth," which refers to a pagan god, worshipped in the Old Testament. *Judges 2:13 "And they forsook the LORD, and served Baal and Astheroth."* Though the author briefly mentions biblical connections to UFO phenomena, it is quickly swept aside as he charges toward his hypothesis. Perhaps handicapping himself before he even sets out by stating: "I am not concerned with beliefs but with the cosmic mechanism which has generated and perpetuated those beliefs." His apparent unwillingness to broach the Bible in any detail is all the more startling if one reads his earlier work, *Operation Trojan Horse* where he makes the following observation: "Did ancient man misinterpret UFO manifestations by placing them in religious context? APPARENTLY NOT. The literature indicates that the phenomenon carefully cultivated the religious frame of reference in early times." Why after this admission that it did not spur the author to make more of a biblical connection in his Point Pleasant thesis is a mystery.

During my research into Astheroth's background, I noted that she was a counterpart to Baal. She encompassed the feminine qualities of life, symbolised by the moon as opposed to Baal, which means "lord" or "possessor" who was the male sun god and was worshipped on the tops of high mountains. As I was poking around for information about Baal I found it somewhat unsettling that constructions such as steeples, turrets, and spires that are normally found as architectural features on most Christian churches today, were originally utilised by pagan worshippers to catch the first yellow rays of their sun god at dawn. Interesting.

Let's return our focus back to Mr. Crowley and his encounter with the alien from Sirius through the act of spiritism. Though the word spiritism seems to have more to do with things of a supernatural nature than it does with space men, channeling appears to be common in serious UFO enthusiast circles. First let me explain what spiritism is. It describes the act of a man or woman self-inducing a trance that produces an altered state during which contact with spirits is made. Now regard the same explanation for channeling except change the word spirits to aliens. Channeling or spiritism can take many forms, but the most common are automatic writing and trance channeling.

Taken Away by Aliens or by God?

There is an active organisation called *Ashtar Command* that believe flying saucers are orbiting the earth ready to intervene in human history. Ex-racing care driver and founder of the *Raelian Movement*, Claude Vorilhon, maintains that aliens will land in Jerusalem in 2025 to usher in the New World Order. The more extreme *Heavens Gate* sect committed mass suicide with the expectation that their souls would be picked up by a gigantic mother ship, which flew near the earth in the shadow of a comet. These are just a few of the many UFO cults that followed or still follow this basic doctrine of a foreign aerial intercession.

Why does it appear that UFO cults, however they may vary in their beliefs from each other, hold this common viewpoint of an intervention or departure onto spaceships at a future time? There is a Bible verse that describes an event that may have had something to do with fueling this widespread fixation. *1 Thessalonians 4:17* says; *"Then we which are alive and <u>remain shall be caught up together with them in the clouds:</u> and so shall we ever be with the Lord."* After reading this verse it becomes apparent that a future departure of the righteous is evident in Scripture and the purpose is uncannily not all that dissimilar to the views of these ridiculed UFO cults.

If a vast majority of the world's population witnesses a future mass vertical exodus of people, this could trigger sympathy toward the authenticity of the Bible amongst those remaining who happen to recall a similar Scriptural event.

The potential threat of such a reaction could be why the mainstream completely continues to dissociate flying saucers from the Godly manifestations described in Scripture. On the whole the average Christian invests no personal time in viewing UFO's in any biblical perspective. In contrast the UFO enthusiast refuses to accept the truth of Scripture when the world has happily ventured so many enticing theories as to their origin. Infusing the perception that the UFO phenomenon is a void subject within the Bible may be a good enough catalyst to further fuel disillusionment of its contents. Finally, this event, looked at through a combination of pre-conditioning and timing, may convince the majority of the world's inhabitants that those who were *caught up* were the victims of a mass alien abduction associated with ufology as opposed to the fulfillment of a biblical prophecy.

Not long after my initial ponderings on this theory, I came across a short snippet from a book called *Cosmic Prophecy* written by the founder of the *Aetherian Society*, George King who claims that he has had contact with Jesus who currently lives on Venus. The final passage of the excerpt shows an interesting method of how the truth is overlaid with a lie. It reads:

"There will shortly come another among you. He will stand tall among men and a shining countenance. This One will be attired in a single garment of the type now known to you. His shoes will be soft-topped, yet not made of the skin of animals. He will approach the earth leaders. They will ask of Him, His credentials. He will produce these. His magic will be greater than any upon earth – greater than the combined materialistic might of all the armies. And they, who heed not his words, shall be removed from the earth."

This excerpt paints a picture of a man of great physical stature that will be dressed in modern garments and will attempt a type of negotiation with world leaders. Though this does indeed address the biblical scenario of a coming deliverer, according to the Book of Revelation, it does not address the correct manner in which he will arrive. In fact an arrival and negotiation with leaders and a granting of power by these leaders to such an individual more aptly fits the manner in which "the Beast" will arrive.

The Doctrine of the Rapture – Truth Left Behind

Though I am sympathetic to a future mass ascension of an elect or remnant, I must clarify that the Scriptures do not necessarily portray it as a pre or mid-tribulation rapture, despite many Bible commentaries and church views to the contrary. Certainly if one interprets the term "rapture" to mean an event that is associated with a type of rescue then such a concept has no biblical basis whatsoever.

The truth is that there was no significant teaching on a rapture of the church before the 1800's. A Jesuit by the name of Emmanuel Lacunza, writing under the alias of a Jewish Rabbi first proposed this concept in his book, *The Coming of Messiah in Glory and Majesty*. This book compounded by the prophesying of a fifteen-year old Catholic girl ignited the appealing idea of "the rapture" which, centuries on has given birth to a series of books that continue to deceive millions to this very day. The Messiah taught in his parable of the wheat and tares that the righteous and the unrighteous would be together until the very end *(Matthew 13:24-32)*.

Scripture teaches that followers will be lead to Israel in the last days and be on or near Mount Moriah (Beit HaMikdash) upon seeing the "abomination of desolation." From there they will flee to a place called "Sela," which is now known as modern day "Petra" *(Mathew 24:15-16, Revelation 12:6,14, Isaiah 16:1-5, 42:11)*. Like the early Hebrews who were present during the unfolding of the plagues in Egypt their latter day descendants will endure a similar situation before reaching the Promised Land.

Alien Invasion Practice

The Bible speaks of a great deception as we read *Mark 13:22; "For false Christs and false prophets shall rise, and shall show signs and wonders, to seduce, if it were possible, even the very elect."* I think most Christians who are familiar with this verse tend to focus solely on a future sequence of events that will be initiated with so much fanfare that little effort will be required to recognise it. They are assured and reassured by their religious leaders that it will occur outside the Christian community, which reinforces this "all is yet to happen mentality." Maybe some churchgoers are even unconsciously in a cycle where they rely on ministers and priests to keep them informed of what to watch out for without any inclination to find out on their own. On top of all this, Hollywood has been more than happy to assist, as most Christians have no aversion in trotting off to watch films that tackle apocalyptic subject matter that sits in complete opposition to the biblical portrayal. There they sit in complete darkness, steamrollered by the opinion of a profit margin concerned industry, beamed onto a three story screen in Dolby surround sound with no right of reply. Then they shuffle away, debating with each other as to the possibility of a world heading the way of the plotlines depicted in such movies as, *Armageddon* or *Deep*

Impact. Then the following day they attend church with a Bible in hand that remains largely unread and misunderstood.

Anyone that has been along to see a special effects based film at the cinemas these days will agree that on screen live action movies can make anything, no matter how weird, massive, or intricate, look completely real. In days gone by the capacity to do this was restricted to animated film or radio broadcasts. Though these two mediums have a unique capacity to entertain and inform, lets look at what else they have the potential to do.

In 1938 Orson Welles' aired a broadcast of an adaptation of H.G. Wells' *War of the Worlds* to six million listeners at The Mercury Theatre. The program would abruptly cut into a normal evening of music mimicking a newsflash about objects shooting out from the surface of Mars and landing on Earth. Despite a disclaimer often presented at points in the show hundreds and probably thousands of people thought that either aliens were really landing or that a foreign power was invading.

Now let's fast forward to the present with our current advances in cinema technology, our booming fascination with UFOs fueled by big budget blockbuster films such as *The X-Files* and *Independence Day* and you have a global population with their thinking already geared to go a certain way should some extreme event take place.

Few people are aware of an incident that took place over Culver City in Los Angeles in February 1942. This information, bizarrely enough, came to my attention after being shown chapter 13 of the *Fire Officer's Guide to Disaster Control,* written by William M. Kramer and Charles W. Bahme. This book is used in the federal emergency management agency's national academy to train new fire fighters. I would not have believed what was in this manual until I saw it with my own eyes. It included statements like, "...you may have engine trouble upon approaching the scene (of a UFO), and radio contact could be lost with your dispatcher," and "...some physical effects have been observed at locations where UFOs have landed..." How would this manual know to include statements like the above ones if this type of thing had not been experienced? It would be like me, never having skydived, and merely heard of and seen footage of people who have, deciding to write a manual on it.

I can't imagine a federal agency including information gleaned from such sci-fi shows as *The X-Files* as gospel when approaching a real crash sight of any kind. Nonetheless this document, to the best of my knowledge, is available in most firehouses around the United States. The chapter in question is entitled, *"Enemy Attack and UFO Potential,"* and in its introduction it relates the 1942 incident in Los Angeles. It says:

"Few Residents of the United States, except for those in Hawaii, have experienced an enemy attack on their hometown in this country; some think they have. The Great Los Angeles Air Raid of February 26th, 1942, began at 2:25am when the US Army announced the approach of hostile aircraft and the cities air raid warning system went into effect for the first time in World War II. 'Suddenly the night was rent by sirens. Searchlights began to sweep the sky. Minutes later gun crews at army forts along the coastline began pumping the first of 1,433 rounds of ack-ack into the moonlight. Thousands of volunteer air raid wardens tumbled from their beds and grabbed their boots and helmets. Citizens awakened to the screech of sirens and, heedless of the blackout warning, began snapping on their lights...The din continued for two hours. Finally the guns fell silent. The enemy, evidently, had been routed. Los Angeles began to taste the exhilaration of its first military victory."

A bit further on, the incident is again referred to:

"But what enemy had been routed? No one ever knew. All the fire fighters saw in the sky were the 15 or 20 moving 'things' which seemed to change course at great speed apparently unaffected by the flak from bursting shells all around them. Rumours that one had been shot down were never verified, nor was the explanation that these zigzagging invaders were weather balloons ever taken seriously."

This incident echos the scene in the sci-fi film *Predator*, when a company of soldiers in South America pump hundreds of rounds in the general direction of an unknown enemy and are promptly informed by a scout that they hit nothing. There was no mention of return fire from the object during the air raid or whether it was hit at all during the ordeal. The only thing that made the UFO eligible as hostile is that it did not identify itself to authorities and did not have permission to be in that particular airspace.

At any rate I recommend getting a hold of the entire *Fire Officer's Guide to Disaster Control* manual, not just chapter 13 (you might need a copy of the whole thing for it to sink in for some people). This is one of very few official government related documents that are available to the general public. It is my opinion that the existence of this subject matter in this type of document, has come about by the military resigning themselves to the fact that if an attack or crash occurs, the first people to be on the scene will in nearly all cases be firefighters. One thing that really amuses me is talk within certain circles about "Top Secret" documents like *Project Blue Book*, that supposedly contain everything the government know about UFOs while UFOlogists could have just visited their local fire station for confirmation.

The above photo featured in the Los Angeles Times. It shows an unidentified aerial intruder that HOVERED over Culver City during the morning of February 26th 1942. It was described by witnesses as being 'enormous' and 'pale orange in colour'. The balls of light surrounding the central object are bursts of anti aircraft shells being fired at it.

Seeing is Not Always Believing

In the course of my research I have watched a fair number of sensationalised videos about UFOs, visitors from other worlds, and alien autopsies etc. It always astounds me when they interview witnesses, contactees, and abductees and how they accept that aliens from other worlds exist because of what they saw. While I sympathise with how horrific, terrifying or exciting their incidences may have been they seem to forget that if the average person observes a top quality magic trick they would, despite being amazed, immediately assume a logical explanation for how it was done. That is why most people badger magicians after they perform and they are usually met with the response, 'a magician never reveals his tricks.' Rarely does an observer instantly accept that the performer has magical powers no matter how convincing the trick. Why should someone accept that a whole other race really exists just because they have had a convincing encounter with little green men or seen a flying saucer? Please don't get me wrong. If I had an encounter like this it would most likely leave an impression on me, yet I would not necessarily associate it with the proof I needed to believe in a superior race of beings that are poised in space ready to save us from ourselves. Seeing is never necessarily believing, especially in this day and age. If technology can be used so effectively to sell believability on a movie screen why then can it not be used off the screen, perhaps to sell what most churches call a "Second Coming." Being witness to a strange event or victim to an unexplainable ordeal does not normally give one the authority to confidently deduce an identity or motive, as the keys to such knowledge are not usually on display within such brief episodes. But how does one correctly react in such a situation if they are an obedient observer of Scripture?

Testing The Spirits

Before I go any further it is important to establish that the English word "spirit," as it appears in Scripture usually translates from the Hebrew word "ruwach" which meant "breath," "wind," "air," "breeze," and in some cases "tempest," or "storm," depending on the context. From this revelation the question immediately arises that if the word means something that there is an English translation for, then why does it appear as an additional word "spirit?" This same principle is found with the word "angel" that is derived from the Hebrew word "malak," meaning "dispatched deputy" or "messenger." The best explanation is that these words became the products of Greek translators that felt a need to add a type of divine emphasis to the meanings to differentiate them from the normal blowing of a breeze or a messenger sent by a king.

This use of the word spirit (breath) may have indicated an ancient linguistic attempt to describe something that has a presence and yet cannot be seen. In a way it could have been like an ancient Hebrew equivalent to the modern word "invisible." It seems to have been a term that was often attributed to God or a series of associated or unassociated beings that maintained a discernable presence when in human proximity whilst remaining permanently or momentarily, partially or completely invisible. In contrast the understanding of what a spirit is within the lay congregation of a church is somewhat vague and ambiguous and is thought of as something almost intangible and indescribable in construct. This subject will be touched on in a later chapter in more detail, but I introduce it here to hopefully illustrate a connection between what many today would describe as sophisticated alien beings that in ages long gone would have been described as angels or spirits.

The Scriptures clearly encourage believers not to be afraid of aerial phenomena as is related in *Jeremiah 10:2; "Do not learn the way of the Gentiles; Do not be dismayed at the signs of heaven, For the Gentiles are dismayed at them."* So if one is able to remain calm in the face of witnessing such an event that may eventuate in a "close encounter of the third kind" (third kind meaning physical or verbal contact) a certain course of action may be required. This course of action is surprisingly beyond the scope of the average Holy Spirit filled Christian. Now if we equate "aliens" with "spirits," there is a mandate that falls on followers to potentially treat the initial phase of such an encounter in a particular fashion. I say "potentially" because there may be an instance where this Holy or Set-Apart Spirit (God's unseen enabler) may instruct a believer to flee or remain if the credentials of a visitor or visitors are revealed in the introduction, as was the case in some angelic encounters throughout the Scriptures. The Bible also tells us in *1 John 4:1;* *"Beloved, <u>do not believe every spirit,</u> but <u>test the spirits, whether they</u> <u>are of God; because many false prophets have gone out into the world."</u>* Testing the spirit is an act whereby we ask the spirit to identify itself and declare its allegiance. *(1 John 4:2; "Every Spirit that con- fesses that Jesus Christ has come in the flesh is of God").* Unless it answers in the name of the one who was impaled and rose from the dead, then this will generally be a good indication that your visi- tor is actually a deceiving spirit. *(1 John 4:3; "and every spirit that does not confess that Jesus Christ has come in the flesh is not of God.").* Satan's minions, once identified, are strictly forbidden to swear allegiance to the name of their enemy. If they are not recognised they may say anything they wish, providing they do this behind an impersonation of some other individual, such as a deceased relative or a terrestrial occupant from a competing interstellar civilisation for example.

Joseph Smith, the founder of the Mormon faith is described as having such an encounter with a shining being who instructed him to locate and translate an ancient text. The result was a manu- script that defied historical findings and boldly contradicted basic Scriptural principles. Throughout the description of the event there is no record of Mr. Smith testing the spirit much less observing the warning in *Galatians 1:8* where it says: *"But even if we, or an angel from heaven, preach any other gospel to you than what we have preached to you, let him be accursed."* If people are not aware of the possibility that a spirit is confronting them or at the very least they are being confronted by a spirit that may not be a messenger of God, how can they test them you might well ask? Well, *1 John 3:24* tells us that we must have the Set-Apart (Holy) Spirit abiding in us. Meaning that not only are we to know it resides in us, but we must be attuned to it as well. The best method of staying attuned can be broken down into three basic principles or pillars. They are: 1) Lov- ing the Name of God (This will be discussed in a later chapter), 2) Keeping the Sabbaths (not just the weekly Sabbath), 3) Hold- ing fast to the Covenants (Teachings of God – Torah) *(Isaiah 56).* These principles should be applied through study, regular personal prayer and interaction with other people who uphold the same val- ues. If most Christians who have a "close encounter" think that they are seeing aliens instead of devils or angels they will struggle to fit their secularly conditioned outlook of such phenomenon within the context of Scripture.

A while ago a couple I know were in a dilemma about whether they would attend a specific church anymore. They had found out that the central church, where a percentage of their own church's offering money went, was sanctioning new doctrine that clashed with Scripture and their pastor was considering breaking his congregation away altogether. They had a fairly close relationship with him and shortly after, the pastor approached my friend and explained that he had a prophecy in a dream. The message he got was to continue an association with this church. That was good enough for my friend and his wife so they decided to stay. When I asked my friend if the pastor had tested the spirit he unfortunately did not know.

The Truth is in There!

So why are people who have sightings or contacts with strange beings seemingly jumping to the conclusion that aliens, as opposed to angels (fallen or otherwise), exist? Simply because the population are not being schooled correctly as to the nature of these entities and how they relate to the Bible. We have been subtly conditioned to disassociate the two subjects. I was reading various statements from abductees on a UFO website and was saddened by the story of one particular person. He described an ordeal of experiencing people standing around his bed, sensations of being pressed down, and being unable to speak. He added that some Christian friends had similar experiences that promptly ceased after a verbal declaration of a belief in God. He concluded by saying that this last suggestion sounded weird. So this person finds the weirdest part of their story being the part that mentions a faith in God. Despite the fact that he has just described beings standing around his bed, an invisible force pushing him down and the loss of the ability to speak. Interesting.

Possibly of more concern than the masses accepting the existence of alien beings is the quiet disassociation of the worldly concept of "aliens" with the biblical portrayal of the "sons of God" (disobedient angels) *(Genesis 6:1-4)*. This latter term as it appears in Scripture emphasises a race of beings excluded from men, made clear by their unnatural union with human females, that give birth to genetically enhanced offspring known as "giants" or "nephilim." This act clearly displeases God *(verse 3)* and brings with it a dramatically reduced life expectancy of the population. I have actually read commentaries on these verses that describe them as a mistranslation or an uninspired portion of text. Very few people are aware of the evidence of UFO activity throughout history depicted in artifacts, paintings, drawings, writings, and primitive religious customs, all of which show evidence of beings with superior technology and/or physical stature. Currently most people that believe in the existence of unexplained objects in the skies are blinded to any connection this may have to the Bible. They believe Scripture does not speak of UFOs or such entities at all, much like the dinosaur issue and therefore is a text that is not true so any reliance on what this book says is outdated and misguided. I'm happy to report that nothing could be further from the truth. If average Christians picked up their Bibles more and looked beyond the limited range of books recommended by mainstream church organisations (that rarely venture much further than teaching the four Gospels) there might be a lot more people coming out of this New Age thinking and receiving the truth. The following verse is just a teaser as to the multitude of references to such flying objects. *Ezekiel 1:16; "The appearance of the wheels and their workings was like the colour of beryl, and all four had the same likeness. The appearance of their workings was, as it were, a wheel in the middle of a wheel."* Dr. Barry Downing who wrote *The Bible and Flying Saucers* in 1968 describes the complex visions of the prophet Ezekiel in about 600BC. He points out that Ezekiel's bizarre account of fiery clouds with wheels and human-like beings is remarkably similar to modern day alien abductions. Former chief of the system layout branch at NASA, Josef Blumrich, after setting out to disprove such implications concluded after careful analysis of the data available, that the vehicle described in Ezekiel's encounter was also indeed a UFO.

All through our human history there is a consistency in these sightings and contacts. And they are not just confined to the Bible. In India the *Vedas*, an ancient *Sanskrit* text describes highly sophisticated flying machines called *Vimanas* (aerial cars), piloted by god-like beings. The text also describes the vehicles being constructed on a triple principle, having three levels, three seats, three supporting poles, and three rotating wheels. The rotating wheels, it appears, served specific functions: one to raise the craft, another to give it direction, the third to speed it along.

As mentioned earlier, the mainstream church's current stance on UFO related phenomena is strictly one of man-made or demonic origin despite many references in their own Bibles of these shapes being commanded by the Lord. I'll give you an interesting example of the church not only distancing itself from this issue but also severely condemning the broaching of it. In 1969, Erich von Daniken wrote a controversial book called *Chariots of the Gods*. He claimed in his book that aliens came down to earth to mate with humans giving their offspring advanced wisdom. He was attacked by the church and scientific institutes alike who claimed that his evidence was poor despite the following verse in *Genesis 6:2-4;* "*That the sons of God saw the daughters of men, that they were beautiful; and they took wives for themselves of all whom they chose. And the Lord said, My Spirit shall not strive with men forever, for he is indeed flesh; yet his days shall be one hundred and twenty years. There were giants (Nephilim) on the earth in those days, and also afterward, when the sons of God came in to the daughters of men and they bore children to them. Those were the mighty men who were of old, men of renown.*" It seems in retrospect that Daniken's biggest crime was using the word "astronauts" instead of "sons of God." The verse indicates that though they were sons of God (angels) they were in fact not obedient angels, but fallen angels with an agenda to breed into the race of men their own rebellious nature. The offspring would eventually steer away at a more accelerated rate mankind's dependency on God and in the process mar the capability of a Saviour by polluting the gene pool. These ancestors not only had the physical stature of their fathers but some were also gifted with increased intellect and beauty, while others possessed massive strength and endurance. Requiring only minor correction Daniken was spot on regarding this point and in my opinion deserves an apology. Also supporting Daniken's theory is the history of the primitive Dogon tribe of Mali in Africa, who have an extensive knowledge of the sky's brightest star, Sirius. You may remember me mentioning Alister Crowley's contact with an alien from this planet. The Dogon tribe believed they were at one time founded by a race of amphibious creatures called "Nommos" that once landed in an ark. Advocates of ancient astronomy hold this tribe's extraordinarily accurate knowledge as being very precious. It is also worth noting that the ceremonial hats worn by popes and bishops, called "miter hats" originate from the high priests of this tribe who wore headpieces that resembled the shape of a fish's head while on their backs they wore a robe that looked like scales.

Many different cultures in fact have similar stories of gods coming to earth and breeding with mankind. It is a sad indictment on the shortness of our memories that our perspective on this issue due to various methods of conditioning has caused us in the current age to call them "aliens."

You'll Never Learn This in Church

The primitive Dogon tribe in Mali, Africa, according to their records, were visited by a being or beings called "Nommo" around 4,500 years ago.

They left images and writings of "Nommo" who specifically came from a planet that orbited the second star in the Sirius system, Sirius being the brightest star in the sky. They related that this being or beings brought down from the heavens great knowledge, which was shared with mankind. The Dogon have a map marked on a large stone, which depicts the orbital period of this apparent mythological secondary star, which they claimed has a cycle of 50 years.

Up until 1970, Europeans believed Sirius was not a double star system, contrary to the Dogon tribes' belief. In this particular year however, a telescope was built that was powerful enough to finally see this secondary star and measure it's orbital period, which ended up being, yes, you guessed it, 50 years.

Another name for the Nommo (which is both singular and plural) is "The Monitor" or "Monitors." This is very similar to the term "Watchers," beings that are referred to throughout the Bible. *Daniel 4:17, "This decision is by the decree of the watchers, And the sentence by the word of the holy ones, In order that the living may know That the Most High rules in the kingdom of men..."* and *Jeremiah 4:16, "Make mention to the nations, proclaim against Jerusalem, That the watchers come from a far country And raise their voice against the cities of Judah."*

Chapter Four

Head in the Clouds

"The chariots of God are twenty thousand, Even thousands of thousands; The Lord is among them as in Sinai, in the Holy Place." – Psalms 68:17

ONE AFTERNOON I remember looking out the passenger window of a friend's car and gazing up at a massive cloud in an otherwise clear sky. The cloud's enormous lenticular shape, its unusual colour and its density reminded me of something otherworldly. At the time my frame of reference was Hollywood and my natural inclination was to liken its appearance to a flying saucer. This got me thinking. By contrast a Hebrew, Egyptian or Greek looking at a similar object 3000 years ago would have had a completely different frame of reference. Could failing to align ourselves with the same frame of reference as ancient scribes lead us to compartmentalise aerial wonders in the Bible and the UFO phenomenon today?

It is not my intention to endorse the origin of weird lights flashing in the sky or disk shaped objects zipping off into the horizon as demonic or man-made. On the contrary there is equally the possibility that such aerial anomalies could be of a heavenly nature. In fact if Scripture is used solely as one's frame of reference then (with the exception of the last century) this third option is more probable. In the Book of Numbers where it relates the story of Moses leading the Israelites out of Egypt there is extensive mention of a cloud. *Numbers 9: 16-17 So it was always: the cloud covered it (the tabernacle) by day, and the appearance of fire by night. 17 Whenever the cloud was taken up from the tabernacle, after that the children of Israel would journey; and in the place where the cloud settled, there the children of Israel would pitch their tents.* This chapter goes onto describe in some detail this cloud under the command of the Lord and how it would move with the Israelites and ascend or descend in accordance to making camp or continued movement and by night it would give off light. To the best of my knowledge clouds are neither able to ascend of descend much less give off an appearance of fire by night!

It is crucial to understand that Scripture uses a particular type of speech called "Phenomenological language." This language describes things as they appear as opposed to using scientific terminology. For example, if I was to say, "the sun sank in the horizon," we know that the sun did not actually descend. Because the Bible is written in this way it enables it to be understood by all cultures throughout the ages. Other examples of phenomenological language can be found in science fiction movies to do with time travel. In the film *Army of Darkness* with Bruce Campbell, his character is dropped from the sky, smack bang into the Middle Ages with his car. Some knights react to the vehicle very aggressively and clang it with their swords. One knight can be heard shouting, "It's some kind of metal beast!"

Lets consider (figure 1a) in terms of phenomenological interpretation. The two "Missile Launching Fixtures" visible in the top image are, though unusual in shape, recognisable by the average person as military weapons of some kind. However, to a person who has lived in a non-technological environment, these things would be totally foreign to them and could only be described in relation to things that they are familiar with, such as a type of animal or beast. The real difficulty with identification of these particular weapons is the lack of separation between the operators and the missile launchers themselves.

Imagine, if you would, that you lived in biblical times and saw a row of these protrusions (guns) mounted on moving platforms (armoured vehicles). Then to your absolute horror each of them bellowed forth with a deafening sound, spewing out fiery objects, which rocket thousands of yards away and explode with earth shattering impact. If you examine the top illustration in detail with a totally alien viewpoint you will notice there are features that align with the anatomical requirements of an animal, such as eyes, snout, mouth, ears, and body. To the uninformed, the second silhouetted image (figure 1b) of the same picture shows the outline of animals that resemble the shapes of dragons, hounds, or pigs.

figure 1a   Phenomenological view of Military Technology

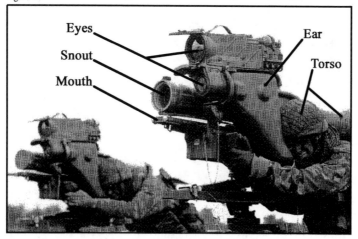

figure 1b   Silohouttes of Gun Fixtures with Operators

Aside from the sun, moon, the occasional comet, stars and clouds, people 2000 or 4000 years ago would presumably not have seen much else. Today, an overhead plane or helicopter, balloon or even a kite are commonplace things. Only as recently as the American Civil war were manned balloons used at various heights to observe the positions of enemy units. The frame of reference for the physical description of any aerial object would have been quite limited to people in Moses' day. Whatever this cloud was, it led and sustained this exodus of people out of Egypt for four decades. The New Testament tells us that the Messiah ascended into a cloud and that he will return in the clouds. I'm not about to try and convince you that our God gets around the place in a flying saucer (and to do so would diminish His magnificence), but I am convinced that on the other hand mainstream churches have been conditioning us to believe that our concept of God should be a fuzzy, shinning orb-like entity. A concept of just a blurred shapeless deity does not seem to gel with the declaration in *Hebrews 1:3*, which describes the Messiah as not only being His "expressed image," but also the physical manufacturer of many worlds *(verse 2)*. Any bipedal manifestations of God in the Old Testament are that of the preincarnate Messiah. This is why in *Exodus 33:11, "the Lord spoke to Moses face to face[10], as a man speaks to his friend,"* and yet in *John 6:46* it says, *"Not anyone has seen the Father..."*

Clouds do indeed appear to play an integral role throughout Scripture. Angels appear clothed in them *(Revelations 10:1)*, God made a formal appearance in one *(Exodus 19:9-11)*, God endorses His Son's ministry from one *(Luke 9:35)*, Daniel and John are lifted up inside one *(Revelations 11:12)* and the Messiah was taken up *(Acts 1:9)* and will return in one *(Matthew 21:27, Mark 13:26)*. Billy Graham writes in his book, *Angels – God's Secret Agents*, when referring to Jesus' ascension, "I believe that the word 'cloud' suggests that angels had come to escort Him back to the right hand of God the Father." Also in his book he refers to some UFO sightings that occurred on January 15th 1975, in Japan when thousands of curious

---

10   The Scriptures say, "no one will behold the face of the (Father) God and live" (**Exodus 33:20**). Jesus is the "expressed image" of God and was created before the earth was made. He is therefore the physically interactive God that is present in much of the Old Testament. His "oneness" with the Father is in "unity."

onlookers witnessed "from fifteen to twenty glowing objects, cruising in a straight formation inside a strange misty cloud."

Sifting out the Angels from the Devils

Patrick Cooke, author of the book, *The Greatest Deception* reveals many biblical facts that the church has managed to dumb down over the years and while I am a subscriber to many of his observations I had one major concern with his work. I felt his calling to reveal that all UFOs are of Godly origin was too narrow a view. He has supported his stance by saying that Satan and his minions are earth bound and therefore cannot achieve aerial deceptions. His response to the title of Satan as "the prince of the power of the air" in *Ephesians 2:2* is that it is the result of a poor King James translation and "air" is more correctly translated as "breath." Here is the verse as it most commonly appears. *Ephesians 2:2; "In which you once walked according to the course of this world, according to the (Satan) prince of the power of the air, the spirit who now works in the sons of disobedience..."* For myself, the use of the word air as opposed to breath paints an entirely different picture and to my knowledge no modern English Bible translation carries this more accurate wording. It was from this single seemingly simple observation in Mr. Cooke's work that I first realised the absolute importance in tracing all Scripture back to its Hebrew or Greek root word meanings. Also in his defence of maintaining Satan's grounding, I did happen to remember a verse when Satan asks for permission to test Job. *Job 1:7; "And the Lord said to Satan, 'From where do you come?' So Satan answered the Lord and said, 'From going to and fro on the earth, and from walking back and forth on it."* Interesting. But the thing we have to remember is that Satan is forever trying to be like God. He is a cheap imitation, a plastic copy. He can appear as an angel of light *(2 Corinthians 11:14)* and even quote Scripture to achieve his own ends *(Matthew 4:6)*. It is my feeling that to maintain a stance that Satan does not have anything to do with UFO related phenomena (period), especially in this point in time is extremely dangerous. Firstly, anyone familiar with the works of the late scientists, Nicola Tesla and Townsend T. Brown, will not find it difficult to believe that we have had the capability of achieving anti-gravitational propulsion since (at the very least) the 1940's. Therefore if man can build a craft that can utilise this phenomenon, Satan who influences man, can in effect, now resume construction of one as well.

In *Stan Deyo's* book the *Cosmic Conspiracy* he includes extensive information on Electro-Dynamic Propulsion and goes on to take the reader through a basic step-by-step explanation of such a craft that employs antigravity principles. Echos of achievements in this field eerily spring up one after the other throughout history with findings from different men at the same level of progress who after receiving interest from the aviation industry, fall silent.

An article that appeared in an Air Force magazine, Jane's Defence Weekly in July 24, 2002 displays an example of this trend. It talks about extensive and successful tests in the field of "anti-gravity" propulsion with the use of a device known as a "Lifter." The feature goes onto say:

"...officials from a small Alabama-based research company Transdimensional Technologies (TDT) [who have] strong links with the National Aeronautics and Space Administration (NASA) – lifted the lid on a set of experiments they boldly claimed would "change virtually every aspect of our daily lives." Under laboratory conditions, TDT had just tested a tethered subscale model of a device it called the 'Lifter' that had demonstrated its ability to 'fly' using a propulsion methodology that science is grappling to explain."

It then goes on to explain some technical aspects and how via the internet a French physicist, Jean-Louis Naudin replicated the experiment, but with a larger scale model, which led to dozens of amateur engineers getting in on the act also. Naudin stated that: "[the vehicle] is able to accelerate upwards very quickly and silently and is very stable during hovering." At this point an article so recent might appear to contradict the afore mentioned scientists merited with achieving the same results much earlier, but the feature continues by adding:

"The TDT work has sparked further controversy via claims that it is not a new effect at all but a reworking of a phenomenon discovered by US inventor called Thomas Townsend Brown in the late

1920's. Brown postulated a novel form of lift based on the assertion that an 'asymmetric capacitor' – a disc shaped plate, slightly domed on one side, capable of retaining a large electrical charge – would experience thrust in the direction of its positive pole when charged negatively on one side and positively on the other. Intentionally or not [the current] Lifters are actually three dimensional representations of Brown's asymmetric plates..."

The most impacting portion of the article is mentioned here in the following two excerpts. See if you can work out why.

"In 1952, Brown went on to submit a proposal for a joint services' technology demonstratio program, 'Project Winterhaven', that was designed to lead to a   shaped interceptor powered via electro-kinetic propul   A series of tests demonstrated to the US Air Force   in which 3ft diameter disc-shaped capacitors   rged at 150 kV, were said by some contemporary so   exhibited results 'so impressive as to be highly classified....   there are signs that after years on the shelf AS A TABOO SCIENCE, electrogravitics – antigravity by another name – is under the microscope of government agencies and aerospace companies as they seek to find breakthrough propulsion technologies that could catapult aviation into a new era..."

Then the feature moves into describing allegations that Boeing have been funding activities in this area for years and concludes:

"The reason for Boeing's interest in the...impulse gravity work remains unclear, but it is apparent, just as it was in the mid-1950's – when ...US aerospace companies revealed their deep involvement in gravity-led research programs, THEN FELL SILENT ON THE SUBJECT – that a quest for radically alternative methodologies is firmly rooted in its agenda."

Subtly revealed in these two examples is a pattern of men making breakthroughs in this field, their ideas being picked up by companies then mysteriously falling into obscurity. Questions that arise from the article are why is it a taboo science? Why did research programs fall silent? It is also important to mention that this article did not appear in a conspiracy magazine, but a certified Air Force publication.

I checked the credibility of the author of the above article and found that not only was it penned by one of the world's leading military affair journalists, but also the head aviation Editor of Jane's Defence Weekly, Mr. Nick Cook.

I since found out that Mr. Cook is the author of a book called, *The Hunt for Zero Point*, which chronicles the history of antigravity research. A major feature of this work explores the reality of harnessing zero point energy and its global implications. Despite his claims, within the work, of Nazi Germany's role in utilizing this technology, Mr. Cook is still a respected editor of this popular defence journal.

Considering the above information it would not be such a leap to assume that if men are capable of achieving this form of propulsion and can be influenced by Satan, then the air would also become an accessible domain for the forces of evil; whether by son's of God or men. Most accounts I have read and heard claim that it is not the technology that is lacking to construct such vehicles, but the cost and negative impact to the world's economy once these things hit the market. In certain government simulations, (programs set up much like the popular *Sims* PC game) scenarios that involve the addition of super technology cause massive problems to global stability within these test environments. I find it hard to accept that God would send down angels to abduct people for terrifying experiments and drop them traumatised in remote locations, engage in weird and inappropriate conversations, ask obscure questions, or give them cryptic warnings about future catastrophes, or impart contradictory information. Yes, when Satan appears in the Bible there does not appear to be any aerial phenomena described with him. Yet God and his angels are almost exclusively depicted as being airborne. However if we are to believe that Satan has a strangle hold over the world system and his influence reaches into government and military institutions, then it would be reasonable to assume that he is able to utilise their resources to eventually construct and use such craft for his own ends. It is also important to point out that *The Book of Revelation* describes a future war between God and Satan. Though God is victorious, a war is a description of a conflict between two opposing sides, so by this definition there will be, however ineffective, an evil force of a size and capability that will attempt to repel of the forces of good. Satan reads his Bible too and he is very familiar with the fact that God will be coming in the clouds, but in the meantime he may just try something in the air as well. Could it ever be the case that Patrick Cooke's very correct notion that a future aerial invasion of UFOs actually being God and his angels, gains enough popularity that Satan reacts to this growing outlook by accordingly initiating an earlier similar aerial performance?

"Don't be Afraid, I'm an Angel"

When angels are dispatched for destructive or helpful purposes in the Bible they do indeed strike fear into the heart of men when they appear every time. But in nearly all instances they quickly explain to those they are assisting not to be afraid. The angel in Revelations even humbly rebukes John who drops to his feet to worship him and assures him that he is a fellow servant and that any praise should be directed to God accordingly. Angels are essentially messengers who don't fit the characteristics of beings that partake in abductions that cause life-long trauma or mislead people by baiting them with prophecies that sometimes eventuate and sometimes do not eventuate. Whitley Streiber states that during his ordeal he had personally witnessed these beings fumble around and make errors during their experiments on him, which portrays beings, regardless of their advances, that are capable of error. It is also evident that a vast majority of abductions seem to have a purpose related to reproduction and breeding that resonates with the same purpose as the son's of God. Could it be true that when the Messiah stated that his return will be in a time that will be just as in the days of Noah, also mean that such interbreeding with son's of God will resume as well *(Matthew 24:37)*?

If God's heavenly angels do have the capacity to make error the Scriptures a devoid of any such incidences. On the contrary these messengers have a consistent record of being completely adaptable and reliable. The following verse shows a portrayal of an angel under the command of God to facilitate a specific combative purpose. *2 Kings 19:35; "And it came to pass on a certain night that the angel of the Lord went out, and killed in the camp of the Assyrians one hundred and eighty five thousand; and when people arose early in the morning, there were corpses-all dead."* It is difficult to picture an angel as one of those renaissance style, white robed, and feathery winged youths after reading that verse. Now in contrast, let's look at the angel that appeared before Mary. In this instance we know it was the arc-angel Gabriel sent with a specific purpose to inform her that she would soon be pregnant with the Messiah. Indeed she was initially afraid but promptly assured not to be. *Luke 1:30: "Then the angel said to her, 'Do not be afraid, Mary, for you have found favour with God.'"* When an angel confronted the three wise men they were filled with fear also, but again reassured. *Luke 2:10: "Then the angel said to them, 'Do not be afraid, for behold, I bring joy which will be to all people.'"* The Bible shows us that these messengers are always sent to interact with mankind for a direct purpose. They don't generally zip around the sky and drop in on us of their own free will.

News at 10 – Roman Soldiers Flee From Alien

However, a lot of these angelic encounters within Scripture are understood through the benefit of hindsight, which can slightly hinder our perspective when we try to draw comparisons with modern day UFO encounters. It isn't until we strip hindsight away and examine the reaction of a witness inside a cultural setting that we see hard similarities with angels then and aliens now. Imagine that you were a Roman soldier ordered to guard the body of recently impaled ringleader of a disruptive Jewish religious sect. You're basically an average kind of guy; you have a family, you're loyal to your Emperor and you know only too well that if you abandon your post this evening it would mean instant death. The night moves on uneventfully, there is a slight unease among the other men and talk of a possible attempt by fanatics to remove the body of this so called King of the Jews and you look forward with great expectation to being relieved from your shift. Suddenly a very bright light shines down on all of you from the heavens. A very tall glowing human-like being descends from this light and stands in your midst. It strides boldly toward the tomb that holds the deceased. All hearts freeze. Some of your comrades collapse from fear and others run for their lives. You don't know what exactly it was you saw that night but even thinking about it years later still chills your soul. To sum up you don't know exactly what you saw and you hope that you never have to encounter such a frightful being ever again.

Lets now fast-forward to 1989, around the same time as the Challenger disaster and look at a small park located in Voronezh, Russia. This case was reported in the United States by the St.Louis dispatch and the story was originally published on October 11th. This strange event occurred one afternoon while some school children were happily playing ball near a group of adults waiting at a bus stop. Little did they know the normalcy of that day was about to be shattered when a large shining sphere descended onto the park from above. Shortly thereafter three tall human-like beings that emanated a brilliant glow emerged from the craft. Everyone started to panic. A small boy who was standing near one of them was frozen with fear. The beings proceeded to take what appeared to be some samples of earth then casually left without physically harming anybody. There were dozens of eyewitnesses to this event. None of the statements about the incident had much range of variation. To sum up they too don't know what it was that they saw. The media that the majority of this people are exposed to have called them aliens from another world, so without a better explanation the witnesses cry alien when the idea of their being angels is the furthest thing from their minds.

In both of these examples neither group of interacting beings bothered to let witnesses know what was going on and in many ways this parallels military procedure in that work is conducted on a need to know basis. In the first encounter these Roman soldiers were the enemy and we have the advantage of knowing the circumstances that led up to this event. But the motive in the second example is barren of external information except the description of the event itself. Putting the reader in a Roman soldier's shoes forces a popular story to be experienced divorced of the knowledge of the angel's origin and purpose. Though angels may be observed there is often no necessity or earnest on their part to equip potential witnesses of their intentions.

How often would a father find it necessary to share with his two-year-old son the details of a bad day at work to explain his short temper or bad mood? Does this father love his son any less at that moment when he walks through his own front door and turns down a hug or appears not to acknowledge him at the end of a day? No! *Isaiah 55:8-9: "'For My thoughts are not your thoughts, Nor are your ways My ways,' says the Lord. 'For as the heavens are higher than the earth, So are my ways higher than your ways, And My thoughts than your thoughts.'"*

Conclusion

UFO sightings of any kind can only originate from three possible sources:

Man-made origin   – (Usually influenced in a greater or lesser capacity by demonic forces)

Demonic forces   – (Beings, whether in bodied or disembodied states that oppose God)

Heavenly   – (God or beings under His direct authority that oppose evil)

God retains absolute discretion as to whether He allows a witness, participant or victim to recognise or learn the nature of any unusual encounter. Remember with little warning Ezekiel was violently taken by a lock of his hair into the upper atmosphere to receive a mission from God *(Ezekiel 8:3)*. On the flipside, Satan usually operates in a gentle and seductive manner to persuade men to do his will.

One thing worth considering is that Satan's cunning carries on through generations. He wears and grinds slowly away at the truth. By clever slight of hand or smooth seduction he has influenced certain men of power to institute major change throughout history to fulfill his final plan to ascend to the place of the Most High. Therefore we can quite confidently deduce that much of the machinery of this coming deception has already been set in motion. I recommend that we be of the mindset that no matter how long we've believed this or practiced that, that if an observance is found, beyond any reasonable doubt to have no basis, that we do everything in our power to correct the error. If we do not do this and instead play things down, ignore them, or ridicule them because of ego, we stand to be counted with the subjects described in the following verses: *2 Thessalonians 2:11-10; "...and with all unrighteous decep-tion among those who perish, because they did not receive the love of the truth, that they might be saved. And for this reason God will send them strong delusion, that they should believe the lie..."* This verse IS NOT talking about non-believers, it is talking about a great multi-tude that do in fact have a belief. This belief however, is an ongoing unrighteous deception, which is the foundation that is necessary to believe the coming lie.

A good start in turning around the ignorance that the aver-age Christian has, is to educate them to avoid instantly dismissing things because they do not appear to be dealt with by the collection of books that we call The Holy Bible. We should always be mindful of the fact that the Bible wasn't originally written in English and didn't go through a marketing process before its release like mod-ern versions do today. To blindly assume that every Bible transla-tor that has appeared in history has come under divine inspiration is irresponsible. What I hope to do in the following pages is to lift the veil of lies that have stopped dead the truth at the roadblock of men who have taken it upon themselves to be God's editors.

You'll Never Learn This in Science Class

In 1882 Nicola Tesla caused a Second Industrial Revolution by harnessing the power of the alternating current (AC), that lead to the AC motor and radio, the basic principles of which are still in use today, yet his name is absent from school textbooks, omitted from technical journals, and even unknown to some engineers. Even less well known is his invention of the rotating magnetic field principle that if utilised correctly today could provide unlimited electrical power worldwide.

People like Thomas Edison and Marconi are the men history remembers for the invention of electricity and the radio, yet these men only expanded and demonstrated such technologies and in reality were little more than entrepreneurs.

In a paper written by John W. Wagner he relates that: "Tesla's four-tuned circuits secured the U.S. patents #645,576 and was the basis of a U.S. Supreme Court decision (Case #369 decided June 21, 1943) that overturned Marconi's basic patent on the invention of radio.

And it was Edison who merely set up a factory at Menlo Park, New Jersey and from there invented practical wonders such as the incandescent lamp, phonograph, and picture machine, which all worked on an already established technology.

In his private journals Tesla revealed that in 1899 he intercepted radio signals that he believed to be from extra-terrestrial beings that he referred to as "martials." A term that sounds similar to the Dogon tribe's "nommo" meaning "monitors."

Chapter Five

Dark Age – This Age

"For the time will come when they will not endure sound doc-
trine; but according to their desires, because they have itching
ears, they will heap up for themselves teachers; and they will
turn their ears away from the truth and be turned aside to
fables."– 2 Timothy; 4:3

THE DARK AGES ARE most commonly defined as a period in
history where the church willingly withheld great portions of biblical truth from the general population to maintain certain priv-
ileges and advantages for the nobility of the day. The dictionary
defines the dark ages as a time in history from about 476AD to
about 1000AD. This is known as the "Middle Ages," a time before
the "Renaissance period," a state of backwardness or unenlighten-
ment. In truth the departure from enlightenment by teachers of
the Gospel commenced sometime earlier than this and as I will
hope to reveal within this chapter, extends well into today's modern
culture.

The Rise of the True Father of Christianity

The truth is the dark ages commenced through the initial actions of an ambitious Roman who rose to power in the wake of much political unrest and civil war. He became the emperor of Western Rome in 307AD and by 312AD won a decisive victory in the nation's capital and assumed absolute power. His defeated enemy was notorious for his persecution of Christians[11] and this conqueror, being deeply religious and superstitious attributed his victory to their God.

Yet despite his sympathetic view toward the faith his motives for instituting toleration of it seemed to be more driven by political need rather than genuine concern for a persecuted people. This man was Constantine I and his actions became so influential that some of the laws and customs he instituted are still kept to this very day, which many modern-day Christians mistakenly believe resulted from Jesus' teachings.

Constantine effectively accomplished goals where his rivals had previously failed by not immediately converting to Christianity, but assimilating or merging it with existing pagan practices. Prior to Constantine the Nazarene sect of Judaism had already fragmented into many diluted splinter faiths and in the meantime the followers of the true vine disappeared into the background of history. In its place Christianity, a severely Greco-Romanised version of this original faith claimed the sole mantle of the sovereign religion of almighty God.

Soon Constantine not only became the head of Rome, but the head of Christianity and hence a quasi-political-religious leader. This duality afforded him not only the roles of judge and jury, but also executioner. Prior to his rule, paganism assumed an essential role in a Roman citizen's life and religion was used as a means of influence by the government. Christian persecution had reached its peak and after Constantine's victory an opportunity arose to combat its persistent practice in a more elaborate and gradual way.

---

11   In this context I refer to Notsarim and various other sects of Jews. In fact wherever I use the term "Christian," prior to Rome's newly established religious order, I refer to the Jews and the Notsarim. Notsarim comprise full-blooded messianic descendants and grafted-in former Gentiles. Pagans initially rounded up both the "persecuting blinded Jew" and the "awakened Notsarim," because their walks looked virtually the same.

The prevailing attitude as quoted from *The New Advent Catholic Encyclopedia* was: "Probably many of the more noble-minded recognised the truth contained in Judaism and Christianity, <u>but believed that they could appropriate it without being obliged on that account to renounce the beauty of other worships</u>." This end seemed appropriate to them despite the God of this faith equating paganism with vomit and teaching repentance of such ways as a requirement for forgiveness. Also the fact that the noble class may have regarded truth in that way and arrogantly chose to ignore its entirety seems an even graver travesty than lesser-informed Romans failing to abandon former practices because they were not convinced of any alternative truth.

Halt, Friend or Foe?

Before I proceed it is important to establish that to prevail over an enemy, hostile confrontation is not the only available avenue to achieve such a result. In fact hostilities can be the most costly form of attack to an initiator. Years ago in a whole other life I purchased an album by a punk rock singer called Henry Rollins. For years I was a devoted fan of his hard-hitting music and lyrics. Recently as I was examining Rome's method of assimilation to Christianity, the following lyrics from one of his band's songs sprang to my mind. This was strange because in recent times it was usually Bible verses that tended to do this. The lyrics read:

> **You tell me you're my friend**
> **You say I know you**
> **I'll trust you just as far**
> **As I can throw you**
> **Now I don't know you**
> <u>**I know my enemies**</u>
> <u>**They show themselves to me with honest eyes**</u>

This song illustrated to me the concept of knowing where one stands with a known enemy as opposed to one who proclaims friendship yet is in fact also an adversary and the complications that arise from the second scenario. For example, if a force comes charging fiercely down a hill with bayonets at the ready toward an opposition, that opposition can appropriately react by taking defensive or evasive action. But if that same enemy comes walking down the hill with warm smiles and white flags waving, with the same intention, that is a different matter.

There is a popular motto among members of the Fabian Social-ist society that appears to support an allegiance to this concept of a slow, subtle, silent and invisible confrontation. It states: "What has been achieved with the mailed fist will now be achieved with the velvet glove." This method of slow gradual attack is achieved through initial support, slow assimilation, gradual disbandment and slow overlapping implementation. This objective is the primary role of the order of Jesuits and will be discussed later in this chapter.

"Come into our lair," said the Pagan to the Israelite.

Not only did the persecution of Christians evaporate under Con-stantine, but so to did the level of their poor social status. The emperor swiftly moved to institute the *Edict of Milan*, which put the faith on equal footing with paganism, provided its Judaic roots where suitably diluted. An already increasingly Greco-Romanised congregation (now called the church) went from being persecuted to becoming a legal part of the Empire almost instantly. Constan-tine and his newly formed church functioned in a symbiotic rela-tionship. He relied on the church for support and the church relied on him for protection. Though Constantine may have felt a genuine fondness for Christianity, which he attributed to his victory, it did not compel him to the point of converting to it, not least until he lay many years later on his own deathbed.

His pagan religious advisors met with him not long after his conquest and revealed the benefits of lulling Christianity into Rome's confidence. They convened a council to settle disputes among the religion's various sects and in the process refashioned key issues within the faith so that it could be controlled from Rome.

The quarrelling rival sects of Christianity were about to blindly stumble into the path of a powerfully ordered pagan Rome.

The Watering Down Effect Commences

Constantine through the diplomatic use of an especially appointed council removed vocal supporters of the original biblical laws. He changed holy days, outlawed the Sabbath, and overlaid old pagan festivals with Christian names and meanings. For example he changed the birthday of the pagan sun god to the official holiday to celebrate the birth of the resurrected Jewish Messiah and officially declared the concept of the Trinity. Trintarianism or the philosophy of a triune god first appeared in pagan religions and is not specifically mentioned in the Bible. For example the Babylonians had "Baal, Ishtar, and Tammuz;" The Egyptians had "Amon Ra, Isis, Horus," Greece had "Zeus (Apollo), Demeter, and Porsephene (Nike)" and then Rome subsequently had "Deus (Zeus), Venus, and Cupid (also referring to Nike)." The reckoning here is that unconverted pagans would more easily adapt to Christianity with this familiar addition of a Trinity. Critics have pointed out that there was some measure of acceptance in the trinity and an observance of Sunday worship by certain sects prior to the council's commencement. While this is true, it should not detract from the fact that the council's official endorsement would have only served to further authenticate their observance to a wider audience. The fact that the Scriptures speak of God, the Holy Spirit, and the Son and that YHWH (God's name) means "I was, I am, and I will be," made this Trinitarian doctrine with a slight spin effortlessly acceptable to the pagan market. Constantine also settled on an Arian nature for the Messiah and the embalm of the Sun god, the cross of light, was adapted officially to Christianity. The *1965 World Book Encyclopedia* states the following: "Cross forms were used as symbols, religious or otherwise, long before the Christian era in almost every part of the world…This Symbol had a wide diffusion before the Christian era in Europe, Asia and America and is <u>commonly thought to have been an emblem of the sun,</u> or fire; and hence, of life." Before a crucial battle against rival emperor Maxentius, Constantine beheld the skyward vision of a cross set before a blazing sun accompanied with the words, "In this sign conquer." Seeing this as a good omen he gave orders for the symbol, which was originally called an "ankh," found in Egyptian religion, to be painted on his army's shields.

Later that day victory smiled upon his army and he entered the capital with his enemy's head skewered on a lance. Shortly there after he would convene a council of religious unity with a closing speech at which he declared himself "a fellow Bishop." He would then go on to murder his son from a former marriage and boil his wife to death in her own bath.

The Council of Gentle Persuasion

All that aside, commentaries on certain issues covered by this first council become quite alarming if we take note that Scripture needs not be added to or taken away from. Such unbiblical topics that were at the forefront for consideration by the church included the Greek philosophical concept of "homoosios," which meant giving Jesus (as the Messiah was later called) the same physical substance as God, and the formulation of an oath that encompassed the acknowledgment of all these doctrines and a statement of allegiance to the Universal (Catholic) Church, called the "Nicene Creed." Some statements recorded of the council's many challenges say it all: "...it became quite evident that there was no Scriptural vocabulary which would correctly express (this) orthodox teaching," and "...they still needed a formula to summarise and convey their meaning." So like fools they bent Scripture to meet their own ends instead of discarding them because they had no biblical support. The very personage of Jesus was the main casualty as he was to be acknowledged as a God with no regard to his human side. His mother Mary (formally known as Miriam) also failed to keep her identity intact and was promoted to "Queen of heaven" and also able to forgive sins. The horror continued with the sanctioning, confiscation and destruction of all works that challenged Roman Christian orthodox teachings, which set a chain reaction that caused eighty percent of the Scriptures to be removed by the twelfth century.

This first official council was held in "Nicaea" in the Roman year 325AD and was attended by around three hundred bishops, some of whom carried the scars of persecution inflicted on them by members of the same legion that stood guard. Some elders are recorded to have fled the meetings after hearing the nature of the proceedings. No Jews, whether sympathetic to the Messiah or not, were officially present. This council was the first in a long line of meetings that ended with the council of Trent in 1563. The first council of Nicaea lasted nearly seven weeks and 84 subjects were debated and voted on. The purpose was to establish a new definitive church doctrine as opposed to realigning the many divisions of the existing ones to "the (true) way." Constantine was primarily concerned with unity and regarded it as the "mother of order." His desire to retain theological truth ran a close second to maintaining the peace and stability of Rome. Biblical truth was not the forte or intent of the Roman Empire by any means. The underlying agenda of the meetings was to eradicate the Jewish feel of the Bible, classifying anything relating to Jews as an abomination. Eusebius' quote from a letter written by Constantine about the festival of Easter plainly supports this view in this statement: "...it was declared to be particularly unworthy for this holiest of all festivals to follow the custom of the Jews. We ought not therefore, to have anything in common with Jews. WE DESIRE TO SEPARATE OUR-SELVES FROM THE DETESTABLE COMPANY OF THE JEWS for it is surely shameful for us to hear the Jews boast that without their direction we could not keep this feast." Is it any wonder after reading this that centuries later Adolph Hitler gained a measure of support from Rome during his horrific regime? To clear any doubts on this accusation might I recommend a book entitled *Hitler's Pope*, written by John Cornwell. During the course of these Roman councils some two hundred and seventy books were initially scrutinised. It is estimated that out of approximately six hundred books of the Bible, by 1611AD only eighty had survived. It is also worth pointing out that the act of destroying books was also later adopted by the Third Reich. Furthermore a reduction by the Protestant Reformation brought the number of books down to sixty-six. Unbelievable. The result is that the existing Bible that is found in most households contains references to at least eighteen other books that do not appear. These references or footprints as I like to call them support at the very least that the common Bible found in mainstream churches is incomplete. While there are no strong records of exactly how many books should appear in the Bible it is apparent that a considerable chunk of wisdom and history has been forgotten. Yet in the face of all this, God's word remains largely intact, despite mankind's best efforts to gently erode or brutally eradicate it. But just as a public speaker is capable of verbally twisting and omitting Scripture to meet his own ends, so to is a scribe able to achieve the same by the written word. Therefore it stands to reason that a council of men could also be equally capable of wrongly discrediting certain Scripture. Today, through a combination of compartmentalised thinking and stark ignorance, Christians believe that modern Bible translations are complete and have minimal errors. A minister will boldly hold aloft a leather bound Bible before his congregation and proclaim that it is the infallible word of God. He will do this without enlightening the masses as to its source or the background of the organisation that compiled and published the particular translation.

Hebrews 4:12 says that the word of God is a lethal weapon, *"For the word of God is living and powerful, and sharper than any two-edged sword, piercing even to the division of soul and spirit, and of joints and marrow, and is a discerner of the thoughts and intents of the heart."* But to copies handled by dishonest translators the Scriptures have this to say: *Jeremiah 8:8; "How can you say, we are wise, for we have the law of the LORD, when actually the lying pen of the scribes has handled it falsely?"*

Below are some examples of verses that point to other biblical texts that are not found in the average Bible:

1 Chronicles 29:29; "Now the acts of David the king, first and last, behold, they are written in the book of Samuel the seer, and in the book of Nathan the prophet, and in the book of Gad the seer." – The book of Samuel the Seer

1 Kings 11:41; "And the rest of the acts of Solomon, and all that he did, and his wisdom, are they not written in the book of the acts of Solomon?" – Acts of Solomon

Joshua 10:13; "So the sun stood still over Gibeon; And Moon, in the Valley of Aijalon. So the sun stood still, and the moon stopped, Till the people had revenge Upon their enemies. Is this not written in the book of Jasher? So the sun stood still in the midst of heaven, and did not hasten to go down for about a whole day." – The Book of Jasher

2 Chronicles 12:15; "The acts of Rehoboam, first and last, are they not written in the book of Shemaiah the prophet, and of Iddo the seer

concerning genealogies? And there were wars between Rehoboam and Jeroboam all their days."– The Book of Shemaiah

2 Chronicles 20:34; "Now the rest of the acts of Jehoshaphat, first and last, indeed they are written in the book of Jehu the son of Hanani, which is mentioned in the book of the kings of Israel."– Sayings of the Seers

Exodus 24:7-8; "Then he took the Book of the Covenant and read in the hearing of the people. And they said, "All that the Lord has said we will do, and be obedient." And Moses took the blood, sprinkled it on the people, and said; "This is the blood of the covenant which the Lord has made with you according to all these words."– Book of the Wars of (YHWH) the Lord

1 Samuel 10:25; "Then Samuel explained to the people the behaviour of royalty, and wrote it in a book and laid it up before the Lord. And Samuel sent all the people away, every man to his house."– Book of Samuel the Seer

The Council Of Laodicea

The Council of Laodicea in 336 (364) AD made the greatest reduction to the Scriptures in history. Many books that are now known as the infamous "lost books of the Bible," met their demise here. The major agenda of this council was to finalise which books were to be considered canon. Godly inspired books were decided upon by a voting system. This meant that any book not deemed worthy would not be read or taught within a church environment. Sixty canons in total were published. Any works that did not make the grade were burned under a regime completely driven by anti-Semitism. Adhering to anything that was in common with the Jew was called "Judaising" and was punishable by death. This racist thinking was at the heart of the assembling of books that are now called "The Holy Bible." This no doubt is why most members of the (Ku Klux) Klan own a Bible and happily go to church. In 1989 Christian fundamentalists ministers occupied 26 positions of a total body of 39 Klan lecturers in the United Sates.

The nature of a reference to the Jewish Sabbath (Saturday) observance, portrayed in chapter 13 in The Epistle of Barnabus, posed a major problem for the council. As already noted this Jewish custom had to be eliminated and refashioned so as to not bear any relationship to the original practice. This Epistle contained an explanation of why "one shouldn't trust going to a building made of hands as part of Sabbath worship." This teaching made it difficult for an Orthodox Roman hierarchy to maintain big brother like control and was thus considered the dead weight that dragged the book down into the depths of obscurity. *Leviticus 23:3* is all that remains as a hint of this original God ordained requirement of us to remain in our respective localities when it says; "*Six days shall work be done, but the seventh day is a Sabbath of solemn rest, a holy convocation. You shall do no work on it; it is the Sabbath of the Lord in all your dwellings.*"

Though many verses depict the Messiah customarily attending synagogues, this word simply meant assembly of people. In some Bible translations the word "synagogue" is mentioned once in the Old Testament in *Psalms 74:8* and is translated from the Hebrew word, "mowed," which means an "assembly." The Greek word "sunagog" means "assemblage of persons." During the Babylonian captivity of the Jews, physical structures began to spring up supposedly in accordance with *Ezekiel 11:16; "Therefore say, "Thus says the Lord God: "Although I have cast them far off among the Gentiles, and although I have scattered them among countries, yet I shall be a little sanctuary for them in the countries where they have gone.*" Since this period of Jewish dispersion the word synagogue has become associated with a building. Whether one agrees with the above interpretation or not its implication as sanctuary is certainly implied as temporary.

List of books banned at the council of Laodicea

Barnabas	The First Book of Adam and Eve
I Clement	The Second Book of Adam and Eve
II Clement	The Secrets of Enoch
Christ and Abgarus	The Psalms of Solomon
The Apostles' Creed	The Odes of Solomon
I Hermas-Visions	The Fourth Book of Maccabees
II Hermas-Commands	The Story of Ahikar
III Hermas-Similitudes	The Testament of Reuben

Ephesians	Asher
I Infancy	Joseph
II Infancy	Simeon
Mary	Levi
Magnesians	Judah
Nicodemus	Issachar
Paul and Seneca	Zebulum
Paul and Thecla	Dan
Philippians	Naphtali
Philadelphians	Gad
Polycarp	Benjamin
Romans	
Trallians	
Letters of Herod and Pilate	

Chop, Change, Hack and Add

"Let no one read it; and not only so, but we judge it worthy of being commited to the flames." – Amphilochius (The Second Synod of Nicaea 787AD)

In the initial phases of these Roman councils, biblical doctrine inevitably became changed with little or no regard to its own edict. Constantine set up a foreign church hierarchy made up of anti-Semitic bishops who persecuted anyone who followed Jewish customs (whether they revered the resurrected Messiah or not). He continued to worship other gods and maintained his pagan title "Pontifex Maximus" to appease his former supporters. In *A History of the Christian Church*, by W. Walker, it records that he had a prayer-room that contained the busts of Jesus and several pagan gods.

Even today, the Catholic Church distribute printed matter and hang plaques that contain an abbreviated version of the Ten Commandments. The law against idol worship is blatantly OMITTED and the last Commandment is split into two to make up the ten. *Daniel 7:25; "He shall speak pompous words against the Most High, shall persecute the saints of the Most High, And <u>shall intend (think) to change</u> times and <u>law</u>."*

The current edition of *The Catechism* states that though there is a commandment against the construction of graven images, the Old Testament contains God ordained permission of the making of images that pointed symbolically toward salvation. The "bronze serpent," "The Ark of the Covenant," and the "cherubim" were examples. Really? These were three objects that were used for specific purposes and situations. Few if any other idols appear in the entire Old and New Testament history of the Hebrews. Nor is there any evidence of an ongoing manufacturing of idols or images of any type associated with God's people. *Isaiah 45:16b; "They shall go in confusion together, who are makers of idols."* Implying that from these three instances that God changed his mind on a direct commandment is a far cry. Particularly when the New Testament assures us that there is no new Commandment except to observe all the existing ones with love. *1 John 2:7; "Brethren, I write no new commandment to you, but an old commandment which you have had from the beginning. The old commandment is the word which you heard from the beginning.* And *John 13:34; "A new commandment I give to you, that you love one another: as I have loved you, that you also love one another."*

The Sabbath change is also supported from *The Catechism* as being the Lord's Day because he was resurrected on the first day of the week. Again if there had been a change in this law it is not recorded throughout the entirety of accepted Scripture. If I knew what day of the week Jesus brought the dead girl back to life on and I decided to choose that day to worship him then this would be no different to the example that Constantine set here. It is a case of retrospective justification in a ruling that alters a Commandment by adding meaning to a wonderful scriptural event. Consider the implications in light of the following verses. *Exodus 31:13; "Speak also to the children of Israel, saying: 'Surely My Sabbaths you shall keep, for it is a sign between Me and you throughout your generations, that you may know that I am the Lord who sanctifies you.* And *Deuteronomy 4:2 "You shall not add to the word which I command you, nor take from it, that you may keep the commandments of the Lord your God which I command you."* Sabbath worship is a special sign that is to be kept by ongoing generations and is not to be added to. We are to worship on God's terms, not ours. The argument that the

Sabbaths or the Commandments were only given to the Jew come unraveled in the face of *Isaiah 56:3-4; "Do not let the son of the foreigner who has joined himself to the Lord speak saying, 'The Lord has utterly separated me from His people...For thus says the Lord; 'To the EUNUCHS who keep My Sabbaths...Even to them I will give in My house...an everlasting name that shall not be cut off."*

Dear reader, full-blooded Egyptians stood alongside Jews as the Commandments were received at Mount Sinai. If you are a Christian who observes a first day of the week worship and you have just clearly read God's terms in this area, the earnest is now on you to investigate this issue. If you have read and understood the above verses you have just lost the luxury of hiding behind the statement, "God only judges us on how we act in accordance to what we know." Living only by some truths and disregarding others because they are not convenient, will be the most common stumbling block to the religious on the Day of Judgment.

The Birth of Esotericism Christianity

Not commonly known was the inclusion of the books of The Apocrypha in the 1611 edition of the King James Bible. These books appeared between Malachi and Matthew and span approximately 450 years of Bible history. There were 13 books in total, which were removed at the Synod of Dordrecht in 1619.

The word "Apocrypha" means hidden or concealed and was a name later given to a collection of books by certain men that regarded the intentions of these writings to be viewed and understood only by an initiated few, despite Scripture itself having nothing corresponding to the idea of a doctrine for a privileged minority. In other words it means any portion of writing that is reserved for a select few.

Introduction of this esoteric view had been unleashed and the foundations of a secret society were laid. Gone were the days when the gospel was to be preached to the poor and ignorant and so too the reading and studying of the Scripture in its entirety. *Isaiah 45:19; "I have not spoken in secret, In a dark place of the earth; I did not say to the seed of Jacob, 'Seek Me in vain'; I the Lord speak righteousness, I declare things that are right. And Luke 8:17;*

"For nothing is secret that will not be revealed, nor anything hidden that will not be known and come to light." And *Matthew 13:35 "...I will utter things kept secret from the foundation of the world."*

The Apocrypha Debate

The term "Apocryphal" is often used with a connotation to being heretical, but is more accurately employed as an indicator of a collection of books that were not deemed acceptable by certain religious councils. It is important to establish that there are a number of different religions that recognise the authority of the Bible and have over time used special councils to measure the authenticity of its contents. Through different and at times absurd processes the books that we are familiar with today were assembled and defined from a considerably larger collection of works. The organisations that partook in these councils were all independent of one another. The three main periods of canonisation started with the Jews, then the Catholic Church and ended with the Protestant movement. Though I use the term canonisation here, I do so in a looser sense in regard to the Jewish assemblies. Because the Council of Jamnia as it is called was merely made up of an informal group of Jewish Scholars who established a non-authoritative assembly to discuss the status of The Book of Ecclesiastes and the Song of Solomon. Though the list of scholars that claim this group also rejected the works of the Apocrypha is exhaustingly extensive NO RECORDS EXIST FROM THAT PERIOD TO CONFIRM THAT THIS WAS THE CASE. On the contrary Jamnia was a school for studying the law and the rabbis who ran it met to discuss the merits of these afore mentioned books alone in terms of there suitability within their local community. The myth that this council met and subsequently rejected the books of the Apocrypha is believed because of a majority rules principle. That is to say that if enough notable scholars confirm it even though no concrete records from that time are evident, then it must be true. The fact is that THERE ARE NO KNOWN RECORDS OF BOOKS THAT WERE OUT RIGHTLY EXCLUDED AT JAMNIA. *The Oxford Dictionary of the Christian Church* cuts straight to the chase on this issue:

"After the fall of Jerusalem (A.D.70), an assembly of religious teachers was established at Jabneh (Jamnia); this body was regarded as to some extent replacing the Sanhedrin, though it did not possess the same representative character or national authority. It appears that one of the subjects discussed among the rabbis was the status of certain biblical books (e.g. Eccles. And Song of Solomon) whose canonicity was still open to question in the 1st century A.D. The suggestion that a particular synod of Jebneh, held c. 100 A.D., finally settling the limits of the Old Testament canon, was made by H.E. Ryle; though it has had a wide currency, THERE IS NO EVIDENCE TO SUBSTANTIATE IT."

Therefore any supporters who claim that the Old Testament was formally established at Jamnia (which would have had to include the rejection of the works of the Apocrypha) hit a brick wall after the claim of H.E. Ryle.

Those that still cling to the view that the Jewish Council of Jamnia decided on a formal canon of Scripture between 90 and 92AD must at any rate accept the notion that there was not a single unified canon of Scripture until sometime after the formation of the congregation as described in the Book of Acts. This point has implications that run in opposition to the teaching within the New Testament. One has to wonder what books Jesus was referring to when he said to the devil, *"It is written,"* in *Mathew 4:1-4*. If Satan had questioned this authority he would have responded with "written in what?" One also has to wonder what books are worthy of instruction when Paul writes in *Timothy 3:16; "all Scripture is given by inspiration of God (God Breathed), and is profitable for doctrine."*

As discussed there is much conjecture as to whether the Apocryphal books were accepted by the Jews. The problem is that the majority of the books themselves are very Jewish, both in style of writing and content. The Jewish liturgy contains certain aspects that are based purely on the vocabulary and framework found only in the Apocrypha. It consists of the most important of all Jewish prayers; the "amidah" that is found in the *Book of Sirach. 1 Maccabees* is also cited by Jewish scholars as being a highly reliable history and Josephus also used it in his writings on the history of the Maccabbeean revolt. Various ancient Jewish sects, such as the "Essenes," as pointed out in the "Dead Sea Scrolls" included much of the Apocrypha as Scripture. While it is true that certain Jews today may not accept them as concrete Scripture, to say that Jews never accepted them defies logic.

By the end of the first century the Jewish faith had splintered into many rival hellenised sects and the Scriptures, most of which were originally written and compiled in Hebrew around 350AD, subsequently underwent a translation into Greek that was called the Septuagint. These hellenised sects in turn tried to use these Greek translations to convert the Jews, which they detested. Later through history it has been assumed that the Jews rejected them because they were never written in Hebrew, which is completely false. It is also believed that the Council of Jamnia also excluded books because they were composed later (between 200BC and 100AD) than other accepted books. The truth is that the Jews saw the Greek language as too cumbersome a dialect for marshaling the accuracy of the passionate organic Hebrew script and in addition took deep offensive to having been presented with their own teachings in a foreign tongue. Yet the claim that they forbade these translations, in particular the Apocryphal books stuck, and perhaps in an effort to help differentiate themselves further from the Jews, the Roman Council of Trent sometime later in 1546 decreed that the canon of the Old Testament should include much of the Apocryphal writings. Amusingly modern Catholic scholars have done an about face in wishing to avoid the unpopular stance of anti-Semitism and now claim that they were included in their Bibles because the Jews originally accepted them.

At the end of the day it should be up to the individual to decide whether these "Johnny come lately" councils all functioned under the complete inspiration of God, particularly when the agenda included sanctioning which books would or would not be acknowledged as inspired. Unless books contain information that may cause one to be led into temptation, is it necessary to decree strict bans on their reading or engage in massive campaigns to destroy them? Is it Biblical to have an organisation take it upon themselves to exercise discernment on the individual's behalf? Should it not be the job of an organisation to train the individual to able to discern for themselves through the consultation of the Set-Apart Spirit what is or isn't the inspired *written* Word of God? I have noticed that when discrediting is made in a formal environment people tend to be satisfied that a correct decision has been made on their behalf.

Without the books of the Apocrypha, a reader launches from Malachi to Matthew completely unaware of the cultural and social evolution that took place within this four and a half century timeframe. Some recent editions of the King James Version have attempted to remedy this situation by including a considerable portion of notes between the two Testaments. In total there are fifteen books that make up the Apocrypha of which only the Roman Catholic Church accepts eleven as canon.

Books of the Apocrypha

1. The First Book of Esdras
2. The Second Book of Esdras
3. Tobit
4. Judith
5. The Rest of the Chapters of the Book of Esther
6. The Wisdom of Solomon
7. Ecclesiasticus or the Wisdom of Jesus Son of Sirach
8. Baruch
9. A Letter of Jeremiah
10. The Song of the Three
11. Daniel and Susanna
12. Daniel, Bel, and the Snake
13. The Prayer of Manasseh
14. The First Book of the Maccabees
15. The Second Book of the Maccabees

Find Out for Yourself

The danger is the ignorance most Christians have as to the origin of the books that are found in the Bible and the complete disregard of any other sources outside these canon approved texts. I know the mindset, I was in it and it was a very closed view. I am not talking about accepting everything as Scripture, but making judgments using our own individual investigations rather than relying solely on the strength of an opinion from a pastor, a minister, a chaplain or a person with a theological degree. Salvation may be instant, but the journey by no means ends there, because in the long run our need to get to know God cannot be fulfilled by one hour at church and one hour at Bible study per week. It is up to individuals to grow from their own discerning findings.

Years of unnecessarily stunted growth can be avoided by resisting the lazy urge to cease our findings at the word of our religious leaders, and examine the historical evolution of Scripture and church doctrine for ourselves. My wish is that people not instantly make up their minds on the assurance of one person. You wouldn't do it if you were buying a car so you certainly shouldn't dream of it in regard to subjects pertaining to eternal life. People often seek a second or even third opinion on a medical issue. Patients even access the Internet to find books or articles about illnesses, and therefore how much more thorough should opinions and information be sought concerning our salvation?

It is interesting to note that in 1904 two encyclicals were issued that opposed any scholarship that delved into the early origins of the history of Christianity. In 1907 another encyclical was forwarded that condemned the very questioning of church doctrine. These facts alone should be enough to motivate anyone to investigate the church that they may be attending and the origin of the doctrines being promoted.

Forget Uncle Sam, God wants you…Apparently

Why has the control of religious matters been so important not only to Rome, but also to other societies across the globe throughout the centuries? The answer lies in being able to convince a person to do certain things by promising something that transcends the finality of death. During the Middle Ages when a peasant wondered into the complex architectural wonder of a grand cathedral he would be literally awe struck by what he beheld. He would be completely convinced that he had stepped into a place that was so magnificent that it had to be associated with God. The combination of coloured light streaming in through stained glass windows combined with choirs singing hymns all set the scene. And in many countries when the time came for these peasants and farmers to go to war a white robed Cardinal would stand on an elevated platform and endorse their salvation for their military service.

One of the advantages in withholding certain elements of Scripture from the masses comes into play when there is a requirement for the rounding up of a large body of men for a war of choice. I say a war of choice as opposed to a war of necessity because a war of choice requires more motivation for human beings to risk their lives for this cause. To get men to fight without any immediate threat is achievable by a host of methods. In the Middle Ages aside from professional soldiers, the most common men, farmers, made up numbers on a battlefield to fight for their king or else they would face the threat of being removed from their lands. But when the chips were down and a government needed men fast who would fight to the last, the most successful method was to have them believe in an eternal reward for such an action.

Even today we often hear that suicide bombers are motivated by the promise of an eternal paradise. If you can convince a soldier that if he meets death in combat he will be rewarded in an afterlife and he believes you, you have for yourself a Lemming style killing-machine. The atrocities of the Crusades were the result of ignorant masses who believed that Salvation was solely dependant on a successful land grab. So successful was this belief that it even spawned the formation of the fanatical Knights Templar. Convinced as they were of this promise beyond any reasonable doubt, these armies ploughed headlong into a state of degeneration and lawlessness, convinced that they could do no wrong, and many thousands lost their lives over a war that was ultimately about land.

The Language of the Poor – Our Enemy

"So much are they afraid of the light of the scripture, that they will not trust the people with it, no not as it is set forth by their own sworn men, no not with the license of their own Bishops and Inquisitors."
– Excerpt from the Preface to the *1611 King James Bible*

The Catholic Church's initial stance on the question of having the first Bible printed in English is also something worth noting.

This cause, which was pushed most strongly by John Wycliffe and was seen as a prelude to the Reformation, was nicely addressed in the closing remarks of a statement by Henry Knighton.

"As a result, what was previously known only by learned clerics and those of good understanding has become common, and available to the laity-in fact, even to women who can read. As a result, the pearls of the gospel have been scattered and spread before swine."

Nice one Henry. Could it be that the flock being able to read the word themselves might discover a massive discrepancy between certain bishop's lifestyles and those practiced by the apostles and the Messiah himself?

Furthermore the separation of the Protestants (kick-started by Martin Luther who read through the book of Revelations and found convincing parallels with the activities of the Antichrist and the papal system) caused only a physical split as many of the original Constantine laws continue to be observed. The Catholic Bible known as the Douay Bible consists of 73 books and the Protestant Bible has 66 books approved by the Synod of Dordrecht in 1619, which today is known as the "Authorized King James Bible." You might be asking yourself goodness knows how a Reformation could have caused a further dwindling of the Scriptures. It came down to the Protestant's view of the aforementioned collection of Apocryphal texts. While there appears to be no doubt that the books of the Apocrypha <u>were not fraudulent</u> documents later compiled to attack Scripture, there are strong arguments for and against their inclusion in the Bible. Citing that Jesus never quoted from them is not strong enough, as it is recorded in Scripture that he only quoted from around 22 books during his ministry anyway. Depending on your stance on the authenticity of the Apocrypha its exclusion was the reason for this diminished number. Though opinions are divided, it doesn't change the fact that 450 years are missing between Malachi and Matthew with little indication of such a leap in time. Though this author is sympathetic to these books, he is not at all (as you've probably noticed) sympathetic to the Catholic movement despite their obvious endorsement of them as Scripture.

What's more alarming is that after this Reformation, which in retrospect was the equivalent of a popgun going off, came the

Vatican's institution of a countermeasure that would reach its tentacles into the core of almost every major movement we know today.

The Jesuits, the C.I.A. of the Vatican

"This Wickliff, albeit in his lifetime he had many grieves enemies, yet was there none so cruel to him, as the clergy itself." – John Foxe's Book *of Martyrs*

Pope John Paul III approved the formation of an order of priests called the *Society* or *Company of Jesus* (later known as the Jesuits), founded by Ignatius De Loyola who was initially arrested by the Spanish Inquisition some years earlier on suspicion of heresy. Having a soldier's background himself Ignatius took admirable note of the Inquisition's almost military like precision, which later inspired him in his proposal of the formation of a similar order under the Pope. According to extensive accounts by Alberto Rivera, who is to date the highest-ranking Jesuit to leave the order, this group was to become the spear-head of the Counter-Reformation and they were charged with the principle tasks of reinterpreting Scriptures and trained to infiltrate secret societies, religions, and cults. Ignatius was also the initiator of the Spanish branch of the Illuminati, which was at that time called the Alumbrados (Spanish for "enlightened"). There is much confusion as to whether he, or a man by the name of Adam Weishaupt, founded the order. So conflicting is some of the data that I have examined on this issue, that I will discuss this in detail in a later chapter.

The Jesuits were thus known as the intelligentsia or secret militia of the Vatican. It has been heavily documented that through their actions under the umbrella of the Vatican they planted the seeds of the current structures of the Illuminati, The club of Rome, International Bankers, The Mafia, The New Age movement, the Masons, and many more organisations. This order are also said to have been the initiators of many major conflicts across the globe. I initially thought that this last claim was getting a little far fetched (even for me) until I started doing some research in this area.

In 1861 Abraham Lincoln made the following admission to a former law client at the White House that seemed to support an unseen Jesuit hand behind the American Civil War:

"I feel more and more every day that it is not against the Americans of the South, alone, I am fighting. It is more against the Pope of Rome, HIS JESUITS and their slaves. Very few Southern leaders are not under the influence of the JESUITS, through their wives, family relations, and their friends."

"Several members of the family of Jeff Davis belong to the Church of Rome. Even the Protestant ministers are under the INFLUENCE OF THE JESUITS without suspecting it. To keep her ascendancy in the North, as she does in the South, Rome is doing here what she has done in Mexico, and in all the South American Republics; she is paralyzing, by civil war, the arms of the soldiers of liberty. She divides our nation in order to weaken, subdue and rule it..."

"Neither Jeff Davis nor any one of the Confederacy would have dared attack the North had they not relied on the promises of THE JESUITS that, under the mask of democracy, the money and the arms of the Roman Catholics, even the arms of the France, were at their disposal if they would attack us. I pity the priests, the bishops, and monks of Rome in the United States when the people realize that they are in great part responsible for the tears and the blood shed in this war. I CONCEAL WHAT I KNOW, FOR IF PEOPLE KNEW THE WHOLE TRUTH, THIS WAR WOULD TURN INTO A RELIGIOUS WAR, AND AT ONCE, TAKE TENFOLD MORE SAVAGE AND BLOODY CHARACTER."

The first cannon shot that roared toward Fort Sumter (which started the American Civil war) was ordered by a Roman Catholic.

You may think that this all sounds like a James Bond film. And for those of you that think these guys aren't that bad, here is an excerpt from an oath taken by Jesuits of minor rank who are inducted into the Chapel of the Convent of the Order:

"I furthermore promise and declare that I will, when opportunity present, make and wage relentless war, secretly or openly, against all heretics, Protestants and Liberals, as I am directed to do, to extirpate and exterminate them from the face of the whole earth; and that I will spare neither age, sex or condition; and that I will hang waste, boil, flay, strangle and bury alive these infamous heretics, rip up the stomachs and wombs of their women and crush their infants' heads against walls, in order to annihilate forever their execrable race. That when the same cannot be done openly, I will secretly use the poisoned cup, the strangulating cord, the steel of the poniard or the leaden bullet, regardless of the honor, rank, dignity, or authority of the person or persons, whatever may be their condition in life, either public or private, as I at any time may be directed so to do by any agent of the Pope or Superior of the Brotherhood of the Holy Faith, of the Society of Jesus."

After reading the above statement it might not come as much of a surprise that Alberto Rivera, the man who renounced the order of Jesuits and blew the lid on the whole scheme, died of poisoning in 1997.

Another ill-fated ex-Jesuit was Malachi Martin. A scholar, translator, and speaker of over 17 languages, Martin released a final book called the "Windswept House," and shortly afterward met an untimely death. In the book he examined and exposed the ritual enthronement of Satan and the avalanche of Masonic and Luciferian infiltration within the Vatican. His account is chillingly authentic and extensively details this Satanic ritual that took place in 1963 in the Vatican's chapel of St. Paul.

Today the Jesuits are one of the largest religious orders in the Catholic Church. It was founded in 1540 and today there are over 20,000 Jesuits serving in the church in over 111 nations. Believe it or not, the Inquisition still exists today under the title, "The Holy Office."

Mithraism & Christianity

"...Many of the emperors yielded to the delusion that they could unite all their subjects in adoration of the one sun-god who combined in himself the Father God of the Christians and the much-worshiped Mithras; thus the empire could be founded anew on unity of religion."
– *New Advent Catholic Encyclopaedia.*

Until now I have been labeling the ancient Roman religion with the general title of "paganism," when in fact this term, according to its modern definition, is the practice of any religion that is not Christianity, Judaism or Mohammedanism. Lets get specific. The dominant religion during Constantine's day was called

121

"Mithraism," from the title *Mithras Solis Invictus*, meaning "Mithras, the unconquered sun." It was first recognised by Emperor Aurelian and followed right through to Diocletian, who burned many of the Christian Scriptures in 307 A.D.

It was the dominant religion in the known world at that time, effectively spread by Rome's legionnaires on the ground-level and Rome's wealthy Emperors at the top, no doubt accelerated by the mass construction and meticulous mapping of roads. Now it sits as a forgotten word attached to a religion apparently conquered by Christianity, yet sadly it is only the title of this religion that has become forgotten and the meaning is now manifest in the heart of its rival. Some of the doctrines of this religion bear a strikingly close resemblance to what we now see boldly displayed and practiced in Catholicism. For example, the headquarters of Mithraism was found in Rome. The leaders of the ritual services were called a "pater," Latin for "father," who wore black costumes with "Nehro" collars. A "Pater-Patratus" who resided over the paters was also known as a "papa," or "pope." It was a "men only" religion, which also observed a trinity concept of the Mithras, Rashnu, and Vohu Manah, being three persons in one. The Sun-day was to be kept as a hallowed day and in it no work was to be done. December 25th was to be celebrated as the birthday of the Sun-god. Newcomers to the religion were laid under a cut bull and saturated or sprinkled with the animal's blood. Members of this faith were promised entrance into a paradise called the "Eleusian Fields." The pater (father) would also administer a sun-shaped wafer disc to the assembly who often knelt in unison. This practice was formally used by Egyptian temple priests who would lead followers to believe they were eating a portion of their gods Isis, Horus, and Seb. To this day the letters IHS are coincidently evident on the Catholic wafers.

Mithraism evolved primarily from a religion that began in Persia around 628BC, where a multitude of gods were worshipped and like Christianity in the time of Constantine, absorbed aspects of other practices as well. Beyond this point, similarities to Christianity have been claimed to stretch into such realms as the amalgamated God "Mithra," being born of a virgin woman and crucified for the sins of the world.

Who Made Who?

In stark opposition to commonly held Christian belief is the content of a book released in 1875. *The World's Sixteen Crucified Saviours: Or Christianity Before Christ*, written be Kersey Graves, makes the bold claim that not only Mithra, but "Krishna" and 14 other gods came as mediators, performed miracles, and not only died, but rose again; with the most damning claim being that the majority of them predated Jesus' ministry. These crucial aspects on which the basis of Christianity clings are driven through with a sword by his conclusion that Christianity is merely a construction of pagan religions.

Indeed there are small smatterings of truth in some of Graves' claims. As I have already pointed out in my opening chapter there are glaring similarities within Christianity to many of the world's diverse cultures and religions. However, to draw such an abrupt conclusion to this particular faith in the manner that he does, reads like a witch-hunt. Ultimately few concrete records exist that support his claim of sixteen crucified Saviours. Only beyond vague references, with conclusions and theories delivered without a trace of humility and truckloads of unflinching bias. The question of which religion influenced which is commented on by one scholar: "Graves often ignores important questions of chronology and the actual order of plausible historical influence, and completely disregards the methodological problems this creates." When evidence on this topic is presented in Graves' book, it nearly always derives after the commencement of Christianity, suggesting the opposite is true.

However, while there should be no debate about whether or not the church practiced syncretism, as the evidence is indisputable, there should be a definite distinction between this and a total a piece-by-piece construction of a religion. Indeed it is difficult to find the existence of Iesus Christos (Jesus Christ) prior to the earliest Roman records for the simple reason that he was made deliberately unrecognisable. The motive was that by effectively absorbing the faith and slowly transforming it, its origin gets lost and a new false origin can be founded. In doing this, a lie is gently placed over the truth while the truth fades into obscurity.

I recommend getting a hold of a book called *Fossilized Customs*, by Lew White for a more detailed look into the chillingly familiar practices that most Christians today faithfully adhere to. If you cannot find something that your church practices in the pages of the New Testament, find out why and find out what the origin of it is. Most Christians don't even query a pastor; because they don't know any better because they don't read their Bibles, and those that do query their pastor because they do read their Bibles, gutlessly let them be the final authority, and not the inspired Word of God.

The Truth – An Annoying Friend that you Seldom Invite Over

Before I dig any deeper I am very aware that this information may be difficult for some people to accept and even be deemed offensive by others. It is not my intention to level an attack at practicing Roman Catholic people in general. Some of the nicest and most genuine people I have ever met have been Roman Catholics. My motive for compiling this work is to clearly show an attempt by an order that is growing stronger and more influential every year to make of little or no effect the teachings within the Hebrew Scriptures. I also wish to expose cleverly concealed pagan doctrine that flows through the veins of the modern church, which inhibits and retards the spiritual effectiveness of genuine believers today who for whatever reason follow the skin of the truth stuffed with a lie.

I also feel compelled to make a plea with readers who are struggling at this stage. In the past I developed a very defensive view of rumours of lost books or additions to existing Scripture. It may have come from encounters with people who supported such views and were not committed believers. I would argue that the assembly of books we have at present where comprised by a council of men who acted under the inspiration of God. In defending my stance I had in reality done little more research than ask a passing chaplain a few questions regarding the issue who gave me an answer I wanted to hear. My ego failed to let me see that I was not equipped to defend this topic. In fact the basis of my emphatic rejection of hidden Scripture came from fears that if there were a possibility of missing texts that this would perhaps not allow people to fully know the Messiah. Thankfully, due to multiple testimonies this is not in any danger of happening as the fulfillment of the Law through Jesus' is not only still very clear, but written from the four viewpoints of Mathew, Mark, Luke, and John. It is important to be reassured that God is still in control. He has never lost control, given over control and therefore never tried to regain control. *2 Corinthians 4:3-4; "But even if our gospel is veiled, it is veiled, to those who are perishing, whose minds the god of this age has blinded, who do not believe, lest the light of the gospel of the glory of Christ, who is the image of God, should shine on him."* He has a battle plan in which the foundation of victory has already been won through His Son's death and resurrection. The choice is ours if we want to play a part on the winning team. We should also be reminded that people can receive Jesus without even hearing, let alone reading a single word of Scripture. The Bible says nothing of a necessity to read or recite specific words to be accepted into the kingdom. Examples of this could occur in unexpected crisis situations or even during last minute deathbed confessions. If someone embraces the Messiah in a normal situation however, it is crucial that they develop a love of Scripture and read the word as regularly as circumstances allow.

I believe that while the truth is still available, some of the records of the facts have certainly been shuffled to the back of the pile and forgotten about. The New Testament Gospels are great baby food to throw at a new Christian, but as Christians mature I see too many of them still unable to chew solids and venture into prophetic books with any level of confidence or interest. I spent a year in one church, going to nearly every service without hearing a sermon on *Revelations* or *Daniel*. These books are the books of our age and anyone with any level of expertise or enthusiasm for them are seen either as radicals or crackpots, putting weight into the phrase "ignorance is bliss." Ignorance may be bliss, but there is no excuse for it when it is openly chosen over seeking knowledge.

The dark ages are still with us, but that doesn't mean we have to continue living in them. Ask your church pastor questions, find out about the current church's sermon protocol, ask why the Apostle's Creed (statement of belief) mentions belief in the Holy Catholic (Universal) Church, what Bible basis do they have on worshiping on Sundays and so on. Complacency is the biggest killer. *ACTS 17:11; "these were more fair-minded than those in Thessalonica, in that they received the word with readiness, and searched the Scriptures daily to find out whether these things were so."* Granted books do appear to be amiss. Some are lost for all time and I am no more of an authority on the authenticity of lost books than the average person, but should that mean that I cease and desist with my research? Definitely not! If you were choking to death you would not ask someone assisting you for their first aid credentials.

The Corporate McDonald's Church

The generic a-frame or cross emblazoned church structures that we usually see in any town or city are run by the local community, but are owned by another body that forms a hierarchy that if followed to the top reaches to the Vatican. These church bodies utilise a portion of their funds raised from weekly tithes to go toward the upkeep of these buildings who in turn receive tax exemptions despite the instruction in *Matthew 22:21; "...Render therefore unto Caesar the things which are Caesar's."* A further percentage goes to various missionary groups, who in turn use the money to maintain and upgrade the church structure that has been built smack bang in the middle of a third world slum. Little or nothing of these tithes goes directly to meeting the basic needs of the poor.

It is these mainstream churches that bear a rapidly declining resemblance to the congregation mentioned in the New Testament. For example outreach functions are minimised in favour of internal church activities and social group outings usually contain no component of Gospel sharing to outsiders. Helping the poor, widowed, orphaned, disabled, and underprivileged is at best a token function and no longer forms the basis of the congregation's focus. We are well reminded of the basis of our duties when we look at Jesus' last command to Peter in *John 21:15-17; "...He said to him (Simon Peter), 'Feed My lambs.'* (again) *...He said to him, 'Tend My sheep.'* (again)...*Jesus said to him 'Feed My sheep.'"*

Martin Luther made the claim that in the near future the Prince of Darkness would be as God in the church, which would call itself of Christ and in turn undermine its theological position. Of this future ruler of the church, the Apostle Paul writes that he (Satan) *"2 Thessalonians 2:4; "...opposes and exalts himself above all that is called God or that is worshiped, <u>so that he sits as God in the temple of God, showing himself that he is God.</u>"*

Many Christians are content with feathering a comfortable nest for themselves and happily maintain the status quo of rocking up to church, attending a few additional functions, and going to a weekly Bible study group. There seems to be an emphasis on internal church needs and this usually results in a Christian lifestyle that only allows short bursts of contact with the needy at best. The next verse nicely sums up our true agenda. *James 1:27; "Pure and undefiled religion before God and the Father is this: to visit orphans and widows in their trouble, and to keep oneself unspotted from the world."*

Chapter Six

Two Floods in Scripture

"And the earth __WAS__ ... " (Genesis 1:2)

MANY CHRISTIANS AND non-Christians know the story of Noah and the great flood. How he and his family were seen in favour with the Lord who instructed him to build an ark upon which he would retain two of each species of animal and seal up in preparation of a great flood that would destroy the rest of mankind. Sadly many people including some Christians see this as a fable. Scientists are eager to inform us that the current atmosphere is unable to sustain a forty-day and forty-night continual downpour. Archaeologists insist that the ancient bones of extinct animals found in drifting formations were the victims of small-localised floods.

To prepare a researched argument in support of a worldwide flood for sceptics of this event is beyond the scope and aim of this book. I suggest if you're honestly looking for material about this event that you seek other more specific sources.

I would prefer to shed light on perhaps a more controversial matter and one that I hope will also support the points I have made in the previous chapter. Close examination of all the references in the Bible of Noah's flood will before long show some minor inconsistencies and to the ill informed could plant seeds of contradiction. Keep the flood in mind, which seems to be the topic of the following verse, and carefully look at the underlined words. *Jeremiah 4 23-28; "I behold the earth, and lo, it was without form, and void, and the heavens, and they had no light. I behold the mountains, and lo, there <u>was no man</u>, and all the <u>birds of the heavens were fled</u>. I behold, and lo, the fruitful place was a wilderness, and <u>all the cities thereof were broken down</u> at the presence of the Lord, and by his <u>fierce anger</u>. For thus has the Lord said, the whole land <u>shall be desolate</u>; yet will I not make a full end. For this shall the earth mourn, and the heavens <u>above be black</u>; because I have spoken it, I have purposed it, and I will not repent, neither will I turn back from it."* The prophet Jeremiah informs us quite clearly of an earth that is without form or void and contains darkness. In the same beat he tells us that birds had fled and cities where broken down (destroyed). If this indeed is telling us of Genesis 1:2 then how can there have been cities that are broken down? *Genesis 1:2; "And the earth was <u>without form</u> and <u>void</u> and <u>darkness</u> was upon the face of the waters."* We know that this takes place well before Noah's time and the passage goes on to say that there was no man or bird. Yet there is a desolation caused by the Lord's fierce anger. What is the reason for this fierce anger? Who else is He angry with? It can't be something man has done if he isn't there. And the account can't possibly be referring to Noah's flood because Noah and his family were still present before and after the event, and there is no mention of darkness in that flood. In fact there is no indication at all that the days during the flood remained blackened and yet many Christians believe there is only one incident of a global cleansing in the Bible. The account can't be jumping from creation to the flood because after the desolation described in the verse the heavens are still black.

The Contemporary English Bible's tackling of verse 2 in Genesis 1 is also worth noting, as it seems to immediately acknowledge the existence of a land beneath vast waters. *Genesis 1:1-2; "In the beginning God created the heavens and the earth. The earth was barren, with no form of life; <u>it was under a roaring ocean covered in darkness</u>. But the spirit of God was moving over the waters."* With the exception of the water, all other stages of creation that follow this verse are given an introduction.

The Strange Appearance of the word "Replenish"

The next verse has a particular choice of word that should ring alarm bells with anyone possessing a King James or Cambridge Amethyst Bible. *Genesis 1:28; "And God blessed them, and God said unto them, be fruitful, and multiply, and replenish the earth, and subdue it: and have dominion over the fish of the sea, and over the fowl of the air, and over every living thing that moves upon the earth."* *(CAB)* The key word here is "replenish," meaning, "to refill" or "fill again." Most other modern Bibles render the same word in this verse as "fill," which comes from the more correct Hebrew root, which begs the question why in Genesis 1:22 is "fill" found there and six verses later in 1:28 "replenish" used? The common explanation is that the word "plenish" was an old English term for "fill" that later only survived in modern English as *re*plenish. It is said that ultimately this word was a stylistic choice. "Re" gradually became a prefix for many words giving them the meaning of a repeated action. Interestingly, six verses later the rendering of "fill" appears from the same Hebrew root apparently devoid of such an evolution. My experience with various choices of words found elsewhere in the Bible shows that translators nearly always decide upon particular words for a practical purpose, such as adding emphasis, deliberately changing a meaning or hiding something. For example the word "cross" is added to a Hebrew root that means "upright pole," or "stake," while the word "church" comes from the old English word "Kirke" that means pagan place of worship, replacing the more correct translation of the word, "assembly." Nonetheless, the appearance of such a word as "replenish" is at the very least mysterious, as its origin, going by the above explanation, is the product of three obscure coincidences with no practical purpose except the ambiguous choice of style. Coincidence #1, it supports the notion of a prior creation (though devoid of man). Coincidence #2, it survived in its old English version "plenish" with a later addition of "re," when six verses away it did not. Coincidence #3 even though it survived in its English version, it only did so by receiving a modern addition to the word "re" that added to its meaning.

King David also appears to write about at least two floods in the Psalms. *Psalms 24:2; "For He has founded it (the earth) upon the*

seas, and established it <u>upon the floods</u> (notice the plural)."And *93:3;
"<u>The floods</u> have lifted up, o Lord, the floods have lifted up their voice;
the floods lift up their waves.*" And *98:8; "<u>Let the floods clap their
hands</u>: let the hills be joyful together.*" So why this vague mention of
an initial flood before the time of Noah? Remember the agenda of
Constantine's appointed council and how they set a precedence of
hacking and cleaving out books from the Bible. Well in doing this
they have left gaps that may not hinder our salvation, but certainly
make it difficult to build a complete picture of a cohesive story in
some places within Scripture.

I'll give you another illustration of what is going on here. A man
goes to the local shop and buys a loaf of bread. On his way home
he stops and realises that he needs two loaves for some guests he
is expecting later that evening. So he promptly returns to the shop
and purchases another. A bit later his next-door neighbour's dog
takes off with one loaf. Fortunately only half of the guests that the
man is expecting arrive, so he has enough bread after all. Nice little
story. What if I decided to pull out the bit when the man returns to
buy a second loaf? We have an anomaly. How did he feed his guests
if a dog took off with his only loaf? Poor latter-day Christians have
been fielding well-researched and structured Bible contradiction
attacks for years without being equipped with the knowledge of
what went on at the blasphemous council mentioned above.

Deadly Deception, Desperate Devil

To understand the reason for the first flood it is necessary to shed
some light on Satan's background and what his role was. Satan was
originally called Lucifer who was the highest ranked angel of all the
free-will beings, created long before Adam and Eve. He was a steward (administrator) of Earth, presiding over the original Garden of
Eden and was the chief trafficker of the praise of heaven. *Ezekiel
28:5,18; "By thy great wisdom and by thy <u>traffic</u> hast thou increased
thy riches, and thine heart is lifted up because of thy riches: [12] Thou
hast defiled thy sanctuaries by the multitude of thine iniquities, by the*

---

12 Excerpted from *The Complete Multimedia Bible based on the King James Version.* Copyright
© 1994 Compton's NewMedia, Inc.

iniquity of thy <u>traffic</u>; therefore will I bring forth a fire from the midst of thee, it shall devour thee, and I will bring thee to ashes upon the earth in the sight of all them that behold thee."[13] Unfortunately the *New King James* does away with the word "traffic" and inappropriately inserts "trade." Most people know that Satan fell from God's grace through pride and a desire to exalt himself above the Most High. But the exact reason for his fall came about by his redirecting the traffic of praise onto himself instead of God, and the accumulation of independent resources. He even managed to rally the support of one third of the heavenly host (angels) to assist him in this rebellion *(Revelation 12:4)*. His force attempted an invasion of heaven but was pushed back. Satan being a former steward of earth regrouped there after the defeat. From here he tried to replenish his numbers by engaging in various crossbreedings with his angels and earth animals, thus defiling one of his sanctuaries. Great cities and complexes were constructed and it is from this age where we get stories of fabled creatures like centaurs and the lost city of Atlantis. The following verses describe the vastness of Satan's former beauty and responsibilities. *Ezekiel 28:12-17; "You were the seal of perfection, full of wisdom and perfect in beauty* (originally a good guy). *You were in Eden, the Garden of God; Every precious stone was your covering: The sardius, topaz and diamond, Beryl, onyx, and jasper, Sapphire, turquoise, and emerald with gold. The workmanship of your timbrels and pipes was prepared for you on the day you were created* (evidence of musical instruments built into Lucifer's original form). *You were the anointed Cherub who covers* (administrator); *I established you; You were on the holy mountain of God; You walked back and forth in the midst of fiery stones. You were perfect in your ways from the day you were created, Till iniquity was found in you. By the abundance of your trading You became filled with violence within, and you sinned; Therefore I cast you as a profane thing Out of the mountain of God; And I destroyed you, O covering Cherub, from the midst of the fiery stones. Your heart was lifted up because of your beauty; You corrupted your wisdom for the sake of your splendor; I cast you to the ground, I laid you before kings, that they might gaze at you.*"

---

13   Excerpted from *The Complete Multimedia Bible based on the King James Version.* Copyright © 1994 Compton's NewMedia, Inc.

God saw that Satan and his minions would not repent. So He sent down a wave of cataclysms that culminated in darkness and a mighty flood. All the hybrid angelic offspring who were the product of flesh and spirit unions perished along with all their cities. Satan's armies were then forced to flee to another sanctuary. Eventually God replenished the earth and this time populated it with new beings called "humans" beginning with Adam and Eve. Satan returned to earth with a portion of his fallen angels who quickly set about concealing themselves within various earth animal DNA. In time members of Satan's forces began to confront and interact with these new occupants. Eve was quickly challenged by one of these concealed adversaries and succumbed to go against a Commandment from God. Adam and Eve's relationship with God became damaged which led to all of them, including the serpent, receiving various forms of punishment. Contrary to popular belief, Adam and Eve's flesh became perishable through being denied access to the tree of life as is clearly stated in *Genesis 3:22-23; "Then the Lord God said, 'Behold, the man has become like one of Us, to know good and evil. And now, lest he put out his hand and take also of the tree of life, and eat, and live forever.' Therefore the Lord God sent him out of the garden of Eden to till the ground from which he was taken."* Despite the fact that these verses get commonly wheeled out to support the notion that Adam and Eve were not meant to be eternal beings, the presence of the tree of life in the garden itself does suggest that it would have been on offer, perhaps if they had rejected Satan's challenge. The presence of a tree in one of the more pleasant moments of *Revelation (22:2)* suggests its use as a mechanism that generates eternal existence. In achieving this objective of deceiving the pinnacle of God's creations, Satan thought he had won a great challenge. God was disappointed in Adam and Eve, but told them they could have eternal life once again if they repented of their deed and resumed their obedience toward him. God then told Satan that from the seed of the very pair he deceived would come a physical and spiritual Son that will be born on the earth in a flesh body and eventually defeat him. Satan did not give up after hearing this and convinced himself that his next move would be a masterstroke, the outcome of which would lead inevitably to the next flood.

Chapter Seven

Send in the Giants

I REMEMBER A TIME when I was very young where I attended Sunday school. I vividly recall being rounded up at one point during the church service by a teacher and following her off to a classroom with a whole bunch of other kids like the Pied Piper. There we were told stories about Moses and Noah, the flood and even the mighty Samson. Leading up to primary school I started learning about and became fascinated with dinosaurs. That interest led me, as I'm sure it did nearly every small boy, to the question of why they became extinct. The popular theory was a meteor shower, which I gently digested. Primary school soon turned into high school and in the last couple of years there I remember thinking that the things I was taught in a church contradicted the things I learned at school. There was nothing in my science textbook about a world flood, let alone two, let alone a theory about a flood. Unbeknownst to me, the story of the dinosaurs had served as a distracting precursor to the secular school curriculum theory of evolution, which at the time replaced any validity I held in a concept of creation.

It is a blessed person that has managed to unravel the tangled cord of mish-mashed concepts to come to a clear understanding of man's history in the grander scheme of things. But even after years of weekly Bible study and church attendance the following truths are at best vague to the average Christian.

Dinosaurs According to God

The word "dinosaur" first appeared in 1841, more than three thousand years after the Bible referred to these creatures as "Tanniyn" which occurs twenty-eight times in the Hebrew Bible. There are in fact three specific references. They are tanniyn, bahemowth (behemoth), and livyathan (leviathan). The last two references are still used very sparingly in our language today. However for the twenty-eight times the word tanniyn appears it is replaced specifically as "dragon," "serpent," "great creature" etc. From descriptions in the Bible of the behemoth it is believed that it refers to a brachiosaurus (1903AD). *Job 40:15-24; ... "eats grass like an ox"... "moves his tail like a cedar"... "bones are like beams of bronze, His ribs like bars of iron"... "He lies under the lotus trees, in a covert of reeds and marsh."* Some Bibles and study Bibles will translate the word as elephant or hippopotamus. Note: neither of these creatures have tails like a cedar (tree trunk). *Job 40:19; "He is the first of the ways of God;"* This phrase in Hebrew implies that he was the biggest animal created by God. Also note: A whale is bigger than an elephant or hippopotamus. The Leviathan from its biblical description is believed to be a kronosaurus (1901AD). *Job 41:14,18-19,26; "Who can open the doors of his face," His sneezings flash forth light, And his eyes are like the eyelids of the morning. Out of his mouth go burning lights;" "Though the sword reaches him, it cannot avail; Nor does spear, dart, javelin."* In contrast to the behemoth, the leviathan is a real live wire (i.e. it would eat you just as soon as look at you). Again some Bibles misinterpret this creature as a crocodile or alligator even though *Job 41* goes on to describe the creature as a deep-sea dweller that cannot be penetrated by sword, javelin, spear, dart and *"regards iron as straw."* Reminder Note: crocodiles and alligators though fond of water are considered land animals and I've seen an arrow penetrate four layers of (chain) mail armour, so goodness knows what one would do to the scaly hide of a crocodile. Last time I checked they don't breathe fire either unlike the Leviathan. By the way if you think it is just a fable that animals can breathe fire then you don't

...erican bombardier beetle. It shoots out

...temperature jet of gas for protection.

...or Men Walking with Dinosaurs?

...ation is the imagery depicted in some

...ered in the area of Peru in South Amer-

...collection. Among the most startling of

...picture of a *Tyrannosaurus Rex* pursuing

...otable characteristic is the creature's cor-

...nless we are to believe that ancient men

...te pictures of dinosaurs by restoring fossils,

...alk or in this case run from dinosaurs. The stones form part of a collection of over 11,000 intricately etched pieces called "gliptoliths" done 13,000,000 years ago, believed to be the records of an advanced race. The former owner Dr. Jevier Cabrara made them available to the public at his Stone Museum in the village of Ica. Some of the stones show captured dinosaurs, what appears to be the use of telescopes and images of the earth as it appears from space. Though the BBC has done a successful documentary on the artifacts, the secular archaeological world stubbornly continues to ignore their implications.

Sceptics like to point out that if some of the images show surgery and even organ transplants, then why are these records primitively carved in stones? Sadly the claim that the stones originated from an advanced race could be misleading, as a more likely explanation is that they are evidence left by a primitive race in close association with an advanced one, in which case the depictions could simply be eyewitness observations of an advanced race or attempts at mimicking their superior techniques.

There has been a new technique in use since just prior to the year 2000 called "the chlorine 23 method" that accurately pinpoints dates of worked stone. I wonder why some of these artifacts have not been formally subjected to this testing? Prior to this, stone has been virtually impossible to date compared to wood and this author waits with bated breath for any news of these artifacts undergoing such analysis. If and when a test occurs and the findings show the stones were made a short time ago by a farmer that managed to belt out 11,000 of them over the course of his lifespan, I will retract the subject of these artifacts from a later edition of this book with an apology. However, if the tests show otherwise then these are 11,000 little headaches for the secular science world to try and explain away.

God Bless Cartilage

Another curiosity is the images displayed on a Mesopotamian Cylinder Seal from approximately 3300 B.C. that came to my attention from the pages of a volume called *The Art of Ancient Mesopotamia*, by Anton. Moortgat, (New York: Phaidon, 1969).

The creatures displayed on this artifact (left) are almost 100% anatomically correct to the appearance of an Apatasaurus, which previously went by the name Brontosaurus. The shape of the legs alone is a signature that these could not be any other type of animal. The muscle definition in the renderings is very similar to a modern day artist's drawing (pictured right) and even the harshest sceptic would have to ask where an artist so long ago would have gotten the idea to draw such accurate depictions unless he observed one in the flesh.

The only extreme difference appears to be the angular heads. Various commentaries on this observation reveal that more and more archaeologists are admitting that the presence of cartilage (unable to withstand the test of time like bones) could have been the reason for the discrepancy.

The Hidden Truth About Giants

Even far less known than the existence of dinosaurs in the Bible is the evidence of giants who came about after Satan heard God's plan to send a deliverer from the seed of the two humans he successfully deceived. Satan reacted by deploying around two hundred of his minions to breed with the daughters of Adam. *Genesis 6:2-4; "The sons of God...took wives for themselves of all whom they chose..."* and *Jude 6; "...the angels did not keep their proper domain, but left their own abode..."* Their progeny were known as the "nephilim" or "men of renown." They were abnormal super-beings; most were large in stature, and all having inherited the rebellious natures of their angelic fathers, were capable of much wickedness. Even today there is a steady increase in reports of alien abductions that are associated with crossbreeding. With this in mind, *Daniel 2:43* has an expanded meaning when we read, *"...they will mingle with the seed of men..."*

After this initial wave of unions the rapid rate at which they spread throughout the land and their rebellious nature accelerated the inherited sin of men and this is regularly overlooked as being the chief reason God sent the flood. We read this in *2 Peter 2:4-5; "For God did not spare the angels who sinned, but cast them down to hell and delivered them into chains of darkness, to be reserved for judgment. And did not spare the ancient world, but saved Noah, one of eight people, a preacher of righteousness, bringing in the flood on the world of the ungodly..."*

Any indication that giants were the root cause of the flood, not just the general wickedness of men in contrast to Noah's righteousness, is never mentioned at any church I have ever attended. Neither is the fact that Noah's bloodline was pure from Adam. Satan knew that if he could infect all men with a gene containing his like mindedness that a Saviour from his army's very own offspring would have a poor chance of succeeding. God let his plan go unchallenged until only eight purebloods were left. Making for a very close shave. Further information about the lead up to this period and shortly after is scattered throughout the Bible and generally goes unnoticed. But there is a source that shines much light on this unknown age. It comes from Cain's firstborn, Enoch. *Jude 14; Now Enoch, the seventh from Adam, prophesied about these men also, saying, "Behold, the Lord comes with ten thousands of His saints, ..."*

The Book of Enoch

It is interesting to note that we are told in the Bible that the Lord was so pleased with Enoch that He took him. *Genesis 5:24; "And Enoch walked with God; and he was not, for <u>God took Him</u>."* And in *Hebrews 11:5a; "By faith Enoch was taken away so that <u>he did not see death and was not found, because God had taken him</u>."* Then later in Jude we read that he prophesied and yet there are no records of these prophecies found elsewhere within the Scriptures. Could it be that one of only several humans to be directly taken by God said prophetic words that were not interesting or relevant enough to be recorded to any degree in the Bible? Of course not.

The Book of Enoch was discovered in Abyssinia (now Ethiopia) in 1773 by Scotsman James Bruce and eventually saw translation into English by Archbishop Richard Laurence. Its contents indicate that it did indeed contain prophecies as cited by the Apostle Jude. Archbishop Laurence expresses this in an introduction of a translation of the work by saying:

"Modern research sees in the Epistle of Jude a work of the second century: but as orthodox theologians accept its contents as the inspired utterance of an Apostle, let us diligently search the Hebrew Scriptures for this important forecast of the second Advent of the Messiah. In vain we turn over the pages of the sacred Canon; not even in the Apocrypha can we trace one line from the pen of the marvelous being to whom uninterrupted immortality is assigned by apostolic interpretation of Genesis v. 24. Were the prophecies of Enoch, therefore, accepted as Divine revelation on that momentous day when Jesus explained the Scriptures, after his resurrection, to Jude and his apostolic brethren; and have we moderns betrayed our trust by excluding an inspired record from the Bible?"

The book's origin dates back to around the Seventh or Sixth century BC, roughly around the time when the Old Testament was chronicled and it was deliberately left out of canonised Scripture at the council of Laodicea for political reasons.

Within its pages it goes into great detail about the plot of the angels and the flood. What unfolds in this book is a story of mutant giants out of control and the decision of God to end the carnage. It also shows that though the physical bodies of these nephilim are eventually destroyed their spirits remained on the earth and are the origin of the demons encountered by Jesus.

When one begins reading the Book of Enoch there is an early hint in the text that suggests its long absence from Scripture may have been a part of God's plan. It describes information that is not fit for its current generation, but for a future generation. But at the end of the day it is up to the individual student to decide the merits of its authenticity and this author makes no guarantees of such except to say that it has undergone extensive scrutiny by many scholars and serves as a clear underscoring of the existing Scripture in the relevant area. It is certainly at the very least a text that adds muscle over the bone of the Scriptures as it harks the same tune as the rest of the known Gospel. I will however, in this instance, refrain from including any passages from the text here, as it is not my purpose to use anything outside the known Gospels to convince the reader on the subject of giants and their history. Suffice it to say that I do recommend acquiring a copy of the Book of Enoch to anyone who wishes to examine this subject more closely.

How Long Can a Giant Tread Water?

One of the most challenging questions I was asked once was, "if the flood wiped out all flesh including the giant nephilim, why after that event do the Israelites say they saw descendants from Anak which came from the sons of God?" Which indeed the Bible does say in *Genesis 7:23; "So He destroyed all living things which were on the face of the ground: both man and cattle, creeping thing and bird of the air. Only Noah and those who were with him in the ark remained alive." Numbers 13:33 "There we saw the giants (the descendants of Anak came from the giants); and we were like grasshoppers in their own sight."* This one stumped me. At the time, I came up with a half-hearted answer like, "Maybe one of Noah's family members was a descendant." Which in turn strips away one of the main purposes of the flood in the first place. So that couldn't have been right.

The person that posed this question should have received a special award. Not all of us get stumped with questions this clever, but with the correct study we can bounce answers straight back and move on to talking about the Messiah.

The answer to this question is found in *Genesis 6:4*, where we read: *"There were giants (Nephilim) on the earth in those days, and also afterward (after that), when the sons of God came in to the daughters of men and they bore children to them".* "Afterward" or "after that" refers to after the flood, so there was a second dispatch of these fallen angels, evidently smaller in number and limited to the nations of Canaan of which the subclasses of races were enumerated. Since God promised that He would not flood the earth again Israel was granted the use of the sword to eliminate them. They failed. We read this in *Joshua 13:13; "Nevertheless the children of Israel did not drive out the Geshurites or the Maachathites, but the Geshurites and the Maachathites dwell among the Israelites until this day."* Thus the giants did the bolt in all different directions and settled in other lands to escape the sword.

References to giants are extremely frequent throughout the Bible. Even the New King James Version has the heading in a break at *Chronicles 20* between verses 3 and 4 entitled, *Philistines Giants Destroyed.* (Note that these headings found in most Bibles never appeared in much earlier translations and therefore can be a help or a hindrance.) The chapter goes onto describe *Lahmi*, the brother of Goliath in *1 Chronicles 20:5; "Again there was war with the Phillistines, and Elhanan the son of Jair killed Lahmi the brother of Goliath the Gittite, the shaft of whose spear was like a weaver's beam."* And *"Yet again there was war at Gath, where there was a man of great stature, with twenty-four fingers and toes, six on each hand and six on each foot; and he also was born to the giant."*

There are approximately 19 different tribes of giants or hybrids mentioned in the Bible. By the term "giant," I mean beings that range from between 8 to 30ft (or greater) in height. Below is an extensive list of references to them:

Nephilim (Means Tyrants or Bullies) – Genesis 6:4; 14:5,6; 15:19-21; Exodus 3:8,17,23; Deuteronomy 2:10-12, 20-23; 3:11-13; 7:1; 20:17; Joshua12:4-8; 13:3; 15:8; 17:15 and 18:16

Kenites – *Genesis15:19; Numbers 24:21; Jude.4:11; 1 Samuel 15:6, 27:10, 30:29; 1 Chronicles 2:55*

Kenizzites – *Genesis.15:19*

Kadmonites – *Genesis.15:19*

Hittites – *Genesis15:20; Exodus 3:8,17; 13:5; 23:23; Numbers 13:29; Deuteronomy 7:1, 20:17; Joshua 1:4, 3:10, 12:8, 24:11; Jude1:26, 3:5; 1 King 9:20, 10:29, 11:1; 2 Kings; 2 Chronicles 1:17, 8:7; Ezra 9:1; Nehemiah 9:8*

Perizzites – *Genesis 15:20, 34:30; Exodus 3:8, 17; 23:23; Deuteronomy 7:1, 20:17; Joshua 3:10, 12:8, 17:15, 24:11; Jude 1:4,5, 3:5; 1 Kings 9:20; 2 Chronicles 8:7; Ezra 9:1; Nehemiah 9:8*

Rephaims *(Means Giants)* – *Genesis14:5; 15:20*

Amorites – *Genesis 14:7, 15:16,21; Exodus 3:8,17; 13:5; 23:23; Numbers 13:29; 21:13,21,25,26,29,31,32,34; 22:2; 32:33; Deuteronomy 1:4,7,19,20,27,44; 3:2,8,9; 3:28,9; 4:47,47; 7:1; 20:17; 31:4; Joshua 2:10; 3:10; 5:1; 7:7; 9:10; 10:5,6,12; 12:2,8; 13:4,10,21; 24:8,11; 24:12,15,18; Jude 1:34,35,36; 3:5; 6:10; 10:8,11; 11:19,21,22,23; 1 Samuel 7:14; 2 Samuel .21:2; 1 Kings 4:19; 9:20; 21:26; 2 Kings 21:11; 2 Chronicles 8:7; Ezra 9:1; Nehemiah 9:8; Psalm 135:11, 136:19.*

Canaanites – *Genesis 10:18, 19; 15:21; 24:3,37; 34:30; 50:11; Exodus 3:8,17; 13:5,11; 23:23; Numbers 13:29; 14:25,43,45; 21:3; Deuteronomy 1:7; 7:1; 11:30; 20:17; Joshua 3:10; 5:1; 7:9; 12:8; 13:4; 16:10; 17:12,13,16,18; 24:11; Jude 1;1,3,4,5,9,10,17,27,28,29,30 ,32,33; 3:3,5; 2 Samuel 24:7; 1 Kings 9:16; Ezra 9:1; NEH.9:8,24; OBA.20*

Zuzims – *Genesis 14:5*

Emims – *Genesis 14:5; Deuteronomy 2:10*

Zebusites – *Genesis 15:21; Exodus 3:8,17; 13:5; 23:23; Numbers 13:29; Deuteronomy 7:1; 20:17; Joshua 3:10; 12:8; 15:63; 24:11;*

Jude1:21; 3:5; 19:11; 2 Samuel 5:6,8; 2 Kings 9:20; 1 Chronicles 11:4,6; 2 Chronicles 8:7; Ezra 9:1; Nehemiah .9:8

Hivites – Exodus 3:8,17; 13:5; 23:23; Deuteronomy 7:1; 20:17; Joshua 3:10; 9:7; 11:19; 12:8; 24:11; Jude 3:3,5; 2 Samuel 24:7; 1 Kings 9:20; 2 Chronicles 8:7

Anakims – Deuteronomy 1:28; 2:10,11,21; 9:2; Joshua 11:21,22; 14:12,15

Horims – Deuteronomy 2:12, 22

Avims – Deuteronomy 2:23

Caphtorims – Deuteronomy 2:23

Anakims – Deuteronomy 1:28; 2:10,11,21; 9:2; Joshua 11:22, 22; 14:12,15

Zamzummims – Deuteronomy 2:20

Forbidden Archeology

The remains of giants have been discovered all over the world, from Southeast Asia, China, North America, Australia and New Zealand, yet no one seems to have heard about them. If so much as a dinosaur toenail gets dug up it's on the six-o'clock news. Full replica skeletons of dinosaurs decorate museums all over the globe, but just a thighbone from a giant or the remains of a massive tool or implement are as rare as hen's teeth. By the way there was no mention of giants in my high school science book either. Gigantopithecus (bigfoot) and Misanthropes (Java man) are names given to two giant humanoid remains found by paleontologists. These remains never get much attention, as they tend to throw a spanner in the commonly accepted evolutionary worldview.

Here is an excerpt from an article that appeared in *The Globe and Mail* on the 9th of Feb 2000:

"As indelicate as it sounds, a rare pair of nearly complete pelvic bones has thrust anthropologists up against the impressively large bodies of human ancestors. More than 200,000 years old, these pelvic fossils – one newly unearthed in Spain and the other extensively analyzed for the first time, although it was discovered in 1984 in China – belonged to individuals whose reconstructed physical build makes most people living today look puny," said Science News last summer. "Separate investigation of (the) fossils now suggests that modern humans have shrunk from the ample anatomical norm of their fossil ancestors, which include a long broad and thick pelvis for both sexes."

And over half a century earlier in 1947 an interesting story appeared in the *Nevada Citizen*, entitled, *Mummified Remains of Giants Found in Caves*. An excerpt from the article reads:

"August 5, – A band of amateur archaeologists announced today they have discovered a lost civilization of men nine feet tall in the California caverns, Howard E. Hill, spokesman for the expedition said the civilization may be, 'the fabled lost continent of Atlantis.' The caves contain mummies of men, animals and implements of a culture 80,000 years old, but 'in some respects more advanced than ours,' Hill said."

I have uncovered literally scores of news articles around the world with similar findings of giants. Apart from the obvious similarities of these findings, another more unnerving commonality is evident; there are usually no follow up articles or records of published findings from extensive examinations of the remains, nor any other explanations of the origin of the findings, which might contradict this evidence of giants. The pattern is that the anomalous discoveries are dug up, described in local history journals or newspapers, and then shipped off to museums, never to be seen again.

The Smithsonian Institute –
The Warehouse That Devours Treasures

Due to an extensive list of catalogued records by professional and amateur archeologists who have successfully excavated the remains of giants, there exists' a vast number of relevant paper trails that seem to literally hit a brick wall at the point of transfer to an organisation called the Smithsonian Institute.

In a 1992 issue of *The Stonewatch Newsletter* there featured a story about a collection of large stone coffins that were discovered in 1892 in Alabama and were promptly shipped off to the Smithsonian Institute and never seen again. The official explanation from the institute was that the coffins were actually wooden troughs and could not be released, as they were stored in an asbestos-contaminated warehouse.

David Hatcher Childress, Author of *Vimana Aircraft of Ancient India and Atlantis*, in an article for Nexus Magazine, attempts to explain why these unfortunate incidents seem to continue to occur:

"Most of us are familiar with the last scene in the popular Indiana Jones archaeological adventure film *Raiders Of The Lost Ark* in which an important historical artifact, the Ark of the Covenant from the Temple in Jerusalem, is locked in a crate and put in a giant warehouse, never to be seen again, thus ensuring that no history books will have to be rewritten and no history professor will have to revise the lecture that he has been giving for the last forty years.

While the film was fiction, THE SCENE IN WHICH AN IMPORTANT ANCIENT RELIC IS BURIED IN A WAREHOUSE IS UNCOMFORTABLY CLOSE TO REALITY FOR MANY RESEARCHERS. To those who investigate allegations of archaeological cover-ups, there are disturbing indications that the most important archaeological institute in the United States, the Smithsonian Institute, an independent federal agency, has been actively suppressing some of the most interesting and important archaeological discoveries made in the Americas."

The Smithsonian Institute, as does mainstream archaeology, supports the concept of "isolationism," which means that most ancient civilisations were completely isolated from one another. This view began to gain acceptance in the 1880's, as did the absurd notion that contact was rare between Ohio and Mississippi Valleys.

The supported concept prior to this one was called "diffusionism," which held that all through history there has been cultural dispersion via contact by sea vessels and major trade routes. Certainly, despite massive diversities, similarities in different cultures, which have always been evident, support this notion.

Not surprisingly the only other institution that comes under as much fire as the Smithsonian for attempting archival cover-ups is the Vatican archives in Rome.

In Europe there is an account from the Middle Ages, which involves St. Christopher. Modern stories make him out (at least physically) to be an ordinary man. Those who actually saw him know differently. According to personal accounts he was a giant, evidently belonging to a tribe of dog headed, cannibalistic giants. Jacques de Voragine in the *Golden Legend* wrote of St. Christopher: "He was of gigantic stature, had a terrifying mien, was twelve coudees tall." A coudee is an antique measurement equal to or larger than the English measurement of a foot. St Christopher stood from 12 to 18 feet tall. The church has ignored this observation, as Western icons do not picture St. Christopher as a giant, Eastern churches however do not appear to have a problem with depicting his enormous stature. His name was originally Offerus and though he was of great size and strength, he had a sensitive nature and travelled the land in search of the greatest god. His search led him to the strange occupation of a human ferry. He would carry people across deep rivers and legend has it that Jesus was one of his customers. Jesus apparently remarked that he carried the sins of the world on his shoulders.

The suggestion is seen in historic accounts that St. Christopher was possibly of royal birth and the product of a tryst between a human being and an Anubis (a demon-like creature based on the Greek Anoubis which came from the Egyptian's jackal-headed god who was believed to lead the dead to judgment.) The sad fact is that the accepted worldly view is that giants are relegated to myth and folklore, children's fairy tales and B-grade horror flicks.

Could it be such a far stretch of the imagination to equate these "*...men of renown...*" as they are referred to in *Genesis 6:4* as the explanation of the origin of Greek Mythology? Or is it easier to accept that the mythology was a mere invention rather than a tradition that grew from memories and legends of demi-gods, which gradually evolved out of the history of the nephilim?

Is it also mere coincidence that in chapter three of this book when I wrote about how some aliens revealed their names to contactees in *The Mothman Prophecy* that they originated from Greek gods, which also originated from gods mentioned in the Bible?

Rocking the Boat of Popular Science

Often I have posed the question, "Do you believe in giants?" to many people and they often say, "Big ones?" and I say, "Yes, big ones," and they promptly say, "No." Then I ask, "If I invited you down to the local museum to see an exhibit on giants, would you be interested?" and they nearly always say, "If it was real, yes, I would." This suggests to me that there is a market for displaying such fossils and certainly the subject would genuinely ignite public interest. Yet years of relegation to myth and folklore have left a burden even too heavy for giants to bear, to see them loosed from the pages of a fairytale and set into the history books. Adding to this, the subject has not passed without its fair share of hoaxes such as the "Cardiff Giant," which turned out to be little more than a chiseled statue conceived by a New York Tobacconist who wanted to strike it rich. And most recently the 'Saudi Arabian Giant photo' that depicts two occupants the size of mice excavating the massive partially unearthed remains of an enormous man, when in fact it was an entry that appeared on a website for an advanced Photoshop competition. The common trend in findings that run against the evolutionary model are nearly always met with silence from scientific institutions. However, hoaxes have also left their mark on more widely accepted areas of science, like "The Piltdown Man" incident, where an opposite reaction by the scientific community to a bizarre discovery is worth noting. The early part of the twentieth century saw men of science eagerly engaged in seeking evidence of 'the missing link' that would support an evolutionary relationship with man and ape. In 1912 an amateur paleontologist by the name of Charles Dawson discovered part of a skull and jawbone that bore striking similarities between each species that set the scientific community abuzz. Eventually his finding was eagerly entered into textbooks as the *Eoanthropus dawson* or "Dawson Man," and it wasn't until 1953 when a team of British researchers subjected the skull and jaw to extensive testing that they found out that they were completely fake, being both no more than a few decades old. It became one of the most damaging scientific hoaxes of all time and set the development of evolutionary theory back decades after researchers toiled to have it first integrated into fossil records, then had it removed.

It is clear that the steady shuffling forward of anthropological sciences, orthodox history, and academia generally tends to make scientists look the other way, cover their ears, or take a wide berth around anything relating to giants, wanting no part in rocking the boat of the neatly defined prehistory model and in doing so shamelessly ignoring astounding discoveries such as the "Antrim giant." "The who?" I hear you ask. Please, let me explain. This finding has become one of the most compelling examples of archeological cover-ups I have noticed, admittedly in some part due to the compelling nature of the photograph that accompanied the article, which originally appeared in the British Strand magazine in December of 1895. The discovery in question quite frankly reduces 'Ripley's Believe it, or not', to the realms of a boring nature documentary. The story of a full sized fossilised giant has since been reprinted in a book called, *Traces of the Elder Faiths of Ireland*, written by W.G. Wood-Martin. The story goes that a Mr. Dyer uncovered it in an iron ore mine in County Antrim, Ireland and it had a length of 12 ft 2 in, girth of chest, 6 ft 6 in, length of arms, 4 ft 6 in, and six toes on the right foot. Its total weight was 2 tons 15 cwt and required a crew of six men and a powerful crane to prop it up at North Western Railway Company's Broad street goods depot (see photo).

The giant was initially displayed in Dublin, before coming to England where it had an exhibit in Liverpool and Manchester. The entry price to view the massive corpse was set at sixpence and it attracted hoards of astonished onlookers including various members of the scientific community.

The exhibits eventually caught the attention of a wealthy entrepreneur named Kershaw who entered into a partnership with Dyer and in 1876 the giant was shipped by Dyer from Manchester to London, a decision that his new colleague Kershaw was apparently oblivious to.

From this point on the story becomes very vague, with Kershaw approaching London solicitors to determine ownership of the artifact before it was to be handed over to another company. No legal action ever came about and nothing more ever became known of the Antrim giant or its original owners. Bizarre.

Giants, Lizard-Men, and Mermaids

The range of names in the Bible that refer to beings that are not of earthly origin or are ancestors of such are as follows: "angels," "fallen angels," "demons," "Hosts of Heaven," "stars," "creatures," "Sons of God," and the "nephilim," also known as "rephaim." The inclusion of "demon" here may come as a surprise, yet when we examine non-Catholic canon approved Scripture we see that it is a broad term used to describe both deceased fallen angels, and their deceased aberrant hybrid progeny, such as the nephilim. This subject was briefly looked at earlier in this chapter and deserves a more thorough explanation here. Alas, the common "where's that in the Bible?" question is a tedious one to piece together an answer for, unless one is familiar with the book of Enoch. Even before an explanation can be administered, Christians will demonstrate their conditioning to remain focused only on the Catholic and Protestant approved books. The mere suggestion of additional books of the Bible being rejected usually come as a complete surprise or is a notion that is often supported by the same people that say they oppose Catholicism.

If one knows what to look for, the Bible exhibits not only a few verses but also an overall theme that forbids members of different species to interbreed. If a son of God mixes with a human, which results in progeny, their genetics are not only borrowed from a fallen Adam, but a fallen angel as well. Therefore this offspring are denied the ability to be raised in the resurrection, due to the genetic properties that fall outside the gift of salvation. This is simply because the Messiah died for the sins of men and not the sins of angels. After death, their forms remain in a non-corporeal aspect that work in tandem with each other and additional corporeal allies to continue deceiving men. This is why there are no evil spirits prior to the flood. This notion is looked at in further detail in Chapter Nine, which thoroughly examines the concept of ghosts.

It is important to understand that the term "nephilim" does not exclusively refer to beings that are of enormous physical stature. Some sources claim that it means "fallen ones," while others say it is the plural Hebrew word that comes from "nephil" (nphiyl) meaning "bully" or "tyrant." The term can cover a host of hybrid-nations bearing a variety of inhuman characteristics. Some of these physical characteristics include an elongated (cone headed) appearance that was found in the skulls of some tribes in Peru. These skulls were brought to the attention of the west by the efforts of Robert Connolly who photographed dozens of alien shaped skulls during the 1990's. Evidence in ancient cultures worldwide has also shown a commonality in the depiction of reptilian bipeds that all appear to be regarded as either ancestors, gods, or both. These were known to the ancient Sumerians as The ANNUNNAKI, meaning "Those who from heaven to earth came." Ancient Central American cultures also depict "Quetzalcoatl," a winged serpent god, like the Hopi Indians who have their plumed serpent god "Boholinkonga," and even the Egyptians who had a serpent called "Kneph." This notion of reptilian or amphibian ancestors is a theme surprisingly well supported in secular museums, yet it usually comes attached with the convenient tag of myth, legend or symbolism that effectively keeps the boat of normality steady. The Dogon tribe from Africa claim that their forefathers were sea dwellers, having both the anatomy of a man and a fish, and appearing on land to have dealings with men. *Genesis* perhaps has this very race in mind in verse *10:5; "From these the <u>coastland peoples</u> of the Gentiles were separated into their lands, everyone according to his language, according to their families, into their nations."* Other Bible versions render coastland peoples as "mariners." Stories amid Jewish legends specifically tell of dolphins and other sea animals around the time of the flood that were also part men. One possible scenario that could have caused nephilim to be present after the flood may have been due to these sea dwellers surviving the catastrophe. Though the Bible is very specific on all flesh not being spared it would be ridiculous to assume that Noah had every form of sea life we have today kept in fish tanks aboard the ark – particularly when scientists are still discovering deep sea animals to this very day.

Ultra Mega Super Patriots of the Sky Country

Often America is accused of having citizens that are overbearingly patriotic and I remember hearing a statistic that the nation contains the highest concentration of extroverted citizens in the world.

People at present are put off by America, perhaps fueled by the country's refusal to avoid an assault on Iraq and then to be later found that the basis for that assault had no grounds. Whatever the case, imagine the level of patriotism, pride and feeling of superiority inherit in a people who knew that their forefathers came from the sky. Imagine the delusions of grandeur from a race of men that knew they were the most physically and mentally dominant race on the earth. Hitler's vision was indeed based on this same concept. That of a "super race."

Some time after the second flood various tribes of these superior beings began to emerge once again, and once again they became a nuisance to pure blood humans as previously discussed. For a second time their presence had made the playing field uneven and a God assisted solution was formulated.

The Old Testament reveals a striving of God to maintain a relationship with mankind, until fallen angels began to cause human women to produce abnormal offspring. Then and only then is a drastic measure of mass elimination implemented. In the case of Noah it came down to himself and his immediate family, so a more absolute solution was called for with a mass flooding, whilst the ark served its dual purpose of isolating them from the destruction and ferrying them on to a new land. In the latter case a more long-term solution was called for as many nations of purebloods who still willingly served God remained. The solution was full-scale open warfare. It is important to realise that this action did not constitute genocide, because the enemy where not completely human.

While I was reading through various parts of the Human Rights Commission's official WebPage I read a speech by Dr. Sev Ozdowski that was delivered at the Armenian Genocide Commemorative Lecture in April of 2004 that showed a great example of men's ignorance of the Bible. While I do strongly condemn the act of genocide a portion of his speech disturbed me. It read:

"'Old Testament Tales' – But as you know, genocide is not a phenomenon limited to a particular time or location. And here is another example to illustrate this. Going even further back in time…those of you present today who have recently read the Bible may be surprised at the language. For instance in the Old Testament in the first Book of Samuel, Yahweh directs Saul through

Samuel to: '...go and strike down (the enemy tribe of) Amalek; put him under the ban with all he possesses. Do not spare him but kill man and woman, babe and suckling, ox and sheep, camel and donkey.'"

Dr. Ozdowski concludes this biblical interlude with the following statement: "I will leave the interpretation of such utterances to biblical scholars, much better qualified than I for such a task."

Sadly even most ministers and chaplains do not know the truth about these tribes and simply say, "yes these were bad people, and God decided their time was up." The fact is they were not people, they were hybrids infected with the corrupted hearts of their fallen angelic fathers. Even a nephil infant taken and brought up in a righteous house would eventually gravitate toward unrighteousness, as its genetic makeup would still remain intact.

Conclusion

One afternoon I found myself enjoying a lovely meal in an Indian restaurant. By chance I happened to look up at a wall hanging of a traditional Hindu depiction of a blue man clad in expensive robes with his arm firmly around a beautiful and scantily clad Indian woman. This image was nothing new. I have seen such pictures and statues decorate relevant restaurants and homes many times before, but this time I was curious about something. I asked a friend, why the man in the image had blue skin. She promptly replied that it was because he was a god. I looked more closely at the image and saw the man's hand was firmly grasping her breast and the look on her face was one of submission or servitude. For the first time the reality of the sons of God and their taking of wives in the Book of Genesis and its remembrance down through the ages by various religions and cultures hit me like a sledgehammer. Wherever you go, whether it is a traditional Indian, Chinese, Thai or Greek establishment the visual records are still very much evident today. It is as if various lines of Chinese whispers have spanned out from an initial event and depending on the cultural influence of the line, the truth is slightly changed yet still bears similarities with other stories which are now regarded as fables. It is further interesting to acknowledge that all cultures and beliefs speak of a beginning with a man and a woman and a worldwide cataclysm of some sort.

The information about our true history and the giants that once roamed the earth with or without the book of Enoch is still available for all who have a mind to look into these subjects. Maybe one day you may find yourself confronted with a tough Bible history question as I was and a strong yet softly delivered answer might mean the difference between planting a seed or giving that person another reason not to look into Scripture any further.

Article that appeared in August 2004 National Geographic Magazine

The following is an article that appeared in National Geographic and a rather heated letter I sent to the organisation in response. In hindsight, I feel that I may have conveyed my point a lot clearer with less emotion, towards the end, but I was at a really exciting point in my research when I found this particular issue strategically placed on the dining room table by a housemate. Anyway, here are both the pieces as they were finally rendered.

"'They Might Not Be Giants' – Reading the bones of a mythic race."

"Ancient Greeks believed in giants – mythic heroes and semihuman creatures many times bigger than ordinary folk. Atlas, the Cyclops, and the Titans were among them, but possibly the greatest of them all was Pelops. Poets envisioned him as a handsome interloper from the east, with a shoulder blade made of ivory. After winning a rigged chariot race, Pelops was said to have founded the Olympic games as a way to honor the gods for his victory. He also reigned over Greece's southern peninsula – the Peloponnese, whose name means "Pelops's island." At the peninsula's northwest corner stood Olympia, a religious complex that was the site of the Olympic games and of a shrine that claimed a relic of the mighty giant himself – his massive, ivory-white shoulder blade. During the Trojan War, the relic was reportedly shipped to the walls of Troy, as a talisman to bring the Greeks victory."

"Greek writers, from the fifth-century B.C. historian Herodotus to the second-century A.D. travel writer Pausanias, chronicled sightings of other bizarre remains of giants. Immense, disarticulated skeletons appeared along unstable shorelines, and huge, jumbled bones poked from weathered hills and cliffs."

"Today most scholars shelve stories of giant bones under fiction. But Adrienne Mayor, a folklorist and historian of early science, takes the Greeks at their word. "Since the 19th century," Mayor says, "modern paleontologists have discovered rich bone beds of giant, extinct mammals in the same places the ancient Greeks reported finding the bones of heroes and giants." She thinks what the Greeks actually found were isolated fossil bones of creatures like the southern mammoth, a relative of the woolly mammoth. With no other way to explain the bones, the Greeks may have conceived them to be skeletal remains of giants."

"Such mammoth bones would have dwarfed any living creature native to the lands of the ancient Greeks. The fossil beds that studded the Greek and larger Mediterranean world included those of mammoths, elephants, and other animals that had lived tens of thousands of years before the Greeks. More fragile bones, such as skulls, often didn't survive. But denser remains – shoulder blades and thighbones, which bear a resemblance to human bones – did."

"They also found fossil ivory tusks from extinct mammoths in the ground," Mayor says, "and they assumed the ivory was produced by the earth, like gems and minerals. In fact, the ancient Greek word for ivory, *elephas,* was the name they gave to elephants once they did encounter them." That first encounter probably didn't happen until the fourth century B.C., when Alexander the Great and his army advanced on Babylon and were met by a phalanx of Persian war elephants."

"By that time, though, the myths of superhumans and giants were well established in the Greek mind. Could some of these characters have been inspired by finds of enormous fossil bones that couldn't otherwise be explained? Or did the myths come first—and when confronted with the bones, did the Greeks imagine them reassembled as the villains and heroes of the larger-than-life mythic world?"

—Joshua Korenblat

My response:

Dear Joshua Korenblat and NG staff,

RE: 'They Might Not Be Giants' Article

I was sorely disappointed by, not only the limited breadth of the information sourced, but the overall implication alluded to from locally and vaguely referenced discoveries of mistaken remains of giants in ancient Greece.

How quickly we selectively forget such cases as the city of Troy and the Trojan War written of in the Greek poem *The Iliad*, by the Poet Homer that was believed to be a myth for many years and only recently is now accepted by most scholars as no imaginary Shangri-la but a real city, and that the Trojan War did indeed happen.

And lets not forget The Dogon tribe of Mali, Africa, who kept a record of the secondary star in the Sirius system, which they claimed has an orbital period of 50 years, which up until 1970, Europeans believed was untrue. This was due to the construction of telescope powerful enough to finally see this secondary star and measure it's orbital period, which ended up being, yes, you guessed it, 50 years.

There is also the Mesopotamian Cylinder Seal, displaying the detailed forms of intertwined Brontosaurus', from approximately 3300 BC, which show that either men did walk with dinosaurs or archaeology was up to speed with today's technique, as the shape, proportion and even muscle definition in the renderings exceeds the detail of many modern illustrations today. In addition their triangular shaped heads have caused archaeologists to admit that the presence of cartilage (unable to withstand the test of time like bones) could have been the reason for the discrepancy.

Either way you play it, the first option goes against all modern accepted archaeological thinking and the second option goes together with your theory of Greeks not being able to discern skeletal segments of animals from humans like chocolate topping on a salad sandwich.

All these examples of mysterious ancient knowledge aside, your hypothesis that the mighty skull of a Mammoth cannot survive over other portions of its skeleton because it is more fragile, border on lunacy and wreaks with desperation at an obvious attempt to water down the continued evidence of these anomalous discoveries that boldly threaten to unravel the tattered theory of evolution that modern science is so hell-bent on clinging to.

And as for Adrienne Mayor, I think she should get out more, and if I drew the same conclusion in a murder trial as to the proximity of Mammoth bone discovery in the alleged vicinity of giant's remains to disprove the existence of them, I would be laughed out of the courtroom.

I grow weary of these types of meagre articles that are just tokenly thrown out there in an attempt to respond to a particular buzz that does not fit with mainstream archaeological thought. If I, in contrast, published an article of the same depth and magnitude about the existence of giants, I would also be laughed out of the classroom.

Shame on National Geographic for publishing such a stupid and ill in-formed article that literally must have dripped from the pen of a blinkered academic with a selective memory. And I haven't even mentioned the evidence of the Gigantopithecus or the Misanthropes discovered by paleontologists in South East Asia and Australia, both of which clock in at around 12 feet each. Oops, I mentioned them.

National Geographic of all magazines should not allow an author to push his or her BIAS or SLANT on the article's chosen topic (even if it does agree with the top brass of the magazine).

Regards,

Jason Jordan.

Chapter Eight

The Second Tower of Babel

MY FIRST SERIOUS thoughts about embracing Christianity, which later led to my walk as a Nazarene Israelite, came about through the information that I wish to share in this chapter. As a consequence this topic has been a personal area of interest for some years. While I do not claim any qualified expertise in the subject, I have spent some considerable time researching and studying a broad range of world news articles that seem to confirm like clockwork the sequence of events that are set down in the Book of Revelations.

I will try to make the points I wish to bring forward as clear as possible to equip the reader with basic information, the purpose being to share with others knowledge about this topic and gently direct all conversation to the subject of Salvation. Please be thoughtful enough not to use this information to scare people or as "show-pony" discussion, but remind them of the joy and fulfillment that is to come.

New World Order Explained

During the time of the Gulf war President George Bush introduced the term *New World Order* to the public during a speech about Saddam Hussein's attack on Kuwait. This was subsequently used in public addresses over 200 times and even the media admitted that no one fully understood what he meant by the use of the term.

Following the collapse of the Cold War there emerged a disintegration of the Soviet states that threatened to have worldwide repercussions in the form of a breakdown in the world capital movement (world wide economic collapse). The stabilisation of this threat laid the foundation for the United States to become a leading world power. Then travelling in the wake of the Gulf War came the solution of The New World Order. This same regime used the September 11 attacks as a platform to marshal the global populace into a state of total paralysis by gradually eradicating civil liberties and increasing the powers of all police and military agencies. This "Order Out of Chaos" or "Problem, Reaction, Solution" model was also used to elevated Hitler's Nazi party to power after the freak burning of the German parliament building in Berlin (Reichstag).

New World Order's Purpose

Its purpose is to achieve global economic and social stability, streamlining all nations to follow the same agenda under a single ruling body. To do this all countries must be subjected to the external control of three specific areas, politics, economy, and religion.

Everything from the surrendering of a country's constitution, the acquisition of internally owned companies, to heavy losses in liberty; freedom, privacy and even possessions are the requirements of such a regime, until ultimately leading to the death of the economic independency of all nations, all for our own good of course. Right! The reality is that this is a blueprint for a system of world communist fascism under the dictatorship of an as yet unknown global leader.

Who's Behind This Plan?

Firstly it is important to understand that this plan has been in the works for a very long time. The group that achieved the first noteworthy steps of this global agenda went by many names, but are today known as a secret society called *The Illuminati* (No, not the bad guys in the Lara Croft movie!).

The sole individual behind the formation of this order is a topic of much debate. Most sources claim that Adam Weishaupt formed the organisation in Bavaria; fewer sources insist that this is a lie perpetuated by the Catholic Church and that the founder was the man responsible for the Jesuit movement, Ignatius De Loyola. Indeed it does appear that nearly all the sources that cite Weishaupt say that though he occupied a Jesuit position in the early years, he was not a member of that order. Further sources claim there was a Bavarian and Spanish branch of the order; one headed by Weishaupt, the other by Ignatius consecutively. From here it gets silly with a host of variables like Weishaupt was a nobody or he was actually a Jesuit or an ex-Jesuit etc. At any rate if Ignatius was the initiator it would mean the order got kick started much early than recorded considering he lived from 1491 to 1556 and Weishaupt passed away in 1830. This author was interested by the fact that while all references to Ignatius were accompanied by his year of birth and death, Weishaupt, where mentioned, was only accompanied by the year of his death.

After much research I have come to the conclusion that I am more lenient to the Ignatius story, though much historical information of Weishaupt's activities during the alleged formation, exposure and growth of the order do appear to have some basis in fact. To the point that certain beats are hit accurately with other evidence that leads me to think that this man (whether his name was Weishaupt or not) was a Jesuit protégé of Ignatius' (the original founder). Alternatively it could be information about Ignatius' activities with alterations to dates and some events. Whatever the case the following scenario is the more popular theory and the most detailed blow-by-blow information available.

According to most sources the order started in Bavaria on the 1st of May 1776 (Note: This is the same date of the formation of the United States of America.) by Adam Weishaupt. He was originally elected to the chair of Canon Law at the University of Ingolstadt, which was usually reserved as a Jesuit position (thus possibly marking his point of contact and influence with the Vatican). In 1778 he managed to infiltrate the Masonic Lodge as a fully initiated Master Mason and gradually meshed his own Illuminati philosophy there as well. By 1783 he had formed a 600 strong party of influential men that threatened the framework of the established order, which led to a battle for control that started in Bavaria and spread to France.

It was presumed that Weishaupt's order ceased to exist after a police raid in 1786. All details of the order were seized and published, exposing an objective of world domination by any means. If this is starting to sound like bad science fiction, you'll find a detailed description of the organisation in a copy of Webster's Illustrated Encyclopedic Dictionary, but don't bother looking in your Encyclopedia Britannica. For some reason better known to the editors, the details have been removed from the latest editions.

Gone, but not Forgotten

Eventually Weishaupt passed away in 1830 and seemingly so too did his grand plans for world domination. However, if we refer to his manifesto, which is available, there is little doubt that his plans are beginning to see fruition today. The document relates an objective to instigate violent worldwide revolutions and global instability to yield a New World Order.

After his death, American postgraduate students who supported this agenda and were studying in Europe brought Illuminati philosophies back home and proceeded to indoctrinate other students with this way of thinking. This resulted in the formation of an Inner Order at Yale University called *The Order of Skull and Bones* although the official name was *The Russell Trust*, of which George Bush Sr. and George W. Bush were both members.

The Weird Pictures on the US $1.00 Bill

During Weishaupt's career he was fortunate enough to make the acquaintance of Thomas Jefferson who though in disagreement with several New World Order principles did support his views on a republic. While Jefferson was serving as an American Ambassador in France in 1784 he saw that Weishaupt's Illuminism was the best method of uniting the competing philosophies of Masonry, Jacobinism and Jesuit teachings.

When he returned home to America five years later he became the Secretary of State and shortly after participated in the drawing up of the U.S. Constitution and the construction of the Great Seal of the United States, the front and back of which appear on every American $1.00 bill.

These images have dual meanings. The first meaning appears to show the birth of a new social order from the thirteen colonial states. At first glance one can be forgiven for thinking that they represent a Christian nation, which supports freedom, strength and unity. The following quote from "The Secret Teachings of the Masonic Lodge by John Ankerberg" tells a different story. "European mysticism was not dead at the time the United States of America was founded. The hand of the Mysteries controlled in the establishments of the new government, for the signature of the mysteries may still be seen on the Great Seal of the United States of America. Careful analysis of the seal discloses a mass of occult and Masonic symbols chief among them, the so-called American eagle. ...the American eagle upon the great Seal is but a conventionalised phoenix..."

A phoenix is a mythical bird from the East that is said to set itself on fire when it senses the end of its life approaching. From the ashes a worm emerges which gradually grows into a bird of unparalleled beauty. Notice the reference to it setting <u>itself</u> on fire. Back in Chapter One I referred to an American Air Force badge that depicted an eagle over a circle with arrows coming out of it in all-different directions. To the learned eye this is a phoenix rising from a chaos symbol, thus echoing the same principle of "order out of chaos" depicted in the Great Seals.

The Latin phrases on the first Seal mean the following:

"Annuit Coeptis" – "Announcing the birth, creation, or arrival"

and

"Novus Seclorum" – "New Secular* Order"

* = (Secular) meaning without God.

The Latin phrase on the second Seal means:

"E Pluribus Unum" – "One out of many"

There is much more enlightening information contained in these Seals than the explanations provided above, but it is not my intention to get bogged down with too much detail. Lets move on to a time where cash will be obsolete.

A Cashless Society – Prelude to the Mark

"The motive was robbery as both victims were found decapitated and missing their right forearms." – Future police statement to the media

Before I begin this subject it seems appropriate to let the Bible have the first word on the ultimate aim of the digital monetary system that is emerging in our lifetime. *Revelations 13:16-17; "He (antichrist) causes all, both small and great, rich and poor, free and slave, to receive a mark on their right hand or on their foreheads, and that no one may buy or sell except one who has the mark or the name of the beast, or the number of his name."*

Currently there is a system in place that through a gradual process will diminish the circulation of physical currency worldwide. We have reached a point in history where one would have to be particularly naive to not agree with that statement. That much is evident with introductions such as EFTPOS (electronic funds transferal at point of sale), phone banking, E-way (automatic funds deduction when passing through a road toll), Internet purchasing, phone cards, bonuses when purchasing with credit cards and so on.

Where there was a point in time that "the mark" was a topic of wide speculation and interpretation, it appears that the function and manner in which it will be worn is the last bastion available for argument by the sceptics. Unfortunately the exact word or concept of a microchip was not known at the time of writing Revelation and though the physical location and ultimate purpose of such an object was, people are still finding feeble grounds for conjecture.

An excerpt from an article in the Sydney Daily Telegraph 2002 defends any relation of an implanted mark to biblical prophecy by stating the following:

"But its use (the *Verichip* as it is called) has outraged religious groups who claim a direct connection to the book of Revelations and its "mark of the beast" passage. It reads: 'He also forced everyone, small and great, rich and poor, free and slave, to receive the mark on his right hand or on his forehead, so that no one could buy or sell unless he had the mark, which was the number of the beast or the number of his name.' ADS (Applied Digital Solutions) disagrees, arguing that it has designed its chip to store vital and medical information. The information can only be read using a scanner within 1m of the chip."

The ADS spokesperson must have thought the average IQ of a person that reads a newspaper was below 50 when this pathetic response was compiled. Firstly, after a chip has had the information stored and is then implanted into the occupant in case of future changes in that person's condition it would have to be able to have the existing information altered, added to, or deleted. That being the case, what is stopping this chip down the track also encompassing social security or tax files numbers in addition to the above mentioned details? Secondly, the ADS response goes on about the use of a scanner and its proximity to the chip for activation, which has nothing to do with their argument.

Through personal experience I can testify that unless you are being paid in cash, without the submission of a tax file number to an employer, there is extreme legal difficulty in receiving payment. Some years ago I was most distressed to learn at the end of a hard days work with an employer far from my home that I would not be paid until I submitted this number. Still being quite new to things I was very scared that the phone number this contractor gave me to call once I acquired the number was fake. Fortunately I was eventually paid and the incident serves as reminder of things to come with the mark. Once I became familiar with the above verse I could see how easy the transition of a number on a piece of paper which wielded so much power could do exactly the same thing if it were contained in a chip under the skin. *"Rev 13:17...and that no one may buy or sell except one who has the mark..."* Therefore just as it is difficult to find legal employment without a tax file or other relevant work number so to will it be for those who choose not to receive the mark. The best way to inhibit any sort of participation in the market place is to deny an occupant the right to earn money in the first place.

But The Mark Seems Very Convenient!

It is true the mark will reduce the need to carry a wallet. Gone will be the days of worrying about your wallet when you hit the beach or going through the hassle of paying for a locker before indulging in water rides at a theme park. Even travelling the streets at night will be devoid of the fear of being mugged. Not to mention the psychological freedom that comes with purchasing items without the physical act of parting with money as this article in The Daily Telegraph boasted:

"**'Chipping in for drinks'** – Glasgow: A nightclub is to become the first in Britain to offer customers cash-free drinking by having a microchip implanted in their arm. The Verichip – the size of a grain of rice – will guarantee entry to the Bar Soba and let revelers buy drinks on account. It is scanned as the bearer enters the bar."

So there you have it. The annoyance of small change and having to go to an ATM at the last minute will be gone. So what's the problem with this new invisible form of currency? I'm glad you asked. There are short-term dangers in accepting this system, as an individual is more likely to spend more money if the chore of making a physical transaction is cut in half. That is to say that the negative process in the transaction (withdrawing money from a wallet) is knocked out and all that remains is the receiving of the service or item. A press of a button on a poker machine produces a beer, as patrons of pubs or casinos potentially could have the entire content of their bank accounts drained as opposed to just the cash filled content of their leather wallets. The morning after a night of excess or a carefree weekend away may yield an unexpected surprise.

But Why Can't I Just Take The Mark And Still Serve God?

More importantly the Scriptures appear to speak of the horrific long-term effects of this technology, as is the case in *Revelations 16:2; "So the first (angel) went and poured out his bowl upon the earth, and a foul and loathsome <u>sore came upon the men who had the</u>*

mark of the beast and those who worshiped his image." One of the delays with the embedding of these chips into people is the lithium contained in the chips and its long-term negative effects. Though it appears chip insertion in pets is okay, humans have considerably longer life spans than domestic animals.

The Bible says quite clearly that if you take the mark, you're in big trouble. **Revelations 14: 9-10; "Then a third angel followed them, saying with a loud voice, "If anyone worships the beast and his image, and receives his mark on his forehead or on his hand, he himself shall also drink of the wine of the wrath of God, which is poured out full strength into the cup of His indignation."**

The Bible also speaks of a promise to those who refuse to take the mark, though such a course of action could prove fatal. **Revelations 20:4; "And I saw thrones, and they sat on them, and judgment was committed to them. Then I saw the souls of those who had been beheaded for their witness to Jesus and for the word of God, who had not worshipped the beast or his image, and had not received his mark on their foreheads or on their hands. And they lived and reigned with Christ for a thousand years."**

Quite simply your forehead is reserved for the Name of God. If you bring up the issue of a future mark that ultimately enables us to buy and sell to the minister of your church and he calmly says that he would accept such a scheme, I urge you to educate him, leave that church immediately or refer to the scenario related in **Revelations 14:11; "And the smoke of their torment ascends forever and ever; and they have no rest day or night, who worship the beast and his image, and whoever receives the mark of his name."**

As of October 2000 the chip unveiled by Applied Digital Solutions was known as "Digital Angel", however it appears the product has undergone a name change for some reason and is now known as the afore mentioned "Verichip." The Florida based company now awaits the approval of the Food and Drug Administration for the device and intends to limit the marketing of it to a voluntary basis. This is important to note as Bible prophecy maintains that receiving this mark will be a conscious choice. In the initial phase of refusing the mark there will be the inconvenience of being unable to openly participate in the economy and at the later stages refusal by an occupant will result in execution by beheading.

Heads Will Roll

Revelations 20:4;" ...Then I saw the souls of those who had been beheaded for their witness to Jesus and for the word of God, who had not worshipped the beast or his image, and had not received his mark on their foreheads or on their hands..." Now before you throw this book at a wall please consider the following piece of information. As of 1996 a new legislation in the State of Georgia was proposed to have execution by guillotine be offered as an alternative form of capital punishment for inmates on death-row.

Guillotine Proposed As Means Of Execution In Georgia

Georgia lawmaker Doug Teper (Democrat, 61st Dist.) has proposed a bill to replace the state's electric chair with the guillotine. Teper's reasoning? It would allow for death-row inmates as organ donors, he says, since the "blade makes a clean cut and leaves vital organs intact..."

For decades there has been trouble associated with lethal injection and electrocution. Prisoners have died excruciating deaths and in some cases withstood initial administering of dosages and electricity, causing witnesses trauma and gathering the attention of human rights organisations that threaten lawsuits and abolition of capital punishment. Procedures as they stand require large teams of very highly paid trained personnel and even without hiccups is clumsy and time consuming. If a single crewmember is unable to perform their duties this can cause delays that drag on for days, weeks, or even months.

Here's how the plan to introduce the guillotine appears to look. I've broken it down into a 5-step program.

Five Steps to the Guillotine

Step 1.   Clinton Administration sets up capital punishment for anyone who ATTACKS a Federal Building or Personnel in the wake of the Oklahoma City bombing.

Step 2.   Have a Senator explain that Guillotine is the ONLY FORM OF EXECUTION that does not DAM-AGE THEIR ORGANS...and have him add that these ORGANS could be used to save lives.

Step 3.   Introduce specially televised executions that show the current forms of capital punishment.

Step 4.   Show an execution by ELECTRIC CHAIR that goes horrifically wrong.

Step 5.   Air radio broadcasts and run newspaper reports that show new initiatives/laws ready to go into effect in both Georgia and Florida...to USE GUILLO-TINES AS AN ALTERNATE FORM OF CAP-ITAL PUNISHMENT!

What has the Mark got to do with The New World Order?

Tracking devices have been proven to be effective in nearly any arena, including inanimate objects, pets, livestock, prisoners, mental patients, elderly, and soldiers. To have them change from a brace-let, anklet and even mobile phone form to being a feature of the implanted chip technology is no mean feet. The tragic event of missing or kidnapped children and run away criminals will both be angles played on to encourage the public to accept this technology, hopefully overshadowing the creepy reality of being able to track down any individual anywhere in the world should the need arise. If you think it's all sounding too much like George Orwell's "1984," you'd be spot on. The name of the game is control.

And The Tower of Babel Connection is?

Believe it or not the world is again conforming to a single language for the sole purpose of effective economic trade. English is the standard school curriculum language taught worldwide. There are approximately 1400 languages left in the world today that are still used and less than a dozen used globally for the purposes of sci-ence, government, business, and trade. An interesting fact in Barry

Smith's book, "...better than Nostradamus" is that in Melbourne the words *"One Government, One Religion, One Language"* and *"The English Language – Improved by the Best Words of all other Languages"* appeared mysteriously along with other One World Government slogans on the face of redeemable coupons back in the 1940's issued by a firm called E.W. Cole. It is recorded in **Genesis 11:1,4 & 6**; *"Now the whole earth had one language and one speech.... And they said, 'Come, let us build ourselves a city, and a tower whose top is in the heavens; let us make a name for ourselves, lest we be scattered abroad over the face of the whole earth.'...And the Lord said, "Indeed the people are one and they all have one language, and this is what they begin to do; now nothing that they propose to do will be withheld from them."* The verse shows the obvious value of a community speaking one language with a goal to achieving the economic independence of maintaining a great city that could possibly rival God's kingdom. When God comes down to take a look, it is apparent that He does see evidence that their advances (if left alone) could see them having no limits to what they can achieve. Notice also the reference to God acknowledging that the *"people are one"* in the verse also. The point is that the Creator is displeased with this people's unwillingness to rely on or acknowledge Him and in the process they try vainly to be like Him. This is not at all unlike the current global climate today.

With the amount of time mankind has occupied this planet it is truly remarkable to see how relatively recent devices such as cars, televisions, computers and mobile phones have changed people's lives. Take a minute to think about how much time you spend in front of a TV on a daily basis, then how much time you spend inside a car, follow that thought by reflecting on how often you use a computer, and conclude by pondering the frequency of your phone use. It its hard to believe that all these things have sprung up well within the last one-hundred years since mankind's comparatively long existence on earth. An endless source of information now sits easily accessible to billions of people worldwide with the emergence of the Internet. While illiteracy rates and poor education rise in vast numbers of third-world countries, continuingly increasing knowledge, which leads to technological advancement, moves at a frightening speed in others. The average frequency and distances of global travel in one week exceeds an entire year of global travel a mere century ago. These trends are evident in *Daniel 12:4; "...many shall run to and fro, and knowledge shall increase."*

Mankind unwittingly follows a perfect "Babel Model" as the foot of progress pushes down on the accelerator of technology unable to look out effectively over the dashboard, beckoning a familiar scenario, but with a more brutal solution than scattering us and confusing our languages as is evident in The Book of Revelations.

What's "... the Number of his Name..." Stuff all about?

In the closing passages of *Revelations 13:17* it says: *"...one who has the mark or the name of the beast, or the number of his name."* And the next verse *(18)* goes on to say: *"Here is Wisdom. Let him who has understanding calculate the number of the beast, for it is the number of a man: His number is 666."* Ask any Iron Maiden fan about the Mark of the Beast and they will recite that last verse without batting an eyelid. Ask what it means and they won't have a clue. To be fair it is safe to say most Christians don't have a clue what it means either. Careful study of this verse sequence reveals the following:

"Here is wisdom"
(This is the knowledge or information).
"Let him who has understanding"
(Let a person proceed if he comprehends
this knowledge or information)
"calculate the number of the beast"
(Find the numerical value of the antichrist's name)
"His number is 666"
(The numerical equivalent to the letters of the
correct candidate's name should equal 666)

I do advise that if the reader seeks to find out possible contenders among the various leaders today, that assistance be sought by someone with not only an understanding of ancient Greek and Hebrew, but also a thorough knowledge of the Scriptures.

Dangerous School of Thought

It has come to my attention that there is a particularly dangerous conclusion that is being drawn by some Seventh Day Adventist communities in regards to "The Mark of the Beast."

Their stance is that due to Chancellor C.F. Thomas' quote that, "the Catholic Church claims that the (Sabbath) change (to Sunday) was her act. And the act is a "mark" of her ecclesiastical power and authority in religious matters," that this is the Mark of the Beast. While I agree that this is certainly an act that shamelessly tramples over God's Sabbath, it is not a sign of the mark of the beast, it is one sign of two, as I will show very clearly from Scripture. There are <u>two</u> very clear signs in the people that go after the beast – "The mark" and "the worshipping." This is a very clever move by Satan as he rolls both these traits into one with the hopes of having at least the more permanent characteristic come to fruition.

Revelations 15:2; "And I saw Something like a sea of glass mingled with fire, and those who have victory over the beast, over his <u>image</u> and over his <u>mark</u> and over the number of his name, standing on the sea of glass having harps of God." There is a victory to be had in avoiding two traits, the image and the mark. It is the image, which is worshipped, and the mark that is the number value of his name.

Revelations 16:2; "So the first went and poured out his bowl upon the earth, and a foul and loathsome sore came upon the men who had the mark of the beast and those who worshipped his image." One of the stumbling blocks of perfecting a microchip to go into human beings is the lithium contained in them. Because humans have a remarkably longer lifespan than chipped domestic animals the long-term affects of receiving these implants can have a detrimental effect on the skin, such as irritations, boils around the implanted region and sores. If we follow the train of thought that "the mark" is an act of worship how is one supposed to develop sores if they do not attend church on a Sunday? This type of thinking reminds me of a concept similar Pinocchio's nose growing longer when he started lying.

Revelations 19:20; "Then the beast was captured, and with him the false prophet who worked signs in his presence, by which he *deceived those who <u>received</u> the mark of the beast and <u>worshipped</u> his image.*" The above verse shows two distinct traits inherent in the people who follow the beast, "the buying and selling enabling mark" and "the (Sunday) worship." It angers me at the straight forwardness of this information and the blindness of a denomination that sits close to the truth but not in it.

Revelations 20:4; "Then I saw the souls of those who had been beheaded for their witness to Jesus and for the word of God, who had not worshipped the beast or his image, <u>and had not received his mark on their foreheads or on their hands</u>." There are two anatomical localities of "the mark" clearly mentioned in the above verse. It states that it will be either located in the forehead or in the forearm. The practicality of these two locations is made overwhelmingly clear as people in cold climate countries, who wear the mark, need only remove a hat or take off a glove for the scanners to read the chip when they make a purchase. Again there are these two characteristics, "the worship", and "the mark."

Chapter Nine

"I See Dead People, Because That's What They Tell Me"

Note: The following Chapter is in no way meant to be the final word on the subject of spiritual affliction. This author is still learning and strongly warns against using this material in preference to study of the Scriptures, prayer, Mikvah (water immersion), and seeking the council of suitably equipped brethren. Please understand that this work is the product of my own personal search for truth on a subject that is saturated with misinformation.

Introduction

The concept of ghosts and hauntings is a topic that has both frightened and fascinated people all over the world. Down through the generations stories are passed on, of ancestors wandering the empty corridors of lavish mansions or figures on roadsides posing as hitchhikers only to vanish in the back of cars after accepting rides to legitimate destinations. The origin of ghosts has been the subject of literally hundreds of explanations and has undergone much heated debate between scientists and advocates of the paranormal. Aisles and aisles of books devoted to the subject fill library walls.

The accepted biblical view of this phenomenon is unknown or regarded as outdated by the world and at best shakily understood by the average Christian. I have never received any solid teaching from any minister on what the Bible says on this subject. My initial findings came from casual conversations with Christian friends or recommendations to check out the few hard to find books that tackle the subject.

The General Worldly View of Ghosts

The common view of ghosts is that they are apparitions of dead people. They may be associated with a specific place and be seen more than once and by more than one witness in a single haunting. The phenomenon can also be described as a phantom or poltergeist if it involves the movement of inanimate objects or any sort of invisible contact. The mechanics of such phenomena fall under the description of the paranormal that describes behaviour that lies beyond the explanation of psychology or known physical principles.

Depending on what Bible translation is used, the word ghost appears most often in reference to the "Holy Ghost" or "giving up the ghost"(meaning to die). However there are a few occasions when the dead or living appear to display interaction with the environment in an unexplained way and are assumed by witnesses to be ghosts or spirits (such as appearing alive after death or walking on water). Most of these are the incorrect conclusions of initial reactions to bizarre events. Even the Apostles mistook Jesus as a ghost when they saw him walking on water and were promptly assured that it was indeed their master. *Mark 6:49; "And when they saw Him walking on the sea, they supposed it was a ghost, and cried out: for they all saw Him and were troubled."* Also after the resurrection, Jesus again set them straight. *Luke 24:39; "Behold My hands and my feet, that it is Myself. Handle Me and see, for a spirit does not have flesh and bones as you see I have."* He then went on to make a point of eating in front of them to confirm the physical nature of his being. Some interpret this verse as evidence that Messiah himself believed that ghosts were real and assures otherwise to his disciples. Understandably Christian scholars have responded by claiming that he is merely telling them he is flesh and blood unlike the ghosts of fables. However, as I hope to point out, there is slightly more to this phenomenon than is effectively addressed by siding with either of these views.

The Biblical View of Ghosts

The question arises, "Why were these unlikely appearances mistakenly assumed as being visits by ghosts or spirits?" In the Old Testament witchcraft and the divination of what were called "familiar spirits" were rampant until King Saul had all practitioners of such arts banished or killed. *1 Samuel 28:9; "…you know what Saul has done, how he has cut off the mediums and spiritists from the land."* Prior to this, these mediums as in current times would call up the so-called spirits of dead human ancestors for the purposes of communicating to the living. The reasons for such séances were as many and varied as the reasons people consult with tarot readers and the like today.

The usual objective of a medium is to have a client contacted by a deceased relative or loved one when in fact they are actually calling up what the Bible calls a "familiar spirit." They are called familiar because one of the methods of justification of contacting a specific person is for confirmation or familiarity of a personal detail, an intimate name or event for example. In reality the deceased is the product of information gathering by a familiar spirit to whom the medium has developed close communication, which also has in turn contacts with fellow spirits. The origin of these entities that are commonly referred to as demons can vary and will be discussed shortly.

Saul's Final Solution

The following biblical example shows one instance of how the charade of calling on the deceased was abruptly closed down when God sanctioned a dead man to rise to the horror of his caller. As Saul's kingship seemed to be slipping from his grasp, in an act of sheer desperation, he managed to track down one of the few witches left that survived his purge and enquired of her to contact Samuel.

For he knew Samuel had a close relationship with God when he was alive and hopefully he would be able to consult his spirit for advice. What the witch did not expect however was Samuel to actually appear instead of one of her demons. *1 Samuel 28:11-12; "Then the woman said, 'whom shall I bring up for you?' And he said, 'Bring up Samuel for me.' When the woman saw Samuel, she cried out with a loud voice."* Why would this woman have cried out in a loud voice after she saw the fruits of simply doing what was asked of her?

Though the Apostles initially observed Jesus to be a ghost he was not. Within Scripture, hauntings of structures and geographical locations is not found and is restricted almost exclusively to the inhabitance of people and animals. What I hope to show in this chapter beyond any reasonable doubt is that paranormal activity is not the product of a grief stricken deceased person that didn't make it to "the light." Nor is it the consequence of a disgruntled child that never made it home from school or old Ned Clancy who was hung by Nazis in his own backyard during the war. Certain forces however will work in elaborate tandem to convince people otherwise, even to the point of ceasing their activities if an individual has been reasonably convinced that the source was a restless spirit of a formerly deceased relative. Take for instance the following example. One of the earliest recorded incidents of a haunting occurred in a mansion in Athens around the first century AD. The ghost of an old man carrying chains caused the house to be abandoned. The philosopher Athenodorus who later became a tutor of Augustus rented the house and confronted the ghost one evening and rather than fleeing he followed it outside where it finally disappeared in a courtyard. He then marked the place where it vanished with leaves and had the city's magistrates dig up the ground there the following morning. They found the skeleton of a man in chains and after the remains were given a proper burial, the hauntings promptly ceased. The accepted view is that the old man's spirit was eventually put to rest after his earthly body finally received a satisfactory burial. The concept of a restless human spirit roaming the earth is not supported in either Old or New Testament theology. But to dismiss these activities as the work of deceiving fallen angels may also be an inaccurate explanation, as I will attempt to support.

Bible References Often Misquoted to Support Ghosts

I have listed some of the most notable Bible verses that are believed to directly relate to ghosts and examined them by simply outlining their contents.

A verse that is occasionally pointed to as referring to the existence of ghosts is found in *Hebrews 12:1; "Therefore we also, since we are surrounded by so great a cloud of witnesses, let us lay aside every weight, and the sin which so easily ensnares us, and let us run with endurance the race that is set before us."* While this certainly points out a lifelong observation by unseen witnesses, in terms of the use of the word "cloud" to describe the manner in which they are gathered, it hardly confirms their origin as being formerly living humans.

Another verse that seems to be a preferred source of ammunition for the existence of ghosts by paranormal enthusiasts is *Mark 9:4; "And Elijah appeared to them with Moses, and they were talking with Jesus."* There is no indication when these two men appeared that Peter, James and John mistook them for ghosts as they had done with Jesus. Initially the disciples were afraid because they knew that Elijah and Moses were no longer in the world, nonetheless Peter insisted on making three tabernacles for them, which suggests that they had a solid physical appearance.

The Bible boldly answers the question of whether the dead may interact with the living in the following verse *Luke 16:26; "And besides all this, between us (the living) and you (in Hades) there is a great gulf fixed, so that those who want to pass from here to you cannot, nor can those from there pass to us."* Some people argue that the above verse contains nothing that should be derived as doctrine since it is simply a portion of the parable about "the rich man and Lazarus." Though parables by their very nature are fictional I personally don't see why Jesus would make the above statement if it were not true. It shows a clear lack of common sense to imply Jesus would put information in a parable that contained any doctrinal elements that are contradictory or untrue to Scripture.

The dead, with the exception of one recorded incident in Scripture do not interact with the living and then immediately return to the realm of the dead at the living's request. Other instances of healing and full bodily resurrections are not to be confused with this example. These instances describe the full reappearance or rejuvenation of a physical body or bodies realigned with the spiritual aspect of that person or persons in a totally healed form (though in Jesus' case scars were evident). This includes such examples as Jesus bringing Lazarus back from the dead, healing the dead girl, raising the son of the widow of Nain, and Peter raising up Dorcas.

The Most Forgotten Incident

A particular verse that often escapes any level of scrutiny is the resurrection of the dead saints when Jesus was crucified. *Matthew 27:52-53; "and the graves were opened; and many <u>bodies</u> of the saints who had fallen asleep were raised: and coming out of the graves after His resurrection, they went into the holy city and appeared to many."* The image that these verses conjure up would not look out of place in a B-grade horror film, yet they are recorded here as happening nonetheless. There is no further reference as to whether these formerly dead saints eventually ascended into the heavens or not, but the verse goes on to say that this event along with the earthquake shook the centurion and his companions enough to deduce that "Truly this was the Son of God." Here in *Isaiah 26:19* the incident is foretold: *"Your dead shall live; together with my dead body they shall arise. Awake and sing, you who dwell in dust; For your dew is like the dew of herbs, And the earth shall cast out the dead."* These dead are fully resurrected saints and should not be confused as ghosts or demons.

Friendly Deception and a Shift in the Spiritual Battlefield

Through the example of the witch of Endor and her interaction with Saul as well as the Messiah's ongoing inclination of releasing people from their spiritual afflictions, it becomes quite clear that an organised evil intelligent third party is at work.

This intelligence's agenda as we saw earlier is not necessarily to frighten, kill, or injure, but to deceive. On the contrary, ground could be won by administering comfort and reassurance to a victim.

The New Testament states quite clearly that the origins of these torments do not come from dead human ancestors, but are inferior disembodied entities responding to orders passed down through rank under an ordered command structure. But again it must be stressed that these entities should not to be confused with the fallen angels. Their origin will be discussed shortly.

Various methods of attack include mental affliction, physical disorders, complete bodily possession (or transformation), moral depravity, the exercise of power in government, idolatry, encouragement of sexual immorality, inspiring false teachers, and in general the lending of assistance to Satan's cause in direct opposition to the way angels assist God. The Old Testament does not speak of these entities until after the flood and they are not formally cast out until Jesus performs the first brief exorcism in the New Testament. This suggests an additional location to the battlefield, a subsequent public awareness of it and a much later public awareness of the correct manner to effectively engage on it. In *Isaiah 13:21* they are portrayed as "hairy creatures" (demon-satyrs) dancing in the ruins of Babylon. *"but wild beasts of the desert shall lie there; and their houses shall be full of doleful creatures; and owls shall dwell there, and satyrs shall dance there.[14]"* Unfortunately the New King James lets us down here as well by replacing satyrs with "goats."

Although the term "demon" can be found in most modern Bible translations it does not appear in this manner in earlier texts. The word comes from the Greek term "daemon" and is more accurately described as "familiar spirit" or "inferior deity." In the New Testament they carry the characteristic of inhabiting or being in close proximity with a human body. It is interesting to note that the term "demon possession" does not appear in the Bible and was originally coined by Jewish historian Flavius Josephus, in the first century. In the New Testament, victims are more appropriately described as people whom "have a spirit," a "demon," "demons" or "an unclean spirit." Multiple numbers of six thousand (legions of) demons or familiar spirits can cohabit a single human body at one time down to as few as one. Mary Magdalene even had a small number plague

---

14   Excerpted from *The Complete Multimedia Bible based on the King James Version.*
      Copyright © 1994.

her as is described in *Mark 16:9*; *"...He (Jesus) appeared to Mary Magdalene, out of whom He cast seven demons."*

DNA, Demonic Influence, Possession and Visitations

In the course of investigating destructive spiritual influence I believe I have gained a miraculous insight into a possible scientific aspect of demonic possession that came from a most unlikely source. Anthropologist and author, Jeremy Narby, makes an astonishing observation in his book, *The Cosmic Serpent – DNA and the Origins of Knowledge,* when he investigates the source of a primitive Amazonian tribe's extensive knowledge of the medicinal properties of local plants that have long mystified Western culture. His book examines the source of the Ashananca tribe's complex pharmaceutical knowledge that is said to be derived from the practice of shamanism, which is a ritual involving the ingestion of a hallucinogenic brew. The challenging aspect to Western thought is that advocates of this brew claim to be able to attune to the inhabitants of a usually unseen world and are able to gain insights into the origin of life itself. In the course of his book he makes a rather startling revelation from the writings of fellow anthropologist, Michael Harner. Harner writes of his experiences in the Peruvian Amazon in the early 1960s after drinking a third of a bottle of "ayahuasca," and goes on to relate an experience that emanated from "giant reptilian creatures" that allegedly showed him scenes usually reserved for the dead or dying:

"First they showed me the planet Earth as it was eons ago, before there was any life on it. I saw an ocean, barren land, and a bright blue sky. Then black specks dropped from the sky by the hundreds and landed in front of me on the barren landscape. I could see the specks were actually large, shiny, black creatures with stubby pterodactyl-like wings and huge whale-like bodies...They explained to me in a kind of thought language that they were fleeing something out in space. They had come to planet Earth to escape an enemy. The creatures then showed me how they had created life on the planet in order to hide within the multitudinous forms and thus disguise their presence."

As I read through this account I immediately recognised a similarity with Satan's fall to earth and an indication of a motive for his appearance as a serpent when he confronts Eve. I couldn't believe that I was picking up information that backed up a Genesis account from a hallucination. I brooded for a long while as to whether I should add these observations in this book, because of the risk of coming under fire from citing biblical basis on the effects of an occupant's drug induced hallucination. However as I delved deeper into these findings I realised that these observations were worth noting, particularly if anthropologists, despite their ignorance of the scriptural connections, saw some concrete evidence of an outside force at play. Harner goes on to say that he learned, "the dragon-like creatures were thus inside all forms of life, including man," and added in his footnotes that they were "almost like DNA." Narby then reveals that the visual records of many ancient cultures depict twin serpents or entwined shapes connected at intervals by strands like a twisted ladder that resembles the modern day image of the double helix that symbolises DNA. Even the ancient Egyptians spoke of a double serpent that was the provider of attributes and the key of life. According to his research, DNA is the same for all life and it is merely the order of its letters that change. He also relates one of its most astounding mysteries:

"Scientists have found spread out among the non-coding parts of (DNA) a great number of endlessly repeating sequences with no apparent meaning...They have called this apparent gibberish, which constitutes the overwhelming majority of the genome, 'junk DNA.' In this junk, one finds tens of thousands of passages like this: ACACACACACACACACACACACACACAC... There is even a 300-letter sequence that is repeated a total of half a million times. All told, repeated sequences make up a full third of the genome. Their meaning so far, is unknown."

He then lets molecular biologists, Chris Calladine and Horace Drew, sum up the situation: "The vast majority of DNA in our bodies does things that we do not understand." Another staggering truth he imparts is that some biologists refer to DNA as an ancient high biotechnology that carries over a hundred trillion times as much information by volume as modern man's most advanced information storage device. I found this information astounding

and after reading through his book I spent many weeks researching the immediate hallucinatory effects of drugs, keeping an eye
out for any continuity in recipients experiencing visualisations that
carried any similarities to biblical phenomenon. My motivation was
ignited because this information dared to show a snapshot of the
physical and mechanical principle behind some of the more bizarre
events in Scripture such as Eve talking to a Serpent and a crazed
man inhabited by a countless number of malevolent entities. During my research into various fields I had encountered a pervasive
consistency of reptilian-like beings that seem to reside at the heart
of many legends and encounters. UFO circles continue to bubble
over with eyewitness accounts of such creatures, ex-Satanists recall
seeing high level members of certain sects transform into lizard
men, people of bygone eras left carved images of them interacting
and cavorting with human beings, and ancient records tell of prominent civilisations being founded by them. Even the Bible casually
describes the serpent as though it were a fellow dweller in the Garden of Eden. To my astonishment formal research into the effects
of ayahuasca or the more concentrated extract "N-dimethyltryp-
tamine (DMT)" was almost non-existent. But thanks to the work
of Dr. Rick Strassman, author of the book, *DMT: The Spiritual
Molecule*, the appearance of Jeremy Narby's serpents was a common
theme. Unlike Narby, Strassman managed to get permission and
funding from a university to conduct an experiment that consisted
of administering DMT to sixty closely monitored volunteers. In his
book he records their vivid and frightening accounts. Almost half
of the experiences were negative. One recipient explained that they
felt as though their very DNA was being manipulated by strange
beings while another described being violently raped by crocodiles.
On the flipside recipients reported being no longer afraid of death
or feeling comforted after the experience, which led me to relate
the ingesting of the drug as having the same effect as conducting a
séance or using a ouija board.

Despite the well-documented singer and drug user Jim Mor-
rison referring to himself as "The Lizard King" due to his hallucinations, visions of serpents were less dominant in modern Western
geographical locations, which was due to the prevalent synthetic
content of drugs such as LSD, heroine and ecstasy. However the

accounts set down in the book, *Fear and Loathing in Las Vegas*, by the late Hunter S. Thompson also serve as having some significance here. The following excerpt from his novel about his extensive days of drug-taking as a journalist drew my immediate attention: "And suddenly there was a terrible roar all around us and the sky was full of what looked like huge bats, all swooping and screeching and diving around the car, which was going about a hundred miles an hour..." Years ago I also recalled watching a film adaptation of his book that contained a scene in which the occupants of a casino bar consisted of reptiles. These persistent indications of serpents and DNA manipulation left me wondering if I had seriously glimpsed into a window of a small scientific aspect of demonic possession. Indeed all forms of life have this overwhelming surplus of unidentified DNA, which could possibly serve as the perfect habitation for Satan's minions to flourish in numbers that reach into the "legions of legions." Is this occupation of unknown DNA the potential physical location of such entities? Certainly with the current advances in military science's nanotechnology industry and their growing ability to perfect trillions of microelectromechanical building blocks that can work in an artificially intelligent manner to simulate compounds, would support such a hypothesis.

Demons – Who and What are they?

Due to the absence of demons and ghosts prior to Noah's flood and their gradual appearance there after, it has been observed that their origin is vastly composed of the deceased "men of renown," which is translated in Hebrew as "gibborim," who were the chief cause of God's wrath. Therefore, demons and ghosts originate primarily from the spirits of the nephilim (giants or hybrids) because they are unable to partake in the future resurrection of the dead. *Isaiah 26:14; "They are dead, they will not live; They are deceased, they will not rise. Therefore you have punished and destroyed them, and made all their memory to perish."* They are cursed to wander dry places and contend with men. *Matthew 12:43; "When an unclean spirit goes out of a man, he goes through dry places, seeking rest, and finds none."* The reason for their disqualification had something to do with their ancestors, in that one parent was of flesh and blood and the other was made of heavenly properties. *Jude 6-7; "And the angels who did not keep their proper domain, but left their own abode, He has reserved in everlasting chains under darkness for the judgment of the great day. As Sodom and Gomorrah, and the cities around them in a similar manner to these, having given themselves over to sexual immorality and gone after strange flesh, are set forth as an example, suffering the vengeance of eternal fire."* Therefore demons and ghosts are not necessarily the sons of God. In fact the Book of Enoch describes these original offenders as being held captive and it is Enoch who is appointed as an official liaison between them and God. These spirits of the nephilim are to be considered equally if not more dangerous than sons of God in terms of their potential for personal influence, which can lead to gradual loss of free will. Some scholars believe that all the sons of God are bound up in chains already, however if this were true their ringleader Satan would also have to be imprisoned, which would bring into contradiction his attacks in the New Testament and beyond.

Apparitions or strange encounters we may witness from our limited perspective may come from a range of different sources. As with UFO encounters we are not usually privy to the mechanics that bring about such unsettling episodes. With enough time and imagination any individual could artificially orchestrate the presence of a familiar spirit. A friend of mine who has a love for antique books on performance magic and illusion has shown me enough written and pictorial evidence to show that mediums leading séances have been ingeniously fooling clients for years.

Hell, Hades, or Sheol – Would the Real Hell Please Step Forward?

When the topic of hell is studied there can be a danger of playing too heavy on the fear element or going completely the other way if something about it is debunked, which in turn could give rise to a sensation that maybe its not as bad as everyone makes out. Whatever might be the case in regards to the nature of hell, whether or not its aesthetic context is misunderstood, the most central aspect is that it is a place that is absent from the mercy of God, and that alone should be enough of a deterrent.

Hebrews and other civilisations saw the universe divided into three parts. There was the upper realm, which encompassed the Firmament or Heavens (sky), the dwelling place of God, his angels, the sun, moon, planets and stars. It is important to note that when the King James Bible was first written its language represented the speech of the noble class and not that of the commoner. That being the case the word sky was usually referred to more glamorously as heaven. This can be easily seen when the word heaven appears 500 times in the Bible as opposed to the word sky that appears only 11 times. This revelation can cause a somewhat radical shift in perspective as some verses are reread. At any rate heaven was seen as a place where no mortal belonged. The second part is the earth realm, which the first chapter of Genesis calls the dry land. It is the place for all mortal land dwelling life. Thirdly, below the earth was the dark realm of the dead, which was called Sheol or Sh'owl. There the dead slept until the resurrection and judgment. These aspects are evident in *Psalm 13:3; "...Lest I sleep the sleep of death..."* and *Job 26:5-6 The dead tremble, those under the waters and those inhabiting them. Sheol is naked before Him. And destruction has no covering.* In various Bible translations Sheol is also referred to as "hell" and means little more than a hole in the ground which bodies are placed in after death. Yet it certainly does not appear that it's the name for an individual grave when we consider the following information. *Isaiah 4:14* describes it as a place that can be made larger in size to accommodate more dead. *(Therefore Sheol has enlarged itself And opened its mouth beyond measure.)*

Sounds From Hell Recorded by Russian Geology Team

Many ancient cultures believed that the physical location of a place equivalent to a heaven was straight up and physical location of a hell was straight down; an attitude most likely born out of the natural appeal of the expanse of a bright blue sky over the sinister and confined look of a deep dark hole in the ground. Centuries on, the belief in such destinations has either been eroded or abandoned altogether by the masses. This literal concept would have been looked on with sympathy by a particular Russian geological team in Siberia back in 1989. Though this incident is often dismissed as an elaborate urban legend, broad research has afforded me the confidence to at least give the article an amber-green light and therefore I include it here as food for thought. Allegedly the story first surfaced in a Finnish publication called *Ammenusastia* and from there it has appeared in countless Christian and non-Christian publications and websites. It relates a harrowing incident where a team, lead by Dr. Dimitri Azzacov ceased a 14.4 kilometer drilling operation after sophisticated recording equipment seemed to pick up the sound of thousands of human-like screams coming from deep within the earth. An excerpt reads:

"We lowered a microphone, designed to detect the sounds of plate movements down the shaft. But instead of plate movements, we heard a human voice screaming in pain! At first we thought the sound was coming from our own equipment. But when we made adjustments, out worst suspicions were confirmed. The screams weren't those of a single human, they were the screams of millions of humans!" Dr. Azzacov continues, "As a Communist, I don't believe in heaven or the Bible, but as a scientist, I now believe in hell."

The article goes onto also explain that famous explorer Jacques Costeau also reported hearing screams during a deep-sea diving expedition.

Unfortunately the story has been thrown around so heavily that various versions of it appear and skillful researchers have reported hitting dead ends that stop at Christian publications. Some copies of the article are accompanied with photographs of crewmembers and of Dr. Azzacov himself. Dr. Azzacov is recognised in other sources as a world authority on the earth's crust. The story's format is professionally rendered in news article fashion and I found it difficult to believe that it came from a letters section of a magazine or newspaper as some researchers have claimed. Personally I do not doubt that something may have occurred at the site, yet to conclude that this was a glimpse of hell is perhaps a little too hasty in my opinion.

The Hollow Earth

In the course of my own research I have become very familiar with a concept that is called the "Hollow Earth" theory. This is a particular belief that relates stories of a massive network of tunnels and super-caves spanning the whole globe, inhabited by various underworld beings. I see heavy similarities with this theory and Old Testament history. So much so that my findings have led me to ponder whether the majority of these alleged dwellers in the earth could be descendants of various casts of nephilim that came into being after the second seeding of men with sons of God. Their origin could be based on a mass retreat into the depths of the earth when their numbers began to dwindle due to a global purging by pure blood humans. Records of islands and other isolated dwellings inhabited by giants are evident throughout the legends of all cultures.

Forbidden Caves

Another aspect that intrigued me about the Hollow Earth theory was information that I read regarding stringent laws set in various parts of the world that are in the vicinity of major digging operations that deny public access to caves unless special government approval is made. The Scriptures speak very exhaustively about a physical location of a place of the dead. Many verses specify a going "down" or coming "up" of an occupant, rather than just saying going "out" or "passing into the beyond" (a phrase popular in New Age circles). *Psalm 63:9* describes a geographical position when it says: *"But those who seek my life, to destroy it, <u>shall go into the lower parts of the earth</u>."* And *Ezekiel 32:24; "All of them slain, fallen by the sword, Who have gone down uncircumcised <u>to the lower parts of the earth</u>..."*

The Greek term for Sheol is "Hades." *(Acts 2:27; "For you will not leave my soul in Hades, nor will You allow Your Holy one to see corruption.")* Baker's Dictionary of Theology states: " Sheol, the name of the place of the departed." And cites the following verse as supporting this view. *Ezekiel 32:23-24; "Her graves are set in the recesses of the Pit, And all her company is all around her grave...All of them slain, fallen by the sword, Who have gone down to the lower parts of the earth, Who caused their terror in the land of the living;"* There are some vague biblical indications of more uncomfortable parts of Sheol designed for the wicked as described in *Luke 16:23; "...being in torments in Hades."* Translators of the King James Bible *assumed* the unfaithful suffered in a type of "hell" while believers went into a peaceful rest in the "grave" when both of these locations originate from the same word, "Sheol." However there is also mention in **Revelation 6:10-11** of an angel who comforts a congregation of dead who were slain for their obedience to God and await the judgment of the wicked. This depiction does appear to support a segregation theory. Many uninformed Christians support the notion that when Hades is mentioned in the New Testament it is referring to the eternal hell (as in the final place for condemned sinners) yet the following verse supports a pre-hell destination. **Revelations 20:13; "The sea gave up the dead who were in it, Death and Hades *delivered up the dead* who were in them. And they were judged, each one according to his works."** Then verse 14 goes onto say, **"Then Death and Hades were cast into the lake of fire."** So if a belief persists that wherever Hades is mentioned it is referring to an eternal hell, one must ask the question, 'how can hell be thrown into itself and destroyed?'

Another verse in **Revelation 20:3; "and he cast him (Satan) into the bottomless pit, and shut him up, and set a seal on him,"** speaks of a detention area that remains in effect for a thousand years and at the end of this time Satan will emerge to make one last stand against God. There he will be finally defeated and cast into the lake of fire (eternal hell). Again many people get the bottomless pit confused with eternal hell.

In the New Testament there are a few uses of the term "hell" that are derived from the Hebrew word *ge-hinnom* (valley of Hinnom," **II Kings 23:10**) which actually refers to a common refuse dump that burns continually outside Jerusalem. **Matthew 5:22; "...But whoever says, "You fool!" shall be in danger of hell fire."** Jesus was referring to this place metaphorically to invoke an idea amongst his listeners of what eternal hell would be like.

Do the Dead Rest in Peace?

It is a common misconception in the church that when a believer dies they immediately go to heaven. This view of an instant transition into the vicinity of the Most High is chiefly espoused from **Ecclesiastes 12:7; "And the spirit will return to God who gave it."**

190

But how does such a process fit in with a future judgment of the just and unjust, which is a theme that remains constant throughout Scripture. The answer, I believe, is simple. When God created the first man, whom He made from the clay of the earth, He gave him something very special. The Hebrew word for "spirit" in the above verse is more accurately rendered as "breath." When a man dies his breath returns to God who gave it.

Theology Based on a Comma

I was at a funeral once when the minister said confidently to the mourners that, "today heaven is a shining reality to the deceased." A friend of mine told me a story where a minister was even taken aside after a funeral and asked why he was saying such nonsense. He replied that it upsets people to be told anything otherwise. Some ministers use two lines of arguments to justify this lie. The first is by saying that heaven is timeless and while we live in a reality bound by time, heaven is outside that parameter and therefore we are justified in making these announcements. The dictionary definition of "eternal" has absolutely nothing whatsoever to do with timelessness. In fact Scripture clearly describes a passing of time in heaven. *Revelations 8:1; "When He opened the seventh seal, <u>there was silence in heaven for about half an hour.</u>"* The second argument is that when Jesus addresses the thief on the cross he uses the following words. *(Luke 23:43; "And Jesus said to him, 'Assuredly, I say to you, today you will be with Me in Paradise.'")* Notice the placement of the comma in the sentence after the words " I say to you," then it continues with, "today blah blah." Ancient Greek did not contain punctuation of any type and notice the sentence also contains the words "you will." If we look elsewhere in the Scriptures, Jesus would often commence a strong statement with, "I tell you the truth, bluh bluh bluh." Notice the comma here falls after the word "truth." If we apply the same principle to his statement to the thief it would read like this, "Assuredly, I say to you today, you <u>will</u> be with me in Paradise." I recognise that my implication points yet again to a poor translation. I have not found a Bible that has the comma in this alternate position and while I am not an expert in grammar, one must be aware that this is the only implication in the entire

Scriptures with the possible exception of *Luke 16:22*, of an instant transition to a paradise for a believer. Basically it comes down to one comma and a parable against literally hundreds of verses that speak of death being like a sleep prior to the future judgment of the resurrected dead. Some theologians also believe that this paradise that is spoken of is the name of one section of several compartments of the dead in Sheol. I must add that the following verse does appear to support a type of detention area within Sheol in *1 Peter 3:18-20*; *"...being put to death in the flesh but made alive by the Spirit, by whom also <u>He went and preached to the spirits in prison</u>, who formerly were disobedient, when once the Divine longsuffering waited in the days of Noah, while the ark was being prepared, in which a few, that is, eight souls, were saved through water."* Some scholars believe this verse was referring to the angels that are described as being in chains in *Jude 6*, which, if true, takes them out of an influential position with men today. This opens up a whole area of problems because it also implies that fallen angels[15] might be eligible to be saved. *Luke 16:22-23* also supports an immediate segregation of the righteous and unrighteous dead. *"So it was that the beggar died, and was carried by angles to Abraham's bosom. The rich man also died and was buried. "And being in torments in Hades, he lifted up his eyes and saw Abraham afar off, and Lazarus in his bosom."*

The "Apostles Creed" which is recited at some services I used to attend mentions that "Jesus died and went to hell for three days." If this is true he must have gone with the thief into the "paradise section" of Sheol and not the uncomfortable part. Most Christians don't even know about the meaning of Sheol, let alone ever ponder the paradise section issue. And sadly they don't appear to be interested in questioning their pastor as to why they say hell and Jesus says paradise. Interesting.

The above verse does indeed show us a picture of Jesus preaching to spirits in prison after his execution. It also has something to do specifically with the evil spirits in Noah's day and speaks of Jesus being made alive again by the Spirit before this task. The purpose of this seems to be obscure even among theologians and this author has heard many theories. One suggestion is that he goes down to

---

15   See also Watchers in Appendix for more information.

preach to the Old Testament dead, as they did not have the living benefit of his victory.

No Need to Write Your Own Survival Manual, God Already Provided One

Many of us have life experiences, situations that didn't perhaps work out as planned or ones that did and with the knowledge of these events good or bad we move forward in the hope of bettering ourselves in as many areas as possible to cope with life's ups and downs. Depending on where and what age we're at we might have more experiences than the average person or less. Whatever the case to use our own life experiences or even those of others as the central or most preferred measuring stick can be dangerous and no matter how sincere we may be about a topic depending on our knowledge and level of understanding we could find that we are sincerely wrong. The road to hell is paved with the sincerity of religious men, teachers and leaders. This is where the Bible comes in. It is a book that speaks with the utmost authority about man's origin, his history and his purpose. No other book exists that comes nearly as close to explaining the vast array of things not only on this earth but also in the universe itself. To try and explain away paranormal experiences with science or whatever the most commonly held theory of the day is without also consulting the Bible extremely limits one's perspective. It is a fact that people who have encounters with the unexplained are bypassing churches in their quest for assistance. These witnesses or victims seek help from tarot readers; spiritists, sorcerers, cultists and astrologers because they are perceived as a demographic that are equipped to provide suitable answers to such episodes without condemnation or ridicule. This environment allows the demonic world to flourish in a profound way. The members of the spiritual realm deliberately divide their own numbers into rival factions, which cause the majority of mankind to seek refuge with the faction that appears most helpful. This becomes a phantom solution as both the illness and the cure are derived from the same dark forces that work in tandem, not unlike a good-cop bad-cop scenario. To make a problem appear to go away after consulting a medium, tarot reader, or spirit healer is to cement faith in the client's mind of the success and need of such professions. The appeal also increases when the cures appear to come without any real effort or struggle on the recipient's behalf. There are Christian books out there that deal with people struggling with spiritual attacks in the form of manifestations and I believe it is with great care that we approach such books dealing with this subject. This is because the authors of these books some times fail to acknowledge whether they are committed observers of the Scriptures. You'll usually get a list of academic credentials, but rarely do they note a committed relationship with God. For example, books going into sordid details with anything related to demonic activity such as human sacrifices, sex acts, or giving the appearance of sensationalising an issue, are dangerous. *Ephesians 5:12; "For it is shameful even to speak of these things which are done by them in secret. But all things that are exposed are made manifest by the light, for whatever makes manifest is light."* Study of this type of material can ignite a person's curiosity and plant seeds of contemplation that Satan could exploit. Much prayer is needed to see if a work warrants being read through to its conclusion.

The Catholic Church maintain a strict policy of celibacy in the priesthood, but at the same time force its priests to study piles of explicit material to allegedly equip them to better handle confessionals. To make matters worse they have to sit in a confession booth and listen to hundreds of sexual related issues of both males and females and are expected at the end of the day to go home to a house devoid of a wife. Priests are only human too and when they are forced to council the opposite sex on such issues (even if they are married) invariably brings them to breaking point. This format of unrestrained and detailed confession is the main reason that a lot of Catholic priests are being driven to sexual acts with members of their church because they have to follow this crazy doctrine set down by the Vatican.

The Danger of Ignoring The Enemy

Satan petitions for our souls constantly as we see in his challenge to God regarding Job. When he gets enough signatures (so to speak) and we have left ourselves vulnerable, God can withdraw His protection from us to varying degrees. It is not biblical to lead someone to believe that they are completely free of demonic attack once they have received salvation. We see this very thing happening with one of Jesus' very own disciples in *Luke 22:31; "And the Lord said, 'Simon, Simon! Indeed, <u>Satan has asked for you, that he may sift you as wheat</u>. But I have prayed for you that your faith should not fail; and when you have returned to Me, strengthen your brethren.'"*

Some ministers function with the principle that a singular focus on winning souls over to Jesus and ignoring Satan altogether will be a sufficient method to overcoming all spiritual hurdles. I remembering hearing a football coach say, "overcoming fear cannot be achieved by closing your eyes and charging forward, but keeping them open, evaluating the opposition and then moving forward." This is very true and the same principle applies here. Anyone familiar with the Psalms will notice a constant recognition of David's enemies. *Psalm 25:19; Consider my enemies, for they are many; And they hate me with cruel hatred.* If an enemy makes an assault do not try to ignore them, but be ready to bring them into submission under the authority of God who is also known as El Shaddi – The Master of all Mighty Ones. *Ephesians 10:11-12; "Put on the whole armour of God, that you may be able to stand against the wiles of the devil. For we don not wrestle against flesh and blood, but against principalities, against powers, the rulers of the darkness of this age, against spiritual hosts of wickedness in heavenly places."*

Relationship With God and the World

It has occurred to me that whenever I read the Bible there is this constant spiritual battle that overflows into physical confrontations. One of the first notable acts of Jesus when he teaches in Capernaum ends in an encounter with a demon possessed man *(Luke 4:34-35)*. He and his followers on a regular basis encounter this concept of spiritual warfare that is very real and yet I am hard pressed to name ministers or leaders of churches that have had any sort of similar encounters and if we are to truly believe that Jesus' return is near then where are all these devils that are described in *Revelations 18:2; "And he cried mightily with a loud voice, saying "Babylon the great is fallen, is fallen, and has become a dwelling place of demons, a prison for every foul spirit, and a cage for every unclean and hated bird!"* A picture is being painted here of an eventual overflowing and bursting at the seams of demonic activity. The popularity in New Age religion has certainly taken a stranglehold on society as you do not have to go very far before you see fortune tellers, astrologers, and tarot readers on nearly every street corner. This influence has even spilled over into academia with some universities offering accredited courses in occult subject matter.

So what's happening? Why aren't Christians being run off their feet actively rebuking this type of activity? Here's the problem. Most Christians I see have too much of the world in them. Their hearts are fixed on that promotion, the new car, the second home or that holiday. This is encouraged in the churches they attend when becoming "born again" is equated with attaining worldly prosperity and physical fulfillment. One church in my local area carries the slogan, "Making Life Better," which is misleading because choosing to serve God can often bring about varying degrees of physical persecution.

An unnerving emphasis in these churches focuses on giving money, which often provides a backdrop to a particularly moving sermon. The emotional intensity that builds during some of these services can be mind-blowing. This is achieved with a combination of powerful music, testimonies, mass speaking in tongues, the laying on of hands and people hitting the deck. Services are deliberately designed to build an atmosphere that generates purely emotional responses in an audience. I believe a person is not saved by emotion they are saved by fact. To prop up the veneer of the spiritual aspect of a service with apparatus and formula should be reserved for the theatre and not a house of God. I have known people that go along to such services like addicts desperately after the euphoric feeling they remember having when they first arrived. There might appear nothing wrong with this motive, but what happens when the euphoria of becoming a Christian wears off? It is as if the church has become their reliance, not God. This can keep them in a perpetual spiritual infancy and while in this state they don't tend to be much of a threat to the enemy (which is the world) so the world in turn generally leaves them alone or worse, rewards them. Therefore it can hardly be said that the world is against them. In fact they invariably develop a friendship with the world despite the warning in *James 4:4; "Adulterers and adulteresses! Do you not know that friendship with the world is enmity with God? Whoever therefore wants to be a friend of the world makes himself an enemy of God."* This demographic of Christian is growing at an alarming rate as prosperity doctrine after prosperity doctrine is delivered by deceiving motivational speakers who preach the skin of the truth stuffed with a lie. *John 15:18-19; "If the world hates you, you know that it hated Me before it hated you. If you were of the world, the world would love its own. Yet because you are not of this world, but I chose you out of the world, therefore the world hates you. Remember the word that I said to you, 'As servant is not greater than his master.' If they persecuted Me, they will also persecute you."*

Becoming obedient to the Word of God will more often than not alienate your family, cause your enemies to multiply, endanger your job or cause financial instability. It has been widely documented that respected scientific men who have embraced creation over evolution have been ostracised from there peers, ridiculed publicly, sacked out-rightly from their professions and even had their livelihood threatened or taken away.

If you find that you may fit some of the above parameters in the type of Christian I have outlined, before you go off and sell all your cars and give away your boat or Jet Ski, halt! Remember Job was blessed with such abundances and he was a righteous man. The possession of such luxurious items and lifestyle is not the problem. All I'm saying here is that these things may represent some of the symptoms of an unchallenged and ineffective believer. Simply ask yourself "does the world love me?" If you can honestly answer "yes," then why would it be against you?

Hypnotism – Delusion Is The Cure

Any activity that distracts, weakens, exposes or encourages us to clear and surrender our mind can be exploited, because the process of erasing the mind of all things must also include surrendering a belief system as well. Intoxication, Eastern meditation, hypnotism, acupuncture and visualisation are all potential doorways for demonic influence. Anything that induces a person to empty, trick or redirect their mind can leave doorways open for uninvited guests.

One thing that amazes me is the public's ever-growing fascination with hypnotism in the entertainment industry. The basic premise of most performances entails to varying degrees the interaction of audience members with the hypnotist on stage. There, under hypnosis they perform antics at the request of the performer to the amusement of the audience. The main thrust of these shows is to get people up on stage and to do things in front of a crowd that they would not normally do. There is an apparent controversy as to whether a person is doing something against his or her will. One side argues that there are fundamental dangers in an individual possessing an ability to have a subject perform actions against their will. The danger in that scenario is obvious. The other side (usually that of the hypnotists themselves) argues that, "the will cannot be violated." I have great difficulty with accepting this latter line of thought as it becomes quite clear that the main highlight of the shows is the expectations of normal people doing abnormal things (i.e. things they would not normally do) in front of a live audience. You wouldn't find it necessarily funny if old uncle Bob danced around a stage like a chicken if that's what he normally did. Hypnotists seem to display an ability to have subjects believe nearly anything they suggest during these performances, even to the degree of causing the occupants to hallucinate at their request. In effect a type of "trance logic" state takes over in the subject where normality can be whatever the hypnotist says it is.

This practice has also become firmly entrenched in the medical fraternity, with people overcoming childhood disorders, nervousness during exams, smoking, confidence issues and so on by undergoing hypnotism. This author accepts the notion only too well that these methods of treatment at least on the surface appear to have a high success rate. It is not my desire to denounce this act as mere trickery. If it were such, I would not have included this topic in this work. My main concern is that the foundations of hypnotism bear strikingly close resemblances to spiritism and trance channeling mentioned earlier in this book.

The specific danger of hypnotism is that by its very nature a state must be achieved that submerges normal evaluating abilities, heightens suggestibility, reduces rational restraint and leaves the subject's will at best endanger of being violated.

Therefore if a patient's will is rerouted from a certain path that is causing them problems, the hypnotic process could also produce other negative shifts in perspective on certain issues and areas, that may not come to light for years down the track and in addition expose them to spiritual attack.

Posthypnotic suggestion takes the cake in terms of it being down right dangerous as it equips the hypnotist with an ability to cause a subject to do an action such as impersonate Elvis at a later time after exiting a trance. After the subject comes out of this state they act normally, then at a time previously specified by the hypnotist, the person starts shak'n and a mov'n like the King. The subject will be able to provide no explanation as to why they did it or be able to cease the activity unless told to do so by the hypnotist.

I have been interested to read that this type of posthypnotic suggestion is evident in UFO and psychic encounters. In some cases a witness hears a beeping sound and lapses into a trance, later they awaken in a different location to a similar sound. Hours have passed in which they cannot recall any activities. In other cases witnesses see an approaching object, usually a craft of some kind, and begin to read a series of numbers clearly visible on it that immediately triggers the occupant to lapse into a trance. Months or years may pass until the correct set of numbers or letters appear again, possibly on the number plate of a passing car. It doesn't take much brainpower to work out that the discipline of hypnotism should be regarded with the same level of concern as someone with a firearm enquiring about a gun license.

Getting Rid Of Them

Forget the movie *The Exorcist*. Though it may have achieved its original intent as a horror flick it falls grossly short of being any assistance as an instructional video for driving out demons. Jesus is represented by two Catholic priests, one young, but weak in the faith, the other, strong in faith, but physically ill, as they stumble through a ritual based exorcism that seems to rely on fancy words and artifacts rather than the true power of God. This attempt to drive out an unclean spirit stands in stark contrast to the simple and effective way Jesus handled such a situation. When Jesus meets the possessed man, the spirits literally beg him not to send them out of the country, but into a herd of swine *(Mark 5:10)*. Sadly the film fails to deliver anything resembling the correct doctrinal protocol as the two men meet their deaths during the ordeal. I have always wondered about the significance of the opening sequence of the film where two dogs are fighting and an old man speaks words that are subtitled on the screen which say: "Evil against evil." As if the opening words are a subtle disclaimer to what is about to unfold.

Because of the potential number of demons that cause a wide range of afflictions and the fact that they display different intellectual, moral, and spiritual traits they are to be addressed if possible by name. This request is always to be done under the complete authority of the name of God, which will be discussed later. *Mark 5:8-9; "For He said to him, "Come out of the man, unclean spirit!" Then He asked him, 'What is your name?' And he answered, saying, 'My name is Legion; for we are many.'"* It is of absolute importance that such an action never be taken lightly or without the fullest commitment to God. One such incident recorded in the Bible of an exorcism going badly is found in *Acts 19:13-16; "Then some of the itinerant Jewish exorcists took it upon themselves to call the name of the Lord Jesus over those who had evil spirits, saying, 'We exorcise you by the Jesus whom Paul preaches.' Also there were seven sons of Sceva, a Jewish chief priest, who did so. And the evil spirit answered and said, 'Jesus I know, and Paul I know; but who are you?' Then the man in whom the evil spirit was leaped on them, overpowered them, and prevailed against them, so that they fled out of that house naked and wounded."* A forecast of what was about to happen is revealed in the fact that they had to specify the Lord that Paul preached, implying that they were about to command demons in a name that they weren't under the authority of themselves.

It is important to understand that though there are guidelines set down in Scripture in cleansing people from spiritual oppression all cases vary. Jesus' disciples came to him perplexed in *Matthew*

17:19 and asked him why their efforts in casting out a demon were ineffective and he answered them by saying, "this kind does not go out except by prayer and fasting."

Some readers who are familiar with this portion of Scripture might also find it interesting to note that this particular demon was responsible for severe epileptic fits in the boy it was plaguing, which has now been a medically acknowledged disorder for over a century that can be controlled through various courses of medication. As we can plainly see by Jesus' expulsion of demons from the possessed man, they do not like being uprooted from their dwelling places and if a procedure was introduce that not only allowed them to stay as long as they behaved, but also convinced the occupant and others that they are not the problem then they would have succeeded in a valuable deception.

All Power Over All The Enemy

Too much discussion and weight thrown into the subject of ghosts, demons and possession can have a negative impact, which could cause a believer to be overly focused on the enemy and in turn push God to the side. This can have just as damaging an effect as eliminating the presence of the enemy from one's mind altogether. One evening I found myself discussing the subject of demon possession with a married couple I know and we traded stories and encounters late into the evening. As the conversation progressed I could feel my curiosity on the topic mounting. Our motive seemed to move from an innocent exchange to how much we could frighten one another, and when we concluded I began feeling quite scared. I believe that I had opened myself up to a unsettling spiritual presence that night, which was not from God. After turning on some praise music and dwelling on Gods' power I ended up feeling okay. Keeping the Creator as a central focus is the key, but this does not mean switching off the presence of any negative spiritual activity in the process. *Romans 16:19* warns us not to become overly obsessed with the workings or the mechanics of the devil when it states: "... *but I want you to be wise in what is good, and simple concerning evil.*" If I sat up all night reading about witchcraft, spiritism and astral travelling, even though I was against all these practices, it would retard my ability to fight against them, as the requirement of being familiar with the engine room of the occult is not my department. My role as was the Son's role was, in accordance with the Father's will to call down his power through faith and obedience. In doing this we should clothe ourselves in the truth revealed in the following verse: *Luke 10:19; "Behold, I give you the authority to trample on serpents and scorpions, and over all the power of the enemy, and nothing shall by any means hurt you."* We must understand and be encouraged by knowing that God wants us to have an equal partnership with him in this battle.

With all this discussion on the nature of the evils leveled at the believer there can, at times, be a sense of overwhelming futility that robs a servant of the confidence to stand on God's promises. There was a story I heard once about a group of tourists that were taken deep into the bowels of an enormous underground cavern. At one point in the tour, the guide turned off all the electric lights in the cave and plunged everyone into absolute darkness. A second later he struck a single match and the light from that tinny flame managed to illuminate the whole interior. One of the tourists imagined that this light was the hope of a single follower of God amid a sea of darkness; as such a small object affected such a vast space. Days later this same tourist stood in the middle of a huge sporting oval on a sunny morning. In direct contrast to the earlier experience in the cave, the person emptied out a box of matches and carefully peeled back one end of the box, revealing a small black opening, which signified a single worker of darkness in a sea of light. The tourist observed that the darkness inside the matchbox had no effect whatsoever on anything around it, unlike the tinny lit match in the cave. The light in the matchbox not only failed to have any affect on the well-lit oval; but even the little amount of darkness that it had, fled. *John 1:5; "And the light shines in the darkness, and the darkness did not comprehend it."*

Chapter Ten

The Truth About Angels

THE BIGGEST ERROR IN grasping the concept of angels today is to treat them in abstraction from the Scriptures. There has been a concentration of interest and an emergence of newer non-scriptural theories surrounding the guardian angel and nowhere to be found in the Bible is this picture of childlike angels with feathery wings, halos, and harps. In short, prepare to forget just about everything you've seen or heard about them, especially if most of your information has come via Hollywood.

The word angel is derived from the term "aggelos," which is derived from the Hebrew word "Mal'akh" and means "dispatcher" or "messenger." Essentially it is a title that conveys a relaying of information or an enacting of a task on behalf of a superior being. Angel is a term that chiefly refers to the most commonly encountered entity sent by God to interact with men. They are also described in Old Testament translations as "sons of God," which was taken from the Hebrew, "Bnē Elohim," meaning "sons of mighty ones." They are also referred to as "stars," "Men" and "heavenly host," *(Luke 2:13; "And suddenly there was with the angel a multitude of the heavenly host praising God and saying...").*

Though the function of messenger is an angel's primary task, it is by no means their only role as they are recorded as performing many other duties as well. They were not only present to celebrate the creation of the world as we see in *Job 38:7; "When the morning stars sang together, And all the sons of God shouted for joy,"* but partakers in its creation *Genesis 2:1 "Thus the heavens and the earth, <u>and all the host of them</u>, were finished."* They themselves facilitate God's will and protect or sometimes harm mankind. If under God, they always act in a subordinate manner and never as independent moral agents. They are often described as being "clothed in a cloud" or in aerial "chariots" (possibly flying vehicles of some type) and when on land they can appear completely human or be clad in brightness or wearing some form of shining uniform. In *Daniel 4:17* they are also described as "watchers" and they perform the function of giving Nebuchadnezzer the physical attributes of a beast under the "decree" of the "holy ones" as a reminder that God rules over the kingdom of men. This incident is a biblical account of Lycanthropy induced by members of the heavenly host and yet the general Christian looks upon the similar concept of an occupant transforming into a werewolf as a laughable impossibility.

Pseudo-Dionysius' View

Most of what is known about angels comes from a book called *On the Celestial Hierarchy* – supposedly written by "Saint Dionysius the Areopagite," who was a real man mentioned in *Acts 17:34*. He became one of the early believers of "the way" in Athens when Paul preached at the Areopagus, and therefore came to be known as "Dionysius the Areopagite."

The authenticity of this document originating from the Dionysius mentioned in The Book of Acts is very weak and therefore the true author is often referred to as "Pseudo-Dionysius," revealing that Dionysius is a pseudonym. Among other things the document claimed to reveal secret information that Paul learned during his vision of the third heaven recorded in *2 Corinthians 12:4*, which says, *"(he) heard inexpressible words, which is not lawful for a man to utter."* This claim is the icing on the cake of the fraudulent nature of this document as the reader is expected to believe that Paul imparted words to Dionysius that were: 1. "Inexpressible" and 2. "Not law-ful" to speak of. The author also searched painstakingly through the Bible and other non-canon approved texts and reasoned that there are 9 ranks, classes or choirs of angels. He then divided them into three groups or "spheres." The word sphere also appears in Norse Mythology when it relates to three worlds or spheres, the lower of which contains demons, the middle containing men, and the upper gods. The first sphere of ranks contains seraphim, cherubim and thrones. The second contains dominions, virtues and powers, and the third contains principalities, archangels and angels.

First of all I wish to examine the credibility of the inclusion of the seraphim, cherubim, and thrones as ranks and discuss the nature of these entities and challenge their inclusion within the three-sphere model by looking at biblical accounts of them.

A Special Note

As you read the following descriptions of types, ranks, or classes of angels please bear in mind that it is not my intention to dimin-ish the beauty and awe of the angelic host, but simply reason from the Scriptures who indeed falls into the category of angels and who does not. On this subject of breakdowns of ranks and responsibili-ties of angels I do not wish to infer any implication that they are the final authority in the administration of any interventions with mankind. On the contrary they work in complete obedience to God in accordance with his will to facilitate specific actions. If you have no problem with the concept that not only were they present dur-ing heaven and earth's creation, but co-helpers in their construction *(Psalm 33:6)*, then information pertaining to ranks in the form of angelic administrations will not be offensive.

The Seraphim

The word seraphim is the plural of the word seraph, which is trans-lated from the Hebrew meaning, "to be on fire" or "burning," and may have been adopted as an appropriate description because of their appearance. The seraphim appear most prominently in *Isaiah 6:1-7; "In the year that King Uzziah died, I saw the Lord sitting on a throne, high and lifted up, and the train of His robe filled the temple. Above it stood seraphim; each one had six wings: with two he covered his face, with two he covered his feet and with two he flew. And one cried to another and said: Holy, holy, holy is the Lord of hosts; The whole earth is full of His glory!" And the posts of the door were shaken by the voice of him who cried out, and the house was filled with smoke. So I said: "Woe is me, for I am undone! Because I am a man of unclean lips, and I dwell in the midst of a people of unclean lips; For my eyes have seen the King, The Lord of hosts." Then one of the seraphim flew to me, having in his hand a live coal which he had taken with the tongs from the altar. And he touched my mouth with it, and said: "Behold, this has touched your lips; Your iniquity is taken away, And your sin purged."* Most Christians believe that the Archangel is the highest rank of angel, followed closely by the cherubim. But the fact is that people often draw this conclusion because these two ranks appear in the Bible most prominently, particularly in their interaction with men. According to Dionysius these seraphim, along with the cherubim and thrones are the highest ranks because they are mentioned in such close proximity with God. While this may be true is it appropriate to conclude that these three entities are angels? One can be forgiven for thinking at first glance that this is so.

In the above verse we can deduce that there are certainly more than one seraphim as verse 2 says, "each one" and "one cried to one another." They each have six wings, a face and a set of feet. Two wings cover the feet and the remaining set are used for flying. These wings and their positioning are similar to the descriptions of the cherubim that have only four wings. They also appear to stand over the throne of the Lord unlike the cherubim who sit beside or beneath the throne. This throne also matches the description of the throne that Ezekiel saw. The term "glory" suggests an overflowing of God's presence, because the original Hebrew word, "kabod" is more accurately translated here as "weight" or "copiousness." The magnificence of what Isaiah sees is so powerful and overwhelming that he exclaims, *"Woe is me, for I am undone! Because I am a man of unclean lips, and I dwell in the midst of a people of unclean lips; For my eyes have seen the King, The Lord of hosts."* He is quite obviously frightened as he tries to fathom the reality of being in the midst of beings that are in complete contrast to his usual environment.

The seraphim speak, emit noise, produce smoke and have the power to cover sins by the articulate application of a hot coal, which subsequently settles the prophet's nerves considerably.

I am uncomfortable with categorising seraphim, cherubim, and thrones as ranks or titles of angels that make up the first sphere as derived from Dionysius' studies on the basis of their having characteristics of highly sophisticated apparatus that provide a range of functions around a core function of mobility. I am also uncomfortable because in many cases they appear to be little more than embodiments of their mission. Isaiah's language describes the exquisite beauty, graceful movements, comforting vocal or telepathic voice emotion of objects that are extensions of God's will.

Are Some Angels Machines?

Ann Madden Jones, author of the book *The Yahweh Encounters*, puts forward the theory that some angels were actually non-sentient or sophisticated robots or even spaceships sent to perform specific tasks particularly in relation to missions involving possible or inevitable engagement of an enemy. Surprisingly, there are growing numbers of authors who have referred to "God's glory," as being sometimes utilised to describe a fiery discharge from spacecraft exhaust ports that also support this hypothesis. However as noted by author C. J. Koster, in his work, *Come Out Of Her My People*, the appearance of the word "glory" in the biblical texts does not always necessarily denote a bright or glowing image. In fact its origin can be traced back to the name of the Roman god, "Gloria," which the author alludes was added to align the biblical language with sun-god worship. In spite of this valid observation, Scripture does refer to seraphim on occasion as the "burning ones," because they emit such pure and bright light, which could imply discharge from an array of defensive craft that surround a central ship (throne). Mrs. Jones puts forward a fairly strong argument in support of the notion that some angels may have been exquisitely crafted robots as she describes biblical accounts of them denying food, ascending in flame *(Judges 13:20)*, and wearing shiny gold suits, and even speaking with a voice of "a multitude," which she suggests could have sounded amplified or synthetic in nature. This author is very aware of how bizarre this theory might sound. Any admittance to sympathy for it may be theological suicide. However, I am simply discussing appearances; if truth to this theory never eventuates or is disproved, my faith will still remain strong as this subject is far from the basis on which my belief rests.

Other Important Considerations Of the Seraphim

During the Israelites' time in the wilderness, the Scriptures record the peoples' disobedience and displeasure with God. In response to their attitude a wave of hostilities plagued them in the form of fiery serpents. *Numbers 21:6; "So the Lord sent fiery serpents among the people; and many of the people of Israel died."* These incidents of "fiery serpents" attacking the people does not sound too dissimilar to popular fantasy stories and folk tales of fiery dragons swooping down on medieval villages and burning houses and livestock to the ground. The word "Seraph" is also derived from a creature that many believe is symbolic, that is a name for a "copper coloured (fiery textured), poisonous hissing serpent." So we have the derivatives of these things described here in this verse, when in Isaiah, the same Hebrew root meanings are untouched and remain in their transliterated form as "seraphim." No doubt this liberty was taken by translators to disassociate these serpents (whether they were machines or not) from the presence of God. Many well intentioned, yet grossly misguided authors, such as *David Icke* for example, have used this point to support the idea that the original God portrayed in the Bible was a serpent. And onward from this premise he proceeds like a one man wrecking crew to throw the entire Scriptures and the existence of a Messiah out with the bath water. While there is indeed a consistency within Scripture of the appearance of serpent-like creatures especially in reference to Satan and unquestionable evidence of such a race in ancient artifacts found across the globe, a commitment to the stance that human's are the result of an evil sentient, bipedal, dinosaur race (while such a race of beings might have existed) is pushing the envelope. However, this is a topic that deserves more thorough analysis and I will delve into this issue of serpent association with Satan and God in Chapter Seventeen.

The Cherubim

"And He rode upon a cherub, and flew; He flew upon the wings of the wind." – Psalm 18:10

The Cherubim are depicted in popular culture as fat babies or small plump children firing love infected arrows into unsuspecting humans. This depiction couldn't be any further from the truth. We know they have a physical form as their images were incorporated into the design of the Arc of the Covenant and the Tabernacle in the Old Testament. The Bible describes them as guards of sacred places who are accompanied by (not grasping) flaming swords, with four wings and four faces. In *Ezekiel 10:1-15* they surround God's glory with fiery coals beneath them and are described as standing and then moving in formation. Remembering the principle of *phenomenological* language that the Scriptures utilise, many aspects of these cherubim begin to exhibit similarities with the physical description and movement patterns of some UFOs. Don't forget *The Book of Ezekiel* is written from the perspective of a person that is not personally familiar with the mechanics of the things he is seeing, yet has a clarity in description that is driven by the inspiration of God. I think under the circumstances Ezekiel does an exceptional job in setting these things down on paper and as much as I have complained about poorly translated verses here and there, I feel these verses still contain a core essence of what happened before his eyes. Ezekiel's story is fascinating and reads like a modern day alien abduction as it mentions *"...the hand of the Lord"* in *Ezekiel 1:3* literally plucking him up into the heavens and placing him on board a vessel. Being disoriented and awestruck by his new environment he understandably miscalculates that he must be in a "temple in Jerusalem," which is reinforced after he is shown images that take place there. Ultimately he is given the task to warn Israel to turn from its wicked ways or its people will suffer the consequences that are depicted before him. The interior of this temple must have been massive as it depicts the cherubim flying and then "standing" on the south side of it with legs that in *Ezekiel 1:7* fit a description of landing gears as we see when we read, *"Their legs were straight, and the soles of their feet were like the soles of calves' feet. They sparkled like the colour of burnished bronze."*

Notice that the texture of the legs had a look of highly polished copper as well. In *Ezekiel 10:17* it also goes onto say, *"…for the spirit of the living creature was in them,"* which suggests internal occupants (angelic pilots) or symbiotic beings navigating them. The different faces could be his interpretation of various portholes on the craft with the faces of personnel wearing differing headgear, beings just differing in physical appearance or protruding configurations in the craft that sat above the wing expanses. However, I believe the specific mention of four distinct faces occupying each cherub has a very significant meaning. In *verse 1:10* of *Ezekiel* they each bear the image of a man, a lion, a bull, and an eagle. These faces, Man (Aquarius), Lion (Leo), Eagle (Ophiushus), and Bull (Taurus) represent the four brightest stars in the Zodiac. All four of these stars are arranged three signs apart and sit in the four corners of the heavens. Because there is no distinction as to whether these faces moved independently or changed expression, I believe they could have been designs upon the cherubim to signify the authority of the Creator of the universe, similar to sea vessels of yesteryear displaying identifying motifs or insignias. It is also important to add that the symbols in the Zodiac did not originate from Greek thought and even appeared well before Sumerian society. The focus of modern astronomy and the occult principle of astrology serve as affective distractions to the little known truth that the entire story of God's victory and salvation of men is contained in the configuration of the stars. However, it must be made clear that I am not implying that there is an acceptable form of "self-help astrology" contained in the Scriptures. Seeking answers directly from star signs is as dangerous as praying for an angel's assistance instead of God Himself.

Another strange verse (unless we look at them in the light of being like a craft of some type) reads: *Ezekiel 10:8; "The Cherubim appeared to have the form of a man's hand under their wings."* These entities all possessed one appendage that looked like a human hand. Could this have been a retractable claw of some kind similar to the one holding the hot coal that was used to cleanse Isaiah's sins and calm him down by the seraphim? Most respected theologians look upon the *Book of Ezekiel* for obvious reasons as a book of symbolism and metaphor that are all conveniently contained in a prophet's dream, which is supported by the word "vision" in the opening verse. If you hold this opinion, I would like you to ask yourself a question. Could you provide a list of all the corresponding descriptions of the so-called symbolic objects portrayed in chapter 10 and give a clear answer as to what they truly mean? If your answer is, "but these verses are one of the great mysteries of the Bible that are yet to be unlocked," then I would have to agree that these verses do appear to be a mystery to many Christians and that the Scriptures do contain information that will be revealed in a future time. However, this particular event is definitely *not* one of them. Whilst *Ezekiel 8:3* reads symbolically or poetically at first, on closer examination it appears to literally describe what physically happened to the prophet; *"He (God) stretched out the form of a hand, and took me by a lock of my hair; and the Spirit lifted me up between earth and heaven..."* Notice this part of the verse <u>does not say</u>, "the Spirit lifted my spirit up," it says, "lifted <u>me</u> up." This sounds very similar to a modern day alien abduction in the sense that God didn't ask Ezekiel's permission to take him, He just did it. Please note, chapter 3 and verse 14 of the same book also says, "the Spirit lifted me up," but also goes onto say, "and I went in bitterness, in the heat (or anger) of my spirit." This means Ezekiel went (or was taken) against his will.

Additionally, the word "vision" in the Bible *does not always* pertain to the word "dream" when it is used in the context of "he had a vision" or "he saw a vision." The International Standard Bible Encyclopedia also supports this view when it reads: "The vision may come in one's waking moments (*Daniel 10:7; Acts 9:7*); by day (Cornelius, *Acts 10:3*; Peter, *Acts 10:9*; *Numbers 24:4-16*) or night (Jacob, *Gen 46:2*); but commonly under conditions of a dream (*Number 12:6*; *Job 4:13; Daniel 4:9*)."

Cherubim are first mentioned in *Genesis 3:24; "So He drove out the man: and placed at the east of the garden of Eden cherubim, and a flaming sword which turned every way, to keep the way of the tree of life."* In studying this verse I noticed that the cherubim are not specifically described as grasping the sword, but the sword is described as being there with the cherubim. Not only that, *it alone* is "turning every way." We also know that the length of the sword is burning or giving off the appearance of a defined or hard length of a sharp and bright light similar to a blade. So now picture a rotating beam of light and marry this image with the description of the cherubim in Ezekiel and you should have something that looks like a high-tech surveillance device. If you were to draw a picture of these cherubim with all the descriptions written in the Book of Ezekiel you would have something resembling a typical UFO with landing gear extended. Interestingly the original Hebrew title of the first book of Ezekiel is called, "Maaseh Mirkavah," which means, "workings of the chariot." Orthodox Jewish Rabbis call this chapter "illogical" and warn that studying it may cause insanity.

Webster's Revised Unabridged Dictionary 1998 edition says the following about the Cherubim: "A mysterious composite being, the winged footstool and chariot of the Almighty, described in – Ezek. i. And x. I knew that they were the cherubim. –Ezek. x. 20. He rode upon a cherub and did fly. –Ps xviii. 10"

Cherubim on the Farm

An interesting account that reminded me of Ezekiel's encounter came from an incident that occurred on February 14, 1967. At around 7am a farmer in Miller County, USA was walking toward a barn from his house when through a set of trees he observed a bright light about 100 metres away. He placed a bucket of feed in the barn and headed toward the glow. What he saw was a disk-like object five metres in diameter and two metres thick, with a central shaft of light half a metre in diameter emanating from its under-belly to the ground. The surface of it had a grayish-green sheen and was dotted with oblong ports around its rim that changed colour. He also observed ten to twelve smaller objects about sixty centi-metres tall moving in all directions beneath and about the disk. A sketch he made showed humanoid-like beings resembling a pea-nut with an antenna, wide set eyes, beneath a type of visor. Their arms were slender and moved rapidly, yet no feet were noticeable. As he approached, the small humanoid objects moved more rapidly and retreated behind and then into the craft. The story goes onto describe the farmer picking up several rocks and pelting them at it, to no avail. Could this episode have been an encounter with cheru-bim or seraphim?

The Ark of the Covenant

God also instructed the images of the cherubim to be incorpo-rated into the Ark of the Covenant in *Exodus 25:18* and woven into the curtain of the tabernacle in *Exodus 26:1*. The ark itself was a forty-five-inch (1.25m) long and twenty-seven-inch (0.65m) high rectangular box that was made of acacia-wood and clad in pure gold. Scholars are divided as to the purpose of having the cherubim constructed over the top of the ark (or the *mercy seat* as it is called). Some say they were just ornamental, others say they served a spe-cific purpose. It is my personal opinion that the painstaking details of everything that was described to be in the tabernacle served a specific function and very little, if anything, was there for aesthetic reasons alone. One of the main purposes of the ark was for direct communications with God as we read in *Exodus 25:22; "And there I (God) will meet with you, and I will speak with you from above the mercy seat (top of the ark), from between the two cherubim which are on the ark of the Testimony, about everything which I will give to you in commandment to the children of Israel.* One theory, which certainly has strong biblical support at least in terms of the use of gold over wood for conductor purposes, is that the images of the cherubim wings served as reflector plates for oscillating electrons for this device to bring about ionic vibrations to produce an audio frequency. Whatever the case, the shape of these images appeared to resemble the cherubim from the Garden of Eden enough to have them adopt their name. At this point, before you get carried away and prepare to write me a letter of complaint to tell me that all the images of the Ark of the Covenant you have seen have two mag-nificently sculpted angels stretched over the top, I would like you to prepare yourself for a shock. The word "wings" used in the context of verse 20 of Exodus 25 is translated from a Hebrew description that more accurately reads, "edge of extremities" and we can only conclude that they resembled some distinct shape similar to the cherubim wings mentioned elsewhere, which I have shown look like anything but the angelic beings people have come to know and love. In many instances through the ages the theological knowledge of artists who depicted biblical subject matter rested entirely on what the church divulged to them or authorised them to depict, especially if their images were to adorn church structures. However there are a vast number of paintings particularly from the renaissance period that reveal familiar aerial anomalies, which have wonderfully slipped through the cracks and reveal more than churches are willing to admit.

Though I endorse the technical and scientific aspects inherent in the Ark of the Covenant, I do not endorse the view that it was merely a multifunctional self generated technological device in its own right. Its purpose was to represent a heavenly counterpart, provide a visible and tangible means to practice obedience, and train future angels through using it in a range of unusual and unique ways to measure loyalty and faith. God occasionally timed the use of it with unique weather conditions, unique sounds and unique actions to achieve uniquely spectacular results. Only He knows whether any, some or all uses of this apparatus contained a required scientific mechanism.

The Cherubim in Solomon's Temple

The word "cherub" and its plural "cherubim" is very interesting in that it has no other Hebrew root word meaning. Bible Translators down through the ages have seen it a necessity to retain the full character of this word. Why? There are two possible reasons.

Reason Number 1: Everybody knew exactly what they were, so there was never any need to translate it. Or...

...*Reason Number 2:* The meaning became confused, so they had no other choice but to retain the word in full down through the ages.

As I began to research into these things I noticed a very wide range of interpretations and read conflicting and confusing essays and theories, until it became very evident that the majority of scholars were divided on the issue. I am therefore in favour of Reason Number 2. To support this, Jewish historian, Flavius Josephus, who wrote during the first century BC, states that in his time "no one knew what a cherub looked like," which if you think about it, is an astonishing announcement, particularly in the light of him being of priestly lineage, and well versed in the Jewish Torah. Not to mention Ezekiel's painstaking and repeated description of them.

Whatever the case, the cherubim incorporated into the structure of Solomon's temple, like the Arc of the Covenant also served the primary function of communications between God and his people. The only major construction difference between the cherubim in the temple and over the mercy seat of the arc was one of scale.

God Rides a Dragon

It is also worth noting that in *Ezekiel 28:14-15* God also points out that Lucifer was indeed associated with the cherubim, when He says, *"You were the <u>anointed cherub</u> who covers."* This was obviously a title that Lucifer enjoyed when his proximity with the Father was as close as the cherubim. Another challenging theory also arises when we look at the following verses. Bear in mind that Satan is referred to as the cherub who covers and in the following verse a cherub is described as something that God rides on. *Psalm 18:10;* *"And He <u>rode upon a cherub</u>, and flew; He flew upon the wings of the wind."* Now if we bring this information together with the additional verses that describe Satan as a "serpent of old" or "dragon" then an interesting picture begins to emerge. *Revelations 20:2;* *"He laid hold of the <u>dragon, that serpent of old</u>, who is the Devil and Satan, and bound him for a thousand years."* And *Revelations 12:9;* *"<u>So the great dragon was cast out</u>, that serpent of old, called the Devil and Satan, who deceives the whole world; and his angels were cast out with him."*

If we take further verses, which detail his potential to appear as "an angel of light," into consideration, Satan begins to appear as a very intelligent, mountable airborne reptile with the ability to shape-shift and change mass. This all sounds very far fetched, and might be a lot simpler to just be accepted as symbolism, yet is it simply just symbolism? If you think about it seriously, these descriptions may have a fundamental truth. For example, the relationship a jockey or a horseman has with their steed is usually a very close one; they form a closeness with each other that enables them to perform, which could parallel the concept of God and his most beloved angel.

Other Important Considerations

Another intriguing school of thought, yet one I am less sympathetic with, is the connection of the cherubim to the mighty sphinx in Egypt.

In other circles a cherubim is described as: (again) "**Cherubim: Plural. Cherub: singular** or (Kerubim, connected with the Assyrian or Akkadian word karibu, which means, 'one who prays' or 'one who intercedes,' although Pseudo-Dionysius declared the word to mean 'knowledge.')"

It is commonly known that the sphinxes were usually placed at entrances to palaces or temples and their positioning would imply power, authority and protection. The sphinxes' body was usually a combination of at least two of four animals – a lion, and a bull or eagle – with the head of a human. This similar characteristic is described later in the cherubim in *Ezekiel 41:18–19*; *"And it was made with cherubim and palm trees, a palm tree between cherub and cherub. Each cherub had two faces, so that the face of a man was toward a palm tree on one side, and the face of a young lion (cat) toward a palm tree on the other side; thus it was made throughout the temple all around."*

This depiction of the cherubim fits a less mechanical conception and a more organic beast-like interpretation, which I found interesting in the light of Lucifer bearing the same title and the fact that his first and last appearance in the Scriptures is in the form of a serpent. Again the image this brought to my mind was one of occupants riding great dragons as described in the Chinese religion. Again there is this connection of angels serving this dual purpose of aerial transport.

Thrones (Colossians 1:16)

As we have already looked at in *Isaiah 6:1* the "throne" appears to be more than just a polished gold seat as some churches might have you believe or a position of heavenly office as gleaned from the studies of the well-intentioned Dionysius. It is in fact the dwelling place of the core manifestation of the Lord, which is nearly always described as being high and lifted up (that is to say elevated or in the sky). There are around twenty-one references to God's throne in the Bible and nearly every single one associates this throne as being high up or in the heavens. *2 Chronicles 18:18* paints a commanding picture when it reads: *"...Therefore hear the word of the Lord: I saw the Lord sitting on His throne, and all the host of heaven* (angels) *standing on His right and His left."* Biblical evidence shows that the throne or thrones are seen in different places and if we pursue the controversial interpretation of the "throne" having the function of a craft we can glean the following information from the prophet's vision in *Daniel 7:9-10*:

"I watched till thrones were in place,"
(I looked until all the craft were assembled in formation)
"And the Ancient of Days was seated;"
(God was among them)
"His garment was as white as snow,"
(His uniform or craft shone white)
"And the hair of his head was like pure wool."
(His helmet or upper portion of his craft glowed
even whiter or emitted white smoke)
"His throne was a fiery flame,"
(His craft shone with flashing and moving lights)
"Its wheels a burning fire;"
(Outer rings of light spun around the craft)
"A fiery stream issued And came forth before Him."
(A great beam of light stretched out in front of the craft)
"A thousand thousands ministered to Him;"
(A roar of sound emanated from countless other craft)
"Ten thousand times ten thousand stood before Him."
(A massive armada of craft stood suspended in front)
"The court was seated, And the books were opened."
(Final judgment was in session)

I do not for a moment believe that our almighty God's magnificence extends to the limits of what can be achieved from the cockpit of a spaceship. He is the Creator of all things and carries the keys to life and death itself. He merely has to speak and things come into being, or breathe and life commences. Earlier in this book I commented that reducing God to a pilot in a spaceship is a concept that diminishes His majesty and power and to limit Him to such a position does indeed fall horrifically short. However, to be committed to believing that He would not allow an expressed human image of Himself to appear at the head of His army is also dangerous.

My first knee jerk reaction was instant dismissal of such a notion. Then as time passed I began to recall that no man has ever seen the Father at any time *Exodus 33:20*. So the image walking with Adam and Eve and talking with Moses face to face must have been His pre-incarnate Son, Jesus. Who indeed is not beyond any task or trial, appearing from time to time as an angel and finally undergoing ridicule, humiliation, torture, and brutal death.

I began to realise that having this attitude that the God I serve would not be willing to belittle or diminish Himself in this way, flew in direct opposition to what the Scriptures say about Him. This misunderstanding I had of God's character became the very quality that I have grown to love the most.

The Father has a willingness to throw his full weight behind a nobody, a loser, a drifter, a battler, the bereaved, and the broken hearted. He'll send a shepherd boy out to meet an armoured giant and He'll send an exiled man who is slow of speech to confront a Pharaoh. He certainly has a way of surprising us in ways we do not expect, so we must be sure we do not get too comfortable understanding Him to a point and voluntarily drawing the line there and saying, "this is as much as I want to know Lord and this is how much I think I need to know of you to get along in this life. Any new information that challenges me of what I perceive you as, will be disregarded. I've got you in this neat little box over here where I can see you."

Finally, the Bible does not support the throne as a stationary object located in the heart of some great planetary city or a title of office held by angels with regional earthly responsibilities as some authors suggest.

In conclusion, there are two possibilities in regards to the make up of the seraphim, cherubim, and thrones. The first possibility is that they are names used to describe highly sophisticated, beautifully crafted vehicles, or portions of vehicles that on occasion are able to detach and be deployed for combat or reconnaissance purposes and are used by bipedal sentient angels or directly by God. The second possibility, is that they could be organic beings made of virtually indestructible heavenly properties that are capable of invisibility, and shape shifting (thus also being able to serve as mounts). These two options seem absolutely laughable in the light of their similarity to the popular kids cartoons, *The Transformers* and *Robotech*, where giant robots wage war on each other in alternate forms.

Ranks and Offices of Angels

The following entries are various ranks and offices of angels that give an overview of the hierarchy system of heaven. Bear in mind that the enemy also possesses a similar network.

Dominions *(Ephesians 1:21)*

This is a title of office occupied by those angels whose job it is to see that all orders passed down from God are effectively passed on and carried out to the letter. The majesty of God is manifested through them.

Virtues

These are angels of grace that bring miracles and acts of courage and are also referred to as "Brilliant" or "Shining" ones. They maintain equilibrium with the natural world by presiding over the movements of the celestial bodies as well as taking care of more local priorities, such as weather manipulation. Some of these responsibilities have now been snatched out of their hands by the technological advancement of men, who obviously think that they can do a better job. Thus men begin to know the secrets of angels, as is described The Book of Enoch.

Powers (Ephesians 1:21)

This is also another office of occupation by angels that have legal jurisdiction. These angels are believed to have the power to bring about life and death and keep the universe in balance. They make up a type of border patrol between heaven and earth. They are the first line of attack against forward assaults from Satan's armies. They also ensure that souls, which leave the mortal world, reach heaven safely.

Principalities (Ephesians 1:21)

Angels of this rank appear to have the same responsibilities as archangels, but have more central roles focused on specific earth locations. A function not unlike that of a territorial army, therefore performing the central task of watching over the mortal world directly, and when sanctioned, guiding and protecting humans that call upon their master.

The Archangels

Archangels are never spoken of in the Bible as a collective rank. Only Michael is given this title in *Jude 9* and is spoken of as a prince in *Daniel 10:21*. The word "arch" comes from the Greek word "archos" which means "first" or "chief." *I Thessalonians 4:16* is the only other specific reference to an archangel in the whole of the Old and New Testament and describes the Lord descending "... *from heaven with a shout, with the voice of the archangel...*" Despite this title only being attributed to Michael, it does not necessarily mean that only he ever held the position and that other angels never occupied it. However there does seem to be an emphasis on his being the most renowned angel to receive such a title. The job description of Archangel appears to have a bit to do with the dispatching of critical information from God's will to select people and leading open battles with the angelic host against Satan and his armies. In *Daniel 12:1; "At the time Michael shall stand up, The great prince who stands watch over the sons of the people;"* Archangel Michael is described as "the great prince" and in *Revelations 12:7; "And a war broke out in heaven: Michael and his angels fought with the dragon; and the dragon and his angels fought,"* other angels seem to be led by him.

In *Joshua 5:14 ("So He said, 'No, but as Commander of the army of the Lord I have now come.'")* it is unclear whether the angel that appears before Joshua, who is mentioned as a commander of the host of the Lord, is Michael, another angel, or a craft piloted by an angel or even an archangel at all. The use of capitals in reference to the angel suggests it is the Lord projecting His voice through an angel or non-sentient (remote controlled) angel or a "theophany," meaning the Lord Himself. Here we have a definite description of a grasped sword and one that is certainly not "turning" every way as in the Garden of Eden with the cherubim. There is also a command for Joshua to remove his sandals, as he is standing on holy ground. This is similar to Moses' encounter with the burning bush. I have deep suspicions that the holy ground was not in reference to a specific piece of ground that was being tread on at the time, but was more to do with it being made holy or "radioactive" because of the presence of God.

It is commonly believed among Bible scholars that Lucifer once held this position of archangel though there is not much scriptural evidence to support this and as we have looked at before, Lucifer's former title (though he has many names) was "the anointed cherub who covers." It seems that though he may have occupied a differing title to Michael this could have been for the simple reason that there was no conflict during his time as God's most beloved angel and therefore there was no reason for him to serve in a like manner to Michael's military capacity as chief.

Angels In Combat

Angels are most commonly thought of as being friendly harpists that drift around the clouds blissfully looking down on man, yet a quick analysis of some of the more warlike acts recorded in Scripture will show the complete opposite to be true. For example, two angels are commissioned to destroy Sodom in **Genesis 19:13** and when David numbers the people an angel destroys them with a pestilence **(2 Samuel 24:16)** and as previously mentioned an angel is dispatched to destroy an entire Assyrian army in **2 Kings 19:35**.

Another account that speaks of an angel standing with a drawn sword exposes another lethal characteristic. Cases where angels are described as spirits could have been attributed to an ability they had to veil themselves from people's minds so they were not seen until they chose to be. This is neatly illustrated in *The Book of Numbers 22:23-31; "Now the donkey saw the Angel of the Lord standing in the way with His sword drawn in His hand, and the donkey turned aside out of the way and went into the field. So Balaam struck the donkey to turn her back onto the road. Then the Angel of the Lord stood in a narrow path between the vineyards, with a wall on this side and a wall on that side. And when the donkey saw the Angel of the Lord, she pushed herself against the wall and crushed Balaam's foot against the wall; so he struck her again. Then the Angel of the Lord went further, and stood in a narrow place where there was no way to turn either to the right hand or to the left. And when the donkey saw the Angel of the Lord, she lay down under Balaam; so Balaam's anger was aroused, and he struck the donkey with his staff. Then the Lord opened the mouth of the donkey, and she said to Balaam, "What have I done to you, that you have struck me these three times?" And Balaam said to the donkey, "Because you have abused me. I wish there were a sword in my hand, for now I would kill you!" So the donkey said to Balaam, "Am I not your donkey on which you have ridden, ever since I become yours, to this day? Was I ever disposed to do this to you?" And he said "No." Then the Lord opened Balaam's eyes, and he saw the Angel of the Lord standing in the way with His drawn sword in His hand; and he bowed his head and fell flat on his face."* Certainly the donkey's awareness of the presence of an angel before Balaam and the fact that he was not able to see the angel until God opened his eyes supports such a theory of selective invisibility. Furthermore it is worth noting that the Angel here is spelt with a capital "A" and constant reference to it being "of the Lord" suggests it is either God Himself clad like an angel or directly in control of it. Though the author tells us here that the donkey's mouth opened, it is my opinion that if we apply the principle of *phenomenological* language as things are written as they are perceived and not scientifically, then we would deduce that the donkey was possibly the recipient of voice projection. Balaam's direct verbal response to the donkey's apparent new ability to speak and his lack of surprise at an intelligent utterance from such an animal is most likely due to a momentary overriding level of anger that he was experiencing at the time.

In Old and New Testament history many people had a generally dark view of angels and at the very least regarded them with fear, suspicion and hostility. As discussed earlier, when angels came bearing good news they would almost immediately verbally reassure the person or persons to not be overcome by fear, but be joyful. This suspicion could have arisen by the legacy of the disobedient sons of God that took wives for themselves, which gave birth to unusual (nephilim) offspring who in turn caused much havoc on the land. Another reason could have been due to first hand accounts or terrible stories of the dangerous destructive capabilities of angels.

The Man Who Looked and Spoke like an Angel

No other account more clearly shows the inherent fear people had of angels than the story of the martyr Stephen who was, "full of faith and power" and yet was accused of blasphemy. In *The Book of Acts 6:15* it says, *"And all who sat in the council, looking steadfastly at him, saw his face as the face of an angel."* Then he goes onto say to his accusers in *verse 53* "(they) **have received the law by the direction of angels and have not kept it.**" Finally we are told again he was full of the Set-Apart (Holy) Spirit and gazed up to heaven and saw "the glory of God, and Jesus standing at the right hand of God." At this point he cries out to the people, describing what he is seeing and is subsequently dragged out of the city and stoned.

Angels Who Look Like Men

With the exceptions of *Zechariah 5:5-9*, which appears to portray the "wickedness" of a woman in a basket and two women with wings of a stalk carrying her off, and Astheroth, the female counterpart to Baal in *Judges 2:13*, angels (or at least obedient ones) appear as men and there is no biblical depiction of them as female.

The most common type of angel physically and knowingly encountered by people in the Bible look like men. *Mark 16:5* speaks of a young man in a long white robe in Jesus' tomb and *Daniel 9:21* speaks of "the man Gabriel." In nearly all other instances of angels dispatched as messengers or helpers, their gender is distinctively male or at least male in appearance. They are devoid of wings and any other characteristics that suggest they are anything but human. However, in Lot's dealings with the Lord and the two angels in Genesis, an emphasis that there is something special about their appearance is evident, in that Lot recognises them immediately, standing with the Lord. There is no description of what God and the angels are wearing in *Genesis 18:1* or later with just the two angels in *19:1*. I find this interesting because these encounters seem more candid than Mary's visit by Gabriel and the angel in Jesus' tomb, where the author was inspired to describe the manner of their dress. In *Luke 24:4* when he writes of the tomb inhabitants (two angels in this account), they are described as wearing "shining garments." It is my strong opinion that in most cases where they are depicted as having "a radiance" that this is attributed to a uniform of some kind.

Angels – Now You See Them, Now You Don't!

They were often referred to as spirits for one reason. As mentioned earlier, in the incident with Balaam and his donkey it is made quite clear that the presence of the angel was veiled from his mind, then the Lord opened his eyes and the angel became visible. The whole while the donkey is obviously aware of the angel's presence. From what happens here we can deduce that they have an ability, at the authorisation of the Lord, to become invisible to humans alone. How often have you noticed your cat or dog look up briefly at something that is not there? The consistent unobtrusive presence of angels usually does not bother animals unless they move abruptly, first enter a region, or stand guard with a weapon. The same law applies to the spirit world, but for different reasons. This ability to become "visible" is more likely set into operation when they become "invisible." Because physical sightings were and are rare (Jesus only enjoyed the visual company of angels twice during his ministry) people naturally formed the opinion that their prominent state was to be invisible and thus connected them with the spirit world that is inhabited by the dead nephilim spirits. This invisibility is also possible with craft as in Ezekiel's abduction when he refers to the Spirit lifting him up as I have discussed earlier. Using the word "Spirit" at least in this instance suggests that it was at one point not seen before materialising before his eyes. If it remained in the spirit world or were invisible during his ordeal how could he have given such a detailed description of it?

In *Genesis 1:2 ("The earth was without form, and void; and darkness was on the face of the deep. And the spirit of God was hovering over the face of the waters.")* As already touched on in Chapter Three, the word "spirit" in Hebrew is "ruwach," which can, in addition to "breath," mean "violent wind," "tempest" or "whirlwind." The same word also appears in *Ezekiel 1:4*, but this time at least in the New King James Bible is more accurately written as whirlwind. If you are still not convinced that the word spirit can also be used to describe something physical read *1 Kings 18:12.*

When the word spirit or angel appears with a capital letter it means it is directly linked to God. It is also interesting to observe that in *Matthew 3:16*, during Jesus baptism (mikveh), *"...the Spirit of God (was) descending upon him like a dove..."* The verse clearly states that it was <u>like</u> a dove. So therefore we can quite confidently declare that it was a physical manifestation, was not a bird, and yet had the flight characteristics of one. The verse concludes by also saying *"...and lighting upon him,"* meaning that there was light coming from it as well. The following verse also states that there was a voice from heaven (meaning the sky) that said, *"...this is my Son, in whom I am well pleased."* We have every reason to believe from this verse that it was an audible voice that came from the sky and not an inner voice or a telepathically sent message to just Jesus or a select few. This was not only a joyous moment and a turning point, but also a visually extraordinary event. A Dutch artist by the name of Aert De Gelder in the 1700's painted a picture of this event called, *The Baptism of Christ*, which depicts a glowing *saucer* shaped object hovering over Jesus, and sending down thin beams of light onto Him. A close inspection of the work reveals a central light in the underside of the saucer that has a similar shape to a bird that sent shivers down my spine when I first saw it.

We know angels can appear physical enough to be mistaken as human males, they can be wrestled with, they can eat food *(Genesis 19:3)*, and yet they are also spirits as we read in *Hebrews 1:7 And of the angels He says: "Who makes His angels spirits And His ministers a flame of fire."* Or should we more appropriately call them invisible? *Colossians 1:16* says *"For by Him all things were created that are in heaven and that are on earth, visible and invisible..."* and in *2 Kings 6:17* we read Elisha's request to have a man's eyes opened and it was granted and he saw things he formerly could not. *"And Elisha prayed, and said, "Lord, I pray, open his eyes that he may see." Then the lord opened the eyes of the young man, and he saw. And behold, the mountain was full of horses and chariots of fire all around Elisha."*

Anatomical Makeup of The Angels

Another myth about angels is that they are sexless and non-gender based. As I have already discussed their gender is always specified and we know from the account in *Genesis 6:1-4* that "sons of God" came down to earth and took for themselves wives who bore offspring. While it is true the angels were not created to be given in marriage *(Matthew 22:30)* one should be well aware that the age-old assumption that they do not possess genitalia is supported predominantly by this verse alone. Even amongst men, those of us that have the rare gift of singleness are encouraged to adopt celibacy while at the same time still possessing perfectly good reproductive organs *(1 Corinthians 7:2-3, 37-38)*. Angels also appear to be able to consume human prepared food *(Genesis 19:3)*, which also suggests an anatomy that contains a digestive system. There is also a compelling case to support that the *manna* supplied to the Israelites was angel food. *John 6:31* says: *"Our fathers ate the manna in the desert; at it is written, He gave them bread from heaven to eat."* And *Psalm 78:24-25;* *"Had rained down manna on them to eat, And opened the doors of heaven. Men ate angel's food; He sent them food to the full."*

Despite angels having similar characteristics to us *1 Corinthians 15:48* shows that those who are first formed in the heavens are not of the same perishable properties of those whom were first formed from the dust of the earth. Those who are first created in the heavens or in the spirit do not usually die as is conveyed when Jesus answers the question, "of which of many husbands unite with one wife in heaven." *(Luke 20:36; "nor can they die anymore, for they are equal to the angels and are sons of God, being sons of the resurrection.")* An example of an angel's immortality is evident when Gabriel appears to Daniel in *Daniel 8:16* then approximately 500 years later in a similar manner to Mary in *Luke 1:19,26-27*. Put simply, angels do not die, do not age, have indestructible bodies, are capable of becoming invisible, and have an unknown array of abilities and apparatus at their disposal that enable them to effortlessly achieve any ends at the behest of their master. The following verse illustrates their superiority to men. *2 Peter 2:11; "whereas angels, who are greater in power and might, do not bring a reviling accusation against them before the Lord."*

On a particular day I went to a little chapel service at my workplace. During some discussion after the sermon a lady in the small congregation voiced her opinion that angels are unable to eat as they do not have bodies. I rudely trumped in towards the end of her statement, which I apologised for later, and remarked that we tend to often equate angels and God as not having bodies because we subconsciously relate the concept of solid human shaped forms as always being of flesh and blood compound. The Bible clearly shows us that angels have a visual form that can interact with the earthly environment to an even more acute degree than men can. This view is often borne out of the idea that the unclean spirits that inhabit people mentioned in the Bible are Satan's fallen angels, which makes sense because *Mark 5:9* portrays a vast number of these spirits taking up the limited physical space of a single man. The canon approved books from Old and New Testaments have little Scripture to support otherwise. It is from the pages of the Book of Enoch that this author derives his information of their origin. That is, from the spirits of the half-flesh and half-spirit nephilim dead (the men of renown).

Hell – Originally Made for Fallen Angels

With the exception of vary rare cases angels do not die, they are more appropriately detained in a pit or holding pen of some description as is in *Revelations 20:3* where they at a later time can be let loose again. Then in *Revelations 20:10* there is described a more permanent and irreversible environment quite possibly reserved for those that can't take the hint. This is described as a lake of fire.

God prepared this place for Satan and the angels that rebelled. Nowhere does the Bible support the look of this place, which is called hell, as being populated by fiery demons prodding people with pitchforks. The suggestion of such an image elevates these demons (or fallen angels) to having a type of brutal prison warden authority that they would gleefully enjoy. Jesus describes hell as a place where the worm does not die and the fire is never quenched. The information that points out the primary function of hell is described in *Matthew 25:41; "Then He will also say to those on the left hand, 'Depart from Me, you cursed, into the everlasting fire prepared for the devil and his angels:"* Also in *Matthew 13:49* the obedient angels have been given the authority to *"...separate the wicked from the just."* And in *verse 50,* "(they will) *cast them into the furnace of fire. There will be wailing and gnashing of teeth."*

Many people familiar with the following verse understandably read it as a place where there is an eternal state of tormented consciousness derived from being perpetually incinerated. *Revelations 20:10; The Devil, who deceived them, was cast into the lake of fire and brimstone where the beast and the false prophet are. And they will be tormented day and night forever and ever.* There is often a correlation made with Moses' burning bush, in which the fire burned yet did not consume it, that is often used to illustrate the reality of such a horrendous place. However a more contemporary source to support an unquenchable fire is evident if we merely step outside on a clear day and look straight up. It is that of the fiery surface of the sun. To be incinerated continually forever and ever would certainly cause an occupant, even if a victim were in an indestructible conscious state, to be beyond the capacity to perform the actions of wailing and gnashing of teeth. Certainly a subject caught in such a perpetual state of excruciating torment would have to be exempt from experiencing the final phases of fatigue, lest they lapse into unconsciousness as is indicated by the reference to their being no rest in **Revelations 14:11**. **Ezekiel 28:18** may hold some answers to the puzzling concept of this place, when it speaks of the fate of the formerly anointed cherub, Satan. *"You defiled your sanctuaries By the multitude of your iniquities, By the iniquity of your trading (traffic); Therefore I brought a fire from your midst; It devoured you, And I turned you to ashes upon the earth In the sight of all who saw you."* This last statement boldly says, "I turned you to ashes," not "I turned you as to ashes," or "you became as ashes upon the earth." This reduction of Satan to ashes shows a finality to the process and it describes his full departure from the equation as tempter and deceiver. Possibly just as the dead nephilim have a state of disembodied consciousness, so to may be the case with Satan. After he has been effectively erased an ongoing form of tormented self-awareness of his absolute defeat may continue on into eternity.

The Guardian Angel

Matthew 18:10 says: *"Take heed that you do not despise one of these little ones (children), for I say to you that in heaven their angels always see the face of My Father who is in heaven."* This is one of the chief verses that seem to indicate that angels are appointed to people from the time of their infancy. The extent of their protection and actions is also evident in **Psalms 91:11-12** *"For He shall give His angels charge over you, to keep you in all your ways. In their hands they shall bear you up, lest you dash your foot against a stone."* I personally believe that we do receive angels that look after us as Jesus did. I do not believe however that we receive one particular all-powerful angel that does everything, lest there would have been no need for the potential of a whole legion of angels to be available at Jesus' command, as is revealed within Scripture. Just in case you think it dangerous of me to cite something that Satan says to back up a point, I would like to say that Satan did in fact make statements that were true. One such statement is found in **Job 1:10** when he says, *"Have you not made a hedge around him, around his household, and around all that he has on every side? You have blessed the work of his hands, and his possessions have increased in the land."*

I do not think it is biblical to view some angels as having the exclusive role of being guardians to people. The danger here is that we can become occupied with thinking that we have an angel with us and not God. We are encouraged in Scripture to be focused on putting on the full armour of God, which is "truth," "righteousness," "peace," "hope," and "love." In doing this we can be hedged in by God who in turn makes his angels available to us. Angels are not to be prayed to *(2 Samuel 24:17)*, idolised *(Acts 7:43)*, or worshipped *(Revelation 22:8-9)*.

Angels of Heaven All Rejoice

On the flip side of the afore mentioned set up of hell and the angel's role of executing judgment, it is supremely important to understand that they not only acknowledge, but rejoice at the salvation of individual sinners. In *Luke 15:7* Jesus uses the parable of a lost sheep being found by a shepherd that leaves his herd of ninety-nine to find it and he concludes by saying, *"I say to you that likewise there will be more joy in heaven over one sinner who repents than over ninety-nine just persons who need no repentance."* And then in *verse 10* he relates a story of a woman having ten silver coins and her joyous reaction after finding one of them that had been lost. The parable finishes with a glorious picture in *verse 10, "Likewise, I say to you, there is joy in the presence of the angels of God over one sinner who repents."*

Intervention of Angels in Modern Times

Angels have often been responsible for rendering valuable assistance to individuals and directly and indirectly saving people's lives throughout biblical times. In *Daniel 6:22* an angel kept the mouths of the lions closed and in *3:25* of the same book an angel is observed standing with Shadrach, Meshach, and Abed-nego by the king when he peers into a fiery furnace, in which he had cast them. An angel is also recorded in *Acts 12:5-11* as boldly entering the prison cell of the apostle Peter and releasing him amid a group of four soldiers who were assigned to guard him, and a fierce angel is sent to go out before the Israelites into a land that the Lord has prepared in *Exodus 23:20*. With so many references to the activities of angels in the Bible, one can become curious as to whether angels still intervene in such dramatic ways today?

A Time magazine poll showed that approximately 69% of Americans believe in the existence of angels and 46% believe they have their own guardian angel or angels. In a Gallup poll 13% of Americans polled indicated they believe they have encountered an angel or a supernatural being.

All through mankind's history there have been stories of angels going to the extremes of rendering assistance to armies in major battles to simply walking alongside a vulnerable person returning home from work late at night. Below are some bold examples that could be evidence of angelic intervention in modern times. I use the word "bold" in the sense that the beings involved in these encounters made themselves visibly manifest for some reason. I believe angels intervene in our lives quite regularly, yet their visible presence is seldom a requirement.

1915 – The "Comrade in White" as it was called, assisted an unarmed soldier who was trapped in a shell-hole and shot in both legs. The being ushered the soldier into his arms and walked him to a safer location under a hail of German rifle fire.

1940 – Air Chief Marshal Lord Dowding confessed at a celebration after the war to a room full of dignitaries including the King and Prime Minister of Britain, that several of his men's planes that had been badly hit and their pilots had been killed or incapacitated, kept flying and fighting and on occasion other pilots would observe a figure operating the controls.

1984 – A team of Soviet Cosmonauts observed seven bright beings that resembled large men with faces and wings flying alongside space station *Salyut 7* for approximately 10 minutes before vanishing. Then twelve days later they and an additional number of crew also observed the same thing.

In most cases that I have heard or read about angels helping people, there seems to be a set of common characteristics that runs through all the stories. Angels will appear around a person, people, or location that is under threat (whether spiritual or physical) and are usually observed only by the threatening party who later (in some cases) simply describe seeing large men occasionally armed with swords or other weaponry of the time. Other less crucial encounters with angels come in the form of people that may require assistance themselves as is related in *Hebrews 13:2; "Do not forget to entertain strangers, for by so doing some have unwittingly entertained angels."*

The Mystery – A Mystery No More

God longs for a relationship with each of us. He wants to provide for all our needs and longs to see us overcome the world. Think back to His relationship with Adam and Eve in the Garden of Eden prior to the fall. It must have been wonderful as they walked with the expressed image of the pre-incarnate Son. He is not portrayed during this period as having anything in his anatomy or presence that differs to His two new creations. *Genesis 3:8; "And they heard the sound of the <u>Lord God walking</u> in the garden in the cool of the day..."* And He is then described as conventionally looking for them as he calls out in *Genesis 3:9; "Then the Lord God called to Adam and said to him, "<u>Where are you?</u>"*

Before I understood that this was Jesus, I used to find this verse particularly interesting in the light that this is God speaking and therefore he should know exactly where Adam is. Making an assumption that God did in fact know where Adam was and still verbally enquired as to his whereabouts is misleading to Adam and it is not in God's nature to lie. The meaning behind His enquiry is a request and a test to see if Adam would voluntarily reveal himself before God found him. In early Judaic teachings it is said that this act was done to teach Adam a rule of polite behaviour and to never enter a house without the occupant's permission. Either way it is very clear in these verses that He does not appear as an angel of light, since we are also informed in *Genesis 1:27* that His likeness is of Adam and Eve. *"So God created man in <u>His own image</u>; in the image of God He created him; male and female He created them."*

It would be safe to say that the Father and the Son (who are one in unity) don't look like a giraffe or a tryst between an elephant and a man (as in the Hindu religion). If we were to see the outline of the Father we would say (going with the above verse) that His shape resembles Jesus, hence a man, before it resembles any other living thing or image we can concoct from our own imaginations. *John 14:9; "...He who has seen Me has seen the Father..."* This is not to say that God may take a form much removed from a human appearance in a combat or operational situation.

Think of your mother and father or whoever brought you up and how they related to you over the years. Think of the time you managed to tackle your dad and get the soccer ball away from him or when your mum sewed up that hole in your favourite pair of pants. Now imagine your upbringing if your parents where brightly glowing balls of light that floated in the sky or if they were always faces on a mobile TV screen or some other shaped entity. I'm not saying that your parents had to be active to have a normal relationship with you, I'm just trying to draw a parallel with a god that we can relate to and a god we cannot. How we are shaped physically has certain bearings on how we can relate to other people.

Relegating God's form to having the same shape as a man, which is what His word clearly states, is met with harsh criticism from the church. For some reason they maintain a mindset that God's form is either unfathomable or a fuzzy glowing orb of light rather than that of a man, despite Jesus being the exact expressed image of the Father. Maybe this comes from a subconscious level in that if God has the same shape as a man then we attribute man's inherent fallen-ness to Him. We must remember that Adam was not originally built sinful; he chose sin after Eve had already been deceived, thus sin entered into them both. We must also remember that there was not a third party in Lucifer's fall. This may have something to do with the fact that we have a redeemer and Satan does not.

At any rate God wants us to get to know Him and like getting to know anyone there are times when a relationship has its ups and downs. On occasion we might think we know a person, but they may still surprise us in either a good or bad way. Whatever the case, it is always a learning process that involves patience, love, and effort.

As I have briefly looked at earlier I found that my concept of God's character seemed to have strayed from how it is related in the Bible. I was grateful for the wake up call, but it still alarmed me because His character, nature, and wisdom are things that those of us that choose to know Him should strive to understand. I was encouraged when I learned that even the angels are also yet to learn some aspects of God's wisdom. Let me explain.

In Paul's writings in the New Testament he outlines that those in the faith are now a "new creature" as he writes that the body of the Messiah *(1 Corinthians 12:27)* is now not only made up of Jew, but former Gentile as well, which at a future time will be called up (whether asleep in the grave or awake) into the air to be with the Father and the Son. This body was formed for God's secret purpose, which is called "The Mystery," which is now revealed as Paul writes in *Ephesians 3:10 "To the intent that now the manifold wisdom of God might be made known by the church to the principalities and powers in the heavenly places..."* Which means one of multiple purposes of saving us through "the dispensation of the grace of God" is to teach the angels in heaven aspects of God's wisdom that even they never knew.

Conclusion

Angels are God's messengers, they are powerful, they are real, they are dangerous and they look like anything but plump, curly haired infants or white feathery winged, ancient armour clad, Prince Valiant-looking, blonde haired, blue eyed Arian males. They are aids, comforters, guides, allies, adversaries and fellow servants. They pilot aerial vehicles, wear shining uniforms, are able to be engaged in physical combat and can eat human prepared food. They should never be studied in exclusion from God or the Scriptures. Their inclusion within Scripture, depending on the translation, is numbered at 291 to 305 times, with 116 references in the Old Testament and 175 references in the New Testament. They appear in the pages of 34 books, from the earliest Book of Genesis and consistently on into the Book of Revelations. They minister to the Messiah himself during a time of temptation and he refers to them numerous times in his public speakings.

Chapter Eleven

Omnipresence and Timelessness

A CHRISTIAN WOMAN became extremely offended as she read some material I had that dealt with the suggestion that God could be embodied in an aerial craft. This is despite the fact that the Scriptures frequently depict Him in such a way. Relevant verses number into the hundreds. Depending on the translation, there are approximately 360 Bible verses that depict organic or technological airborne modes of transport. Examples: Cherub (organic), chariot (technological). In addition, the Scriptures boldly declare that God (YHWH) chooses to present Himself within an object. *Exodus 19:9; "And the Lord said to Moses, "Behold, I come to you in the thick cloud, that people may hear when I speak with you, and believe you forever."*

As this woman reeled at this bizarre suggestion I heard these words come out of her mouth, "What about God's omnipresence?" Good question, I thought at the time, but was it? Her reaction prompted me to look deeply into the subject of this commanding ability that we understandably attribute to God without flinching. This subject was not something that I originally intended to broach in this book, but some of the information I came across was so compelling that it had to be shared. Again, this information is not deliberately written to offend or diminish the power and greatness of God. I present it here to give clarification on what the Bible actually says about the Creator's presence with us and looks into whether the word omnipresence is the most appropriate term.

Firstly let us look at the definition of the word omnipresent. The dictionary simply describes it as being, "present everywhere at the same time." Let us not confuse this with the term "omniscient," which means, "knowing all things or having infinite knowledge."

Secondly let's look at the most prominent Bible verses that support this ability God has of being everywhere at once.

Proverbs 15:3; "The eyes of the Lord are in every place, Keeping watch on the evil and the good."

Genesis 28:15-16; "Behold, I am with you and will keep you wherever you go, and will bring you back to this land; for I will not leave you until I have done what I have spoken to you."

Genesis 28:16; "Then Jacob awoke from his sleep and said, "Surely the Lord is in this place, and I did not know it."

Deuteronomy 4:39; "Therefore know this day, and consider it in your heart, that the Lord Himself is God in heaven above and on the earth beneath.; there is no other,"

1 Kings 8:27; "But will God indeed dwell on the earth? Behold, heaven and the heaven of heavens cannot contain You. How much less this temple which I have built!"

Psalm 139:1-12; "O Lord, you have searched me and known me. You know my sitting down and my rising up; You understand my thought afar off. You comprehend my path and my laying down, And are acquainted with all my ways. For there is not a word on my tongue, but behold, O Lord, You know it altogether. You have hedged me behind and before, and laid Your hand upon me. Such knowledge is too wonderful for me; It is high, I cannot attain it. Where can I go from your Spirit? Or where can I flee from your presence? If I ascend into heaven, You are there; If I make my bed in hell, behold, You are there. If I take the wings of the morning, And dwell in the uttermost parts of the sea, even there Your hand shall lead me, And Your right hand shall hold me; Indeed, the darkness shall not hide from you, But the night shines as the day; The darkness and the light are both alike to you."

Jeremiah 23:23-24; "Am I a God near at hand," says the Lord, "And not a God afar off? Can anyone hide himself in secret places, So I shall not see him?" says the Lord."

Acts 7:48-49; "However the Most High does not dwell in temples made with hands, as the prophets says: 'Heaven is My throne, And earth is My footstool. What house will you build for Me? Says the Lord, Or what is the place of My rest?"

Acts 17:24-29; "God who made the world and everything in it, since He is Lord of heaven and earth, does not dwell in temples made with hands. Nor is He worshipped with men's hands, as though He needed anything, since He gives to all life, breath, and all things. 'And He has made from one blood every nation, of men to dwell on the face of the earth, and has determined their preappointed times and boundaries of their dwellings, So that they should seek the Lord, in hope that they might grope for Him and find Him, though <u>He is not far from each one of us</u>; for in Him we live and move and have our being, as also some of your own poets have said, 'For we are also His offspring. Therefore, since we are the offspring of God, we ought not to think that the Divine Nature is like gold or silver or stone, something shaped by art and man's devising."

Thirdly, let us look now at verses that appear to show God not being present everywhere at once or at least challenge the belief that He is in equal capacity everywhere simultaneously.

Genesis 11:5; "But the Lord came down to see the city and the tower which the sons of men had built."

Genesis 11:7; "Come let us go down and there confuse their language, that they may not understand one another's speech."

Genesis 3:8; "And they heard the sound of the Lord God walking in the garden in the cool of the day, and Adam and his wife hid themselves from the presence of the Lord God among the trees of the garden. Then the Lord God called out to Adam and said to him, "Where are you?"

Genesis 18:21; "I will go down now and see whether they have done altogether according to the outcry against it that has come to Me; and if not I will Know."

1 Kings 19:11-12; "Then He said, "Go out, and stand on the mountain before the Lord." And behold, the Lord passed by, and a great and strong wind tore into the mountains and broke the rocks in pieces before the Lord, but the Lord was not in the wind; and after the wind an earthquake, but the Lord was not in the earthquake; and after the earthquake a fire, but the Lord was not in the fire; and after the fire a still small voice."

From the above verses we have a picture of God never being far from our reach, being with us wherever we go, and the futility of hiding ourselves from Him, indeed being inescapable and therefore everywhere. Yet also we have God seeking us out with a verbal voice of inquiry, walking like a man *(Genesis 3:8)*, flying in some object that causes a great blast of wind and fire *(1 Kings 19:11-12)*, and responding to a report of anguish not unlike a police chief responding to an incident after being informed by his subordinates *(Genesis 18:21)*.

Those who have studied the apparent anomaly of Moses' face-to-face conversations with God *(Exodus 33:11)* and no man being able to see His face and live *(Exodus 33:20)* know that all physical manifestations of YHWH (God) are always in the tangible preincarnate form of Messiah. But other more volatile encounters appear to be the Father or the post resurrected and glorified Son. These instances are usually defined by disruptions to local geographical areas *(Exodus 33:22-23)* or where the ground turns to sapphire *(Exodus 24:10)*. The Father and the Son are one in unity only and therefore any concept of the Son having any power in exclusion of God is unbiblical. This is why *John 5:19* says: *"...The Son can of himself do nothing of Himself, but what He sees the Father do..."*

Generally when we absorb the notion of God being omnipresent, that is to say everywhere at once, it tends to form an illogical equation. If this concept were true it would render the act of movement counter productive to God. Why would He need to move in any capacity if He occupied every conceivable space? An argument along the lines of, "He moves and interacts with us in such a manner for our understanding and benefit," is quickly countered when we read His Spirit (wind) "hovering over the face of the waters" in *Genesis 1:2* at a time where there is darkness and certainly no man. The need or preference for a countless number of heavenly angels that were not only present, but co-helpers in creation and the administering of the Set-Apart Spirit who was left as a comforter is also diminished with the view that God is in equal capacity

238

everywhere. Quite simply the concept that He is multiplied in a core-embodied sense in any and all situations is not biblical.

This God that we are challenged to come to know and love has made His whole creation available for scrutiny, not only to us, but to the devil as well. There are ample demonstrations of God's dealings with men and many examples of the way He works in the pages of the Bible. Though most people are familiar with this, the current general perception of how He goes about enacting His will today has drifted into territory, which has no biblical foundation. For example angels usually appear to save God's people in individual and group cases, yet it is God that sanctions their intervention and it is therefore God who is to be praised, not the angels. *Hebrews 12:1* speaks of us being "surrounded by so great a cloud of witnesses." This shows us God's continuous presence in the form of the angelic host who represent Him. He is with even those of us that do not belong to Him in the sense that nothing they do will be overlooked by His judgment and at the same time He waits patiently to forgive them. I believe prayers are broadcast directly to God via the work of angels. The following verse may have to be read several times. Pay close attention to the last part. *Genesis 18:21; "I will go down now and see whether they have done altogether according to the outcry against it that has come to Me; and if not I will Know."* Those of us that are his children have in addition His Set-Apart Spirit, which gives us Godly inspiration, direction, power, and comfort.

When a member of a council lobbies to have a road built, which gets approval and is subsequently finished, we will say that he built the road, which is indeed true, yet he did not physically drive a tractor or use a shovel at anytime. If a question was ever asked, "who built this road," we would never seriously answer, "road workers." Notwithstanding the fact that I believe God had a more hands-on orchestration of the architecture of the earth than a councilor would in the technical construct of a road, so too the Lord of the Bible is portrayed in a similar way in creation and interaction with us.

God is indeed everywhere, but not in an equally divided form in every conceivable location. Most of the verses I have quoted that support the concept of omnipresence simply state in various ways that there is ultimately no way to evade Him and nothing will transpire without His knowledge.

If omnipresence is the definition of being in every place at one time, cannot an indication of such a potential be evident in a race of beings who are capable of attaining an awareness of more than one location simultaneously? Is it such a far cry to say that a married couple with a listening device to hear a newborn sleeping in the next room or a security guard surrounded by surveillance monitors are unwitting recipients of a crude initial phase of such a powerful ability? Is this omnipresence of God more tangible than religious teachers through the centuries have led us to believe?

Two Lords in the Old Testament

Most Christians believe that the physical interactive manifestations of God in The Old Testament are the Father, despite Scripture saying that no man is able to see the Father and live *(Exodus 33:20)*. In *Genesis 19:24* there is a curious verse that clearly illustrates the presence of two Gods working in unity: *"Then the Lord (YHWH) rained brimstone and fire on Sodom and Gomorrah, from the Lord (YHWH) out of the heavens (sky)."*

Moses was the only human in the Old Testament that came close to seeing the Father's face. This occurred in *Exodus 33:22-23;* *"So it shall be, while my glory passes by, that I will put you in the cleft of the rock and will cover you with My hand while I pass by. Then I will take away My hand, and you shall see My back; but My face shall not be seen."* The view of a pre-human born Messiah working in tandem with His Father tends to corrupt the concept of a "Second Coming" as there are a host of arrivals and key interactions of Jesus' before His[16] virgin birth, crucifixion and ascension. Without this understanding *Exodus 33:11; "...the Lord spoke to Moses face to face, as a man speaks to his friend..."* and *Exodus 33:20; "...You cannot see my face..."* appear contradictory.

---

16   The use of the upper case "H" signifies the Son outside the period of his human occupation on Earth. At His resurrection He was restored to His former glory, thus I use a capital "H" for "him," "his" and "he" to mark any references, which describe Him in His pre-existent state or His later full restoration.

The Bible shows us in Genesis that His expressed image (the pre-human born Messiah) enjoys interacting with us in a physical sense as He is distinctly described as walking and talking with Adam, Eve, Abel, and Cain. Somehow He was and is able to localise His Son's consciousness in a singular bipedal form and later limit his senses at will to human standards without compromise to His greater attributes. Christians are either not familiar enough with God interacting with His creation in this manner or if they are, they have selective problems with what He chooses to do in such forms as cries of, "God doesn't need to travel around in a craft, because He's omnipresent!" are angrily voiced, yet accounts of His walking and speaking as a man and wrestling in the form of an angel are quietly accepted.

The only sense of an immediate or simultaneous presence of God that we read of in the Bible is through the indwelling of his Set-Apart (Holy) Spirit. There is a definite emphasis within the Scriptures that portrays angels as observers who are willing to render assistance. However, in virtually all documented encounters they act in accordance to God's will, not men's, yet if they do answer to men, they do not answer by their own will, but that of their Master. If someone seeks such a guide, it should be the Set-Apart Spirit that fulfills this purpose. The concept of a triune god (a trinity) as I have discussed earlier, has pagan roots and should not be looked upon as a God existing in three different forms simultaneously. The Set-Apart Spirit is an enabler, a comforter, and a guide and in no way should it be divided into equal parts alongside God and His Son. To accept a simultaneous Father in Heaven and a Father hiding in the persona of a fleshy Son of Himself is stark lunacy, especially when we see the manner in which Jesus prayed to Him in isolation and when he explained quite clearly that he came in the name of his Father, not as the Father himself.

Timelessness

I remember for years I would, without even thinking, say to people that God is timeless. It was a concept I had of God throughout the majority of my life. Indeed the majority of theologians, philosophers, ministers, chaplains, laypeople, agnostics, non-religious, and

Christians themselves consider Him as transcendent to both time and space. Though this is not a negative concept of God, and if anything, is a formidable quality that people attribute to Him, it must be clearly understood that biblical writers always *speak* of God as *in* time and space. In saying this, it does not mean that God's beauty and favour have an expiry date. All things of God have a timeless quality in a poetic sense, but more accurately they are *without end.*

God is referred to as being eternal as opposed to timeless. If He is timeless the Bible never speaks of Him in this sense so there is no foundation for this description of His Being. The dictionary definitions of "eternal" and "eternity" do not mention timelessness or any absence of time whatsoever. What they do in fact mention is "infinite time" and time without beginning or end. The Bible commences with the words, "In the Beginning," and in **Genesis 1:5;** **"God called the light Day, and the darkness He called the Night. So the evening and the morning were the first day,"** we see God naming frames of reference for two aspects that make up an event. Then the account of creation continues in divisions of days. The fourth Commandment by its very nature can only be observed correctly with a measurement of time. The Scriptures point out in **Exodus 20:11** that in the wake of the Lord's rest on the seventh day, His people are to commemorate this glorious event by also resting.

Essentially time is the name men have given to a device that is set in motion before them by the Creator. God does not appear to name this concept, but instead records changes in motion with names such as day and night that dictate intensities of light, warmth and season. Time has no relevance without movement. Arguing cleverly that if this statement were true then sitting motionless in a room makes time irrelevant has no grounds as the body moves against our will quietly toward old age and our organs move to keep us alive. Even in death a corpse will deteriorate under the passage of time. There is also the point when we entered the room and finally leave at another time, which inevitably is marked by a period of time. Movement gives birth to time by default. An image in a photo is a snapshot in time and the properties in the chemicals that make up the picture may deteriorate, but the image of what was caught in the camera will not and therefore is divorced from the parameters of time. But in achieving that, remains frozen and ineffective. As soon as anything moves, including God, a record of differing points in the changes in that movement leave an historical trail. An animator commences with a single image of a character; he then proceeds to draw key frames or points in its overall movement for the entire scene. The scene is then passed onto an "in-betweener" who draws all the necessary in-between points of movement to those key points. Fewer points are drawn between the extremes of the key points to give an impression of quicker movement of the character.

For God to be truly outside of time it would make him frozen in a point and inactive, ineffectual, and non-existent. To come out of and return into this supposed strand of timelessness, He would have to do it at points in that strand which would automatically impose a concept of time and as a result render it inappropriate to call that state timelessness.

God's Foreknowledge Does Not Support a Case for Timelessness

Time is a concept created by (or left in the wake of) God, which records significant points in changes and progressions. It is indeed true that He views time differently as in *Psalm 90:4; "For a thousand years in Your sight Are like yesterday when it is past, And like a watch in the night."* and it seems to pass for Him in the same way as time passes for humans in contrast to the way it passes with their pets. Neither is God's foreknowledge any justification for a concept of timelessness. It is in fact an ingredient that hinders the concept since by the very nature of being able to perfectly foretell an event relies on knowing at what point in time it will occur. Jesus was accurate to the point of being able to gauge when Peter's denial of him came prior to the three crows of a roaster. The notion of God traversing backwards and forwards through time in any form again does not promote any concept of timelessness. We might be reminded that science fiction books that deal with time machines rarely if ever have the inventors or users originally set in a frame of existence outside time. They usually construct the device and go backwards or forwards in time at their own will and after a heroic adventure return to their initial starting point.

243

Not in a very long while have I been as dumbfounded by the logic of a great many learned men on the subject of timelessness as I have when I began to sift through pages of university and scientific grade commentaries on the subject. Great philosophers and theologians such as Augustine (AD 354-430), Boethius (*c.* AD 475-525), Anselm (1033-1109), and Aquinas (1225-1274) are but a few that cling to the concept of a divine timelessness. Some of the more elaborate and interesting theories come from lesser knowns, though perhaps not lesser in intellect. They have written essays on possible models that elevate themselves away from the scriptural depiction of God like a rocket elevates itself away from the earth. The seed of a divine timelessness was earthed in alien origins and as the philosopher Richard Swineburn, one of a few educated men that carry a torch of hope for logic, so aptly points out, "the doctrine of God's timelessness seems to have entered Christian theology from neo-Platonism, and there from Augustine to Aquinas it reigned." And the theologian Oscar Cullmann delivers this blinder when he states, "Primitive Christianity knows nothing of a timeless God. The 'eternal' God is He who was in the beginning, is now and will be in the future, "who was, and who will be' *(Revelations 1:4)*. Accordingly, His eternity can and must be expressed in this 'naïve' way, in terms of endless time."

Miniature Gods Over Sim City

The digitised voice, " would you like to play a game?" echoed across cinemas in 1983 with the release of the film *War Games*, which starred Mathew Broderick. It told the story of a young boy who finds a back door into a military central computer and after confusing a part of its network as a game, nearly starts WW III. It was made at a time when the general public were convinced that nuclear war was a real threat and the Soviet Union were considered "the bad guys." The atmosphere during this time was very much one of fear, fear of mass extermination by a super bomb, not unlike the atmosphere today with "terrorism." Through the premise of that film people began to understand that the military had the capability to conduct computer-simulated war games on a global scale. Shortly after the film's release I remember a period of nationwide unease at the fear of nuclear war as the media told the world we were well and truly capable of obliterating ourselves with the wrong push of a button somewhere.

Believe it or not computer based simulation games originally came about through governmental means to boost a country's national security, increase its warfare capabilities, and analyze community reactions to possible economic changes, whether by wars, famines, natural disasters, civil unrest, or the introductions of new commodities. Now corporate companies and multi-billion dollar industries have access to the same technology, as does the individual in the convenience of his or her own home. An overwhelmingly large market for simulation-based programs occurs in the entertainment industry. Computer games have an ever-growing popularity, which is spearheaded by an addictive ensemble of war-based strategy and urban simulation games that focus on mass or individual progression and acquisition-oriented goals. The most common scenario is to overcome an enemy or enemies or control an individual to attain a secure livelihood by striving for successful work or social status within the game confines. The catch-cry of the very successful game *The Sims* says: "Create and play simulated worlds of your making." It is from a god-like perspective that the occupant plays and constructs the initial attributes of the characters, sets their surroundings, schedules their agendas, and at anytime may pause, save, quit, return to saved locations, or choose to accelerate through game play by viewing highlights. Another very successful game is *Championship Manager*, which puts the player in charge of nearly all the aspects of running world-class soccer teams as they make their way through season after season. Game play consists of hiring and firing players, increasing and decreasing wages, handling media, training, and on field strategy etc. Many, many individuals play these games. Though the products never state this, to get the most enjoyment out of some of the top of the line simulations, players really need to spend blocks of at least four to five hours of consecutive time in game play. By the very nature of the game, the occupant assumes a type of god-like role and this perspective is initiated from a time-based zone. From here the player has the option to save at a specific point, then continue forward whilst observing future variables and at their own discretion return to the saved point with a thorough knowledge of a future sequence of events. From this vantage point the player may choose to send the character down a different corridor or equip an army with a more effective weapon for an engagement. Thus an element of foreknowledge is in the hands of the player.

I remember the first time I realised the advantage of this save option when I first started playing the old first person shoot'em up game, *Doom*. I was able to save at points where I had full health and progress through stages until I got to know when and where monsters appeared. Having played forward from a saved position and despite receiving massive depletions in health, I was able to let my character die and restart from the previously saved point with a foreknowledge of the locations of spare health and ammo that was placed in the environment. In pausing the game a player is in essence able to freeze time in the confines of the digital realm. Notice when the game is paused, time has stopped which causes everything in the game to be frozen and where there is no time there is no motion. Time outside the game continues unhindered whether the game is played in normal time, accelerated time, previously saved points in time or in pause mode. In looking at the range of options available to a player in this setting it can be easily seen how in a very basic sense that this position is a stripped down version of the abilities that a higher or supreme being may have in our reality. At the very least this is an example of how an environment can be manipulated by a person in a time-based location.

This medium of digital entertainment caters to our inbred desire to create, maintain, and interact with things. In the following verse Jesus makes a statement that hints at another point I wish to make. ***John 10:34; Jesus answered them, "Is it not written in your law, 'I said, "You are gods?"'*** As in the Tower of Babel, man attempted to reach up into the heavens and be like God and now we are clearly seeing, in this current age through the advantage of technology, the subconscious desire to assume the role of God ourselves. This desire is inherent in our nature individually, and collectively, as governments provide for more and more of our needs. They are gradually utilising a generic and systematic provision that chokes out a genuine desire to rely on God. Next time you hear yourself saying, "I'm independent," ask yourself what you would do if you became unemployed," and then ask yourself, "where would you go to acquire money to support yourself in the meantime until you get another job?" We rely on the government to educate us, feed us, employ us, pay us, inform us, transport us and secure us. The average urban or near-urban dweller is entirely dependant, in some form or another on the government. Rural people who own farms may lose their businesses through draught or economic difficulties, but at the very least a family will have a measure of rainwater, some cattle to milk, vegetables to grow and chickens to eat etc. Because rural communities usually have more of a sense of camaraderie than city dwellers any produce they might lack is usually bartered or donated by a neighbour.

An interesting point to note is that civilised explorers classed indigenous races of people as primitive if they lived 100% off the land and had no form of economy, which meant that there was no basis for so-called civilised men to introduce the concept of capitalism. These primitive peoples lived on a day-to-day basis and research has shown that they were not left wanting anymore than any civilised community. On the contrary, all major cities that exist today have a large proportion of poor and destitute. The nomadic tribal community had and has a superior lifestyle to urban settlement unison with the ecosystem and all its members enjoying a fairly equal provision of needs, unlike the urban, capitalist, consumer driven mega-settlements.

While the powers that be build their empires, the creative needs of the individual are provided for with the elaborate distraction of a market of sophisticated and highly addictive video games, theatrical releases, and sporting competitions.

Conclusion

I do not wish to imply that God controls everything like a computer game or that computer games are necessarily evil or harmful in anyway, I simply wish to use video game play configurations of some of the more popular strategy games as an example of how foreknowledge is achieved from a time based location.

I also want to show that mankind is merely on a path to becoming like the gods and as we have seen in the Tower of Babel, God did not allow this to happen, nor will He allow it again. As we progress, we reach certain points in our advancement, remain there for a while, and then move on. This is not to say that we should avoid technology. We should just be aware that the ease to misuse it is also the same, as is the ease to use it correctly. I would personally prefer two children to play with an axe than a loaded shotgun. The axe, signifying old world ways, is required to be lifted and swung with some force to fatally injure someone, but a gun, signifying new world technology, only requires to be pointed and a small trigger pulled for an even more devastating result.

Computers and technology in general have well exceeded the expectations of those first responsible for the massive processors that used to fill entire rooms and laboratories. As the boundaries of our own imaginations and technological capabilities widen together, the realms of science fiction begin to diminish. Books delving into the subject of super technologies may have to be gradually withdrawn from the sci-fi shelves of bookstores and local libraries and be relocated to science sections as Defence departments eventually have to own up to possessing machinery that can be best described as objects found between the pages of a H.G. Well's novel. If we were to go back 500 years and try to explain to someone there that we will be able to create an artificial environment, inhabited by artificially intelligent beings, we would have been laughed at or accused of speaking with a devilish tongue. This notion would be looked on as impossible and blasphemous as it presents us in the same manner as a god in that we are creating a type of world and the beings within it. In turn, if we look forward 500 years from our present point in history, there would be considerably fewer things that we might be capable of achieving that would initiate a laughable response. Some of the most extreme examples that I can think of are achieving invisibility, teleportation, and time travel, all of which wouldn't get much of a giggle as various universities are seriously studying them. An article called, *Future wars: the invisible soldier*, that appeared in the Daily Telegraph 2002, said the following: "...officials have unveiled a US army program to develop high-tech gear that would allow soldiers to become partially invisible, leap over walls, and treat their own wounds on the battlefield. The Massachusetts Institute of Technology won a $97 million five-year contract from the US Army to form a centre that develops combat gear. The new Institute for Soldier Nano-technologies will be funded by the US Defence Department with another $77.75 million from corporations."

What we are seeing here is the consequence of living in a reality where, according to systems engineer, *Roberto Vacca*, "Everything grows: everything is on the increase, and every year the speed of that increase is greater."

Chapter Twelve

The Technology of God

IN THE COURSE OF writing this book I have been warned by certain people that I could be in danger of playing down the strength of God's power by suggesting that there is a formula or set of formulas employed by Him in the miraculous act of raising someone from the dead.

First of all, I solemnly believe that the Author of all life and the Creator of heaven and earth knows exactly how to reconstitute the physical properties of a human body and realign it with a former occupant's conscience soul. I also believe that the Son of man did not and was not required to know the technical aspect of such a feat, other than through complete obedience, faith, and instruction from the Father via the Set-Apart Spirit. Every miracle that the Messiah accomplished was done in complete harmony with the Father's will and no such miracles occurred that fell outside this framework as is confirmed in *John 5:19; "Then Jesus answered and said to them, 'Most assuredly, I say to you, the Son can do nothing of Himself, but what He sees the Father do; for whatever He does, the Son also does in like manner.'"* And *verse 21 "For as the Father raises the dead and gives life to them, even so the Son gives life to whom He will."* And *Verse 30 "I can of Myself do nothing…I do not seek My own will but the will of the Father who sent Me."*

Miracles are no less miracles if the technical aspect of them is left open to scrutiny. It would be just as equally a miracle if an individual were rescued on a deserted island by the rare passing of an overhead plane, as a man who wakes up in a morgue after having been certified dead. Newborn babies are often described by parents and relatives as miracles, even though the scientific principle behind the whole concept of birth is completely understood.

If a surgeon with a limited supply of medical equipment stepped from our time into the Middle Ages and was given the opportunity to treat various illnesses, injuries, and diseases, he would be attributed as having miraculous powers as would an elite team of United States marines with all the most advanced weapons if they faced off against an army of ancient Saxon warriors.

It is not my desire to pointlessly speculate on how God performs such grand feats as parting the waters of a sea or enabling his Son to walk on water, but to simply say that He does not awkwardly bend or break scientific principles to achieve them. The Scriptures clearly say that creation obeys his will *(Job 9:5)* and if the occasion should arise mountains may be even levelled at our request. At one point in Jesus' ministry he makes a fig tree wither before the very eyes of his disciples and later assures them of their own potential to achieve such feats through faith. *Mathew 21:21; "So Jesus answered and said to them, 'Assuredly, I say to you, if you have faith and do not doubt, you will not only do what was done to the fig tree, but also if you say to this mountain, Be removed and be cast into the sea, it will be done.'"*

Jesus' disciples were nonetheless understandably astonished at how he could perform such miraculous feats. He understood their curiosity and even provided a slightly deeper insight into the practical nature of these abilities in *John 6:63; "It is the Spirit who gives life; the flesh profits nothing. The word that I speak to you are spirit, and they are life."* This explanation was so simplistic that his disciples did not understand its deeper meaning. The creation account in Genesis displays this verbalised spirit in the phase-by-phase construction in Chapter *1*, verses *3, 9, 11, 14, 20, 24, 26,* and *29*. It is interesting to note that all the acts of creation appear to commence with the common word "said," which acts like a key to initiating God's building process in the creation of earth and its inhabitants. God speaks as Jesus later does and things come into being. So we see God's Son displaying the same characteristics as his Father when he resurrects, replenishes, rejuvenates, multiplies, or destroys something by uttering a verbal command.

The first part of *verse 63* of *John 6* in more accurately translated Bibles says, *"It is the spirit that quickeneth,"* which means "enables." So therefore if one believes and obeys they are "quickened" or "enabled" with the spirit. One merely has to speak the will of the Father that is brought into effect by the spirit and the request is granted. Though the Messiah would have been deeply grieved by the beheading of John the Baptist, John was not raised because it was not in the will of the spirit. In the case of Lazarus it was, so he was raised *(John 11:41)* and we see why in *John 11:42; "And I know that You always hear Me, but because of the people who are standing by I said this, that they may believe that You sent Me."*

The spirit, as described in this sense, is a very real thing, a form of energy that has a variety of capabilities, among the most precious being to give life. It cannot ever be called upon to do anything outside the will of the Father. However, having said this, I am also convinced that the forces of evil are able to muster a counterfeit version of this spirit that can produce similar outcomes. This falls in line with the beast in the Book of Revelations as it portrays him performing great miracles that deceive many. I am aware of the possibility that some readers might feel as though I'm examining miracles like someone who peeks into the generator room of an elaborate lightshow, but I simply wish to point out that they are wielded and passed on by beings far more attuned to the natural world than we are.

The word "miracle" in the dictionary is described as such: "An effect in a physical world, which suppresses all known human or natural powers and is therefore ascribed to supernatural agency. A wonderful thing; a marvel."

We may *ascribe* supernatural origin to a miracle, but to validate a belief in supernatural phenomena based on an observation of something that appears to defy understanding is unnecessary.

When Jesus was asked how he performed such feats, he never once said, "its magic" or "it's a mystery." He told the simple truth. He said by whom and how he derived such an ability and importantly added that it was available to anyone who believed, repented and followed him.

An Ever-Changing Technology vs. A Never Changing One

To suggest that God utilises some sort of aerial vehicle is also to suggest that he utilises a form of technology. If grappling with the foreign concept of God in a saucer is difficult, the concept of a Him preceded by technology takes the cake.

The first stumbling block in accepting this notion is our current view of technology today. We live in an age of ever-changing and ever-advancing technologies, a super information highway that once steered onto with the purchase of a computer, one is subject to the ever-evolving upgrades and updates of a tool that becomes obsolete before it leaves the warehouse where it was manufactured. For every computer monitor that is built another one becomes outdated. Cars, while the process is a little slower, are no different, televisions are no different, white goods are no different, DVD's, CD's, the list goes on. If it is electrical it will one day become obsolete. Therefore it is difficult from the above perspective to envision pure and non-upgradeable technology. Indeed as a friend pointed out to me, commodities are often repackaged in newer more appealing casings with minimal actual advances to the unit itself, to appease to the changing trends of a consumer driven market. Along with leaving the concept of a continuously upgraded medium at the door as we try to absorb this aspect of Godly technology, the aesthetic construct of these media, which are also steered by trends in the market place, are to be shelved as well. Human beings can be very fickle as our collective desires of what is trendy or looks good evolves and changes throughout the years. This is evident when we look at how people dressed in the seventies or the way cars looked in the sixties. Yes fashions come back into vogue, but usually with slight variants from their original look.

Human technology is in a constant process of exponential growth and Godly technology resides happily at its destination without need for improvement or alteration. To subject anything associated with God as having room for improvement would be to admit imperfection in His foundational elements.

God frequently commanded His people to construct apparatuses for practical and at times unusual purposes with earth materials. Metals had to be pure and specific measurements were required, as was the case with such items as the Ark of the Covenant, Solomon's temple, and Noah's Ark. The purpose of such objects ranged from healing snakebites to communication with God to providing protection and assisting in warfare.

To suggest to the average Christian today that God uses a form of technology to achieve mobility would be considered heretical, despite numerous verses describing God in a chariot, riding a cherub, lifted up in a throne, or coming in a cloud. This particular stance inevitably leads to the response that God doesn't need to travel in a vehicle, and though this is a valid statement, we should also realise that God doesn't need to rest, but in **Genesis 2:2** He did. God does things not because He needs to, but because He chooses to. There is deliberation and meaning behind everything He does. We should think in terms of what He chooses to do and less in terms of what He needs to do. Thinking that He needs to do anything presents an element of a God that has a dependency or reliance on an external force, which immediately reduces His value to less than whatever that outer component is.

To support this concept of a conscious choice by God to utilise a vehicle, at least in His interactions with us, lets look at Bible verses that mention chariots in relation to God.

Psalms 68:17; "The chariots of God are twenty thousand, Even thousands of thousands; The Lord is among them as in Sinai, in the Holy Place."

Psalm 104:3; "He lays the beams of His upper chambers in the waters, Who makes the clouds His chariot, Who walks on the wings of the wind..."

Isaiah 66:15; "For behold, the Lord will come with fire And with chariots, like whirlwind, to render His anger with fury, And His rebuke with flames of fire."

2 Kings 2:11; "Then it happened, as they continued on and talked, that suddenly a chariot of fire appeared with horses of fire, and separated the two of them; and Elijah went up by a whirlwind into heaven."

Zechariah 6:1; "Then I turned and raised my eyes and looked, and behold, four chariots were coming from behind two mountains, and the mountains were mountains of bronze."

Chariot Definition

The word chariot is derived from the Hebrew word *rekeb {reh'-keb}* which means vehicle, cavalry or (upper) millstone. It is interesting to note that a millstone is a thick disc-shaped rock, which has a similar look to the accepted appearance of UFO's today. Author, Jeff A. Benner makes a very interesting observation in his book, *His Name is One*, when he examines the Hebrew root of the word "Spirit" as it appears in **Genesis 1:2; "And the _spirit_ of God was hovering over the face of the waters."** He notes that the same parent root of this word also resides in the Hebrew words, "moon," "traveler," and "millstone," which he concludes all carry the common characteristic of a prescribed path. I also noted that all three words could be easily used to describe a range of characteristics. For example the moon describes a bright "colour," the traveler describes a "use," and the millstone describes a "shape." This further validated my view that, within some Scripture, the word "spirit" can also be understood as being the physical presence of an aerial chariot or UFO. The word chariot is also used extensively in its normal sense throughout the Bible to describe the mobile infantry of the Egyptians and many other armies. These vehicles were a highly feared and effective addition to any military force and were among the most prized acquisitions to the victors of major battles. Throughout the Bible the word chariot is used in equal effect to describe horse drawn military vehicles as it does the manner in which God or his angels appear or intervene in the affairs of men. Due to the absence of specific words that currently describe unusual aircraft, witnesses in biblical times could have only attributed the aerial appearances of God and His heavenly host as coming or contained within chariots, clouds, dwellings, cherubim or thrones etc.

Cloud Definition

The word cloud is derived from the Hebrew word *anan {aw-nawn'}* which means covering the sky. It must be pointed out that prior to Noah's flood clouds did not exist in their current form, because an upper atmospheric layer of water originally covered the earth called the firmament *(Genesis 1:7)*. This firmament would have made the sky appear much different to how we perceive it today. In addition rainfall would not have occurred in the same manner. Many scientists have theorised that the earth would have been showered in a daily mist, giving the same global environmental effect as is generated from a greenhouse. This early type of pre-flood biosphere, according to archaeologist Dr. Carl Baugh, would have incidentally also been a far more favourable environment in promoting optimal genetic forms of all species on the earth at that time, giving them greater physical stature and longer life spans. However, normal cloud coverage would have certainly been a reality for the majority of the time periods covered in the Bible.

The references to clouds with aerial appearances of God and His angels is so frequent that unless we concede that they are usually used in reference to craft of some kind, then God would have appeared 95% of the time on overcast days. This includes appearances of clouds at night that also in some cases burn with fire.

Flying Vehicles – Evident in Many Diverse Religions

YHWH is far from the only god that is recorded as using an aerial vehicle. Though flight is certainly a common attribute of the different gods of the world's religions, an additional component is also nearly always evident. Early Chinese texts speak of immortal rulers that fly fire-breathing dragons as records from the Ming Dynasty show: "Come in Thy precious chariot to the altar. Thy servant, I bow my head to the earth reverently, expecting Thine abundant grace…" The Tibetan Kantyua mentions pearls in the sky and transparent spheres that carry the forms of kings who originally came from the stars while ancient Sumerian tablets tell of gods that fly in Shems, which are described as rocks that emit fire. The Indian *Mahabharata* portrays gods riding bright celestial cars upon cloudless skies and the *Yantra Sarasva,* written by the sage *Maharshi Bhardwaj,* describes aerial craft that have the capability to travel from country to country and from planet to planet. Among these ancient pages are described military planes that featured the following characteristics:

∞ Impregnable and non-combustible structures

∞ Able to come to an immediate halt at high speeds

∞ Sophisticated camouflage (Invisibility)

∞ Listening to conversations within enemy planes

∞ Visual and audio recording facilities

∞ Capable of emitting destructive projectiles

∞ Temperature regulation within planes

Why Are They Evident?

If we look back to the incident at the Tower of Babel and how God confused the languages and scattered men, we can see the birth of a diversity of peoples. This act of injecting different dialects into the population with a flourishing economy would have had a devastating effect. However, there would have been scattered groups of people amid the infrastructure of Babel that spoke familiar tongues. But groups could not communicate with other groups because no one was bilingual so it would have been ineffective to continue as a whole community. The component parts of the economy could not link back together so dispersal of the different groups into isolated locations was the only solution. As the years passed stories of the creation account passed from generation to generation within each new settlement of peoples. The new language, geographic location, and isolation from the past meant that settlements grew enormously in diversity and even their histories began to change until like Chinese whispers stories of the origin of man began to evolve to fit the cultural sovereignty of the differing settlements. This is why we see such a diverse range of ancient religions in the world, yet upon closer inspection, they all carry significant similarities. Even Islam carries many customs that are acknowledged and practiced by Christianity. Greek mythology also contains a chillingly similar story to Genesis as it speaks of Deucalion and his wife floating in a chest for nine days and nights while Zeus floods the planet to destroy men in the Bronze Age.

Evidence of a Forgotten Technology on the Ground

I have attempted to list and briefly explain some of the more unexplainable technological abnormalities that have been widely documented yet consistently ignored by relevant mainstream institutions. Collectively, they build a compelling case of an ancient world of men that rubbed shoulders with an advanced race. The hypothesis of self-acquired knowledge to achieve some of the things that I wish to share has two major stumbling blocks. They are:

1) In dealing with many strange artifacts, no evidence has been found of an evolution of their designs. In fact, author, David Hatcher Childress, in his book, *Technology of the Gods – The Incredible Science of the Ancients*, points out that in the case of ancient Egypt, its sciences, arts, architecture, and hieroglyphics are devoid of any evidence of a period of development. It is almost as if the entire civilisation just appeared full-blown on the surface of the earth.

2) We simply do not have the technology to duplicate the construction of the Giza Pyramid or the technological know-how to cut, excavate, and move some of the rocks that have been found elsewhere in certain parts of the world. No apparatus has ever been found, intact, partially intact, or in tiny component parts that could have even half believably moved such enormous objects, some of which range in weight from 1000 to 3000 tons. I can rattle on about ancient flying objects, giants, and prophesied technology until the cows come home and a half skilled sceptic may still come away relatively unscathed, yet with the single evidence of these massive chunks of stone hewn from one piece of rock laying on the earth, the world of a clearly thinking sceptic trying to attack the concept of outside intervention comes crashing down hard.

Without any further ado here are a few of the contenders:

∞ The remains of a piece of machinery consisting of no less than 40 cog wheels with a centre wheel consisting of 240 teeth was discovered in 1900 in a submerged Greek shipwreck by a diver. It (the artifact, not the ship) has been dated at 3 to 4 million years old. It is called the "Antikythera Machine."

∞ What was initially thought of as being merely an ancient pot, later, after careful examination appeared to contain smaller parts that resembled a crude form of battery dating back to the first century B.C. Willard Grey, a scientist specialising in electrical energy concluded that with the addition of citric acid, an electric current could be produced from the artifact. It is known as the "Baghdad Battery."

∞ "The Baalbek Stones" are hewn from one solid piece of rock and weigh 1200 tons. Two stones with beveled edges weighing in at 1000 tons make up a portion of the base of the "Temple of Jupiter." This temple is considered one of the largest structures in the world. Somehow these blocks were accurately cut, dressed, and moved from a stone quarry ¾ of a mile away. At the quarry is a monolith of erect limestone that weighs 2,000,000 pounds. By comparison the largest block that makes up the Giza Pyramid weighs 400,000 pounds. Baalbek also means (Baal) of the Beqaa', and refers to the fertile Beqaa plain. It is interesting to note that The Book of Enoch refers to an opening in a desert called Dudael where the fallen angel Azazel is to be cast. Rough and jagged rocks are to be placed there to keep him entombed forever.

∞ Recently in China, an ancient artifact has been discovered that supports the notion that, "craftsmen were using complex machines to work jewellery long before such devices are traditionally thought to have been invented," to quote from the BBC News UK edition that appeared on Thursday, 10 June, 2004, 22:26 GMT 23:26 UK. The article goes onto say:
"Dr Peter Lu claims spiral grooves on 2,550-year-old jade rings must have been made by a precision "compound" machine.

As the name suggests, compound machines comprise two or more machines with different motion that have been linked together to perform precision work. Dr Lu, of Harvard University, US, has published his research in Science. Previously, the earliest known historical references to compound machines come from writings attributed to Hero of Alexandria that are dated to the First Century AD.

Carved decorations on jades from ancient China are generally thought to have been made by hand, or with simple machines that worked with a single movement. The ornamental jade burial rings reported in Science come from the so-called Spring and Autumn period (771 to 475 BC) and have been excavated from hoards and from tombs belonging to ancient officials and nobles. The machine that carved the grooves would have linked rotational and linear motion, perhaps using a stylus suspended over a rotating turntable, says Dr Lu.

'The complex machine that created these spiral grooves may also be among the ancestors of the crank in China... sculptures to have mechanised a variety of agricultural processes such as milling and winnowing,' Dr Lu writes in Science magazine."

∞ A large stone slate called the "Dashkin Kamen," uncovered by scientists in Russia that shows a sophisticated relief map of a specific region carved between 90 to 120 million years ago. An excerpt from an article in April 30, 2002, in an online news site called "Pravda.ru" said:

"This seems to be impossible. Scientists of Bashkir State University have found indisputable proofs of an ancient highly developed civilization's existence. The question is about a great plate found in 1999, with (a) picture of the region done according to an unknown technology. This is a real relief map. Today's military has almost the same maps. The map contains civil engineering works: a system of channels with a length of about 12,000km, weirs, (and) powerful dams."

And further the article reads:

"'The more I learn the more I understand that I know nothing,' – the doctor of physical and mathematical science, professor Bashkir State University, Alexandr Chuvyrov admits."

Initially, scientists thought some of the inscriptions found on the plate were of Chinese origin, however, closer examination yielded hieroglyphic-symbols of an unknown origin.

A follow-up press conference carried a statement by Chuvyrov that contained a considerably watered down version of the find, contradicting some of the earlier claims by saying that the inscriptions were indeed of an ancient Chinese dialect used about 3000 years ago. The significance of the rest of the findings remained intact, which is still unbelievable enough, yet to this author, the article read like a whitewash, enforced by the wider scientific community. I couldn't help but think that it was a trade-off to ensure the finding retained suitable funding, with the proviso to adhere to generally accepted archaeological views.

Archaeological evidence found across the globe that shows inconsistencies with the general worldly view of human linear progress certainly supports the existence of superior beings (sons of God) that co-existed, influenced, dominated, and out-rightly ruled men. Now technology has found a home, not only with these gods, both good and bad, but also with men.

Other Forms of Godly Technology

Apart from air transport the Bible painstakingly relates countless other instances where the technology of God is evident. These include any events of a miraculous nature no matter how big or small from a global flood to producing money from a fish *(Matthew 17:27)*. To provide an extensive list of all such wondrous irregularities would require a volume of work that would wear down the hardest sceptic. Though there are some points we differ on, the author Patrick Cooke includes an extensive listing of such verses in his book *The Greatest Deception* and offers a clear and concise argument into the subject of the "technology of the gods". What follows is a short list of various technological feats of God that appear in the Bible with corresponding verses. As a more in-depth resource, Cooke's book is the most comprehensive I have seen to date and is therefore an essential addition to any serious researcher's library.

Beings that glow and emit light – *Ezekiel 1:27; "Also from the appearance of His waist and upward I saw, as it were, the colour of amber with the appearance of fire all around within it; and from the appearance of His waist and downward I saw, as it were, the appearance of fire with brightness all around."*

Projected light, lights and sound emission – *Revelations 4:5; "And from the throne proceeded lightenings, thunderings, and voices. Seven lamps of fire were burning before the throne, which are the seven spirits of God."*

Heat ray – *Leviticus 9:24; "and fire came out from before the Lord and consumed the burnt offering and the fat on the altar. When all the people saw it, they shouted and fell on their faces."*

Craft exhaust emission (Glory) – *Isaiah 2:19; "They shall go into the holes of the rocks, And into the caves of the earth, from the terror of the Lord, And the glory of His majesty, when He arises to shake the earth mightily."*

Mechanised Movement – *Ezekiel 10:11; "When they went, they went toward any of their four directions; they did not turn aside when they went but followed in the direction the head was facing. They did not turn aside when they went."*

Control over planetary rotation – *2 Kings 20:9-11; "Then Isaiah said, 'This is the sign to you from the Lord, that the Lord will do the thing which He has spoken: shall the shadow go forward ten degrees or go backward ten degrees?' And Hezekiah answered, 'It is an easy thing for the shadow to go down ten degrees; no, but let the shadow go backward ten degrees.' So Isaiah the prophet cried out to the Lord, and He brought the shadow ten degrees backward, by which it had gone down on the sundial of Ahaz."*

Light control over localised areas – *Exodus 10:22; "So Moses stretched out his hand toward heaven, and there was thick darkness in all the land of Egypt three days."*

Cloning – *Genesis 2:21-22; "And the Lord God caused a deep sleep to fall on Adam, and he slept; and He took one of his ribs, and closed up the flesh in its place. Then the rib which the Lord God had taken from the man He made into a woman, and He brought her to the man."*

Superhuman strength – *Judges 16:3; "And Sampson lay low till midnight; the arose at midnight, took hold of the doors of the gate of*

the city and two gatepost, pulled them up, bar and all, put them on his
shoulders, and carried them to the top of the hill that faces Hebron."

Final Thoughts

As I browse through various articles on the world's latest technologies I read unnerving leaps ahead in the fields of computers, genetic engineering and nanotechnologies. These new technologies differ from previous luxuries we've enjoyed such as cars, televisions, and telephones in that unlike these that accelerated for a while in transforming society and then settle to a reliable condition known as "lock-in," computers, biotechnology and nanotech do not work in the same way. They self accelerate as old computer chips are put to work in developing newer and more powerful ones. Breakthroughs in discoveries of bioengineering and nanotechnologies lead to the spiraling process of exposing literally endless possibilities. It is no secret that technology is getting more convenient, sophisticated and advanced, but the speed of its advancement has rarely been witnessed by men at the rate it moves today. Satan will soon think himself suitably equipped to enter a bolder position on the stage as earthly advances in technology move into a more efficient and controlling direction in a vain attempt to replace God. A good friend once said to me "with knowledge comes responsibility and with responsibility comes accountability." Sadly it is the last word of that statement that mankind has the most trouble with.

So Many Bibles, So Little Time

Bible Translations, Versions & Editions

It is important to differentiate between the term "edition" and the terms "version" and "translation," which can be interchangeable. Version or translation usually pertains to Bibles that are written in a specific style, varying from basic to more advanced English, containing a wider vocabulary, and usually claiming greater accuracy and clarity of wording, than existing translations.

Editions include Bibles that are literal, amplified, paraphrased, interlinear, multiple translation, study format, reference format, chronological, etc. Different editions of Bibles can appear in different translation formats such as an NIV (New International Version) and an NIV study Bible and a multiple translation may contain a KJV (King James Version), NIV, and amplified translation. The following chapter will look at Bible versions and in particular examine the New International Version and King James Version heavyweights.

The following is a list of the major Bible translations and editions available today. These lists exclude multi-media Bibles of which many more varieties are available. Less well-known, but no less scholarly in execution are a growing range of Sacred Name and Restoration Bibles. Two of the most popular in this range are the "Restoration Scriptures" by *Your Arms to Yisrael Publishing* and "The Scriptures," published by the *Institute For Scripture Research* in South Africa. An explanation of these editions will be examined at the close of this chapter.

Translations – New International (NIV), New Revised Standard (NRSV), New American Standard (NASB), King James (Authorized Version or KJV), New King James (NKJV), Living Bible (TLB), Good News Revised (GNB), Contemporary English Version (CEV), The Message, The Revised English Bible, New Jerusalem Bible, The Amplified Bible, The New Century Bible, God's Word.

Editions – Dake's Annotated Reference Bible, 1963. (KJV), The New Oxford Annotated Bible. (NRSV), The Open Bible, 1978. (KJV & NKJV), The Ryrie Study Bible, 1979. (NASB & NIV), The New Schofield Reference Bible, 1967. (KJV), The New Chain-Reference Bible, by F C Thompson. 1934. (KJV & NIV), The NIV Study Bible, 1985, The Life Application Bible, 1988. (Available with the Living Bible, the NIV, the NRSV and the NKJV.), The New Jerusalem Standard Edition, 1985, The Harper Collins Study Bible, 1993. NRSV, The Serendipity Study Bible. NIV, Quest Study Bible, 1994. NIV.

Please Bear the Following in Mind

To be in a part of the world that even has a Bible translation, let alone a few to choose from is a privilege, and to inhabit a location where one can read a Bible without fear of persecution or death, let alone teach openly from it, is not only a privilege, but a blessing as well. Therefore no matter what the issue with a translation, a Christian Bible of any sort is worth more than none at all. Having said this I am also aware that some of us live in a part of the world where we are literally saturated by different Bibles and this can have a negative effect as well. These are a few global statistics on Bible translations that are available worldwide.

World Population as of 2004 – More than 6.3 billion
Languages currently spoken in the world – 6,809 (approx)
Languages that need Bible translations: 3,000
Number who speak a language with no Scriptures
(neither Bible or parts thereof) – **250 million**
Languages that have a whole Bible – 383
987 just have the New Testament
(Source: Lutheran Bible Translators of Canada Volume 29 – Winter 2002 – Number 1)

To avoid any confusion on what my stance is on Bible translations, let me start by making it clear that I do favour the Authorized King James version over the New International Version. But I am also aware of how grossly short it falls down in quite a few areas. I own quite a few different Bibles and I usually use a New King James in non-messianic circles, despite knowing many of its translatory flaws. The advantage here is to be able to share Scripture with people without the added alienating concept of coming at them with some obscure study Bible that they've never even heard of. I am not a King James only advocate and I believe there is no perfect English translation in existence. However, logic says that there has to be a single English rendering somewhere that nudges over the head of it's nearest competitor in terms of accuracy. For example there can't be two different translations that are equally accurate. Or for that matter equally non-accurate. Because the majority of KJV readers and the NIV readers are divided over which Bible is more accurate I have chosen to explore some of these issues to equip the reader with some of the facts.

Introduction

The subject of Bible versions and which ones are to be encouraged or avoided is a massive issue and a subject I was hoping to avoid in this work. But it is so obviously a concern with many people that it deserves mention. No doubt some of the things that will be presented here will add to the fallout I will receive from some Christians, but sticking with a Bible because the English is plainer should not excuse illegitimate omissions, additions, or changes to Scripture.

Burning Poorly Translated Bibles is Unadvisable

I do not advocate the incineration of any versions of the Bible, nor do I any book unless it deals with witchcraft, Satanism or pornography. If I received a phone call from a friend at an outpost in Antarctica that declared he wanted to commit his life to God and he had started reading the only Bible version there that in my opinion was a poor one I would be a fool to advise him to burn it. My explanations of why would most likely dishearten him and this action would cut off his only source of direct knowledge about God. I have read many enlightening articles and essays on Bible versions that fall short by encouraging readers to burn specific Bibles. These types of requests always tend to unnecessarily sensationalise the issue and alienate the reader. The practice of burning books period clouds my conscience with the unsettling regimes of the Catholic Church and Nazi Germany. Some people become so consumed by this issue that the Bible becomes an idol and they fail to realise that the words themselves do not save, but the Saviour that they speak of. We should be reminded that though the circumstances may be rare, a man might receive salvation without ever having sighted a single verse of Scripture. A relationship with a favoured Bible version should not climb above a personal relationship with God. The Bible merely points us in the right direction and it has no magical properties itself. It is not and should not be looked upon as an enchanted artifact and be held tightly to one's breast in the hopes of gaining protection. Its power comes from its contents being read, understood and obeyed.

Amid the vast range of different versions available we can make two simple deductions. Firstly, there must be one that contains the fewest errors and secondly there must be one that contains the most errors. Knowing where the KJV or the NIV fit in this equation is the objective of this chapter.

The NIV vs. The KJV

In the mainstream Christian arena the two versions that I believe lead the way in displaying some of the best and worst features in a

Bible are the KJV and the NIV. I will examine each volume in order of preference and look at the negative and positive aspects of each.

It is important to point out that though these two versions happen to contain the widest discrepancies in their text from one another, the worst of the two does not parade the product of translations from manuscripts that differ seriously from one another.

The Authorized King James Bible

The positives – The King James translators were unparalleled in scholarly discipline and had attained a level of study that still far exceeds modern day Bible translators today. There were 54 translators, which were organised into six groups. Each of these groups tackled a particular book and when a translation was completed they were passed on to each other group in turn.

The KJV has enjoyed a track record of being widely used for over four centuries and it is so well known that it has influenced the English language to the point of inspiring poets, dramatists, artists and politicians alike and is often quoted by people that do not know they are quoting from it at all.

The negatives – Firstly the Authorized King James Version differs from the original 1611 version that also contained the books of the Apocrypha, and differs in 421 notable places, though there have been claims by some authors that differences reach into the tens of thousands.

As discussed in an earlier chapter, the language of the court of King James was a language of royalty. It contained a very proper form of court English that exhibited not only many words unused in today's language, but also many different words to the common speech of the day. This was done to give it an effect of sounding ancient and authoritative when read aloud to the masses. A casualty of this ideology was the word "sky" and its replacement with the word "heaven." As a consequence many churches preach the word "heaven" as being the place with the pearly gates and streets paved with gold rather than the sky. This is exemplified when heaven is translated so frequently from the Hebrew word "shamayin" which means "the sky."

An error that occurs in the KJV that particularly disturbs me is the inclusion in a single instance of the word "Easter" in *Acts 12:4; "And when he had apprehended him, he put him in prison, and delivered him to four quaternions of soldiers to keep him; intending after Easter to bring him forth to the people."* The original Greek word that appears in the verse is "pascha," which means "Passover" and to the average Christian there would be nothing that unusual about replacing it with the word Easter. This is because the observance of Easter is and has been looked upon for centuries as the traditional day to celebrate the Messiah's death and resurrection. In reality the name originally signified the celebration of a pagan festival in which worshippers would engage in sex acts and display symbols of eggs and rabbits as signs of fertility. As you might have guessed this was another great idea of Constantine's in his quest of sanctification by assimilation. The *1934 edition of Encyclopedia Britannica* relates, "(Easter) or Eastre, was the goddess of Spring in the religion of the ancient Angles and Saxons. Every April a festival was celebrated in her honor. With the beginnings of Christianity, the old gods were put aside. From then on the festival was celebrated in honour of the resurrection of Christ, but was still known as Easter after the goddess Eastre."

The fact that this word does not appear anywhere else in this version is unusual enough and thankfully most scholars are in agreement that this is an error in translation.

The most notable flaw of all modern mainstream Bibles, and the KJV is no exception, is the almost total omission of the name of God – YHWH. As this practice is not confined to any one particular Bible, the topic will be discussed in the following Chapter.

The New International Version

The positives – It meets the current level of the general standard of English spoken today and for this reason it currently enjoys the widest range of readership.

The negatives – Due to the current theologically blinded climate and accepted social trends within mainstream Bible colleges I believe that it would be difficult to find a sizable enough community of spiritually disciplined and highly trained scholars that match the level of scribes centuries ago. Records we have today show that early Hebrew scribes and copyists would rewrite entire pages of Scripture over just one minor error and rewrite entire books if they, in a single instance, misspelt the name of God. Notwithstanding that, another element is at large today that plays a very big role in the final format of the modern Bible; that is capitalism. A factor that is often put on equal standing with accuracy is presentation of language that appeals to a wide audience, to avoid offending some groups for the purpose of selling more Bibles and making more money. Often books have a heavy emphasis on commentaries, which at the end of the day are often quoted to support non-biblical based doctrines. Commentaries are often given credence because they share the same page as Scriptural text. A footnote or a commentary is simply someone's theological opinion and should not be esteemed over God inspired Scripture. The Bible is its own commentary. The NIV falls like a professional stuntman into all these potholes, as I will show.

It is a reasonably new translation completed in 1978. It is often argued that this version was required because, "changes in the English language affect the language of Scripture." This line of reasoning comes undone when one looks at the bigger picture as the chief aim of language today is to aggressively evolve into a means-to-an-end dialect with its principle purpose being to vehicle open-ended meaning where applicable. Language is being hacked and cleaved by abbreviation and acronym as mobile phone text messaging escalates and schools fail to equip students with a good grasp of language by the time they leave school. Publicly schooled students become unable to comprehend clever rhetoric or fine print while privately schooled students become equipped with an ability to mislead and overtly generalise when the occasion calls. Bill Clinton's, "I did not have sexual relations" comment is a prime example of this misuse of modern English. Children need to be taught how to read and write correctly instead of receiving new Bible translations that cater to a barely literate population too often easily deceived by generalities and cleverly used words.

The Earlier the Manuscript the More Accurate Fable

I have had chaplains, ministers, and Bible students boldly tell me that this is the most definitive version of the Bible ever printed and the argument that is often wheeled out to support authenticity of texts is that the work is based on older more authentic Greek manuscripts. And indeed this version does make these claims in the footnotes. I do not dispute that some of the source manuscripts predate those of other Bibles. It is alarming that earlier translations are always assumed to have greater accuracy. It does not take much brainpower to realise that the oldest manuscripts are not necessarily the more correct ones. Let us look at a simple example to illustrate this. Imagine a translation of the Book of Matthew is made in around 200 AD from the original manuscript, however the author is influenced by external philosophical disciplines and subtly alters some aspects of the text to align with these beliefs. Then 260 years pass and another scholar acquires that same original text and makes a flawlessly faithful reproduction. The date alone of a manuscript should not determine its accuracy. The amount of alterations found in the NIV of "God" reduced to "Him," "Holy Spirit" reduced to "spirit," complete omissions of "Jesus" and "God" and the absence of critical verses are mind-blowing. The irony of all this is that the words "God," "Jesus" and "Holy" are corrupted terms anyway, because they are transliterations of pagan deities (i.e. They can be traced back to the names of fallen angels and have another or no meaning when converted back into the Hebrew words they allegedly espouse). More will be explained on this soon. Below are just a handful of examples of this more recent phase in the meltdown progress of truth. I encourage you to check other sources to see if this information is correct, and if it is, ask the question, "is it more difficult to detach oneself from the use of a favoured Bible or more difficult to detach oneself from hell?" This is in no way meant to imply that I believe NIV users are going to hell, but if you have been given good reason to avoid this particular translation then you be the judge.

Some Random Verse-by-Verse Comparisons

One of the most intriguing verse omissions evident in the NIV is found in the Book of Acts.

Acts 8:36-37; (KJV) "And as they went on their way, they came unto a certain water: and the eunuch said, See, here is water; what doth hinder me to be baptized? 37 And Philip said, If thou believest with all thine heart, thou mayest. And he answered and said, I Believe that Jesus Christ is the Son of God."

Acts 8:36-37; (NIV) "As they traveled along the road, they came to some water and the eunuch said, 'Look, here is water. Why shouldn't I be baptized?'" 37 (omitted)

The omission of verse 37 is the most intriguing for the simple reason that it relates a portion of conversation that is critical to the act of baptism (mikveh). To accept that this verse was omitted is to assume that an overly creative translator somewhere down the track had invented a portion of conversation.

The following two verse comparisons are interesting considering the subject broached.

Revelation 22:18-19; (KJV) "For I testify unto every man that heareth the words of the prophecy of this book, If any man shall add unto these things, God shall add unto him the plagues that are written in this book: 19 And if any man shall take away from the words of the book of this prophecy, God shall take away his part out of the book of <u>life</u>, and out of the holy city, and from the things which are written in this book."

Revelation; 22:18-19 (NIV) "I warn everyone who hears the words of the prophecy of this book: If anyone adds anything to them, God will add to him the plagues described in this book. 19 And if anyone takes words away from this book of prophecy, God will take away from him his share in the <u>tree</u> of life and in the holy city, which are described in this book."

I'm sorry, but no matter how hard I squint when I look at a book it never looks like a tree. The concept of having a place in the tree of life (which I assume is the tree that was in the Garden of Eden) is a brand new concept that is never mentioned anywhere else in Scripture and just makes it in here, two verses from the end of the entire Bible. The word "And" has also been removed which weakens the sentence.

1 Timothy 3:16; (KJV) "And without controversy great is the mystery of godliness: <u>God</u> was manifest in the flesh, justified in the

273

Spirit, seen of angels, preached unto the Gentiles, believed on in the world, received up into glory."

1 Timothy 3:16; (NIV) "Beyond all question, the mystery of godliness is great: <u>He</u> *appeared in a body, was vindicated by the Spirit, was seen by angels, was preached among the nations, was believed on in the world, was taken up in glory."*

God is booted out and replaced with He.

Romans 14:10; (KJV) "But why dost thou judge thy brother? or why dost thou set at nought thy brother? for we shall all stand before the judgment seat of <u>Christ</u>.*" Romans 14:12 (KJV) "So then every one of us shall give account of himself to God."*

Romans 14:10; (NIV) "You, then, why do you judge your brother? Or why do you look down on your brother? For we will all stand before <u>God's</u> *judgment seat." Romans 14:12 (NIV) "So then, each of us will give an account of himself to God."*

The title Christ is replaced by the title God.

Micah 5:2; (KJV) "But thou, Bethlehem Ephratah, though thou be little among the thousands of Judah, yet out of thee shall he come forth unto me that is to be ruler in Israel; whose goings forth have been from of old, from <u>everlasting</u>.*"*

Micah 5:2; (NIV) "But you, Bethlehem Ephrathah, though you are small among the clans of Judah, out of you will come for me one who will be ruler over Israel, whose origins are from of old, from <u>ancient times</u>.*"*

According to the NIV, eternity has an origin point somewhere in ancient times instead of everlasting.

1 John 4:3; (KJV) "And every spirit that confesseth not that <u>Jesus Christ</u> *is come in the flesh is not of God: and this is that spirit of antichrist, whereof ye have heard that it should come; and even now already is it in the world."*

1 John 4:3; (NIV) "but every spirit that does not acknowledge <u>Jesus</u> *is not from God. This is the spirit of the antichrist, which you have heard is coming and even now is already in the world."*

Christ is omitted and confirmation of his arrival on earth in the flesh is apparently no longer required.

Matthew 27:35; (KJV) "And they crucified him, and parted his garments, casting lots: that it might be fulfilled which was spoken

ALL LIGHTS ON IN THE MASTER'S HOUSE

by the prophet, They parted my garments among them, and upon my vesture did they cast lots."

Matthew 27:35; (NIV) "When they had crucified him, they divided up his clothes by casting lots."

Over half of the verse has hit the cutting room floor. The Old Testament's foreshadowing of this event doesn't seem to be important enough to mention here.

Mark 15:28" (KJV) "And the scripture was fulfilled, which saith, And he was numbered with the transgressors."

Mark 15:28 (NIV)

The absence of the above verse speaks for itself.

Romans 1:29; (KJV) "Being filled with all unrighteousness, for-nication, wickedness, covetousness, maliciousness; full of envy, murder, debate, deceit, malignity; whisperers…"

Romans 1:29; (NIV) "They have become filled with every kind of wickedness, evil, greed and depravity. They are full of envy, murder, strife, deceit and malice. They are gossips…"

Fornication has been removed.

1 Corinthians 16:22; (KJV) "If any man love not the Lord Jesus Christ, let him be Anathema Martanatha."

1 Corinthians 16:22; (NIV) "If anyone does not love the Lord – a curse be on him. Come, O Lord!"

Jesus Christ is completely omitted.

Ephesians 3:9; (KJV) "And to make all men see what is the fellowship of the mystery, which from the beginning of the world hath been hid in God, who created all things by Jesus Christ…"

Ephesians 3:9; (NIV) "and to make plain to everyone the administration of this mystery, which for ages past was kept hidden in God, who created all things."

Again Jesus Christ is removed.

The Final Straw

The following piece of information was eventually gleaned from a snippet of information that claimed one of the editors of the NIV was a lesbian. Upon reading this claim I found stupefying confirmation of the saying, "where there's smoke there's fire."

I must stress, for whatever reason that you cling to that NIV, whether it be because your pastor swore on his life that it was the best, whether the entire congregation uses one (indeed 70% of churches do), whether you assured scores of people over the years that it was the best, or whether you just can't bear the heartache of being wrong, put it away (you may need it in the future to set other people straight) and buy yourself a different one. Which one? I will get to this shortly. If you must cling to an NIV, try to get yourself an NIV Hebrew Interlinear Bible, these have every Hebrew root word available for scrutiny and I recommend this version at least in terms of it being a first step in weaning off the NIV as a personal study Bible.

The following is an extensive report written by Mr. Michael Penfold on November 1997, which contains a statement by Dr. Virginia Mollenkott and sheds some light on the background of Dr. Marten Woudstra who was the chairman of the NIV's Old Testament translation committee. I encourage the reader not to skip, skim or partially read this section.

"James White's book The King James Only Controversy (Bethany House Publishers, 1995) includes a question and answers section. One of the questions reads, 'I've been told that there were homosexuals on the NIV translation committee. Is that true?' On pages 245-246 of his book James White gives the following answer."

"'No it is not [true]. But due to the consistent bearing of false witness by KJV only advocates, Dr. Kenneth Barker, Executive Director of the NIV Translation Centre, had to write a response to the accusation, which I quote below:' [Dr. Barker writes]: 'It has come to my attention that false rumours are circulating, in both oral and written forms, that the NIV was soft on sodomy (that is, homosexual sins). The alleged reasons for this is that some NIV translators and editors were homosexuals and lesbians. These charges have no basis in fact. Thus they are simply untrue. And those who make such false charges could be legitimately sued for libel, slander and defamation of character. Here are the facts. It is true that in the earliest stages of translation work on the NIV (in the late 1960s and early 70s) Virginia Mollenkott was consulted briefly and only in a minor way on matters of English style. At that time she had the reputation of being a committed evangelical Christian with expertise in contemporary English idiom and usage. Nothing was known of her lesbian views. Those did not begin to surface until years later in some of her writings. If we had known in the sixties what became public knowledge only years later, we would not have consulted her at all. But it must be stressed that she did not influence the NIV translators and editors in any of their final decisions'"

"This is a very cleverly worded statement and one, which we can allow Virginia Mollenkott to answer herself. In a letter to me [Michael J. Penfold] dated Dec. 18th 1996, in reply to my investigation into her true role on the NIV, Mollenkott wrote the following revealing letter:"

[Virginia Mollenkott writes]

"'I worked on the NIV during the entire time it was being translated and reviewed, although I was never free to attend the summer sessions even when I was invited to do so. Elisabeth Elliot and I were the Stylistic Consultants: out job was simply to make sure the translation would communicate clearly to modern American readers, and that the style was as smooth and understandable as possible. I was never removed, sacked, or made redundant from my work on the NIV; If I were, my name would not have appeared on the list sent out by the IBS. It was Dr. Edwin Palmer, who lived near my college, who invited me to work on the NIV. He had heard me speak and respected my integrity and my knowledge. So far as I know, nobody including Dr. Palmer suspected that I was a lesbian while I was working on the NIV; it was information I kept private at that time. Dr. Palmer always sent me batches of translation to review, and I always returned them (with my comments) to him. I have not kept track of which of my suggestions made it into the final version; I am a busy person, and it was a labour of love in the Scriptures. I do not think anything concerning homosexuality was in the batches I reviewed. I do not consider the NIV more gay-friendly than most modern translations, so I do not understand why anybody would want to bash the NIV because a closet lesbian worked on it. I was not a translator; If I were I would have argued that the word/concept "homosexual" is too anachronistic to be utilized in translating an ancient text. But I was a stylist and nobody asked me. I no longer have any contact with NIV-CBT, but

I am often amused to remember that I frequently refused my $5 an hour stipend because I heard the project was running out of money. At the time I was naïve about how many millions of dollars are made by successful Bible translations! Please tell Kenneth Barker for me that although there is much controversy about homosexuality among Bible scholars, to my knowledge nobody denies that the Bible condemns lying about other people. He should be ashamed of his attempt to rewrite history. Somewhere in my files is a letter I got thanking me for my work on the NIV when the project was completed. I also have the slipcase version sent out to the whole NIV team in 1978 by Zondervan; and I have the tenth-anniversary edition sent out to the whole team in 1988 by the International Bible Society. Various other editions were also sent out gratis to the translation committee and stylists, but I have received nothing since 1988 that I can remember. Because I am idealistic and sincere, it never occurred to me that anyone would lie about my contributions, so I was not meticulous about keeping records. Thank you for anything you can do to set the record straight. You may utilize this letter to do so, and I'd appreciate you sending me a copy of anything you generate. Sincerely, Virginia Ramey Mollenkott.'"

"Why could not Dr. Barker have told the truth in the first place? Taking Mollenkott's words at their face value, the NIV publicity machine has nothing to worry about. Does their anxiety to distance the NIV from homosexual associations reveal something more sinister?"

"In the light of the following, I believe it does, as it has now come to light that THE CHAIRMAN OF THE NIV'S OLD TESTAMENT TRANSLATION COMMITTEE, DR. MARTEN H. WOUDSTRA, WAS A HOMOSEXUAL. This is much more serious than Mollenkott's involvement. Here we have one of the leading scholars on the NIV CBT who is a homosexual. Obviously this fact comprises the whole project, especially as this fact was well known by his colleagues for many years. However, only now is this fact coming to the notice of the general public through articles like this one you are reading."

"Dr. Woudstra, who died in the early 1990s, was a long-time friend of Evangelicals Concerned Inc. This organization was founded in 1976 by New York psychologist, Dr. Ralph Blair, as a nationwide task force and fellowship for gay and lesbian 'evangelical Christians' and their friends. ECI's address is 311 East 72nd street, New York, NY 10021. They can be found on the internet at http:/www.korpi.com/ECWE/"

"It was during a series of research phone calls to Dr. Blair that I first confirmed the fact of Dr. Woudstra's homosexuality. Blair and Dr. Woudstra were friends. Dr. Woudstra had been on the mailing list of Evangelicals Concerned from its conception, and although he had no formal ties with ECI, on one of his many trips to New York he called in and had tea with Dr. Blair. Dr. Blair told me that Dr. Woudstra shared the viewpoint of ECI that lifelong "loving monogamous relationships' between gay men or women were acceptable to God. He believed that there was nothing in the Old Testament (his special area of technical expertise) that corresponds to 'homosexual orientation'. The 'sodomy' of the OT simply involved temple rites and gang rape (Gen 19)."

"Notice the similarity of the view and that of Virginia Mollenkott. Dr. Blair clearly stated to me on the phone on the 23rd of September 1997 that Dr. Woudstra, a lifelong bachelor, was a homosexual. He intimated that other members of the NIV translation committee were also quietly supportive of ECI, but he was not able to tell me who they were (for obvious reasons). He later called them bigger names than Dr. Woudstra."

"As to Dr. Marten Woudstra theologically, he was once the OT Professor at Calvin Seminary, the college of the Christian Reformation Church (Dutch Calvinistic). Over 70% of this denomination's churches now use the NIV. Dr. Woudstra was considered very 'conservative' with Calvin Seminary. He wrote the Joshua Commentary in the New International Commentary on the Old Testament (Eerdmans), which was also contributed to by such illustrious 'evangelical' names as F.F. Bruce. "In 1973 the Christian Reform Church published their official position relative to homosexuality."

"There is currently discussion, debate and disagreement over the issue of homosexuality within the CRC as in wider Reform denominations. For instance, the CRC's sister denomination, the Reformed Church of the Netherlands, took the position in 1979 of actually approving homosexual behaviour within certain bounds. This is a more liberal position that the CRC has ever taken. Is it not incredible to think how far the CRC has traveled over the years when one considers some of the former teachers, professors, and presidents Calvin Seminary had, such as Harry Bultema, Herman Hoeksema, H.J. Kuiper, Louis Berkof and William Hendrikson, to name a few."

"In 1970, the CRC Synod appointed a six-man committee to study homosexuality. Its report was adopted by the same Synod in 1973. One of the six, Clarence Boomsma, was four times moderator if the CRC and pastor of two CRC churches. In fact Boomsma held the record for the longest pastorate in the CRC; 35 years in the CRC church in Grand Rapids, near the Calvin Seminary.

I called Clarence Boomsma on the phone in October 1997, and had a long talk about Dr. Woudstra since he had known him for many years and had been his friend. HE TOLD ME THAT DR. WOUDSTRA ASSISTED IN WRITING THE REPORT ON HOMOSEXUALITY. I have a copy of the complete reports in my office. It takes a compromised 'middle line' between the biblical anti-homosexuality absolute, and the Reformed Church of the Netherlands liberal acceptance of homosexual behaviour within certain bounds."

"Let me quote a few lines from the report (Report 42, Art. 53, 1973): 'In fact, its [homosexuality] origin is so unclear as to be finally a mystery' (page 613) 'As the cause of homosexuality is uncertain, so is the possibility of correcting it' (page 614) 'Responsibility and the possibility of personal guilt for the homosexual arises at the point where he must decide what he will do with his sexuality. It is here that the Christian homosexual must ask what God's will is for him in the same way as the Christian heterosexual must ask what he must do in obedience to God with his sex drive' (page 616) [Note here the clever but wrong comparison being drawn. For a man to desire sexual relations with a woman is not wrong within the marriage relationship. However, for a man to desire sexual relations with another man is always wrong in all circumstances]. From this story [Genesis 19, Sodom & Gomorrah] read as an isolated incident we cannot conclude however that homosexualism is here condemned (page 617). [Note that this report took the position that a person may be a homosexual by birth (homosexualism) due to the fallen and irregular nature of humanity, but should not

practice homosexual acts (homosexuality)!] 'In how far the prohi-
bition of homosexualism [in Lev 18:21 & 20:13] is binding on us
is therefore a question that remains' (619). 'It has been suggested
that the use of these words [malakoi and arsenokoitai in 1 Cor 6:9-
10] stresses the activity rather than the condition of homosexuality' (page 619) "[Note this vital belief of Dr. Woudstra. This is the
reasoning behind the very clever translation in the NIV in 1 Cor
6 'homosexual offenders'. Thus the NIV here allows a person to be
a homosexual, as long as they don't offend.] The report refers constantly to the 'Christian homosexual', and urges that he 'deserves
the same acceptance, recognition, compassion and help that is given
to any person' (page 626). Since the report urges a fully functional
place in the church for 'Christian homosexuals' is it any wonder
that, according to Boomsma, the CRC has currently (1997) one
openly 'celibate' homosexual minister who has 'come out'."

"All through the report one is struck with similarities it bears
to the views of Virginia Mollenkott. Even the title of her book, 'Is
The Homosexual My Neighbour?' finds an echo on page 631 of the
CRC's Homosexuality Committee's 1973 report where paragraph
2 begins 'Love for the homosexual neighbour...' The 1973 report
advised homosexual ministers to seek pastoral and psychological
help to cope with their desires, but stopped short of condoning
homosexual practice. Boomsma felt that although the CRC should
understand and 'sympathise' (page 630) with the struggle homosexuals faced, for which they may bear minimal responsibility (page
631), it could not make an exception and allow such people to
engage in 'homosexual activity' that is wrong. This is still the view
of the CRC in general."

"Taking the scriptural principle of two witnesses, I will now
add the comments of Clarence Boomsma regarding the sexuality
of his friend Dr. Woudstra, the chairman of the NIV Old Testament Committee. Boomsma made the following statement to me
on the phone on 25th October 1997; I wrote it down verbatim: 'It is
generally believed among [Christian Reformed Church and Calvin
Seminary] that Dr. Woudstra was a homosexual.' I asked Boomsma
if Dr. Woudstra was an 'active' homosexual. Although he knew Dr.
Woudstra's views on homosexuality very well and holds in his possession a written dissertation by Dr. Woudstra on the subject, he

did not feel free to comment on its contents. However, he did tell me about a '[homosexual] incident' in Dr. Woudstra's career in which his professorship was at stake. Woudstra survived and was not fired from the Seminary. "Boomsma also spoke of Dr. Woudstra's frequent trips to New York 'which like all large cities has a large homosexual population.' On his return Woudstra would tell Boomsma how much he enjoyed the 'plays' in New York. I asked were these 'gay plays.' Boomsma would only say that New York has a large gay culture and is dotted with gay bars, and it was his impression that his friend, Dr. Woudstra, took part in this side of New York's social scene."

Michael Penfold goes onto say that in his opinion the above research "has a direct bearing on how the NIV treats homosexuality." It is a fact that "sodomy" and "sodomites" are specific words that describe specific acts and people who willingly perform such acts, and the NIV has no equivalent words rendered in their absence.

Below are two such examples:

Deuteronomy 23:17; (KJV) "There shall be no whore of the daughters of Israel, nor a <u>sodomite</u> of the sons of Israel."

Deuteronomy 23:17; (NIV) "No Israelite man or woman is to become a shrine prostitute."

1 Kings 14:24; (KJV) "And there were also <u>sodomites</u> in the land: and they did according to all the abominations of the nations which the LORD cast out before the children of Israel."

1 Kings 14:24; (NIV) "There were even male shrine prostitutes in the land; the people engaged in all the detestable practices of the nations the LORD had driven out before the Israelites."

I was in total disbelief when I first read through Virginia Mollenkott's statement and her apparently oblivious attitude to the motives of supporters and representatives of the NIV who had attempted to distance her from the project. She seemed more concerned in retaining the credit for her input than about having worked on a document that fundamentally opposes the particular lifestyle that she willingly maintained throughout the duration of her involvement. I got the sense that she views her work on the NIV as equal to editing any other academic manuscript or book in her career. The fact that millions of people across the world read the Bible and attempt to live their lives accordingly on the promise of eternal salvation, with one of the provisos being not to participate in homosexuality, has not seemed to sink in or concerned her in any way even years down the track. In my opinion this adds another reason for her unsuitability for the task. I also found the use of the term "Christian homosexual" as perplexing as referring to someone as a "Jewish Nazi." If it is completely impossible to walk in righteousness whilst leading a homosexual lifestyle, how much more inappropriate is it to become involved in the consultation process of a book that so dogmatically opposes such a concept. However, it must be said that the Scriptures hold homosexuality (sodomy) and fornication (those who practice sexual relations outside of marriage) as equally damaging acts of sin. Neither road is less spiritually destructive than the other.

Homosexuals and fornicators in general should be allowed an opportunity to hear a Sermon. Churches are understood to be accessible domains for this opportunity. But accepting sinners within a congregation to hear a teaching was never initially encouraged. In fact the act of welcoming sinners by the droves into synagogues is the main reason that these places of worship now resemble Babylonian mystery cults. The Scriptures say that "the word" was primarily taught (to unbelievers) from "house to house" *(Acts 2:46, 5:42)*, on temple steps and in open areas and nearly everywhere else accept Synagogues. Only a fully repentant individual who has turned away from former wrong doings such as fornication can dwell among and participate legitimately in the activities of a congregation. Michael Penfold concludes his article with a resounding quote from *Matthew 7:17; "A corrupt tree bringeth forth evil fruit."* Indeed.

Switch Title – Switch Character

There is a very interesting alteration to *Isaiah 14:12* in the NIV that upon serious study causes all sorts of problems. Firstly lets look at the verse as it appears in the KJV, paying special attention to the underlined words. *Isaiah 14:12; "How art thou fallen from heaven, O Lucifer, son of the morning! How art thou cut down to the ground, which didst weaken the nations!"* And elsewhere in *Revelation 22:16* we read: *"I Jesus, have sent my angel to give you this testimony for the churches. I am the root and the offspring of David, and the bright Morning Star.*" Notice Jesus is referring to himself as "Son of the Morning Star," which is similar to Lucifer's title, "son of the morning." So we have:

"Jesus" – "Son of the Morning Star"
"Lucifer" – "son of the morning"

Also in *2 Peter 1:19* and *Revelations 2:28* Jesus is also referred to as the "morning star." Bearing this in mind, a close inspection of how the NIV tackles a verse in Isaiah becomes extremely interesting. *Isaiah 14:12a; "How you are fallen from heaven, O morning star, son of the dawn!"* Now have a look at how the KJV handles the same verse. *Isaiah 14:12a; "How art thou fallen from heaven, O Lucifer, son of the morning!"* The NIV drops the name "Lucifer" and adds, "star," which reverses the meaning. We now have Jesus in the place of Lucifer.

For those of you that have just looked inside your copy of Webster's dictionary and are preparing me a letter of complaint because it says that Lucifer is the morning star, halt! Most good pre-1970's encyclopedias will correctly contain no such meaning. In fact what they will say is that Lucifer was the name given to the planet Venus by ancient astronomers. It is a Latin name meaning "light bearer" and though it will sometimes appear as "morning star," Venus is not a star at all; it is a planet that reflects the light of the sun.

The Verdict

As you can see once the NIV goes under the microscope it has trouble even standing up as a creditable document let alone a contender as a superior translation. But it is important to point out that comparing these two versions is not entirely fair either, due to the fact that the KJV had the benefit of sweeping in on the transforming winds of a new technology known as printing in an age where youngsters learned to read from the pages of the only book their families owned. For many years after its release it was the only English translation of a Bible available and many people grew up knowing countless Bible passages by heart as a consequence. Alister McGrath, author of *In the Beginning, The Story of The King James*

Bible points out that, "Without the King James Bible, there would have been no *Paradise Lost*, no *Pilgrim's Progress*, no *Handel's Messiah*, no Negro spirituals, and no *Gettysburg Address*."

So where does a discerning believer turn, to get a good Bible?

Is the KJV as good as it gets for the English speaking Westerner who wishes to study the Scriptures? The answer is no.

Restoration Scriptures

In recent times there has been a steady stream of people that have emerged from various Messianic and Christian fringe groups who have done extensive research in various biblical related fields. New discoveries and breakthroughs in the areas of archaeology, technology and Biblical Hebrew and Greek languages have led to a vast increase in knowledge. This knowledge has led to the appearance of various Bible publications that claim to have restored aspects of the Scriptures that have been hidden from the English-speaking world for centuries. The secular and mainstream Christian communities have largely ignored this claim and where possible debunked these assertions in reactionary publications or websites. Nonetheless these editions are beginning to gain unprecedented recognition by many Hebrew scholars. These works display a meticulous, thorough and honest presentation that unapologetically goes back to the roots of Hebraic thought. While the new believer may find these volumes difficult to read through at first, due to the heavy appearance of Hebrew words and names, they are refreshingly devoid of the Greco-Roman replacement language that saturates the Bibles most of us have grown up with. A principle aspect that continues to gain my admiration for these Bibles is their humility, which is displayed in the preface to an edition called, *The Scriptures* where it states: "We stand in awe and fear before the Most High, knowing that every word rendered in this version, *The Scriptures*, shall be accounted for. Much is going to be required from those to whom much has given *(Luke 12:48)*...we do not offer our labours to the public as the "last word" on these matters, and welcome feedback and useful input from any who have insight or information relevant to the improvement of this translation."

The restoration works feature a number of characteristics that set them apart from the common Bible. The most obvious feature is the departure away from the tradition of substituting the name of the Father and the Son with names of gentile pagan gods. Instead of reading the terms "Lord," "God" or the name "Jesus," the Hebrew characters that bear the title "Elohim" and the names "YHWH" and "Yahushua" appear in their rightful stead. Due to the immensity of the controversial pagan name issue I will delve into this subject with more detail in the following chapter. In addition the much loved terms "cross" and "holy," stemming from pagan origin, are replaced by the more accurate English translation "execution stake" and "set apart." Another feature is that the translations do not blindly follow a Greek or the Aramaic text exclusively, which is a practice that usually sacrifices context.

No Scripture is deleted from the Restoration or Sacred name Bibles that was not part of the first century texts. The missing texts as indicated by the "LXX," "Dead Sea Scrolls" and "Brit Chadasha" are completely restored. Another noteworthy characteristic is the retaining of what is known as the "the two house message." Admittedly a concept that I was not initially familiar with is perhaps one of the most central themes contained in the Scriptures. That is YHWH's (God's) convent promise to restore the house of Ephraim and the house of Judah *(Ezekiel 37)* by re-uniting the 12 tribes of Israel, the majority of which are currently dispersed throughout the gentile nations.

Another helpful aspect of these volumes is easy-to-find contact details of the editors and those directly responsible for the works. *The Restoration Scriptures – Sacred Name Edition* thoughtfully provides a bibliography, which alone is a concept foreign to most other Bibles.

The Hebrew Roots Version Scriptures (HRV), by James S. Trimm is a truly unique rendering, because it claims to be entirely translated out of the original Hebrew and Aramaic scripts. It is composed of a revised translation from the Tanak (Old Testament) portion of the JPS 1917 version and is combined with a literal translation of the Hebrew and Aramaic books that make up the Brit Chadasha (New Testament). In this volume's extensive introduction there are clear examples presented that show how Hebrew words were irregularly mistranslated when rendered into Greek and how this has carried through into English. Verses I'd been familiar with for years transformed before my very eyes like this one:

Matthew 19:24; "...*it is easier for a camel to go through the eye of a needle than for a rich man to enter in the Kingdom of God.*" – The word "camel" in the Aramaic manuscripts translated as "camel" can also mean "large rope." Clearly the better translation is "large rope."

There is also an impressively long list of early church fathers that unanimously support a Hebrew origin of the majority of New Testament books, such as:

"Clement of Alexandria (150 – 212 C.E.) 'In the work called *Hypotyposes,* to sum up the matter briefly he [Clement of Alexandria] has given us abridged accounts of all the canonical Scriptures...the Epistle to the Hebrews he asserts was written by Paul, to the Hebrews, in the Hebrew tongue; but it was carefully translated by Luke, and published among the Greeks.' – Clement of Alexandria; Hypotyposes; referred to by Eusebius in *Eccl. Hist.* 6:14:2"

Recommended Versions:

The Scriptures – (1998) Institute for Scripture Research – South Africa Web Page: **http://www.messianic.co.za**

Restoration Scriptures – (2005) True Name Edition Study Bible (Second Edition) Your Arms to Yisrael Publishing **www.yourarmstoisrael.org**

The Hebraic Roots Version Scriptures – (2004) The Society for the Advancement of Nazarene Judaism **http://www.nazarene.net**

Chapter Fourteen

Tongue Tired

"For then I will restore to the peoples a pure language, That they may call on the name of the Lord (YHWH), To serve Him with one accord." – Zephaniah 3:9

THE STUDY OF VERBAL and written language is a truly fascinating subject. Few people had such devotion for ancient languages as linguist and popular author, J. R. R. Tolkien, whose vast knowledge and love for real languages formed the basis for many different dialects in his books, which added a unique richness and believability to the characters in his *Lord of the Rings* epic. It should come as no surprise to note that the most popular fantasy authors are those who borrow heavily from reality. Yet in the real world, the complexity, variety, and beauty of language is often overlooked or taken for granted by many people today. As I have already touched on, the diversity of languages worldwide is disappearing at an alarming rate, until eventually, like at the time of the Tower of Babel, one language will stand victorious.

Firstly, what is language? Common dictionaries describe it as: "Communication by voice in the distinctly human manner, using arbitrary auditory symbols in conventional ways with conventional meanings." Other sources also add:

∞ A system of words used in a particular discipline – *WordNet*

∞ The code we all use to express ourselves and communicate to others – *Speech & Language Therapy Glossary of Terms*

∞ A set of (finite or infinite) sentences, each finite in length and constructed out of a finite set of elements – *Noam Chomsky*

Language is a beautiful tool, now so commonly misused, abused and mangled as it hurtles, like everything else, towards the stripping down process of the New Age. According to an *Associated Press* article by linguist, Darlene Superville, languages are "...dying at an alarming rate..." 83 year old Alaskan, Marie Smith is one of the last to be able to speak the native 'Eyak' language:

"'It's horrible to be alone,' she told The Associated Press on Monday. 'I have a lot of friends. I have all kinds of children, yet I have no one to speak to' in Eyak. Eyak isn't the only language with a grim future. Among the world's 6,800 tongues, HALF TO 90 PERCENT COULD BECOME EXTINCT BY THE END OF THE CENTURY, linguists predict. One reason is that half of all languages are spoken by fewer than 2,500 people each, according to the Worldwatch Institute, a private organization that monitors global trends. Languages need at least 100,000 speakers to survive the ages, says UNESCO, the United Nations Educational, Scientific and Cultural Organization. War and genocide, fatal natural disasters, the adoption of more dominant languages such as Chinese and Russian, and GOVERNMENT BANS ON LANGUAGE also contribute to their demise."

And in another article, written by Michael S. James, which appeared in *ABC News Online*, we read:

"In the United States, fewer than 150 Native American languages out of hundreds that once existed remain, according to UNESCO. And every single one is in some jeopardy, as are hundreds of other native languages in Canada, Mexico, and Central and South America. The same is true for languages in locations as far-flung as Africa, Scandinavia, Siberia and Taiwan. In Australia, for example, the Jiwarli language's last native speaker died in 1976, according to Peter K. Austin, a professor at the University of Melbourne. In fact, after decades of government suppression into the

1970s, dozens of Australian Aboriginal languages are just about finished, according to UNESCO."

Mr. Kiplangat Cheruiyot, National Coordinator of the *Centre for Endangered Languages* (CEL) in Kenya shares the same view:

"16 out of Kenya's 42 languages are at serious risk of disappearing...The fear being expressed today is that some of these languages, in view of their degrees of adulteration or outright abandonment, may not live to see the 22nd century. In fact, it is estimated that only ten percent of the present languages in the world will survive. THE FEAR IS THAT OF A HOMOGENOUS WORLD, WHERE EVERYBODY SPEAKS THE SAME LANGUAGE, WEARS THE SAME STANDARD CLOTHES, AND THINKS THE SAME STANDARD THOUGHTS."

G. Aaron Broadwell, a linguist at the State University of New York at Albany also comments:

"'ALL THE EVIDENCE THAT WE HAVE SEEMS TO SUGGEST THAT THE RATE OF LANGUAGE EXTINCTION IS ACCELERATING," said Broadwell, WHO BLAMES GLOBALIZATION.' All the people who were living in the corners of the world sort of isolated from the nation-states are now in contact with the rest of the world. As contact increases, it becomes harder for people to get along WITHOUT LEARNING AND DEALING EXTENSIVELY IN THE LANGUAGE AND ECONOMY OF THE DOMINANT CULTURE."

The Monster That Ate My Language

While languages drop like flies all over the world, one seems to keep swallowing them up, literally. Though dominated by Greek and Latin, English borrows shamelessly from nearly every other language to a greater or lesser degree. Many people I speak to on the subject of the English language are quick to boastfully remind me that it is an ever-changing dialect that undergoes shifts in meanings and additions at an ever-growing and expanding rate. One thing that astounds me is the notion that this is actually a positive concept. Continual evolution and expansion of a dialect suggests weaknesses and inadequacies in its previous forms, as this process of adaptation moves it to a point of increased potential. The result is a desire for accuracy and speed of delivery at the expense of aesthetic beauty. An obvious weakness in a language that undergoes such change becomes apparent in the following illustration: A man is isolated for an extended period of time due to serving a prison term and is eventually granted permission to return to his native speaking environment. He sets out from the prison gates and crosses a busy main road without looking. An old street buddy waiting faithfully to pick him up calls out for him to stop as a large truck roars towards him. The phrase his friend uses to warn him is a relatively new street slang term for "stop." The ex-inmate is completely unfamiliar with the term and thinks it is just another form of greeting. There the story chillingly ends.

A simple example of a changed meaning in a term is the use of the word "gay" becoming associated with "homosexual" and thereby losing its association with the word "happy." The elderly in particular struggle with words due to popular slang, combined word meanings and new industry related names. New terms and phrases are often deliberately hybridised to veil truths for advertising purposes and used for entrapping consumers into various ongoing repayment schemes.

The Incredible Shrinking Word

Mobile phone text messaging has pushed language into a new arena of abbreviation and acronym that sees users making up the rules as they go along. Only time will tell if this new ultra compact form of word downsizing leaves further scarring on an already battered and bruised dialect. The rapid rate of technological advancement has been a major factor in the increase of an absolute barrage of words such as "Email," "cyberspace," and "internet" to name a few. One particular friend commented by saying, "So what if a language changes. Adaptation is a positive characteristic and it makes communication more efficient." While that point may be true in the current technologically advanced communications age that we live in, this characteristic can cause confusion and alienation to isolated communities and an aging population as they become unable to make sense of a language that is constantly guided by cheap trends and fads. This person went on to add, "So what if all the other languages are dying out, as long as we've got one that does the job." My answer to his last statement was in the form of a demonstration. I held aloft an intricately designed glass, full of water in one hand, and a plastic cup, full of water in the other and said, "Imagine if you had just invited the girl of your dreams over to your house and she asked for a glass of water. Which cup would you give her to drink out of?" He naturally said, "the glass." I asked why, at which he replied, "because it looks better." "Precisely," I concluded. Both of the things I held up did the same job. They carried water, yet the glass was more beautiful. The same can be said for a language. While it serves a core purpose of verbal communication, it should not have to sacrifice its original beauty to keep pace with ever-accelerating social and economic pressures. If bankers, brokers, and businessmen want to scale it down, then that version should remain on Wall St. in the same way soldiers recognise a form of communication that respectfully remains on the battlefield.

The Language of Mathematics

One thing often overlooked in topics of this nature is the universal language of mathematics. J.P. Changeux and A. Connes, in their study of *Conversations on Mind, Matter and Mathematics*, said: "Mathematical language is plainly an authentic language. But is it therefore the *only* authentic language?' (Changeux) "It is unquestionably the only *universal* language." (Connes)

The very core characteristic of mathematics, an aspect that drove me up the wall at school, is that it works on the basis of being absolute, and this is the very thing that has maintained it as a constant companion to man throughout history. However, its use throughout history has been largely dependant on the apparatus of the linguistics used to wield it.

In ancient times, Chinese mathematics, referred to as the "art of calculation" (suan chu), served both practical and spiritual uses, covering a wide range of subjects from religion and astronomy to water control and administration.

The great Pyramid of Giza is a mathematical wonder that displays many aspects of mathematics that, by secular historical reckoning, were not officially discovered until centuries later. Each block of this Pyramid was tailored from the beginning to fit exactly into a 2.5 million piece, 481 foot high, 90 million cubic foot, 13 billion pound, amazingly accurate puzzle that contains two narrow shafts that point directly to the polar stars.

The Origin of English

What is English? Where did it come from, and is it indeed going to be the final language of mankind? The origin of English can be accurately traced as far back as the 5th Century AD, spawned from three Germanic tribes, which moved into the British Isles. The inhabitants of Britain had previously spoken Celtic and most of the users of that tongue pushed up into Wales, Cornwall, and Scotland. The "Angles," one of the Germanic tribes, spoke "Englisc," which is where English is derived. It can be then somewhat less accurately traced from these "Teutonic" tongues to "Indo-Aryan" languages of the Middle East and beyond. The English spoken today is very different to the old English "Anglo-Saxon" dialect and is predominantly made up of pagan words. This is not to imply that speaking this language is sinful. One should bear in mind that even Japanese, Chinese, Arabic (from its predecessor Aramaic) and many other languages are also predominantly pagan.[17] While God was the author of the countless languages given to mankind at Babel, we have to understand that the pagan component of them came about by the influence of "sons of God" (fallen angels) who later supplanted these human languages with corruptible words. This administering of a vast array of languages at Babel was a punishment to bring mankind into submission. God is not the author of pagan languages, because He cannot create languages that oppose His own character. The substitution of names and key words of these many linguistic variations of a Set-Apart (Holy) dialect with words that originate from names of fallen angels are essentially what characterise pagan languages. After the Babylonian captivity of Israel, even Hebrew dialects became partially corrupted, but it is the actual verbal utterance of words, which identify fallen members of the heavenly host that is the issue.

---

17   That is languages, which are predominantly made up of the transliterated names of pagan deities.

I am not saying we should discard English; on the contrary, we should work with what we have been given and simply be aware of these things. If we find names that, once their meaning has been established through careful research and prayer, do not glorify God, we then become free to remove them. With the speed and convenience of the Internet we can find clean transliterations and return them to their rightful place with minimal legwork. We should not do this for any legalistic reason except for the love of God.

"Lord God" or "Baal Gwad?"

Let's look at an example of this pagan influence on our language by examining a critical word used throughout Christendom. According to the *Encyclopedia Americana (1945 Edition)*, the term "God" that I have used so frequently in this book originates from the following source: "Common Teutonic word for a personal object of religious worship, formerly applicable to superhuman beings of heathen myth, on conversion to Teutonic races to Christianity, term was applied to Supreme Being." On further investigation we can find that it comes from the German word "Gott," which comes from the word "Guth" and is directly related to "Taurus the Bull." You'll find this revelation in *The Encyclopedia Britannica (eleventh edition)*. According to *The New English Dictionary* it can be found to have two Aryan roots, both written as "gheu," but one of which means "to invoke," the other "to pour," both having an association with religious invocation or of religious worship by sacrifice. Yet further investigation into this word's origin surfaces an even more alarming association. The *Gesenius Hebrew Chaldee Lexicon* of the Old Testament shamelessly equates "God" as the pagan deity of the Canaanites when it states; "(Lord God) was the divinity of fortune, worshipped by the Babylonians and by the Jews exiled among them; elsewhere called Baal." *The Oxford English Dictionary* supports this notion when it describes the ancient Babylonian deity "Baal Gawd," as appears in *Joshua 11:17, 12:7* and *13:5* as later finding its way into the idol worship of heathen Teutonic tribes. Even Christian scholars will admit that "Baal" means "Lord," but fail to acknowledge or draw attention to the fact that "Gawd" means, "God." This revelation is mind blowing when we consider the warning in *Joshua 23:7b; "You shall not make mention of the name of their gods, nor cause anyone to swear by them..."* If this is true, not only are legions of people verbalising the name of a pagan god, but are also unwittingly substituting the title of the Most High with it.

At this point it is important to establish that despite my analysis of the NIV's frequent neglect in the use of the terms "God" and "Jesus" discussed in Chapter 13, it was not my intention to endorse the KJV or any other Bible that may carry these terms in place of the NIV. I examined this issue to merely expose a phase in the watering down process of Scripture. My research has shown that we can travel much further down the timeline of deconstructed Scripture than the NIV.

When the word "God" is used in a responsible manner it is generally understood to be the name of the Almighty Creator. This is fine if one does not know the history of this word. But if someone is very familiar with Scripture and understands the word's true origin and also maintains that God is a valid form of addressing Him, I will demonstrate that they are ignoring a core biblical principle. This might sound a bit hard line, but if we again examine Scripture and see what the Father requires, it becomes clearer. Scripture specifically instructs an avoidance of speaking aloud the names of other gods. *Exodus 23:13; "And in all that I have said to you, be circumspect and make no mention of the name of other gods, nor let it be heard on your mouth."* Now in this age such a task alone seems near impossible, with days of the week, models of cars and even the very clothing we wear bearing the names of pagan gods. We are living in an age where there are so many things within our environment that, when examined closely, are a complete mockery to the Creator of the Universe. This climate has come about by the introduction of two primary factors that commenced hundreds of generations ago. One is the slow and gradual replacement of His Name and the second is the failure to observe the distinct command to avoid the verbal use of the names of others gods. His Name has faded into obscurity by the implementation of a strict ruling that it was too sacred to utter or even write down in spite of the biblical requirement to verbally call on it. The logic in this move is obvious when I use the following example. If I was in an ongoing war with someone and I knew that if they simply called a certain name they would always prevail over me, I would seriously explore the option of having them forget that name or at the very least confuse the name by adding another one or two into the mix. The concept of God's name and the logical alternatives of this title will be examined shortly. For now let's get back to the subject of English.

Mandarin and English at the Head of the Pack

Now we know that English is a Germanic offshoot of Indo-European dialects, we should also know that it is at present the second most used language in the world. The first is the Chinese dialect Mandarin. Be that as it may, its usage is predominantly restricted to China and other localised areas whereas English is spread across the globe. It is the language of the Asian trade group (ASEAN), the working language of 98% of German research physicists and 83% of German research chemists. It is the official language of the European Central Bank, even though the bank is in Frankfurt and neither Britain nor any other predominantly English-speaking country is a member of the European Monetary Union. It is the language in which black parents in South Africa overwhelmingly desire their children to be educated. It is the official language and co-official language of over 45 countries and spoken regularly in countries where it has no official status. I watch quite a few Indian Bollywood films with my wife and am amazed at how English words often pop up in Punjabi and Hindi languages. Other contenders in high language use are French with 27 countries, Spanish with 20 countries, and Arabic with 17 counties. Half of all business deals done worldwide are conducted in English, two thirds of all scientific pages are written in English, and 70% of all postage is written and addressed in English. Most international tourism and aviation is also conducted in…you guessed it, English. It enjoys an estimated 300 million users, 300 million who use it as a second language, and a further 100 million people are foreign to it.

There is a story I heard once about a German airline pilot who complained about having to speak English on his radio when approaching a runway in his home country. Unknown to him the channel he was communicating on was open and a pilot from an English airline company responded by saying, "It's because Germany lost the war."

So What if More People Speak Fewer Languages?

Apart from coming to terms with the sentimental loss of a language poised on the edge of extinction, it should be painfully clear that human beings can not only still survive with diminished dialects, but will also inevitably experience better mutual understanding across a broader spectrum of people as the obstacle of the language barrier is removed. But are the drawbacks worth this heartwarming convenience?

The pursuit of efficiency is a vicious and merciless quest. The powers that be recognise that the earth 's diverse resources can be extracted and traded with greater ease if every nation, with something to sell, used the same language. Our greatest cities scattered all over the world are but one interconnected organism as they function in a cohesive worldwide economy. If something goes badly in one area its repercussions are felt like a domino effect elsewhere. Whether we believe civilisation has evolved in a perfect linier fashion or not, it is worth noting that our level of current technological advancement has only been with us on Earth for only a fraction of the time against the entirety of man's existence. So much of our time on this planet has been devoid of the things we now take for granted, things that have appeared in just over the last fifty-odd years. Pick up a ruler if you have one laying around. Imagine that the length of that ruler signifies the length of our existence on earth, whether or not you believe its been 3,000,000 years or 7,000 years. Now imagine a measurement of the duration of that time we have used telephones. It would probably be a little less than a millimeter and even then that would be an exaggeration.

The end result of this emergence into a new era of advancement has never been so clearly defined in any other book than the Bible. The following verses appear chillingly prophetic in the light of today's current trends when we read *Genesis 11:1; "Now* *the whole earth had <u>one language and one speech</u>."* And *4 "And they said, "Come, let us <u>build ourselves a city</u>, and tower whose top is in the heavens (sky); let us <u>make a name for ourselves</u>, lest we be scattered abroad over the face of the whole earth."*

You can take your pick from a host of presidential speeches proclaiming our achievements and future potentials with God neatly excluded from the equation. The following is a favourite quote of mine and shows a blatant twisting of the Scriptures.

"As the Scriptures says, our eyes have not yet seen, nor our ears heard, nor minds imagined what WE CAN BUILD...WE CAN DO IT." – From Bill Clinton's speech at a Democrat Party National Convention in New York City.

YHWH (God) recognises, only too well, our fatal potential without Him at the helm as we read in *Genesis 11:6; "And the Lord said, 'Indeed the people are one and they all have one language, and this is what they begin to do; <u>now nothing that they propose to do will be withheld from them.</u>'"*

We have looked at the concept of languages in general and how they may eventually merge into a global economic dialect, but it is important to also examine the use of language within a theological setting and hopefully wrap up some of my previous more controversial implications.

Speaking in Tongues

While there are many doctrines within the Christian community that continue to divide scholars, theologians and denominations alike, the act of speaking in tongues has remained one such practice that is either overly encouraged or overly discouraged in the open assemblies of various churches.

This phenomenon of speaking in tongues is predominantly practiced in the Pentecostal movement, the Shackers and Quackers, and also amongst the Mormon faith. These groups to varying degrees perceive it as a language of angels. It takes two forms, that of "glossolalia," and "xenolalia," the later of which is the act of speaking in languages unknown to the occupant. Both these forms of speaking in tongues appear in Scripture.

Many charismatic churches adopt the belief that the receiving of the Set-Apart (Holy) Spirit will cause the occupant to speak in tongues, that is "glossolalia," which is the form of tongues that is a completely unrecognisable speech. This form can basically sound like anything, and in the initial phase is accompanied with a type of religious ecstasy, often causing the occupant to laugh, cry, and in some cases appear drunk. This state is aptly referred to as being drunk on the Spirit, which is a phrase that I am less than comfortable with. The principle verse that supports this view of lapsing into "glossolalia" tongues is found in *Acts 19:6; "And when Paul had laid hands on them, the Holy Spirit came upon them, and they spoke with tongues and prophesied."* The point to note in the above instance of speaking in tongues, is that it is accompanied by prophecy, an act by its very nature not only requires the speaker to be understood, but to speak of something to do with a future event. Noting the observance of tongues as confirmation of the Set-Apart Spirit by a recipient as a rule of thumb is dangerous, if by no other reason than the fact that speech can be emulated knowingly or unknowingly.

One evening after being encouraged to speak in tongues by a friend, I found myself driving home alone and I eventually decided to have a go. What I can best describe as gibberish in the form of repetitive words and open-ended vowels began to pour out of my mouth. I tried to alter my accent a little to more accurately mimic the sounds I had often heard whilst in group prayer. I noticed it became easier the more I completely lost control of my speech (despite the principle of losing mental or bodily control being discouraged in Scripture) and I felt a sense of release come over me from the verbal discharge. I began to realise a perceived value of such an act in terms of a type of therapy, yet such a purpose is not outlined in the Bible. It felt like the sounds that were being made and exclaimed could have been manipulated easily be an outside force. I was then reminded of having read somewhere that in the Middle Ages Christians saw it as a sign of heresy or possession of demons. From then on I released that speaking in tongues is not something you have a go at, but receive. I do believe that speaking in tongues does occur with the receiving of the Set-Apart Spirit. Yet I do not believe that it <u>always</u> occurs.

Now let's look at another incident in Scripture of an administering of the Set-Apart Spirit and see if speaking in tongues occurs. *1 Samuel 10:10; "When they came there to the hill, there was a group of prophets to meet him; then the Spirit of God came upon him; and he prophesied among them."* With so much emphasis on the Set-Apart Spirit's arrival at Pentecost in *Acts 2:1-4* of the New Testament, it is surprising to note that the above verse comes from the Old Testament and here again there is an act of prophecy after the Set-Apart Spirit manifests. In fact when the "glossolalia" type of tongue is uttered publicly in the Bible, there is always an accompaniment of prophecy. Many people I meet attest to the gift of tongues, which they usually utter in open meetings. Yet the gift of interpreting seems to be barren. I have yet to come across someone who claims an ability in it with the same conviction. A most unsettling incident that I experienced once occurred in a church where a woman opened in prayer and then said to the whole congregation; "now lets speak in tongues," at which point the entire place erupted in an avalanche of senseless babble. After a minute the place went silent and not one word of prophecy or interpretation proceeded. Not having the gift of tongues myself, I just sat during the outburst stupefied, unable to pray, and hopelessly listening to all the weird sounds. I couldn't help thinking that if I wandered in off the street with only a little knowledge about Christianity I would have run for the door. I have found praying with fellow Christians who feel compelled to verbally break into tongues during group prayer to be debilitating. Though I do not doubt for a moment their faith and sincerity, I do believe they should understand from studying the Bible that the Set-Apart Spirit's indwelling is never always strictly marked by speaking in tongues and its use should be as prevalent as interpreting and prophesying. Invariably this indecipherable language, which comes devoid of words of prophecy and absent of crucial interpretations distracts others who are communicating with YHWH. Biblically this "glossolalia" type of tongue was not a regular feature of prayer. When Jesus told the disciple how to pray he never mentioned that they would be struck by a compulsion to speak a heavenly language unknown to men whenever they engaged in such an act.

The over-emphasis on tongues was also a problem in the New Testament era. For if it was not so, Paul would not have included the topic in his letter to the congregations at Corinth. *1 Corinthians 14:6-9; "But now, brethren, if I come to you speaking with tongues, what shall I profit you unless I speak to you either by revelation, by knowledge, by prophesying, or by teaching? Even things without life, whether flute or harp, when they make a sound, unless they make a distinction in the sounds, how will it be known what is piped or played? For if the trumpet makes an uncertain sound, who will prepare for battle? So likewise you, unless you utter by the tongue words easy to understand, how will it be known what is spoken? For you will be speaking into the air."* Speaking in tongues without interpretation is not done for man, but for YHWH. I believe no one should be encouraged to have a go at speaking in tongues in the same way as having a go at riding a two-wheeled bike for the first time; to do so is missing the point. One should be encouraged to receive the Set-Apart Spirit and then this gift, if it is YHWH's will, may be added.

Veiled beneath the layers of modern translations exist other references to this subject that deserve mention here. In the earliest Greek version of the Scriptures, called the *Septuagint*, the "glossolalia" tongue *(Deuteronomy 18:10)* is likened to the pagan practices of witchcraft and sorcery. They read:

"Mantevomenos (manteuomeno V): "he who practices glossolalia" (changed to the more familiar "He who practices divination" in the French translation by Louis Segond);

"Mantian klidonizomenos" (manteian klhdonizomeno V): "he who interprets glossolalia" (changed to the more familiar "he who looks for omens" by L. Segond)

The Name of God

Since my initial disclosure of information under the subheading "Lord God" or "Baal Gawd?" you may have noticed the gradual appearance of the name YHWH as opposed to God when referring to the Husband of Israel. This segment will go into more detail as to why this is done and hopefully shed some more light on the issue.

The following subject has proved to be one of the most difficult ones to put down on paper in terms of maintaining clarity and
focus, as more than one can of worms was opened along the way
that required detailed explanation. But I feel it is one of the most
rewarding topics and deserves possibly more than one read-through
to grasp. The content is such that it can be easily written off as
heretical if just skimmed through and as such deserves a keen eye
with the reader's thinking cap firmly secured.

Consider the following verse as we look at the topic of God's
name. *Malachi 3:16; "Then those who feared the Lord spoke to one
another, and the Lord listened and heard them; So a book of remembrance was written for those who feared the Lord and who meditate
on His name."* The last part of this verse goes beyond describing
someone generally reflecting on God's goodness and specifies contemplation on His Name. Other versions say, "who esteem His
name," or "thought on His name." If names are truly a reflection of
a person's character, then a study into God's name is akin to a study
into His nature.

Calling the Good Guy the Bad Guy's Name

*"They are thinking of making my people forget my name by means of
their dreams that they keep relating to each other, just as their fathers
forgot my name by means of Ba'al." – Jeremiah 23:27 (NWT)*
Not much time passes when two individuals first meet and
become friends before each other's names are known. When we
usually make the acquaintance of people we address them as Sir or
Ma'am, or their family name until we are invited to call them by
their first name. To call someone by his or her given name is a sign
of knowing who that person is. If we do not know someone personally we are less inclined to use their first name in an encounter.
Luke 13:27 is extremely interesting if we are to keep this premise
in mind. Note carefully what this verse says: *"But He will say, 'I tell
you I do not know you, where you are from. Depart from Me, all you
workers of iniquity."* To love someone, you have to know them. It is
for this reason that the words, "I do not love you" is absent from the
above verse. We cannot love someone we do not know; yet there
are millions of Christians across the face of the globe that profess

to have a personal relationship with God and yet do not know, nor have felt compelled to use His Name or contemplate its meaning.

Two Names Working in Perfect Unity that Later Become One

There are many verses within modern Bibles that endorse calling on and asking things in "Jesus Christ's" name as opposed to the Father's Name. Jesus Christ, as I will examine later in this Chapter, replaced the name "Yahushua ha Moshiach," which means, "YHWH is our anointed saviour." The Christian belief that "Jesus" is the name above all names is supported in *Acts 4:12b*; *"...for there is no other name under heaven given among men by which we must be saved."* Yet seemingly in contrast Scripture also tells us that Yahushua came in his Father's Name. *John 5:43*; *"I have come in My Father's name and you do not receive Me; if another comes in his own name, him you will receive."* *John 17:12* again confirms this when the Son is praying to the Father; *"While I was with them in the world, I kept them in Your name."* Then he concludes this prayer in *John 17:26* by saying; *"And I have declared to them Your name, and will declare it, that the love with which You loved Me may be in them, and I in them."* Both the names of the Father and the Son seem to be emphasised. But which name is he to be acknowledged when we pray? The answer is found in the Messiah's instruction in *Matthew 6:9*; *"In this manner therefore pray: Our Father in Heaven, Hallowed be Your name."* Prayer should be directed to the Father and open with an acknowledgment to His Set-Apart (Holy) Name. In *John 14:14* he also says; *"If you ask anything in my name, I will do it."* From this we can confidently deduce that prayer is directed to the Father by opening in His Name and concluding in the character of His Son's name. The Father will not respond to those who accept His Son but deny Him (Christianity in general) and in contrast the Father will not respond to those who accept Him and yet deny His Son (Judaism in general). An example of this inseparable unity is found in the Son's name, "YAH-ushua." There is the heavenly part of the name and the earthly part. The Son also says in *Matthew 28:19*; *"Go therefore and make disciples of all nations, baptizing them in the name of the Father and of the Son and of the Holy Spirit."* Then in the new kingdom, as pointed out in *Zechariah 14:9* they will be acknowledged under the banner of one name: *"And the Lord shall be King over all the earth. In that day it shall be – 'The Lord is one,' And His name one."* As I have stressed elsewhere within this work, the oneness is in unity, as it is YHWH (God) who sits on the throne and the Son who sits at his right hand. Clearly the "Yahu" part of the name is important since without it, the name simply means "rescuer" or "saviour." Modern Bibles also deliberately hide the fact that Yahushua was not a unique name and was given to quite a few other biblical characters such as Isaiah, Joshua, and Jason, which are all derived from exactly the same Hebrew root. The reasoning behind this deception is to add a focal emphasis to the Son's modern equivalent name, "Jesus" and in turn take focus away from the Father's Name.

Sharing the Truth About the Word God

To effectively combat this dilemma, Christians have to be lovingly re-educated and new believers must be correctly informed. The sharing of any initial information to a receptive occupant must have a strong foundation and be completely based in truth. A person who has no church background and inquires willingly of spiritual matters should not be initially deceived about the name of the Father and the Son. This has often been denounced as a cause of some confusion. However to say one thing and then wait till a person matures to tell them something else echoes of level ascension exhibited in Freemasonry and other Esoteric societies. The new believer ought to be encouraged to make some sort of independent inquiry into basic Scriptural matters. On the flip side, sharing the importance of the true name of the Creator with the average Christian can be a slightly more complicated situation and a wider arc of sharing techniques may have to be explored. Ultimately if they are convinced by the truth, they will naturally make an effort to gradually refrain from replacing YHWH's righteous name with the title God when praising, preaching or engaged in private prayer. The sad fact is that churches are full of people ignorant of the very Scriptures that they profess to live by as they blindly sing, preach and praise "God" and a range of other names with a completely sincere yet misguided heart. In saying this I am not advocating that the reader immediately drop these terms from their vocabulary. But I do encourage that independent investigation into a range of sources regarding this issue be carried out at the next available opportunity. From there the reader can make an informed decision. If we completely ignore sharing the wonderful truth about the name of YHWH for the sake of avoiding trouble, we may find ourselves pleasing people over pleasing the Creator and inadvertently perpetuating a misconception, a kind of false status quo. Therefore I do encourage believers and non-believers alike who have ever prayed or sincerely searched for the truth to investigate for themselves and take up this challenge. Ultimately God and Jesus are not God's names anyway. One is a title and the other, as I will discuss, is an illegal translation of a not uncommon biblical name.

Elohim & God

This whole concept of a falling away of a pagan name and the restoration of an eternal heavenly name is evident in the following verse. *Hosea 2:16-17; "And it shall be, in that day,' Says the Lord, 'That you will call Me 'My Husband,' And no longer call Me 'My Master (Baal),' For I will take from her mouth the names of the Baals, and they shall be remembered by their name no more.'"* We should also note that the title "god" is used in reference to Satan in *2 Corinthians 4:4 "... whose minds the god of this age has blinded..."* Another verse that is heavy with the word God is *Deuteronomy 10:17; "For the Lord your God is God of gods and Lord of lords..."* I'm sure you would agree there's a lot of gods and lords being thrown around there. As I have briefly pointed out in Chapter One, god with a capital "G" usually signifies a replacement of the actual name of God, that is, YHWH or YHVH, which appears in the earliest Hebrew and Greek Manuscripts. This name was removed from the Scriptures long ago, because as I have pointed out, was falsely believed to be too sacred to utter. In Hebrew, *Deuteronomy 10:17* reads: *"Ki YHVH Eloheichem Heo Elohei he'elohim v'adonei ha'adonim..."* which is translated as: *"For YHVH your Elohim He Elohim of the elohim and Lord of lords."* Notice the words "Elohei" and "he'elohim." This is where we get the title ELOHIM that appears very sparingly in some modern Bible translations. Though this title has also been used by pagans as pointed out by some scholars who defend the use of the title God, its usage first originated among the Hebrews in reference to YHWH. So a more accurate form of the name would appear as YHWH ELOHIM rather than the more familiar but less accurate "Lord God." ELOHIM means "Mighty One of Oaths" (the HIM part being "Oaths"), "Excellency" or in some circles the family title of supreme beings. This "EL" appears at the ending of many Hebrew names such as ImmanuEL (EL with us) and MichaEL (who is like EL). I occasionally use the term Elohim as a title of the Father in private prayer and conversation, but never as a singular term because it does not refer to a particular being. I simply find this a more acceptable alternative to the English transliteration of the pagan deity, "Gawd," which is now commonly used as a title. Ultimately it all comes down to what you know. YHWH will not judge us on what we do not know, but what we do with the knowledge we have. Do not think for a moment however that an avenue to voluntarily remain in ignorance is an option. *Proverbs 18:2; "A fool has no delight in understanding, but expressing his own heart."* And *19:2 "Also it is not good for a soul to be without knowledge, and he sins who hastens with his feet."*

The Mystery of The Father and The Son

Before we delve deeper into the name of YHWH it is important to define who "God the Father" is and who "God the Son" is, as there are indeed two key figures that are at work here as hinted at earlier. For it is pointless to reveal names when one is still unsure whether to pray to the two as one or acknowledge both in a manner that shows two individuals working in perfect unity.

It has been my custom and also the custom of almost every Christian I have ever met to have a tendency to elevate the Son over the Father or to refer to them almost as if they are one being, that is to say one personality residing simultaneously in the two. On the surface, Scripture does support this baffling notion of the Father assuming an earthly form via His own Son. *Colossians 2:19:12* says, *"For in Him dwells all the fullness of the Godhead bodily; and you are complete in Him, who is the head of all principality and power."* Further supported by *John 2:19 "...Destroy this Temple, and in three days I will raise it up,"* Notice the Son uses the word "I" instead of my Father as he refers to himself raising himself from the dead and yet in stark contrast *Galatians 1:1* states the following: *...("not from men nor through man, but through Jesus Christ and God the Father who raised Him from the dead").* Then the ball bounces back again into the other court with the statement, *"I and My Father are one,"* in *John 10:30* that appears to seal the concept for legions of Christians of the one being residing in two forms. This oneness and the Son's referring to himself or his Father performing the same feat is simply an example of a perfect and flawless unity. They work and think alike, and to deal with one is to deal with the other. In many ways it is like the perfect marriage. To support this lets look at *John 17:11; "Now I am no longer in the world, but these are in the world, and I come to You. Holy Father, keep through Your name those whom You have given Me, that they may be one as We are."* Here the Son is requesting that his disciples share in this complete oneness. Many people struggle with this concept due to the divertive trinity principle, despite this explanation of the mystery of our Creator being totally absent from Scripture. Being "one" and being "the same" is actually different. To be one within the context of this teaching is to be of "one mind" and of "one intent." To be "the same" is to be a complete duplicate or an additional manifestation or extension of the first.

John 14:28 challenges this idea of the Father and the Son being a single entity when it says: *"...I am going to the Father, for My Father is greater than I."* Here the Son is plainly saying that all power comes from the Father. *John 14:12; "Most assuredly, I say to you, he who believes in me, the works that I do he will do also; and greater works than these he will do, because I go to My Father."* The interesting aspect of this verse is that the Messiah is describing future believers who may have the potential to exhibit miraculous works that far exceed his own. Surely this does not mean that those who believe will display greater works than YHWH Himself? Of course not. Many churches often dramatise the Son's miracle workings as though no one who believes will ever match them much less exceed them. They often present his miracle workings as if they were a defining characteristic of his uniqueness. I believe there are men who walk today that have performed magnificent feats in the name of Yahushua. There are many documented cases of people across the globe who have been raised from the dead. Interestingly most of the more dramatic incidences come from Third World countries. Sometimes it happens in a startling way with a patient waking in a morgue or in a completely obvious way with a flat line skipping back to life after defibrillation.

John 14:9 is often mistaken for being a verse that supports the Son as being the Father when it states: *"...He who has seen Me has seen the Father; so how can you say, 'Show us the Father?'"* In responding to Phillip's question, the Messiah does not simply say here, "I am the Father," and if we know the Hebrew mindset on the importance of outward appearances we immediately understand that he is speaking of the manner in which he conducts himself and that it is in perfect union with his Father. He is in effect a perfect representative of the Father. To no degree should we accept a perception that he is the Father in disguise. It is important to understand that the Hebrew thought differs considerably from the modern Western mindset, which is influenced by Greek philosophy. Eastern thought carries an emphasis on the function of things as opposed to an emphasis on mere identification or appearance. The problem here is if we make a judgment on someone's looks we can often be sorely disappointed, yet if we judge on someone's action we can be more confident in our conclusion as to his or her character.

When We Lost Our Father's Name

Have you ever stopped to wonder, when engaged in conversation on spiritual matters, why the God of the Bible is often referred to with a title, and His adversary, Satan is granted the privilege of a name? Not many people ever stop to think about this, having done it many years; some since Sunday school. Satan has many names that are always made readily available. One slightly lesser known name, "Beelzebub," actually comes from the Hebrew word, "BAAL-ZEBUL," which means "Lord of the Flies." After I found this out (which was not that difficult) it further cemented my resolve to abandon the use of the term "Lord." Though I have occasionally used the word "Lord" in this book to now, I will refrain when referring to YHWH from this point on and restore the title "Eloh" or "Elohim"(plural) where applicable, unless "Lord" appears in a quote or in a modern Bible translation.

No individual god can be gleaned by commencing the spelling of a term that defines a non-specific deity with a capital letter anymore than if one uses a capital "J" to single out a particular judge or magistrate. Ancient Hebrew never had capital letters or punctuation. The uses of capital letters in terms like "Lord," "God" and "Father" to indicate references to YHWH evolved over a period of time. During Yahushua's time the name of God was considered by the Pharisees to be too sacred to utter, let alone write, which led to subsequent translations of Scripture replacing it with the Hebrew word "Adoni." This word means "Lord" and appears as such in modern English translations. This practice of capitalisation has been utilised within this work out of respect and to retain a familiar presentation for those familiar with modern Bibles. Sadly we have adopted this methodology of transforming a title into a name over a long period of time. This is very alarming when we consider the depth of emphasis in the Scriptures that encourage us not to bring the Father's Name to nothing. So whenever one comes across the titles "Lord," "Father" and "God" in the Bible it more often than not was a location where the name of the Most High was exhibited. The absence of the name YHWH reaches figures of up to 7000 times in the Old Testament and 1000 times in the New Testament.

Evidence for a Hebrew Origin of The New Testament

Through careful research I have found that God's name is most correctly pronounced as "Yahweh" and written in English as YHWH. However, there is no firm consensus on the English spelling or exact pronunciation. The most dominant versions are YHVH, YHWH, YAHWEH, YAHWEH, and "Jehovah." It is absolutely crucial to add that there is a degree of personal preference involved, because the type of native language spoken by the user can have a bearing on which rendering is adopted.

The name is composed of four Hebrew letters. This is called a Tetragrammaton [Yod, He, Wod, He] or [Yud, hey, vav, hey]. In most contemporary Bibles the only remnants of it appear in the word "Halleluiah," which means, "Praise you Yah." I should emphasise that the English arrangement of this name is done primarily to achieve the right pronunciation.

Why is Hebrew so important? Hebrew is often referred to as "the holy (set-apart) tongue" or "the language of creation." It is the only language that does not carry exact names for human genitalia or sexual relations. The Hebrew word woman (ishah) was taken from man (ish) as is demonstrated in *Genesis 2:23*. Hebrew's root word meanings give deeper insights and validation to Scripture that no other language can bring. If time and a sufficient level of intellect permit, any attempt to become familiar with ancient Hebrew to better understand the Bible is to be encouraged. Respecting and understanding the Hebraic roots of the Scripture is invaluable because without tracing words back to their origin, the reader is forever left at the mercy of a Western interpretation.

In recent times some scholars have slowly awakened to the fact that the greater portion of the New Testament was not written in Aramaic but originally penned in Hebrew. Recent research discussed in the book, *Understanding the Difficult Words of Jesus*, by David Bivin and Roy Blizzard Jr. has revealed that the Hebrew language was very much alive and well at the time of the events recorded in The Book of Acts. The breadth of evidence put forward in this book is absolutely overwhelming. It examines many artifacts and literary documents written in Hebrew around the time of the first century. Most significantly are the conclusions drawn from the discovery of the Dead Sea Scrolls. The written contents of these carry a nine-to-one ratio of Hebrew to Aramaic. The scrolls contain 600 partial manuscripts of both Biblical and non-biblical text that are 1,000 years older than any manuscripts previously found. Abbe J.T. Milik, scholar, archaeologist and Polish priest, pointed out that, "The copper rolls and documents from the Second Revolt prove beyond any reasonable doubt that Mishnaic (Hebrew) was the normal language of the Judean population in the Roman Period." In addition, countless coins bearing Hebrew characters from the New Testament period have also been discovered as well as written accounts that exist from learned men of the third century. Post-Nicean Father, Epiphanius, who wrote about the Nazarenes also stated: "They have the entire Gospel of Matthew in Hebrew. It is carefully preserved by them as it was <u>originally written,</u> in the Hebrew script."

The most compelling case for Hebrew is the Scriptures themselves with the many Hebrew literalisms and idioms stretching the length of the New Testament. As a consequence there is, at times, great difficulty in interpreting many of the Messiahs' sayings when they appear translated from the Greek. Messianic Author, Lew White states on his website that, "Greek is the most cruel alphabet to impose on words from outside, since it lacks the sound necessary to replay words properly." New Testament books originally written in Greek account for less than 13% of the entire Bible. Perhaps this is what Satan had in mind all along when this pagan language commenced swallowing up the Hebrew. In contrast is it any wonder that the richly organic and passionate language of the Hebrew alphabet is known as "the letters of creation?"

"...I'm God's Name!" "...No I'm God's Name!"

Thanks to the legacy of "The Tower of Babel" there has been countless different languages that have attempted to tackle the name of the Father and the name of the Son. This has led to a numerous array of transliterated versions. A transliteration is when a word is written in a foreign language with the purpose of duplicating the same sound of that word in its original written form. A translation is simply the written or verbal explanation of what a foreign word means.

The transliterated names for the Father are: **YHVH, YHWH,** *Yahweh, Yahveh, Yaveh, Yaweh, Jehova, Jehovah, Jahova, Jahovah, Yahova, Yahovah, Yahowah, Jahowa, Jahowah, Yahavah, Jahavah, Yahowe, Yahoweh, Jahaveh, Jahaweh, Yahaveh, Yahaweh, Jahuweh, Yahuweh, Jahuwah, Yahuwah, Yahuah, Yah Jah Yahu, Yahoo, Yaohu, Jahu, Yahvah, Jahvah, Jahveh, Yahve, Yahwe, Yauhu, Yawhu, Iahu, Iahou, Iahoo, and Iahueh.*

The transliterated names for the Son are: *Jeshua, Yeshua, Yahshuah, Yehshua, Yehshuah, Yeshouah, Y'shua, Y'shuah, Jeshu,*

Yeshu, Yehoshua, Yehoshuah, YHVHshu, YHVYShua, Yhvhshuah, Yhwhshua, YHWHShau, YHWHShuah, Yhvhshuah, Yhwhshuah, Yahvehshua, Yahwehshua, Yahvehshuah, Yahwehshuah, Yawhushua, Yahawshua, Jahshua, Jahshuah, Jahshuwah, Jahoshua, Jahoshuah, Jashua, Jashuah, Jehoshua, Jehoshuah, Yahua, Yashuah, Yahshua, Yahshuah, Yahushua, Yahoshua, Yahoshuah, Yaohushua, Iahoshuah, and YAHO-hoshu-WAH.

God Knows Who I Mean, But do I Know Who I Mean?

For those readers who still cradle the opinion that God doesn't require his true name uttered, because He knows who we mean, should think again. Scripture almost from cover to cover is laced with a core principle that completely flies in the face of this non-specific methodology. If a person is an active believer, then they will often find themselves in various types of spiritual combat situations. Worse than that, they will be constantly in the enemy's territory and names are crucial in keeping track of who's who and what's what. As demonstrated by the Messiah in the act of casting out demons, a name is often required and surprisingly will be acknowledged as they depart from an occupant and are cast out into barren places. Within the Hebrew culture a name was a memorial to a person and much more than a mere term of reference as is the extent of the value of names today. Today, especially in the business world, a name is little more than a number and in some cases is of equal importance as a number.

For some reason, YHWH's name is always emphasised in the Bible. Sadly this is difficult to see for the average person because of its mass deletion in later Scriptures. Sentences concerning YHWH and his dealings always heavily exhibit his name. Why doesn't the Bible just say, "In the way of the Lord," instead of "in the name of the Lord?" or "call on you," instead of "call upon your name?" or "I exalt you," instead of "exalt your name?" or "I do this for you YHWH," instead of "I do this in your name YHWH?" An emphasis on names and names themselves appear on almost every page of Scripture. It's almost as if the word "name" has been deliberately squeezed into every possible sentence as is the case in *Genesis 48:16;* *"...and let my name be named on them and the name of my fathers*

313

Abraham and Isaac;" There are names in stones, names on thighs, names in foreheads, names in angels, numbers in names, names being blotted out, disciples named, names being made, names being forgotten, and chapters with lists of names. In the light of this, how could anybody still stand up and say that names are not important, when the Bible says differently?

Not surprisingly, believers who are usually against a specific name are also the same people who subscribe to an "any day of the week Sabbath mentality." At the very least this demographic displays a consistency of an "it doesn't matter attitude," with their spiritual walk. When anything sounds challenging, a usual response goes along the lines of, "it doesn't matter because Christ died for me and that's all I have to know."

Believe it or not, a Sabbath keeper who <u>does not</u> see the value of using a specific name ends up being in worse shape. The reason for this is because he or she practices maintaining the Sabbath because it's a Commandment and yet will disregard another Commandment that warns against making the Creator's name worthless.

For many years I held the belief that the Third Commandment, that is, not to take the name of YHWH in vain, meant to refrain from using it as a swear word. While I still firmly believe that to be true, I was awakened to other such violations in the form of adding or replacing the name all together. Consider the following verse in regards to alterations to the Father's name. *Exodus 3:15; "Moreover God said to Moses, 'Thus you shall say to the children of Israel: 'The Lord God of your fathers, the God of Abraham, the God of Isaac, and the God of Jacob, has sent me to you. THIS IS MY NAME FOREVER, and this is my memorial to all the generations.'"*

Now *Proverbs 30:5-6; "Every word of God is pure; He is a shield to those who put their trust in Him. <u>Do not add to His words</u>, lest He rebuke you, and you be found a liar."*

As I began to understand this concept, verses began literally jumping out at me that had this emphasis on the Father's name. I couldn't believe what I began to read. Initial concerns of legalism, through the subtle murmurings of Christian acquaintances, fell away when this truth revealed itself. Here are just some of the many multitudes of verses that highlight this theme. They show not only the importance of the name of the Father, but the name of the Son.

Proverbs 30:4; "...Who has established all the ends of the earth? What is His name, and what is His Son's name, if you know?" The last sentence of this verse almost rings like a challenge for us to find out what these names are. Note that there are also two names to know as opposed to one.

Joel 2:32; "And it shall come to pass That whoever calls on the name of the Lord shall be saved..." Notice the difference here of the concept of "calling on the Lord" and "calling on the name of the Lord." You may have never really stopped to think about this before. If not, you might want to take some time to do so now.

Psalm 118:10-12; "All nations surround me, But in the name of the Lord I will destroy them. They surrounded me, Yes, they surrounded me; But in the name of the Lord I will destroy them. They surround me like bees; they were quenched like a fire of thorns; For in the name of the Lord I will destroy them." Notice the Psalmist says, "in the name of the Lord I will destroy them" as opposed to, "for the Lord," or "for the sake of the Lord."

Psalm 74:7; "...They have defiled the dwelling place of your name to the ground. And *verse 10...Will the enemy blaspheme Your name forever?"* Again, they have defiled the place of his name, which is different from simply saying they have defiled his place.

Exodus 3:13-14; "Then Moses said to God, 'Indeed, when I come to the children of Israel and say to them, 'The God of our fathers has sent me to you,' and they say to me, 'What is His name?' what shall I say to them?' And God said to Moses, 'I AM WHO I AM.' And He said, 'Thus you shall say to the children of Israel, 'I AM has sent me to you.'" Though the words, "I AM" appear in nearly all English translations of the Bible, this term is more accurately translated from the original Hebrew as "I WILL BE that I WILL BE." In a note in verse 13:14 of The *American Standard Version* it reads: "I will be that I will be," and in the footnote of *The NIV Study Bible* it says: "I will be who I will be." *The International Standard Bible Encyclopedia* (1915) edition (pg. 1266) also agrees with this more correct rendering, as does *The Analytical Hebrew and Chaldee Lexicon*, by Benjamin Davidson. Despite these supporting texts, someone with a thorough knowledge of Hebrew will read it as such anyway.

Perhaps modern translators felt that "I AM" read a lot stronger than "I WILL BE," which in my opinion it does; however it should have never been changed. As if God needs the help of a translator to amplify this truth. After all, their job was to translate the Bible, not to edit it. Don't get me wrong, only a Bible written by the hand of YHWH Himself would be completely perfect, and a Bible written by men under the inspiration of YHWH will inevitably contain looser meanings and eventually, through the ages, outright errors.

I have probably sounded like I have an axe to grind, especially in the translation chapter, but I simply wish people to understand that no written modern Bible is word for word perfect to the Hebrew. This being said, there is a small movement gaining momentum at the moment that has begun circulating several Scriptures that restore the sacred name and contain Hebrew rendered New Testament portions.

John 17:6; "I have manifested your name to the men whom you have given Me out of the world." And *verse 11 "...Holy Father, keep through Your name those whom You have given Me, that they may be one as We are."* Notice the emphasis on the manifesting of God's name to men as opposed to simply manifested him, and the keeping through his name those that have been given, unlike saying, "keeping those whom you have given..."

Mark 9:37; "Whoever receives one of these little children in My name receives Me; and whoever receives Me, receives not me but Him who sent me." And *verse 39 "But Jesus said, "do not forbid him, for no one who works miracles in My name can soon afterward speak evil of me."* The illustration of the action of receiving a child in his name is again promoted and working miracles in his name is clearly encouraged in verse 39.

John 20:31; "but these are written that you may believe that Jesus is the Christ, the son of God, and that believing you may have life in His name." It is up to the reader to discern if the use of the phrase "in his name" has been tacked onto this sentence for poetic reasons or because there is power in it. Most Christians would agree the latter explanation is the case and faithfully proclaim the name Jesus Christ in obedient observance of this truth.

Which brings me nicely to my next topic, the name of the Son. The popular name "Jesus Christ" is widely recognised by most

Christians as the English translation of the original Hebrew name "Yahushua the Messiah." This next segment of the Chapter will investigate if this perception is true. We have to be objective and ask if the name of the Son has picked up any corruptions through the ages in certain tongues. Surely such a widely accepted name has remained unspoiled and cleanly translated and transliterated down through the ages. This type of inquiry might seem pointless yet it should go beyond simply asking your pastor for reassurance or simply referring to a modern dictionary definition. Most modern dictionaries provide a definition that is dominated by its use as a swear word anyway.

The Name of The Son

Throughout the course of this book I have used the name "Jesus" and to a lesser extent "Christ" to indicate the name of the Son of YHWH. Now with the permission of the reader I wish to lift another veil on a topic, which I will do with the same trepidation as someone who has just walked into the midst of a peace march with a T-shirt emblazoned with, "War – The Only Option." For in the exhaustive unraveling of dogma disguised as truth, and the inevitable ferocity of the attacks I may receive from those who once called me their brother, such an analogy may be fitting. From here on in I will refrain from the use of the name "Jesus Christ" and in its stead use the Hebrew name, "Yahushua." Why, I here you ask. Let me explain.

Languages vary in written form in two ways. They are either letter based or symbol based, like Palaeo-Hebrew, Chinese, or ancient Egyptian hieroglyphs. In converting symbol-based languages to letter based characters, the priority is to preserve the sound of the word at the cost of the physical construct of the symbols.

It has become my understanding after careful research that the general rule of a name subjected to transliteration is that its fullest original verbal capacity is to be maintained, providing the language has the appropriate corresponding letters. If this is not the case an alternative representation of a letter or collection of letters must be composed in order to retain at least a similar verbal sound. Outside these parameters, alterations to a name such as additions or subtraction of letters are avoided, as names represent the character of a person and to change a name changes the banner that displays all the crucial aspects of that individual.

It may come as no surprise to find out that the word "name" does actually mean "character and reputation." In Scripture, "name" is translated from the Hebrew word "shem" as we see in Strong's Concordance Dictionary:

Strong's # 8034 Shem; a primitive word [perhaps rather from 7760 through the idea of definite and conspicuous position; compare 8064]; an appellation, AS A MARK or **MEMORIAL OF INDIVIDUALITY**; by implication honor, authority, character: – +base, [in-] fame[-ous], name[-d] renown, report.

The name of the Son as with the Father is a memorial of individuality as the last sentence of *Exodus 3:15* says, *"This is My name forever, and this is My memorial to all generations."*

With these things in mind lets consider carefully the contents of the following verses in terms of the Son's name.

Philippians 2:9; "Therefore God has highly exalted Him and given Him the name which is above every name..." Please notice the verse says "the name," rather than "a name." This verse indicates that the Father has given his Son the right to come in his own name. We should not elevate the Son's earthly name over the Father's heavenly name, because the Father's heavenly name is above every other name. Nowhere in Scripture is there an instance where the Son's name should override the authority of the Father's name.

I find it very interesting that we maintain for example the name "Karate," the martial art, which means "open hand" yet fail to maintain the name of our Saviour in its original verbal form. If the reverse where true we would call that discipline the "open hand" and refer to "Jesus" in the Hebrew/Aramaic equivalent "Yahushua." It is as if we extend more courtesy to an unarmed combat technique than to the Son of YHWH.

Most of the Bibles we have today retain the Hebrew word "Joshua" in the New Testament, and yet they fail to retain the name of the Son. To add enormous confusion to this whole issue, some Bibles in two instances have Jesus in place of Joshua for reasons that I will explain shortly. Before I proceed any further let's start by looking at *The International Standard Bible Encyclopedia* meaning of the name "Jesus:"

"Jesus" (*Iesous*) is the Greek equivalent of the Heb "Joshua," Meaning 'Jehovah is salvation.' It stands therefore in the LXX and Apoc for "Joshua," and in Acts 7 45 and He 4 8 likewise represents the OT Joshua; hence in RV is in these pages rendered "Joshua."

On close examination of the above definition it appears to generate more questions than it answers, as it fails to mention that the name "Jesus" isn't a Hebrew name and has no exact meaning in Hebrew and therefore is not a translation. In fact its closest meaning in Hebrew is "horse." When I first read the encyclopedia definition, I was immediately struck with curiosity as to why a Greek equivalent is used for the Messiah and not the lesser character Joshua (Moses' companion), as Yahushua was originally the name of both these men. Yet only the Old Testament character receives the honour of the transliteration, (Y)oshua to (J)oshua as the 500-year-old letter "J" replaces the "Y." In contrast, the Son of YHWH gets a REPLACEMENT name "Iesous," the origin and meaning of which fails to be discussed in the above description. The explanation here informs the reader that it is a name, which is an "equivalent" to the Son. But if we then source out a definition of Joshua, (a pivotal character in the Old Testament) we find it is a legal "translation." The name of the Saviour being also shared with another is a startling revelation for the average Christian let alone an unknown equivalent being used for the name of the most important man in Scripture. In other words it's like two people who share the same name arriving in a foreign country. One of them is more senior to the other and the less senior is granted the honour of retaining a transliteration of his name, while the more senior gets a recently introduced equivalent name that is meant to mean the same thing, but in actuality sounds a bit like the name of an animal. Many definitions that describe the origin of the name Jesus also fail to point out the reasoning behind the use of the letter "J" over the letter "Y."

Ladies and Gentlemen, Introducing the Letter "J"

Another problem is that the "YAH" sound that represents the Father's name is absent from the Son's name in the Greek version.

The correct rendering is "Yah+shua" not "Joshua." There is no letter "J" in Hebrew or Greek and up until 500 years ago even the English language didn't have it. In Germany the letter "Y" is pronounced as a "J" and it was German Bible scholars that first started writing God's name as "Jehovah." The Jewish Encyclopedia (Volume 7, p.88) states: "Jehovah is generally held to have been the INVENTION of Pope Leo the 10th's confessor, Peter Galatin (De Arcanis Catholic Verties 1518 Folio XLIII), who was followed in the use of this hybrid form by Fagius Drusius." The hard "J" sound began to appear in the wake of the Normandy Invasion of 1066 and yet did not receive wide recognition until the 1200's. It wasn't until 300 years later that it started officially replacing male names that began with "I" or "Y." A simple exercise to test this truth of the "Johnny come lately letter J" is to pick up a reprint of the 1611 King James Version (recently made available again) and look for the letter "J." You will not find it. This introduction of the letter "J" into a language that would eventually overlay key names was the beginning of Satan's master plan. His most effective and least observed attack strategy is to gradually replace. He knows the Scriptures better than most Christian teachers, ministers, and lay-preachers I know, and he knows that only one name is the key to salvation. The "J" rapidly began replacing the "Y" or the "Ieo" sound in most names of males because it sounded more masculine. Try speaking a name that starts with "J" and replace it with a "Y" sound. For instance my name, being "Jason," would sound like "Yason" or "IEason." It is no small coincidence that out of all the 22 letters available in Hebrew that the "Y" gets replaced with "J." This is effectively the second stage of dilution of the Saviour's name.

Words we should always watch out for when explanations are given for arriving at the name "Jesus" are: "It is widely accepted" (meaning: "everybody else does it so we do to."), "equivalent" (meaning: it is not a translation or transliteration, but a replacement.), "In these pages rendered" (meaning: in this instance we do this, but elsewhere could be different.)

To sum up so far, the Hebrew/Aramaic name "Yahushua" means "YHWH (the name of God) is our salvation," and the equivalent name Jesus means, "horse" in Hebrew. The meaning of Yahushua is outlined in *Matthew 1:21; "And she shall bring forth a Son, and you shall call His name Jesus, for He will save His people from their sins."*

Zeus – The Replacement Name

There are many etymologists and scholars who claim that the name "Jesus Christ" comes from the Greek "Je-Zeus Christos" and actually refers to the Greek god Zeus. This certainly appears to be the case as it is well documented that Constantine was a worshipper of Zeus and that this god's attributes were added to the Messiah to appeal to Roman pagans. This implication can cause instant emotional unrest, yet one should look into this claim with a consistent rule of rational measure.

According to author, *Lew White* the "IE," Greek part for "Je" gives off a "Yeh" sound (not a Yah sound), which means "hail." The origins of the "sus" part of the name "Jesus" is explained in the *The Dictionary of Christian Lore and Legend* by *J. C. J. Metford*: "It is known that the Greek endings of sus, seus, sous (which are phonetic pronunciations for Zeus) were attached by the Greeks to names and geographical areas as a means to give honour to their supreme diety, Zeus."

The reader must bear in mind that there are other well-researched claims into the meanings of "Jesus Christ," that when rendered in different languages mean a varying array of insults that defies coincidence. For example "sus" translated back into Hebrew means "horse." As there is no "J" in Hebrew, the name "esus" is rendered, "The Horse." That is why in my private prayer I address Jesus as Yahushua and freely use the Father's name YHWH. I feel a great privilege to be granted the motivation to look into these things that in turn draw me closer to our Father in Heaven. I now have a desire to want to know more about Him on a daily basis and I believe finding out these things is inevitable for someone who desires truth. I am often fired statements from friends like, "that's your thing," or "that's what you're into," as if to say, "well I'm not into looking at that nitty-gritty stuff, but it's good that you are." Another one is, "I prefer to go out and connect with people and share the Gospel," which is really insulting because it implies that I don't. After all, shouldn't we study the truth of the Gospel very carefully, especially if we have the intention of going out and sharing it with people?

"Hail Zeus the Oil Pourer"

Whatever your thoughts on the use of this word in reference to Yahushua, know these two things: "Christ" is not his last name, and there is absolutely no biblical support in adding it to the Son's name in prayer, conversation, or teaching. It is merely a title that has been used to magnify the name and personage of who it refers to, as the name Yahushua itself was not unique. The appearance and slowly developing emphasis on this title has crept so firmly into Christendom that it has effectively replaced even the corrupted name, as those who pray close with the saying, "…in Christ's name." Masses of followers are unwittingly hoodwinked into believing that this specifies the Son of man when it simply means "anointed." History shows that any priest, king, beggar, rich man or poor man has had the potential to receive an anointing, which by its very nature when used alone is specific to no one. With the sheer density of Scripture that supports doing things in his name, this emphasis on a solely used nonspecific title seems like an insult.

When we delve into the meaning of the word "Christ" we soon come across a grey area. According to all reputable sources the title comes from the Greek word "Christos," which means "anointed." The meaning of the word "anointed" is: "to pour oil on one's head" which was traditionally a sacred act that was adopted by both pagans and follower's of YHWH alike. Therefore its application to the Saviour's name gives him no exclusive recognition. Yet nowhere in modern Bible translations is it written, "the people became the Christs," which would simply mean, "the people became anointed ones." The name of the same act is rendered as "anointed" for any reference outside Yahushua.

Delving deeper we find that it is the equivalent (there's that word again) to the Hebrew word "Moshiach," which we say as "Messiah." Some sources claim that Messiah means "saviour" or "liberator," which has nothing to do with "anointed."

Many definitions for "Christ" say it means both "messiah" and "anointed," which doesn't make any sense if one means "rescuer" and the other means "to consecrate." Modern Bibles often use the Greek word "Christ" in place of the Hebrew word "Messiah," based on the understanding that these words mean exactly the same thing. In truth the term Messiah means "Anointed one of Yah (the first syllable of God's name) while the term Christ ambiguously means, "anointed." Let's have a clear look at three different words in Scripture that are used interchangeably that describe Yahushua (sometimes within the same passages):

Translator's Preference	Original Text
Christ — Used over 500 times* (used exclusively in reference to Yahushua) (never used in reference to recipients of an anointing) **Greek word meaning "anointed" (To consecrate with oil / Nonspecific)**	**= Messiah / Mashiyach** **Original Hebrew Meaning: (Anointed one of Yah / Specific)**
Messiah — Used 2 times* (used in reference to Yahushua) (never used in reference to a recipient of an anointing) **(Hardly used specific)**	**= Messiah / Mashiyach** **Original Hebrew Meaning: (Anointed one of Yah / Specific)**
Anointed — Used 98 times* (sometimes used in reference to Yahushua) (used in reference to recipients of an anointing) (not used exclusively in reference to Yahushua) **(To consecrate w/ oil / Nonspecific)**	**= Messiah / Mashiyach** **Original Hebrew Meaning: (Anointed one of Yah / Specific)** **= Mashach** (sometimes used) **(To consecrate w/ oil / Nonspecific)**

* = Depending on translation

The reality is that translators appropriated terminology at their own discretion to add emphasis. In turn "Christ," the equivalent of "anointed," became associated exclusively to the name of Jesus.

To add more pain to the topic there is another commonly held understanding of the origin of the name Christ. In the Hindu religion, "Christos" is the Greek version of the word "Krishna," and when followers of this faith call on their god, they usually address him as "Krsta" or "Krishna" interchangeably. According to the writings of A. C. *Bhaktivedanta Swami Prabhupada*, "When Jesus said, 'our Father who art in heaven, sanctified be thy name,' that name of God was "Krsta" or "Krishna." Actually it doesn't matter – Krishna or Christ – the name is the same. The main point is to follow the injunctions of the Vedic scriptures that recommend chanting the name of God...If you have prejudice against chanting the name Krishna, then chant "Christos" or "Krsta" – there is no difference."

And so the case of Christos meaning Krishna is trumpeted. In-depth writings on this subject are not difficult to find. Nor is material on the association of the name "cretin" with that of "Christian" as discussed in Chapter One.

Whatever your own conclusions as to the true origin of this name, one thing remains sparklingly clear, that is, Christ is not the last name of Yahushua, let alone Jesus. People in that day were known by a single name and defined by the name of the city or the region where they came from, such as Yahushua (Jesus) of Nazareth. Eventually last names started to evolve out of the use of an ancestor's first name that was added to a descendant's name. The Scottish king, "Robert the Bruce" is a good example of this. Sometimes names even became used as titles, such as in the case of the name "Caesar."

To use Christ on its own has no more power than saying, "we pray all these things in the anointed one's name." For even the Scriptures refer to Satan as "the anointed cherub who covers." It's difficult to accept when people deny that this subject is an issue when Scripture clearly documents that it is. Consider the implications of the following verse. *Hosea 2:17; "For I will take from her mouth the names of the Baals, and they shall be remembered by their name no more."*

When I was first shown these truths I did not like them and at first retreated into "God knows what I mean territory," but I could not shake the feeling that this was the same excuse used by those who choose to worship on the Sunday instead of the Sabbath. It has to be a gradual thing and the best place to start is in private prayer. A good start is to thank YHWH for showing you the truth, then gradually introduce these names into your language. Meditate on them and think about what you've learnt and what they mean. You may feel compelled to share this with fellow Christians in a church environment. Be careful, because sharing this knowledge in a public forum could be confronting to a group. The best method I have found is to start using the uncorrupting names in conversation, which usually leads people to ask why you use them. Keep the responses short and sweet and don't try to be too overbearing. Don't try and showboat what you've learnt. Be humble and expect harsh opposition to your conviction.

With the amount of research I have done, I am most confident with the rendering, "Yahushua ha Meshiach," which means "YHWH is our salvation." However we must remember that Yahushua was a common name at the time of his ministry and it is the name of the Father that he ultimately INHERITS. Therefore the true power lies in that name.

The name of the YHWH and his Son can be traced back to the following Palaeo-Hebrew symbols. I present them here out of reverence and in the hopes that being made known again, they might be restored quickly.

ⴴYⴷⵎ

The preserved palaeo-Hebrew Name of the Creator.

The preserved palaeo-Hebrew earthly name of Yahushua.

Amen – The Hidden God Crouching in our Prayers

While on this topic it is worth mentioning that there is another word that is used with tiresome frequency in Christian circles, whose meaning is debatable at best. The almost universally used word "amen" according to most Christian and Judaic source books is adopted directly from the Hebrew root letters a-m-n (aman) meaning any of the following: firm, permanent, so be it, trustworthy, educate, train, true, confirm, confidence, and faithfulness. *Isaiah 65:16* carries the words "truth" in place of the Hebrew aman in this verse: *"...Shall bless himself in the God of truth...Shall swear by the God of truth."* As observed earlier, the same principle of adding emphasis by using different words from the same Hebrew root is the order of the day. Note that "aman" has been subsequently rendered "amen," when amen also appears to have a completely unrelated meaning. When we look at the *1991 Concise Columbia Encyclopedia*: "Amon (a'men, a-) or Ammon (a'men) or Amen (a'men), ancient Egyptian deity. Originally the chief god of Thebes, Amon grew increasingly important in Egypt, and eventually, as Amon Ra, he was identified with Ra as the supreme deity. He was also identified with the Greek Zeus (the Roman JUPITER). (Ed.: Jupiter or 'Zues-Pater – (Zeus our fathers')."

The Official Internet site of the Egyptian Ministry of Tourism makes the following statement about the sun god Amen-Ra: "In hymns to Amen we often read that he is "hidden to his children," and "hidden to gods and men...Now, not only is the god himself said to be "hidden," **but his name also is 'hidden'...**" If we consider this last point, the reality of this word that is used by the mainstream Christian at the close of any prayer, whether done openly or in private, becomes all too chillingly real. Read carefully the most popular closing sentences in Christian prayers and notice the strategic placement of the name:

"We ask these things in your name, Amen."
"We praise your name, Amen."
"Praise the Lord, Amen."

Please also note that any one of the above Hebrew to English translations is not grammatically correct and despite the best of intentions, they can easily be passed off as addresses to something possessing the name Amen.

At any rate this is an attempt at using a Hebrew word that also has precisely the same construct as one of the main deities in Egyptian mythology, while the very name of the Creator is relegated to a weaker equivalent and a non-specific title. Whether there can be found any evidence or not of a link between these two names, the fact remains that this word used in prayer or worship to YHWH shares the name of a pagan god. Once out of the shadow of ignorance on this issue we should let *Exodus 23:13* lead us to more truth. *"And in all that I have said to you, be circumspect and make no mention of the name of other gods, nor let it be heard from your mouth."* We must bear in mind that the context of the above verse is in reference to praise and worship. To not be able to say the name of a pagan god would mean that all of the Torah could not be read aloud as it does mention some of these gods by name.

Subtle Opposition is the Most Dangerous Opposition

In the popular *Harry Potter* films much is made of the students at *Hogwart's School of Wizardry* achieving a specific and correct verbal pronunciation in the utterance of various spells. This theme of word recital and gathering special items is common in nearly all fantasy and horror films where witchcraft is depicted. Over the course of thousands of years these ideas are the product of an original custom that was tilted a degree off centre by an opposing force that led many people today to a counterfeit version of commandments and customs that were never meant to be altered. There are some people who practice arts that are boldly set in opposition to God's statutes and as a result can often be spotted a mile away. Surprisingly they have more in common with their enemies than those who practice the imitation and have a form of Godliness yet deny its true power *(2 Timothy 3:5)*. The reason is they believe in nearly all the same things as a follower of Yahushua, but their allegiance is with Satan. The imitation followers of Yahushua who knowingly have been exposed to the truth, yet reject it <u>are the more dangerous</u>

327

of the two enemies. There are legions of people who openly reject Satan yet through ignorance, born out of complacency or gullibility serve a god that presents himself in a similar manner to YHWH yet it is counterfeit. *John 16:2; "They will put you out of the synagogues; yes, the time is coming that whoever kills you will think that he offers God Service."* Note that the verse does not say: "…their god…" but "God" aka YHWH."

Chapter Fifteen

An Antichrist in the Hand is Worth Two in the Bush

LET ME INTRODUCE THE next topic by turning again to the subject of popular film. In the phenomenally successful science fiction movie, *The Empire Strikes Back*, the hero of the story, Luke Skywalker takes a short interlude on an isolated planet to seek the help of a great warrior, known as Jedi Master Yoda. After his former master is killed, Luke is prompted to find one who is even greater in power to complete his crucial training, in the hopes of defeating his enemy. What is interesting about this segment of the story is the nature of his first encounter with this warrior. Amid the planet's murky swampland surroundings, a short, greenish creature, with pointed ears, emerges to find the young man, tired, frustrated and anxious. The creature appears to be a somewhat eccentric nuisance as he proceeds to rummage through Luke's supplies and scuffle with his robot companion. Finally, Luke utterly dismisses the creature by saying, "Now get out of here, little fellow. We've got things to do." A short time later Luke finds out that this harmless little creature is Yoda, the most powerful Jedi warrior in the known galaxy. Luke apparently had a range of preconceived possibilities of what this Jedi Master would look like, and a little green, pointy-eared creature was not on his list. The truth, through his ignorance, and impatient expectation had overtaken him like a thief in the night. One thing that we can be sure of in reflecting on YHWH's past interactions with men is to expect the unexpected.

A similar incident occurs in *Luke* (no pun intended) *24:13* of the New Testament, when two men, disciples in fact, are walking to a village called Emmaus. It is the third day after Yahushua's execution and they speak doubtfully of his promises as no news has reached them of his resurrection. Before long they are joined by the subject himself during their conversation, but are unable to recognise him. *Verse 15-16* states: *"So it was, while they conversed and reasoned, that Jesus Himself drew near and went with them. But their eyes were restrained, so that they did not know Him."* Innocently, Yahushua inquires as to the nature of their conversation and is swiftly told that they were saddened that he had not yet appeared to redeem Israel. He responds in *verse 25* by saying: *"O foolish ones, and slow of heart to believe in all that the prophets have spoken! Ought not the Christ to have suffered these things and to enter into His glory?"* Soon after, they realise who he is in *verse 31* when it relates: *"Then their eyes were opened and they knew Him; and He vanished from their sight."* *Luke 24:18* describes one of them as Cleopas (Qleophas) but it is only in *Mark 16:12* where their origin as disciples is disclosed. In this more brief telling of the encounter there is also a definite emphasis that Yahushua was in a completely different form. This act was obviously done to draw out the men's level of faith. The same motivation is evident in Yoda's presentation of himself to Luke. It enables him to get a clean view of the nature of a potential pupil. So to, in these days, if we wallow too long in a preconceived rendering of the return of the Saviour, born out of only a diluted viewing of the Scriptures, we may find ourselves in a similar situation as Luke (Skywalker) or the disciples on the road. Wrestling with what Yahushua will physically look like or where, when and how he will show up is unadvisable as it is by his actions that he will be known. It is this subject that I wish to delve into here.

What can tend to happen, when the person of greatest importance is pointed out in a crowded room, is a deliberate posturing toward that individual. Only when that important person leaves will we relax our guard and become ourselves again. In doing that, this person never gets a clear understanding of who we really are. Yet in contrast, if pointed out that there is someone in a crowded room, who is of the greatest importance but we are not told whom, we are not able to impose favouritism on that individual. If we can continue to carry this principle of avoiding favouritism and treat everyone as equals, we will be less likely to turn away or disregard an angel masquerading as a stranger or even Yahushua himself. This will provide a more peaceful existence by requiring less energy in displaying a manner of Godliness for a predetermined time.

The same principle comes into play with naming a time for the second coming. Let me illustrate this with the following example. Imagine that you are housesitting for some friends and you know that they are to return in a week's time. You know that in a week from now that the place has to be tidy and left in the condition you found it. So in the meantime you can throw a few parties, maybe neglect some chores and pretty much do as you please. Now imagine that you are housesitting and you have only a vague idea when the owners will return. Because you don't know the exact time of their return you will have to make sure the house is maintained and in order on an ongoing daily basis. There is less desire for putting things off in this scenario, which ultimately makes for a more practical and ordered lifestyle. Likewise it is commonsense to avoid preconceived notions of Yahushua's appearance and to cease fixations of pinpointing an exact time of his return. To be fully equipped with the knowledge of either is to be encumbered with the temptation of complacency, which retards the desire to stay watchful for him. To seek exacting answers to these things is futile and of no importance, but nonetheless we vainly search and in so doing the enemy happily regales us with answers, and usually the ones we secretly want to hear. Today, we have an idea of the Saviour's appearance that over the centuries has remained somewhat uniform. Even depictions of Yahushua as a black man retain certain characteristics that fit a commonly accepted look.

The Shroud of Lies

For hundreds of years there has been a steady cultivation of a particular physical depiction of Jesus agreed upon in Constantine's day. That of the Aryan and ageless looking figure we see today portrayed in all manner of mediums. In recent centuries the image had received a major boost in its authenticity with the discovery of a fourteen-foot-long piece of linen in 1357. It surfaced after its former owner Geoffrey de Charney II was killed by the English a year earlier at the battle of Poitiers, in France. The linen possessed a steamed image, brought about by grievous wounds mingled with sweat and lactic acid that formed the remarkably clear depiction of a familiar individual. The image was that of a middle-aged man with a medium built six-foot-frame, a face with a narrow nose, hair that was slightly longer than shoulder length with a centre parting, and a full forked beard. Also visible, were the familiar wounds on the hands and feet.

The physical similarities to how Jesus was depicted in that day, coupled with the marks of a crucified man, added fuel to the rumours that it once wrapped his body, and it was to be this view that spread like wildfire throughout the community. Rome acquired it and for many years it was accepted as the shroud that enclosed the body of the Son of God, despite the Vatican's denial. Nevertheless, it was displayed under the strictest security at Turin cathedral where thousands periodically filed past to catch a glimpse of Christ. Finally, in 1988, after extensive carbon-dating tests, Cardinal Anastasio Ballestrero announced that the figure was not that of Jesus Christ. The result was that the shroud could not be dated any earlier than 1260 AD. Even with the Catholic Church's denial and the dating proof, the damage was done. So influential was this artifact on the minds of most believers that even in the Mel Gibson film *The Passion*, the theory is still pursued. In the closing act, Jesus is handed a cloth to soak his blood stained face during a pause in his march to Calvary. When he pushes on, his blood stricken features are evident on the material. This scene was obviously a homage to the Shroud of Turin.

The true origin of the shroud has continued to elude most scholars. However, authors Christopher Knight and Robert Lomas have put forward the most plausible scenario to date. Their conclusion came about during the pursuit of information on the demise of the Grand Master of the Templars, Jacques de Molay. This individual was appointed the position of Grand Marshal of the Knights

Templar in England. This group was a branch of a sacred order that broke away from Rome. Eventually a money hungry French king who had the full support of Rome captured him. He was tortured and crucified but managed to survive. After the Templar made a confession of heresy, the shroud was applied to his body and he was later released.

A little known fact is that the shroud of Turin is one of ten other contenders that carry the ghostly depictions of other wounded or deceased individuals as noted by Collin de Plancy in 1822. I have often wondered at the possibility of these images being various attempts by Satan to set down some sort of familiar depiction of a counterfeit Messiah to cement a look into the subconscious minds of the masses.

The conditioning on the look of the Messiah continues to be pushed, as the longhaired, narrow-faced appearance becomes universally accepted. Occasionally this look is challenged by scholars who get wide publicity, yet eventually these challenges slip quietly into obscurity without debate or conjecture as films, books, televisions, and pictures continue to belt out the Turin style look by the truckloads.

A Picture can tell a Thousand Words, But how Much of them Truth?

The earliest origins of the image of Yahushua could have come about through a number of avenues. Some works of the *Apocrypha, Pseudepigrapha* and *Gnostic* texts have him appearing as a shepherd, the master of a ship, in the form of one of his apostles, or as a young boy. He displays a smile of friendship and appears as a beautiful lad to Peter and Theon in *The Actus Vercellensis*. Yet none of these sources appear to go into great detail or tend to shed any more light on his appearance than the known biblical texts.

The New and Old Testament do not speak at all of a specific appearance, nor do they define any characteristics, of Yahushua's physical form. In fact the Bible speaks very candidly and briefly on the physical appearance of its central character and even then it is argued by some that the majority of the verses contents speak of inner qualities. *Isaiah 53:2-3; "...He has no form of comeliness;*

And when we see Him, there is no beauty that we should desire Him. He is despised and rejected by men, A man of sorrows and acquainted with grief. And we hid, as it were, our faces from Him; He was despised and we did not esteem Him." This verse basically says that his appearance was that of an "average Joe," he was familiar with sadness and experienced rejection.

The subject was of minor interest to the early church fathers, yet interestingly enough they did seem to regard him as a man that assumed whatever form was suited to circumstances. Then in the fourth century, a time when a broad range of Scriptural issues received a bashing, Chrysostom and Jerome laid the foundations of a more beautiful Saviour pathetically supported from a reference in **Psalm 45:2; "You are fairer than the sons of men; Grace is poured out on your lips; Therefore God has blessed You forever."**

One of the oldest pictures of Yahushua appeared on an embroided handkerchief, supposedly made by Mary, depicting him and his Apostles. The monk Arculfus allegedly saw this during his residence in Jerusalem (Adamnan, *De Locis Sanctis*, i. 11 [12]). Not surprisingly this is from a Roman source as are at least four other such stories of his image adorning various ancient artifacts. One source led straight to Constantine himself.

Constantine was reported to have had a brass statue, which was standing in his prayer room among a host of other brass renderings of other gods. A considerable amount of our current perception of not only Yahushua's character but that of his appearance was born out of a forced vote presided over by Constantine at the council of Nicaea. Among some of those attendees who regretfully put their endorsing signatures to paper was Eusebius, who later wrote the Emperor: "We committed an impious act, O prince, by subscribing to a blasphemy from fear of you." Thus a more aesthetically pleasing figure, resembling an image more akin to that of Zeus or Apollo, was unveiled before the pagan populace.

Constantine and his dignitaries knew that the existing status quo meant that idols were an inevitable part of pagan worship. A new all encompassing religion would not take hold without embracing the use of such an accessory. Worse still, an image carrying the visage of a common Jew may have been met with disastrous ridicule by the masses. It is interesting to note that Constantine's combining of Jesus with accompanying sun god imagery is very similar to contemporary cross-marketing advertisements that we often see in the media today. Any imagery you see at a church that depicts a circle or sun behind a cross is unadulterated pagan symbolism. It has no Scriptural basis whatsoever.

The historical reality of Jewish custom at that time was that younger men had short hair. Contrary to the popular portrayal of Orthodox Jews in cinema, only elders possessed beards. Some people claim that Yahushua's long hair and beard was on account of his being a Nazarite. This would be a good argument, but Yahushua was a Nazarene, not a Nazarite. Men who took Nazarite vows would put themselves in isolation for three years and during that time would not lift a razor to their face. Incidentally, even if he were a Nazarite, after the period of isolation he would have cut his hair before appearing in public. Furthermore a Nazarite was not permitted to drink wine or touch dead bodies, which would have presented somewhat of a stumbling block to his brand of ministry. In Paul's first letter to Corinth he states (under normal circumstances) that it is shameful for a man to have long hair *(1 Corinthians 11:14)*.

Yahushua the Messiah – Warrior or Pacifist?

What type of picture do the Scriptures really portray of Yahushua? Is he depicted as a quiet unassuming Gandhi-like character or a passionate and confrontational leader? As a twelve-year-old he is recorded as having a most unusual encounter with a group of Jewish teachers. Being still a child he spoke words that drew in these learned men who were probably three to four times his age. His effect on these wise listeners was to make them enquire about his parents and the source of his knowledge. That being the case, it is important to pause for a moment and look to the Scriptures, rather than consulting popular thought for insights into his character, lest we be fooled like Luke Skywalker was in his first encounter with Yoda.

Yahushua, like his Father, was outspoken, unafraid of confrontation and a professional separator of truth from lie. He was viewed by the governmental and religious leaders of his day as a dangerous rebel, because he threatened to dismantle the oppressive hold that the religious and political leaders had over the masses. However, most people today assume that he was a pacifist, most likely because he never entered into physical combat or put himself at the head of a conventional army. Yet he himself said that he did not come to bring peace, but a sword *(Matthew 10:34)*. Unfortunately most people have trouble envisioning him as a warrior because he didn't fight battles with a physical weapon or use any military might. Nonetheless, like his Father, he was and is well acquainted with war. YHWH himself says that, *"The Lord (YHWH) is a man of war" (Exodus 15:3)*. For a warrior to be truly great in battle he must truly want peace. Thus is the nature of the YHWH Elohim. It was Yahushua's unconventional approach in combating the enemy that attracted the strangest allies.

YHWH's Motley Crew – All Sinners, Yet All Clothed in Righteousness

It is no coincidence that the most popular and enduring storylines are the ones of the ugly duckling variety, where a character that is at first despised and ridiculed, is later raised to hero-like status to the complete shock of his or her peers. It is the endearing story of the underdog, the rogue, the rebel, or as we say in Australia, "the battler." It is the one you never saw coming, the weak and burnt out shell of a man you wouldn't look twice at. The drunken vagrant, the poor widow, the blind beggar, or the quiet and shy school girl who is made fun of, but is then looked up to, by not only her peers, but even by her teachers after a dramatic event. Even notorious villains are potential candidates for truth, as they go through a process of redemption and end up being the biggest supporters of the ones they tried to overthrow. Let's not forget films like the *Magnificent Seven* and *The Dirty Dozen*, where the wildest and most undisciplined crews of men get together to perform impossible tasks. Looks are not important and nor are the degrees of a person's sinfulness. Take, for example, some of YHWH's most pivotal recruits:

Abraham – Slept with a maidservant
Lot – Committed incest

Moses – Easily angered and slow of speech
Noah – A drunkard
Jacob – Deceived his Father and Brother
Samson – Pursued Philistine women (womaniser)
Jonah – Disobedient and headstrong, avoided responsibility
Peter – Consecutively denied Yahushua three times in his presence
David – Adulterer and premeditated murderer
Thomas – Doubted the resurrection
Paul – Former persecutor of YHWH's people

The above individuals were all major players in the Scriptures and all possessed exceptional qualifications to perform their designated tasks, but all had varying degrees of flaws; some ongoing, some singular in nature, and some more extreme than others. We would not normally associate these lists of credentials with YHWH's people, yet here they are. If we don't snap out of the idea that "Followers of The Way" should have this goody-two-shoes Ned Flanders and Hill Song trendy image, we will never understand the mission. One of the most enduring things that was ever said to me was by a councilor at a Christian help group that I attended some years ago. I shared with him the nature of some struggles I had with sin in my life and how it made me feel unable to be of any use to YHWH. He replied by giving me a piece of invaluable advice. He told me to go forward with whatever it was that I felt compelled to do and not let the memory of that sin or the fear of it taking root again hold at ransom everything good I have to give.

Physical appearance, profession, geographical location, education, and even the extent of one's spiritual and physical brokenness are of little concern to YHWH, if that person is willing. The sooner we drop needless speculation on what he looked like or whether we, ourselves, are worthy YHWH material, the sooner we can focus more on His Son's actions and try to imitate them. Another aspect that is needlessly speculated on is the manner of the Son's return.

Antichrists through History

The subject of the antichrist is a topic that has fascinated Christians and non-Christians alike for centuries, but who or what is he? Surprisingly the word "antichrist" never appears in Revelations and only shows up in a total of three passages contained in 1 and 2 John, yet it is central to the apocalyptic theme. In this next verse I will hope to completely shatter the fable that the subject of antichrist is to be confined to a future date, as we know it. Please pay close attention to the underlined passages: *1 John 2:18-19; "Little children, it is the last hour; and as you have heard that the Antichrist is coming, <u>even now many antichrists have come</u>, by which <u>we know that it is the last hour</u>. They went out from us, but they were not of us; for if they had been of us, they would have continued with us; but they went out that they might be made manifest, that none of them were of us."* The spirit of antichrist, that is to say, one who is in direct opposition to Yahushua, yet assumes similar credentials, has already manifested in the hearts of many individuals. The first such individual was Judas, the betrayer. An important characteristic of antichrist is that he was once a member of the brethren. So someone who has never walked with fellow brothers and sisters in the faith, though still considered a nuisance, cannot under any circumstances go by the name of antichrist. That alone narrows the past and future candidates down considerably.

Another interesting aspect of verse 18 is that the last hour is considered to have commenced in Yahushua's day; therefore almost the entirety of the New Testament is in a sense apocalyptical. With this knowledge we are now equipped with the understanding that this is not a term exclusively confined to an elusive future global dictator. This is the roll of the "Beast," or the "antichrist beast," if you like. He will have the spirit of antichrist, but be known more specifically as "the beast," as described in Revelations. He will be joined by another nasty fellow called, "the false prophet." This false prophet will pave the way for the beast.

If Yahushua's day was known as "the last hour," then today we can confidently describe the present as "the last minute."

The Lie Dressed in Truth's Clothes

Yahushua's return has been plainly described in the New Testament. *Matthew 24:30; "Then the sign of the Son of Man will appear in heaven, and then all the tribes of the earth will mourn, and they will see the Son of Man coming on the clouds of heaven with power and great glory."* Notice that the verse says, "and all the tribes of the earth will mourn." This clearly indicates that his coming will be seen as a negative by all the worldly establishments. To nurse a belief that his coming will be greeted by a global celebration, even by a minority of communities, is not biblical. Those that have been well provided for in an economic system that displeases YHWH will be terrified at the prospect of having this system taken away. They will move in full cooperation, *Independence Day* style, to repel an invading force that has come to enact retribution on a wayward people.

The most unsettling thing about the generally held expectation of a Deliverer is that his arrival will put an immediate end to the chaos and corruption that ensues due to the opening of the seven seals. Most Christians who study eschatology overlook the fact that Satan appears to triumph FIRST over these disasters, symbolised by killing the two witnesses. At which point the world rejoices for three and a half days. At the end of this period the world's rejoicing turns to fear and mourning as they scramble to defend themselves against the arrival of Yahushua and the host of Heaven.

Yahushua does not appear until the seventh seal of Revelation is opened. By this time one third of mankind will have been wiped off the face of the earth. Satan will seize the opportunity to appear as a Saviour by killing the two witnesses who preach a message that is contrary to most of the world's view of Scripture.

Prior to this, Satan influenced super-powers will officiate over the most widely spread religion, Catholic Christianity, and move to convert or erase all opposition. The option of the mark or beheading could possibly be instituted in classic inquisition style, which will gain immediate converts from atheist circles, who won't have a problem as long as they don't lose their heads. Then most other religious bodies who don't see anything wrong with accepting such a move will come around.

The true children of YHWH will not be caught up out of the earth UNTIL THESE THINGS HAVE ALREADY COME TO PASS.

The Antichrist Hall of Fame

Satan has been very busy keeping us busy with possible antichrist candidates. Though the Scriptures may discourage the physical search for a Saviour, Satan knows that looking for the beast is not discouraged. As we have already looked at in Chapter Eight there is permission given to count the numerical value of a suspected person or organisation's name to find out whom the antichrist beast will be. Satan has and is doing his best to keep us occupied in chasing down false leads by cleverly exploiting certain verses. Let's look at a list of some of the "beast" and "antichrist" suspects that have been brought forward over the years: (Bear in mind that any people on this list that have expired cannot be the beast and any who were not initially members of the body of YHWH are also disqualified.)

Willy Brandt
Caligula
King Juan Carlos of Spain
Emperor Fredrick II of Germany
King George II of England
Emperor Justinian
Ayatollah Khomeini
Nikita Khrushchev
Sun Myung Moon
Napoleon Bonaparte
Pete Seeger
Josef Stalin
Kaiser Wilhelm
Boris Yeltsin
Yasser Arafat
"The Beast" – Nickname for a supercomputer in Brussels
Jimmy Carter
Bill Gates
Mikhail Gorbachev

John F. Kennedy
Henry Kissinger
Martin Luther
Benito Mussolini
Nero Caesar
Pope John Paul II
Ronald Wilson Reagan
Pat Robertson
David Rockefeller
Anwar el Sadat
Saddam Hussein

Another misconception is that the beast will force his people to worship him through fear of persecution. *Revelations 13* describes a scenario of sympathy, pride and amazement in the world's population toward him, initially brought about through a healing from a fatal wound of one of his organisations (heads) as *Verse 3-4* of chapter 13 states: *"And I saw one of his heads as if it had been mortally wounded, and his deadly wound was healed. And all the world marveled and followed the beast. So they worshipped the dragon who gave authority to the beast; and they worshipped the beast, saying, 'Who is like the beast? Who is able to make war with him?'"* There is true admiration in all the people towards him and they will feel so comforted by him that they will think that he will keep them safe from all harm.

Daniel 2:31-33 also holds further clues as to why he will be so adored by such a volume of people. In these verses it speaks of a symbolic representation of a manlike-image. This image is made up of certain attributes that represent characteristics, normally reserved for YHWH. In this instance however, the image is made up of material of a consistency that show strong compounds such as gold and silver in the upper portions of the anatomy, but eventually end with the lower extremities being made up of the failed combination of iron and clay. This reveals the origin of the image to be that of the beast.

Below is a listing of these anatomical parts, their relevant attributes and supporting verses that are described in relation to YHWH. Each segment also has an appropriate ingredient listed, down to the foundations (feet), which are made up of these two materials that cannot mix together; them being "iron" and "clay." The mixing of these two foreign materials is also symbolic of the failed long-term results of the interbreeding with daughters of men and fallen angels.

> The Head = Wisdom (Colossians 3:10) / Imitator's ingredient = Fine Gold
>
> Breast and Arms = Security (Psalms 91:10-12) / Imitator's ingredient = Silver
>
> Belly and Thighs = Well-being (Matthew 6:24-34) / Imitator's ingredient = Brass
>
> Legs = Strength (Isaiah 54:17) / Imitator's ingredient = Iron (So far so good)
>
> Feet = Healing (2 Chronicles 7:14) / Imitator's ingredient = Iron & Clay

When John sees a vision of a glorified Yahushua in *Revelations 1* he makes mention of his feet. *Verse 15* of chapter 1 states: *"His feet were like fine brass, as if refined in a furnace..."* In contrast to the antichrist beast, the true Saviour has feet devoid of clay.

Could the Negative-Messiah (Anti-Christ) Adopt the Name Jesus Christ?

Revelations 13:11 relates an interesting aspect that builds a more concrete picture of this attempted hijacking of the Son's persona by the deceiver. Consider if you will the implications of the following verse: *"Then I saw another beast coming up out of the earth, and he had two horns like a lamb and spoke like a dragon."* Interestingly the beast is described as having horns like a lamb, unlike his usual symbolic satanic depiction as a goat, which also has horns. The above verse contains a definite allusion to an infiltration with the use of the term "like." Also worth noting is that the symbol of the lamb is used a total of 28 times throughout Revelations and 27 of those times it is use exclusively as the Lamb of YHWH Elohim. Therefore this verse reveals the manner in which this beast surfaces and how there is no point in "coming up out of the earth" and looking like anything else apart from the generally accepted view of the Messiah. We'd all love to believe that this beast will have this obvious look, the way some people view George W. Bush. He'll be powerful, yet there will be something obviously unsettling about him and his whole regime, especially to anyone that attends a church on a semi-regular basis. This scenario has no grounds if the name being used for worship by these churchgoers is perfectly adopted by him, if he is accompanied by a performance of miracles and wonders akin to that of the Son's doings in the New Testament. This will particularly be the case if he physically fits the generally accepted view of what the Saviour will look like. With this in mind it is more than reasonable to assume that the antichrist may seal the deception by boldly assuming the name "Jesus Christ."

Now we know that the Antichrist is not an exclusive individual. Who is the beast and how will we recognise him? Unfortunately this question is still somewhat difficult to answer because The Book of Revelation actually speaks of two beasts, one of whom comes out of the sea and another who comes out of the midst of the earth *(Revelation 13:1 & 11a)*. To be more specific, one might ask what is the identity of the beast who causes men to wear a mark for buying and selling? The answer is that there are many identifying characteristics, which are indicated throughout Scripture. The most impressionable one is that people will adore him. He will be a breath of fresh air and a new hope for countless people. Note that he will come after the catastrophic seals have been already opened to appear to bring stability. The false prophet will usher him in and though he will have an appearance of the lamb the content of his speech should give him away. He will speak with impressive words; yet will have a tongue "like a dragon" *(Revelation 13:11b)*. This type of speech is evident today in the arena of politics and diplomacy, where the English language is deceptively twisted to such an elaborate degree that it can be used to dress up any agenda. For example a speech that promotes an act of genocide could be delivered in a way to make it sound acceptable enough to generate applause from the very community, which the genocide is directed.

Remember that the beast will appear to be the good guy to the majority of the world who will happily follow after him. Yahushua will conversely appear in the clouds as the bad guy. Those of us who are in Messiah will have already fled to the cleft in the rock (Petra) while the rest of the globe is conflagrated *(Isaiah 2:21, Daniel 11:41-42)*. In the meantime the majority of Christians will be waiting in their respective homes for the rapture bus that will never come.

Chapter Sixteen

Mind Control, Mind Guidance & The Holy Spirit

"A seed thought thus lodged in the mind of the other person grows and develops, and in time is regarded as the rightful mental offspring of the victim, whereas it is really like the cuckoo's egg placed in the nest of the sparrow...it destroys the rightful offspring of the sparrow." – Secret Doctrine of Rosicrucian Teachings.

To THE AVERAGE person the subjects of mind control, mind manipulation and brainwashing instantly conjure up images of sci-fi films, fanatical religious cults, or trashy pulp comics. They are topics well beyond the normal boundaries of acceptability and the serious broaching of these phenomena is often met with cynicism or ridicule in casual circles. This is predominantly and understandably due to the stupefying potential of such concepts. They sit on equal footing with the practices of invisibility and teleportation, two other capabilities that are still largely relegated to the fantasy genre. Yet amazingly, the general public seems to have conveniently accepted the practice of hypnotism in the entertainment and medical arena without regard to its disturbing potential elsewhere, like in the defence industry.

In this chapter, I not only wish to answer the question of whether certain government departments have the potential to achieve mind control, but also examine the many and varied avenues that such a state can be pursued. I will also examine how it can be effectively harnessed by these departments and used as an unwelcome and suppressive counterfeit to a form of mind guidance that is better known within the Christian community as the Holy Spirit.

What is Mind Control?

By the term mind control I refer to a receptive mental state where control by an external force is automatic and cannot be rejected. This force can take the form of a specific task or series of tasks initiated by a verbal or mental visualisation that may consist of a command or suggestion. It can also manipulate one's health, mood, desire, and perception. The type of mind control I wish to discuss is one that is not generated by hypnotism or subliminal suggestion. On the contrary, in its optimum state, it works in an exacting and deliberate manner by manifesting an immediate command, physical feeling or emotion in the brain of the recipient. It therefore induces a response that far exceeds the expectations of hypnotism or subliminal suggestion.

How Real is it?

The greater part of the community have no clue as to the reality of the covert use of mind control techniques and its very real threat to civil liberties and basic moral principles. In spite of this ignorance, it has been a practice used effectively on individuals and communities for decades with varying degrees of success. The subject has become real enough to see the formation of a number of protest organisations with the sole purpose of spreading awareness and applying public pressure to ban the use of such technologies. Some organisations include **The Citizens Against Human Rights Abuse, The International Movement for the Ban of Manipulation of the Human Nervous System by Technologic Means, Christians Against Mental Slavery,** and the **Moscow Committee for Ecology Dwellings**.

How Did This Technology Come About?

Breakthroughs in this technology first commenced in the early sixties in the Soviet Union where scientists perfected alterations in the condition and perception of rats by way of transmitting ultra-low electromagnetic microwave frequencies. The research then expanded to the human realm and included the distribution of verbal messages that are carried by these pulsed microwave transmissions that could be completely recognisable by the recipient. The U.S. released a report on surveillance technology in 1976 that responded to material found in Communist literature. It stated: "Sounds and possibly even words which appear to be originating intracranially (within the head) can be induced by signal modulation at very low average power densities." Negative effects that soon became apparent through the use of this technology over extended periods of time included heart failure, atrophy of internal cavities, cancer, cataracts, leukemia, birth defects, same sex attraction, learning disabilities, and death. Positive effects also became apparent, such as giving information that warns or coaches a recipient, healing, and increased mental or physical strength. Not so surprisingly, any research into this field enjoys nearly all it's major funding from military sources. Consider, if you will, the contents of the following transcript from a CNN Special Assignment show entitled "Electromagnetic Weapons and Mind Control."

Mr. Decaro states: "CNN enlisted the help of noted physicist Dr. Elizabeth Rausher and electrical engineer Bill VanBise and test an RF mind-interference machine from data found in Soviet scientific literature. The machine itself was inexpensive and easy to construct using parts from a consumer electronics store. It emits a weak magnetic field pulsed at extremely low frequency. As the subject of the test I was blindfolded and my ears were blocked to prevent inadvertent clues as to what was happening. A magnetic probe was placed about 18 inches from my head. As the experiment began, two signal generators produced waveform patterns that were transmitted by the magnetic probe at about one one-thousandth of Earth's magnetic field strength.

VanBise – watching a chart recorder: Describe anything that you see, if any.

DeCaro: In the control room VanBise varied the waveforms being generated. In another room I could see waveforms changing shape in my mind.

Decaro during experiment: A parabola just went by.

Rausher: A parabola just went by...

DeCaro: ...Later, I asked VanBise what a weapon using this technology could do.

VanBise: Induce basically what would be considered hallucinations in people; direct them to do things against their so-called better judgment...

DeCaro: How easy would it be to assemble a weapon from existing off-the shelf parts?

VanBise: Three weeks, I could put together a weapon that would take care of a whole town.

Decaro: We showed the results of our tests to Dr. Robert Becker, a two-time Nobel nominee for his work in biological effects of electromagnetism.

Becker: This is a very significant experiment because it carries our understanding of how vision is actually performed a step further into the mystery."

Night of the Zombies

In March 2001 the Marine Corps division of the Pentagon announced that they were working on a new "non-lethal" crowd control weapon, using a technique involving electromagnetic radiation at higher than microwave frequencies, which can produce pain in multiple targets without permanent injury. An article in the *Air Force Times* called it "perhaps the biggest breakthrough in weapons technology since the atomic bomb." I find the use of the term "non-lethal" very disarming, because such a device has the potential to unleash a variety of unprecedented atrocities. This clever catchname is utilised in completely the opposite manner to the term "weapons of mass destruction," which enjoys the full pronunciation whenever used in official public addresses.

Perhaps the most threatening form of this technology is known as "wide-field mind control." This refers to a technology that can influence and affect the mental mood of occupants over a large geographical location via the use of electromagnetic fields and acoustic phenomena. Recently I have noticed a wave of Zombie movies hitting the big screens and found an alarming reality to them when I married this knowledge of mind manipulation to their usual plotlines. The premise of these films is that a few lone survivors are caught in a situation where the rest of their local community have been transformed into flesh eating maniacs who wander around eliminating uninfected occupants. The storylines of these films are a population control division's dream-come-true as a whole town vehemently wipes itself out without the need for expensive chemical or ballistic resources.

The new wave of weaponry, currently in covert use, is gradually being introduced to the world, by the use of diffusing key terms such as "non-lethal" and "soft." These disarming names provide the perfect verbal counterweight for "Weapons of Mass Destruction" and the "Global War on Terror." But be warned, they may go by any of the following titles:

Electromagnetic Weapons
Microwave Weapons
Non-Lethal Weapons
ELF (Extremely Low Frequency) Weapons
Directed Energy Weapons
Acoustic Weapons
Psychotronic Weapons
RF (Radio Frequency) Weapons
Soft Kill Weapons
Less-than-Lethal Weapons

Media and News Reports on the Subject

I am always mindful of people who refute hard-to-believe subjects, which lack sufficient evidence and therefore resort to ridicule them. So in view of this I have included a comprehensive list (collected from a website disclosed in the bibliography of this work) of news and media material that has been printed on this topic.

Literally scores of news articles and defence reports have appeared over the last decade from reputable sources containing disturbing information on genuine breakthroughs in the field of psycho-weaponry yet thus far it has failed to make any sort of impact on the wider community. This news scrapes by unnoticed or with readers failing to make any connections of how this technology may be used to devastating effect. The real terror of mass mind control doesn't even rate on par with the recent media driven, and at times ambiguous subject of "global terror." Some excerpts from articles that have appeared in news reports and briefs that are legally and easily available for public viewing include:

Newsweek, 1994 – "'Soon, Phasers on Stun' – ...the list of exotic technologies that could be harnessed for non-lethal weapons is already large and growing. It includes lasers, microwaves, sound waves, strobe lights, electromagnetic pulses, microbes, chemicals, computer viruses – even giant nets..." (Notice again the use of the term "non-lethal," cleverly administered to soften the subject. What better way to fight a war on terror than with non-lethal means.)

Department of Defence Draft of Non-lethal Weapons Policy, July 21, 1994 – "The term 'adversary' is used above in its broadest sense, including those who are not declared enemies but who are engaged in activities we wish to stop. This policy does not preclude legally authorized domestic use of non-lethal weapons by U.S. military forces in support of law enforcement."

U.S. News article, by Douglas Pasternak, July 1997 – "'Wonder Weapons: The Pentagon's quest for non-lethal arms is amazing, but is it smart?' – By using very low frequency electromagnetic radiation – the waves way below radio frequencies on the electromagnetic spectrum – he (Eldon Byrd) found he could induce the brain to release behaviour-regulating chemicals. 'We could put animals into a stupor,' he says by hitting them with these frequencies. 'We got chick brain – in vitro – to dump 80% of the natural opioids in their brains,' Byrd says. He even ran a small project that used magnetic fields to cause certain brain cells in rats to release histamine. In humans, this would cause instant flu-like symptoms and produce nausea. 'These fields were extremely weak. They were undetectable,' says Byrd. 'The effects were non-lethal and reversible.

You could disable a person temporarily,' Byrd hypothesizes. 'It would have been like a stun gun.'"

New Scientist, September 7, 1996 – "'Perfect Sound from Thin Air' – (This refers to a company called American Technology Corporation) The system may also have applications in crowd control. Powerful, low-frequency sound can cause disorientation and nausea. In the 1960s, the US tried unsuccessfully to use low-frequency sound from helicopters to disable enemy soldiers in the Vietnamese jungle. But the sound sources needed were so intense that they almost shook the aircraft apart, and most of the sound was absorbed by those nearest to the loudspeakers. According to Norris, acoustical heterodyning could pinpoint an individual up to 200 or 300 metres away by positioning the interface zone correctly."

World Foundation for Natural Sciences Report, October 17, 1998 – "A weapon which could intrude into the brain of an individual represents a gross invasion of their private life. The idea that these new systems could be created in the next several years should be cause for significant discussion and public debate. On July 21, 1994, Dr. Christopher Lamb, Director of Policy Planning, issued a draft Department of Defence directive which would establish a policy for non-lethal weapons in the United State. The policy was intended to take effect January 1, 1995, and formally connected the military's non-lethal research to civilian law enforcement agencies. The government's plan to use pulsed electromagnetic and radio frequency systems as a non-lethal technology for domestic Justice Department use rings the alarm for some observers. Nevertheless, the plan for integrating these systems is moving forward. Coupling these uses with expanded military missions is even more disturbing."

Defence News, January 11, 1993 – "'U.S. Explores Russian Mind Control Technology' – Washington – The Russian government is perfecting mind-control technology developed in the 1970s that could be used to hone fighting capabilities of friendly forces while demoralizing and disabling opposing troops. Known as acoustic psycho-correction, the capability to control minds and alter behaviour of civilians and soldiers may soon be shared with U.S. military, medical and political officials, according to U.S. and Russian sources…"

Time Magazine, June 26, 1995 – "Time magazine reported on Mike Koernke, of the Michigan Militia, who believes that there are 'Americans enslaved and implanted with microchips.' This is a plausible claim as the government-funded behavioral control research in the 1970s, which included implanting electrodes to control violence by a Harvard Medical School professor and others ... Means are being found in all the crafts and sciences of man, society and life, that will soon make possible precise control over much of people's actions, thoughts, emotions, moods and wills...Radio remote controls over epileptic seizures, sexual desires, and speech patterns are already operational." (I was interested by the use of the term "crafts" which made me ponder what type of crafts this article is referring to.)

The Times, September 21, 1996 – "'Stick'em Up' – As former science-fictions writers, [Janet and Christopher Morris, leading proponents of non-lethal weapons] the couple speak with zeal about a coming age in which the enemy will be disorientated by very low frequency sound waves, dazzled by isotropic radiators, imprisoned by invisible magnetic fields...The Morrises even talk admiringly about a technology that would enable two different acoustic beams to plant a voice in a dictator's head, convincing his subordinates that he has suddenly gone mad."

Scientific American, April 1994 – "Scientific American reported that Janet E. Morris and her husband Christopher C. Morris 'have been involved promoting a psycho-correction technology, developed by a Russian scientist, that is intended to influence by means of subliminal messages embedded in sound or visual images."

St Martin's Press, 1994 – "'Mind Wars' – There is, according to the best resources, a real threat in the electrical manipulation of the human mind. The possibility arose from research that attempted to explain telepathy electromagnetically...According to Barbara Honegger (who was on the Reagan White House staff), 'the fundamental reason for the increased interest' in psychic warfare, and the area where the pentagon spends most of its estimated 6-million-dollar annual budget for psychic or related research, 'is initial results coming out of laboratories in the United States and Canada that certain amplitude and frequency combinations of external electromagnetic radiation in the brain-wave frequency range are capable of bypassing the external sensory mechanisms of organisms, including humans, and indirectly stimulating higher-level neuronal structures in the brain."

Defence and Foreign Affairs Daily, June 7, 1983 – "According to Dr. Adey, who reportedly visited the USSR, the Soviets have used the machine (called a 'Lida,' which bombards human brains with radio waves) on people since at least 1960. The machine is technically described as 'a distant pulse treatment apparatus.' It generates 40 megahertz radio waves which stimulate the brain's electromagnetic activity at substantially lower frequencies."

Microwave News, Nov-Dec 1993 – "...a three day top-secret non-lethal weapons conference which took place in the Applied Physics Laboratory at the John Hopkins University in Maryland. 400 scientists gathered at the university to discuss their work in developing non-lethal weapons technologies, including radio frequency radiation (RF), electromagnetic pulse (EMP) weapons, ELF, lasers and chemical weapons."

Los Angeles Herald Examiner, November 1976 – "The report said that along with microwave hearing, the Soviets have also studied various changes in body chemistry and functioning of the brain resulting from exposure to microwaves and other frequencies of the electromagnetic spectrum. 'One psychological effect which has been demonstrated is heart seizure,' the report said...it has been accomplished experimentally with frogs by synchronizing the pulses of a microwave signal with the animal's heartbeat and then beaming the radiation at the chest area. The document added that 'a frequency probably could be found which would provide sufficient penetration of the chest wall of humans to accomplish the same effect.' –heart attacks."

Bulletin of Atomic Scientists, Sept-Oct, p.44. – "Barbara Hatch Rosenburg, director of the Chemical and Biological Weapons Program of the Federation of American Scientists, writes about electromagnetic weapons: 'These weapons are said to cause temporary or permanent blindness, interference with mental process, modifications of behaviour or emotional response, seizures, severe pain, dizziness, nausea and diarrhea, or disruption of internal organ functions in various other ways.'"

Sunday Telegraph, September 27, 1992 – "'Microwave Bomb That Does not Kill' – The microwave bomb, which works by emitting a massive pulse of radio energy, would render humans unconscious by scrambling neural paths in the brain but would not cause lasting injury."

Military Review, Dec 1980 – "'The New Mental Battlefield: Beam Me Up Spock' – There are weapons systems that operate on the power of the mind and whose lethal capacity has already been demonstrated...the ability to heal or cause disease can be transmitted over distance thus inducing illness or death for no apparent cause...The application of large scale ELF (extra low frequency) behaviour modification could have horrendous impact...mind-to-mind thought induction techniques are also being considered."

Even Satan Knows Performing Great Wonders Convinces Masses

Some mornings I get up early enough to watch an evangelist by the name of Benny Hinn, who presents a world touring healing ministry. His sermons usually take place in the most overwhelmingly large stadiums and auditoriums. The format usually consists of praise music, prayer to anoint the location, a short sermon, and healings. These healings consist of audience members coming forward and giving testimonies of any remission of illnesses they may have experienced during the course of the meeting. I have always held the opinion that many of these individuals experience a tangible type of healing, yet if this is true it should not necessarily support a case that this evangelist has YHWH behind him. Rarely do individuals, once they hit the stage, get healed on command. Not conducting healings that way keeps the proceedings running smoothly and reduces the chance of a failed confrontation presenting itself, as only those who claim they have been affected by a healing will come forward.

After becoming suitably convinced of the capability government departments have to induce pain, fatigue, sexual arousal, anger, euphoria, instant fatal injury and even accelerated healing by way of low frequency microwave transmissions it is with strong resolve that I feel a genuine link exists with this type of technology and these ever expanding crusades. If there is any truth to this theory, there is always the possibility that Hinn may be totally oblivious to the true origin of these healings, and while still perpetuating a bed of deception, he plods on with complete sincerity in his motivation.

The Set-Apart (Holy) Spirit

Linking the subject of mind control to the Set-Apart (Holy) Spirit might seem unusual at first glance, but as I hope to explain, it is the key to understanding the basic communication and guidance structure of the heavens. A communication potential that mankind is within arm's reach of grasping. But as man reaches forward into this final frontier, so too does the twisted and corrupted hand of the deceiver.

As I have already established, the word "spirit" is predominantly used to describe something that originates from YHWH, which is perpetually invisible to the naked eye, or was at one time unseen and yet has a discernable and influencing presence. Just the same as when a wind blows on a person and affects them, but at the same time cannot be seen. The term "ghost" is also used interchangeably with this word when it appears as the "Holy Ghost." However, when this is the case it appears that there is an additional accompaniment of YHWH Himself *(Matthew 1:18)*. Ghost, on its own, can also be described as a person's will or life force. It even enjoys the more traditional use in reference of the fabled non-corporeal apparitions of dead humans as opposed to dead Nephilim as explained in chapter nine of this book. The King James Version favours a use of the term as a type of will in many verses such as: *Job 11:20 But the eyes of the wicked shall fail, and they shall not escape, and their hope shall be as the <u>giving up of the ghost</u>.*[18]

Essentially the Set-Apart Spirit is an infused knowledge and guidance feed that is emitted from YHWH and is freely accessible to any human being that chooses to surrender their own spirit to its authority. It can also increase physical strength *(Judges 14:6)* and

---

18   Excerpted from *The Complete Multimedia Bible based on the King James Version.* Copyright © 1994 Compton's NewMedia, Inc.

clearly exhibits the potential to inseminate *(Luke 1:35)*. It predominantly functions as a highly sophisticated downlink to the Creator and would have lethal potential in the hands of any human civilisation that could manufacture a similar device. *1 Corinthians 12: 7-11* describes a diversity in its manifestations and its overall purpose: *"But the manifestations of the Spirit is given to each one for the profit of all: for to one is given the word of wisdom through the Spirit, to another, the word of knowledge through the same Spirit, to another faith by the same Spirit, to another gifts of healings by the same spirit, to another the working of miracles, to another prophecy, to another discerning spirits, to another different kinds of tongues, to another the interpretation of tongues. But one and the same Spirit works all these things, distributing to each one individually as He (YHWH) wills."*

Human emotions are usually felt in the anatomical location of the heart and stomach regions, yet the origins of these sensations originate in the brain. The conscience is like a type of local receptor that comes with every sentient person at their conception. If a person so chooses, they can later enjoy the benefit of receiving an upgrade in the form of the Set-Apart (Holy) Spirit. While the Scriptures speak of a cloud of witnesses (angels) that watch over us *(Hebrews 12:1)*, who have the potential to minister and guide, there is an ongoing opportunity to log onto a network run by the original Owner and Operator, enabling a closer active relationship with this Being. This logging on or tapping into is not achieved by attaining special abilities to make the manual connection, as is the case with some "mystery schools" and "esoteric societies," but is an automatic process achieved by a single action. It is important to understand that the residence of this Set-Apart Spirit in an occupant is not necessarily always a requirement for salvation. A long time may pass between a person's baptism (mikveh) or conversion to receiving the Set-Apart Spirit as is illustrated in *Acts 8:14-17; "Now when the apostles who were at Jerusalem heard that Samaria had received the word of God, they sent Peter and John to them, who, when they had come down, prayed for them that they might receive the Holy Spirit. For as yet He had fallen upon none of them. They had only been baptized in the name of the Lord Jesus. Then they laid hands on them, and they received the Holy Spirit."* It is also absolutely imperative to understand that complete submission to the Set-Apart Spirit will not always guarantee a preconceived outcome concerning a recipient. This is because as we fluctuate in our submissiveness to it, so to does our awareness of what it may reveal to us. It is by faith that a recipient walks. A physically bad situation may still worsen or a request may not be responded to in the manner or timing that is envisioned. The Set-Apart Spirit in itself is a facilitator and like angels, is not to be understood or accessed in exclusion from YHWH.

Mental Pathways

People have a tendency to follow a number of different mental paths. I will attempt to cover most of them here. They are:

1) Sole reliance on own conscience

2) Shifting reliance between own conscience or some other aspect of guidance (whether Set-Apart Spirit or some other unrelated spirit)

3) Reliance on the Set-Apart Spirit

4) Reliance on some other unrelated spirit (whether demonic or technological in origin)

5) Total disregard for own conscience (short-lived state, may inevitably lead to any of the other options listed)

6) Complete loss of own will (basically a robot)

Satan's Unholy Counterfeit Spirit

These days a great portion of the known world is in comfortable possession of three pieces of technology: a telephone, a radio and a television. The telephone can send out a sound, in the form of a ring tone, to a specific location, enabling two vastly separated individuals to converse. A radio can emit voice and music that travels on waves and can be picked up in vast geographical locations, enabling a great many listeners to receive news and information simultaneously. The television is this again, but accompanies the sound with moving imagery. The introduction of such forms of technology to the world has gradually changed the face of modern society. The marketplace benefited from these advancements in advertising, as also did armed forces with the advent of modern warfare. As of the year 2000 data transfer during wartime hit a rate of .5 million words per minute and it is estimated to reach 1.5 trillion words per minute in the year 2010. Now with the dawning era of shrinking technological apparatus, there is already solid talk of a newer, more efficient device that encompasses all the aspects of existing phones that neatly fits into the rear molar tooth of an occupant. An article by Anne Wall discusses the development of the "tooth implant phone" and how it "may only be a matter of years before the filling in your molar has more byte than bite." It is to function by way of a small long range receiver that turns the phone on and off and can also receive data from a radio or computer. It derives power by converting jaw and head movements of the user into useful energy and relays voice transmitions via vibrations that transfer directly to the inner ear. I am regularly visited by friends with small phones devices wrapped round one ear from which stretches a speaker toward their mouth. I quietly shudder to myself as the evidence of our attainment to the heights of Babel is plainly visible. This, as with all technology, is following a path of diminishing scale and increased efficiency, until it may one day reach the same format utilised by YHWH Himself at the creation of earth and its contents. This format is "speech." It is no coincidence that the only common action of all the stages of creation in Genesis is the act of speaking, written as "Then God said..."

The Use of Mind Control to Eliminate "Middle Grounders"

The Scriptures pound us with the message that there are only two types of people, those that serve one master and those that serve another. Within these two brackets of people there are many divisions of supporters labouring in either camp. One group of people serves either master openly and knowingly, another supports one unknowingly, and within these divisions services can vary in their effectiveness. It is my humble opinion that the most efficient supporters of those in opposition to YHWH are those that appear to follow him, but in secret set out to dismantle his body. We know that the Jesuits (the society of Jesus) were set up for that specific purpose and the fruits of their labours are evident today with so much disinformation and confusion on countless subjects, ranging from everything from Scripture itself to the UFO phenomena. If it were not so there would be no need for any books to clarify these subjects.

The particular type of people I wish to focus on here are the secular, atheist and agnostic population, a cross section of society that has beliefs which amount to living lives devoid of any active reverence to a higher being. They may have sympathy for a particular religion yet remain neutral on a belief system. Such as someone at a party who says they believe in Karma, but on further questioning, haven't got a clue what it's about. They have a vague philosophy that provides the motivation to keep a satisfactory moral mean. Some atheists might display a passion for non-belief on par with a believer, especially if challenged. But ultimately they will have no preference to adhering to any practice or custom that is contingent on a force that falls outside their regular perceived sphere of reality.

Occasionally I pose the question, "If there were no law, and you couldn't be punished legally, would you rob a bank?" More often than not the answer is quite alarming. If I hear the response, "Yes," I make a mental note not to be anywhere near this type of person in case a future world wide economic collapse ensues.

A Possible Scenario

My theory is that mind control will inevitably escalate in use across the globe by way of a steadily escalating bombardment of wide field microwave pulses. These pulses will induce a range of physical and mental reactions such as apathy, inaction and complacency in the population. Most occupants of First World countries own a mobile phone; some even own more than one and many are accepting models that fit into the ear. These make perfect conductors to assist in the transmission of these low frequency beams as mobiles work on the basis of such technology anyway. These invisible transmissions will continue until the population will have unknowingly entered a phase of mind control that sees them disinterested in protest actions, appealing against injustices, or lobbying unfair governmental rulings.

Prior to the manually injected feed of the fear of terrorism, there was already a wide spread attitude of complacency in the west. This was helped along by distractions in the entertainment industry and the relaxing of restrictions in the lending of money via luxurious credit card limits and easy to get loans. The fallout from the fear of terrorism has only served to erase personal liberties as people unwittingly give the government and corporations more power to quell the perceived problem. Once this has subsided and people fall back into this mode of complacency, a new environment of diminished rights will see them in worse shape than before.

The skyrocketing population of Third World countries will be dealt with by population control, which will scale down numbers by way of diseases (Cancer, Aids, Bird-Flue), famines, funding continuing conflicts and initiating what appear to be natural disasters, until human numbers are manageable. It is important to understand that mind control is merely one tool from a toolbox of numerous instruments that are and will work in unison to achieve this outcome. So what is the solution to this H.G. Wells, *Time Machine* like existence, where the hero of the story travels into the future to find a utopian environment lined with manipulators that cultivate it to suit their own unspeakable ends?

The answer lies with submission to the will of the Set-Apart Spirit. It will be the only guaranteed protection against a possible onslaught of an array of very aggressive mental attacks that could be leveled at an individual near the end of the this age. In the past people who did not have the Spirit residing within them could receive protection against spiritual attacks through a number of different means. But gradually the climate could become so saturated with evil, through attacks being initiated by both manmade and purely spiritual sources, that it may become increasingly difficult for the average person to make continued rational or fundamental moral decisions. A type of mental one-sided propaganda continually dogging a person's psyche could soon give rise to a population that will seem to exhibit no workable middle ground of objectivity. Presently there exists the ability to apply personal judgment in decision-making. But if the ability to execute discernment is consistently affected, a person will be unable to select a correct path, even if one is clearly presented.

Ultimately we may be looking at a situation where people are either brainwashed or are followers of YHWH. Whether this theory comes to fruition or not, there will certainly be more aggressive applications introduced to encourage people to swing one way or the other in terms of whom they will obey. People who remain unconvinced of the existence of a God will either have to follow the rules of a world system that does have this belief or follow the enlightened few that also believe in a God, but one who opposes such a regime.

Of course mind control is not a new form of attack. Satan has already been influencing us in this fashion since man's fall. The demon-possessed men in the cemetery serve as a shining example of a more excessive case *(Matthew 8:28)*. Through the use of demons and even humans who are involved in occult practices, people have always been vulnerable to both subtle and extreme mental attacks. The only difference now is that through technological means human-run organisations maybe able to enact the same outcomes. But remember the same admiral is at the helm of the ship.

Chapter Seventeen

"Clothed in Glory" and "Devoured" by the Land or Nano-Technology Suits and Worm Holes?

WITHIN SCRIPTURE THE word "glory" often means much more than a term of endearment. The English rendering is a transliteration of the name of a Roman goddess called "Gloria." It has a connotation of sun radiance or the emanation of an intense light. The original Hebrew word that "glory" espouses is "Kabad," which does not necessarily carry this same meaning. So too in Greek the term "doxa" means "esteem" or "estimation."

Despite this revelation, some verses in Scripture do appear to use the word in a context that denotes the accompaniment of some sort of uncommon visual splendour. In a previous chapter I have even concurred with the extreme view of some controversial authors who have linked the term with craft exhaust emission or the outer hull of some aerial transportation.

There are four translations of the word "glory" used in modern Bibles. The first is its usage in the more traditional sense as a description of a people or an individual's sheer magnificence. The second is the aforementioned fiery exhaust trail and the third is the outer-body of an airborne chariot. The fourth is something that I wish to discuss in some detail here.

I believe that current research programs in the U.S. geared toward designing elite forms of body armour will produce a crude version of something that the Bible occasionally describes as "glory." Military technology is advancing to a state that will enable a specialised soldier to attain a range of capabilities that would not easily be accepted by the general public. They include partial and complete invisibility to the naked eye, fast and silent movement, greater jumping capacity, instant automated medical assistance, continuous acclimatisation, and complete protection from small arms fire, shrapnel and cutting implements. It would not be a far cry to imagine a scenario where a combatant of a Third World country would equate a military engagement of appropriately attired individuals as an encounter with the gods.

Before I launch into the heart of the matter, a major source which first steered me onto this train of thought, needs to be presented. The following extract comes from an abridged version of a Jewish oral teaching called the *Haggadah*. The particular portion I wish to draw attention to details a moment immediately following man's fall in Genesis:

"The first result was that Adam and Eve became naked. Before, their bodies had been overlaid with a **HORNY SKIN** and enveloped with the **CLOUD OF GLORY**. No sooner had they violated the command given them then the **CLOUD OF GLORY** and **HORNY SKIN** dropped from them, and they stood there in their nakedness..."

This extract from an ancient Jewish teaching challenged my original understanding of the story of Adam and Eve. The generally accepted view is that they simply developed a new awareness of the evil potentials of their nakedness as is demonstrated in their former innocence of such a state in *Genesis 2:25; "And they were both naked, the man and his wife, and were not ashamed."* On the surface this ancient Jewish teaching appeared to contradict the biblical account. However an investigation into the Hebrew root of the word "naked" demanded that I maintain this line of inquiry. In an essay on Jewish head coverings, Rabbi Edward Levi points out that there are two Hebrew words used for "naked" in these passages. The first is "arom" and the second, after the fall, is "erom." Neither of which mean completely bare.

A *Bible Heritage Report* by Jim Myers seemed to shed even more light on the subject. The article pointed out that both Hebrew words shared the same root as the translated words "subtle," "shrewd," or "cunning" as in *Genesis 3:1a; "Now the serpent was more cunning than any beast of the field which the Lord God had made."* So *Genesis 3:1a* can be rendered *"...was more naked than any beast..."* and in turn *Genesis 2:25*'s account of Adam and Eve can be rendered *"And they were both cunning..."* This is also the case with the word "ashamed" at the end of the same verse, which can be translated as "confused." On further reflection I also began to realise that to be considered clothed, one has to be dressed in a garment that is from a foreign source. Therefore if a creature wore an outer covering similar to a fur coat or scales that grew from itself, it would still technically be considered naked. With these points noted this slight variation of Adam and Eve's plight in the *Haggadah* seemed to join a few dots that had drifted unanchored amongst my research. A little bit further on I read statements like, "...(Adam) lost his celestial clothing," and "his body was to exude sweat." After I first read these passages, I stood with my mouth gaping and mind racing as the mentioning of this "horny skin," "cloud of glory" and "celestial clothing," taunted me with implications too bizarre to comprehend. I believed I had lifted a dust-laden sheet off a piece of knowledge that many professional scholars and notable theologians had feared to uncover. Or if they had uncovered it, they conveniently failed to share their information with the rest of the world. If the latter was the case, in their defence, maybe fear of ridicule or a savage assault from the church kept them silent.

While the *Haggadah* is not Scripture, it makes up between one-third and one-sixth (depending on the period) of ancient Judaic interpretations on the Bible, ethics, Bible commentaries, sciences, medicine, mathematics, and Jewish history. The *Haggadah* was not generally understood to contain fables or legends, but solid teachings for a wider secular audience. This is no different to commentaries and books that specialise in specific Biblical topics today. The advantage with this ancient text unlike more modern works that seek to amplify Scripture, is that the majority of these teachings were written around the fifth century BC, not long after the Old Testament was also written. This means that these writings do not have to pass over an unfathomable cultural gulf that is often the hurdle for later Greco-Roman interpretations.

"Snakes, why do they have to be snakes?" – Indiana Jones

The description of a horny skin brought my mind back to the familiar characteristic of a reptile. My thoughts went immediately to the seraphim mentioned in *Isaiah 6:1-2*, inhabiting the throne of YHWH and their assault in *Numbers 21:6* on disobedient Israelites where the encounter has them conveniently described as "fiery serpents." The term fiery serpent comes from the Hebrew root seraphim, apparently too hot to use in its translated form in the vicinity of YHWH in the Book of Isaiah. So sitting oddly among the heavenly host is a serpent, in complete opposition to the association the Bible portrays of such a creature. I also vividly recalled ancient biblical images of YHWH portrayed as a serpent and Yahushua also depicted as a wise serpent of wisdom in 2nd century Gnostic Christianity. There is even an illustration of a stone-carved image that has the vertical body of a snake ending in a human head that is an exact replication of the face on the shroud of Turin. A Savant in Napoleon's army drew the image from a relief on an Egyptian temple in 1798. The similarities of this face with the Turin image, which was not photographed until 1888, are virtually identical. This revelation, coupled with my earlier suspicions of the shroud being a smoke screen, brought me spiraling backwards toward an embarrassing contradiction. On the one hand I was saying that it is not a depiction of Yahushua and on the other hand I was implying that the serpent was indeed a symbol of him and the Father, supported by the predated image resembling the shroud figure's head attached to a snake. Thankfully it wasn't long before I found an acceptable solution to my dilemma that allowed me not to back away from either theory. But, at the time, before I arrived at any satisfactory conclusion I took a while to reflect on all the information I had gathered.

You'll Never Learn This in Bible Study

Gnostic Christianity is and was a form of the faith that emphasises a pursuit of knowledge over an emphasis on maintaining a loving obedience to YHWH's commandments. "Gnosis" comes from a Greek word meaning knowledge. Mystery schools adopt many Gnostic knowledge seeking principles with a chief emphasis on finding a Saviour within one's self. To that degree of it I am not in favour, however common Christianity peaks in the opposite direction in that it almost advertises a total lockout of seeking any knowledge at the expense of belief alone. Knowledge seeking is arranged in tailored Bible study groups marshaled by a host, equipped with an ability to march people through verses at a speed that doesn't generally allow too much investigation; making me think that perhaps a correct middle ground between these two unacceptable extremes was once, more correctly, trodden.

Whatever the case, at the time of reading these portions of the *Haggadah*, I needed a reality check. I was not, nor am I a formal scholar or student of theology or biblical history. Where was I going wrong? My understanding was that the serpent or dragon was an almost exclusive form for Satan, and not in any way related to YHWH. I needed to find out more.

Recapping my findings it became blatantly clear that the *Haggadah* described the "horny skin" of Adam and Eve as being likened to "a luminous garment" and being as "bright as daylight." The Bible, despite appearing to carry a contradiction, did not run counter to this claim. Could it have been that, to the unfamiliar eye, the garments appeared similar to a cross between the skin of a chameleon and a crocodile, which in turn could have given them the appearance of an upright serpent? Continuing on this line of thinking I also pondered the reference to the exuding of sweat and how the Genesis account also emphasises Adam's punishment of toiling the land by the sweat of his brow and the relationship this has with animal physiology in the reptile kingdom. Was it possible that this outer skin enabled the occupant to avoid sweating?

I did know, at the time, that current areas of military research were on the threshold of perfecting a suit that could keep a soldier automatically acclimatised to any external environmental condition and also maintain the subject's exertion levels to a degree that eliminated sweating or fatigue. A safety feature would also enable the suit to glow with a brilliant light if the wearer was lost at sea or missing in action.

A few authors, who have noted similarities in ancient records between power inducing garments and man's current technological breakthroughs in perfecting the ultimate survival suit, have forwarded the opinion that our ancestors were reptilian gods. Even as I write a movement is gaining momentum that consists of people who honestly believe mankind descended from reptiles. This is not a popular theory among the Christian or secular scientific communities for obvious reasons. This observation is one that I too am not completely comfortable with, but as I will attempt to show, it is less to do with the fact that Satan is portrayed as such, because we must remember that even he appears as an angel of light.

The White Robe, The Magic Cloak and The Mantle.

Adam and Eve became stripped of an exterior natural garment or outer skin that, despite the application of another covering, would not meet the quality or standard of the original. Whatever they lost it was something that could not be easily replicated and not having it bore them great shame. If I had a favourite set of clothes taken away I would set out to acquire new clothing and the problem would be solved, but with Adam and Eve this seemed not to be as simple. Instead they departed the scene clad in tunics of skin, apparently now clothed once again, yet still bearing their shame *(Genesis 3:21)*.

Many times when an outer garment is mentioned in the Bible it can also be referred to as a mantle, cloak or robe. In 2 Kings there is an important emphasis placed on the mantle or cloak that had fallen from Elijah. *2 Kings 2:13-14; "He also took up the mantle of Elijah that had fallen from him, and went back and stood by the bank of the Jordan. Then he took the mantle of Elijah that had fallen from him, and struck the water, and said, "where is the Lord God of Elijah?" And when he also had struck the water, it was divided this way and that; and Elisha crossed over."*

Another interesting aspect of this emphasis of an outer garment or robe is found in *Revelation 6:10-11* when the souls of those who had been *"slain for the word of God (YHWH)"* cry out *"how long... O'Lord (YHWH), holy and true, until You judge and avenge our blood on those who dwell on the earth?"* In response to this plea these souls are each given white robes with the command to *"rest a little while longer..."* And earlier in *Revelations 3:5* is a promise of being clothed in white garments as well as an assured place in the Book of Life. Could this be a returning of the outer mantle that was once taken away from Adam and Eve?

There is a video game on the market called *Halo*, which is a first person "shoot'em up" game where heavily armoured infantry face-off against a colorful array of combatants. This game is extremely popular and the soldiers that are available within the game all possess a curious characteristic. The sophisticated armour that they wear is green and completely covers the soldiers from head to toe. The armour's texture appears barbed in places and the helmet is quite obviously shaped like the head of a snake. The helmet is configured in such a way that the jaw of the snake is wide open, making a gap where the face sits behind a lit reddish or orange visor. The suit is completely self-contained and offers a numerous array of features to keep gamers entertained for hours. Could the portrayal of such a suit in something as harmless as a video game be a glimpse of the future? In the popular *Dune* novels by Frank Herbert, the inhabitants of the desert planet wear a "still-suit" that allows them to keep cool in the heated climate and even relieve themselves. The suit processes the occupant's urine through a purification system and is later distributed into a bladder that is suitable for drinking. Tabletop war simulation games have also become completely saturated by soldiers in powerful suits called exoskeletons. In fact the idea of super-powered suits, whether they be in movies, books or games is nothing new, but is it set to be a reality? More and more the suits in these games possess an interface that works via implanted microchips that are surgically grafted to the soldier's brain, so that he can activate a suit's features through voice control, movement of his head or even thought. If you think that all this could not break into the realms of reality think again. In 2003 a conference was held in Washington DC that was sponsored by an organisation called DARPA (Defence Advanced Research Projects Agency). The title of the conference was called, "Harvesting Biology for Defence Technology." In an article entitled, "DARPA Bioengineering Program Seeks to Turn Soldiers Into Cyborgs," Author, Cheryl Seal, reveals a 24-million dollar "Brain Interface Program" that is aimed at "developing ways to 'integrate' soldiers into machines – literally – by wiring them (remotely and directly) to their planes, tanks, or computers." Bernadette Tansey, of the *San Francisco Chronicle* also wrote an article in 2003 called, "Molecular Might," that contained some key points that certainly indicate a future not unlike the imagery on show in the *Halo* franchise:

"'Nanotech 'battle suits' could amplify soldiers' powers.' …(Edwin) Thomas (director of the Institute of Soldier Nanotechnologies) said a future 'battle suit' could be more like a car than mere camouflage-and-khaki clothing – with options like radio communication, heating and air conditioning, bulletproof shields and bionic-man-like tools built in. Some of these features could work automatically, like air bags, at the instant they're needed, by a soldier who may be under fire or injured."

It's hard to doubt the overwhelming potential of the future soldier following these claims from a man who is at the head of a company that has the full support of the U.S. army in the form of a 50-million dollar five-year grant. I also happened to notice that this article mentioned a word I was seeing more and more these days – Nanotechnology.

What is Nanotechnology?

While most people have a vague understanding of what computer and biological technologies are and what they can do, the definition of nanotechnology, despite widespread use of the term, is still very much a grey area for many people. Though most of us have heard of nanotechnology and know that it is something to do with the manipulation of extremely small particles, a full definition might leave a person wondering what would happen if such an advanced science fell into the wrong hands. In my search for a basic definition I became swamped with so many different spins on a description from so many publications and websites that it became hard to choose a simple, yet all encompassing explanation. Firstly, imagine an object so small that you need a microscope to see it. Now think of something even smaller than that. Now keep going and think of an object so small that thousands of them can fit in a "full stop." Now imagine that these tiny objects can be redesigned, positioned and manipulated to achieve any defined goal.

Nanotechnology can be best described as individual sub-atomic sized smart matter that work on a combined molecular level and has the capacity to replicate and mimic any material and that material's function. It can also be described as devices that are smaller than microelectromechanical systems (MEMS) that are of nanometer to micron scale and are generally fabricated by chemical processes that result in the growth or formation of certain useful structures. Microelectromechanical systems (MEMS) are devices and machines that are fabricated using techniques generally used in microelectronics, often to integrate mechanical or hydraulic functions with electrical functions. Nanotechnology is a newer way of creating MEMS structures in the "Nano" range, which is 1000 times smaller than the current generation of MEMS devices. These systems of molecular size can emulate the behaviour of larger systems and any life system is potentially creatable in these dimensions, using standard biological or even inorganic components.

If these components were woven as the fabric of a garment they could perform functions at the wearer's command or as a protective reaction to virtually any external force. This could take the form of mimicking any structure density with less than half the associated weight of an equivalent compound, or fabricating any articulating mechanism consistent with natural law, which leaves the term "suit" as a grossly inadequate description of such a device.

371

For example, scientists at The Massachusetts Institute of Technology are in the process of developing a soft, invisible clothing that can solidify into a medical cast when a soldier is injured or turn the forearm into a "karate glove" for combat. Ultimately nanotechnology is atomic engineering with the ability to devise self-replicating machines, robots, and computers that are molecular sized. The possibilities appear limitless. Another article written in 2003 by Abraham McLaughlin, a staff writer of the *Christian Science Monitor* also had some interesting insights:

"'The quest to create a futuristic battle suit, one micron at a time' – ...Another project – which involves medical researchers – would include nano-sized bioweapons sensors. When the battle suit detected chemical weapons it would close up a system of 'pores' that would keep toxins away from the soldier. Indeed, the beauty of nano-tech, (Dr. Ned) Thomas (director of ISN) explains, is that it can include multiple functions all woven into a fabric as thin as a wet suit."

Could it not be such a far cry to deduce that certain men are capable of perfecting a cloak, mantle, or suit that could enable the wearer to do many miraculous feats? Perhaps a suit that is so perfectly designed that it acts in a symbiotic manner to the wearer and virtually never needs to come off, never needs additional clothing to keep the occupant warm, never needs to be cleaned, and forms an appropriate shape and function during times of recreation or conflict. Certainly such a suit with this vast array of capabilities is the goal of many well-funded organisations. An article on December 30, 2004 at a Nanotechnology news site called *News.NanoApex.com* stated the following:

"Scientists have won a 1 million pound grant to help develop clothes that never need cleaning. It will aid research into nanotechnology, looking at the properties of fabrics down to atomic particles. And it could make the plot of the 1951 Ealing comedy, *The Man In The White Suit* a reality."

And a press release that appeared on August 8, 2005 in *Nanotechnology Now* also stated:

"Sending your favourite suit to the dry cleaners could one day be come an infrequent practice. Researches at Clemson University are developing a highly water-repellant coating made of silver nanoparticles that they say can be used to produce suits and other clothing items that offer superior resistance to dirt as well as water and require much less cleaning than conventional fabrics...in addition to suits, the new coating could be applied to hospital garments, sportswear, military uniforms and raincoats."

Are we seeing a glimpse into the beginnings of a covering that will have the ability to shift between a bright uniform, similar in appearance to an angel, and a protective scaled hide, similar in appearance to a reptile? Is the end result of this present technology a fundamental characteristic that was inbuilt into the newly created humans, Adam and Eve?

It would not be difficult to accept that prior to the division of one third of the Heavenly Host, there was once a time when all of the Elohim carried a range of tangible unifying similarities. As the climate moved into a period of war, combatants on both sides could have assumed appropriate warlike attire. Early human witnesses of such beings could have perceived both parties as upright walking or flying reptiles, while if these same beings were viewed today, they might be described more like the characters in the popular video game, *Halo*. However, such a suit would more accurately be described as a malleable organic extension of the occupant, rather than a temporarily donned mechanical suit. So just as a crab is devoid of a foreign covering and is thus considered naked, it is still covered by its own protective shell. Therefore the biblical teaching that Adam and Eve were naked before the fall still holds validity. I think early pictorial records that depict Satan and YHWH as serpents present the same dilemma that was faced in the American Civil war when similar uniforms of opposing sides caused confusion among combatants, militia forces and civilians, which stemmed from a division in a once united nation.

In answering the question of why Satan is consistently and exclusively depicted as a serpent, my answer is two-fold. On the one hand I do believe that it could have been a conscious effort of conspirators to gradually hide the truth. If so, this act might ultimately be turned to good since it might serve to more effectively usher in the Remnant as they recognise the real Saviour by His words and not by His appearance. On the other hand it could have been done to simplify the account.

In the film *Braveheart*, Scottish patriots were depicted in completely different outfits to the English. This was done so mass battle scenes could be accurately followed by the viewer. Historically the Scots wore similar attire to the English, but to portray that cinematically would confuse an audience. The same principle may have been adopted in translating the biblical accounts by diminishing YHWH's association with a serpent and retaining Satan's. In turn the scribes overlooked a golden rule not to add or detract from the Scriptures as they attempted to portray the bad guy wearing black and the good guy wearing white.

The Jewish Prayer Shawl (Tallit)

Within the Torah (the first five books of the Bible) there is a curious command set down that speaks of "fringes" or "tassels" to be worn from a particular garment.

Numbers 15:37; "Speak to the children of Israel, <u>telling them to make themselves a fringe (Tsitsit) on the corners of their garments throughout the generations;</u> to the fringe (Tsitsit) on each corner they are to give a blue cord. And it will be to you as a fringe (Tsitsit), and you will see Him, and you will remember all the commandments of the Lord (YHWH), and you will obey them, and you will not go after (the lusts of) your heart or your eyes, prostituting yourselves after them. Then you will remember and obey all My commandments, and you will be holy ones to your God (Elohim)." And in Deuteronomy 22:11; "Make for yourselves tassels (g'dilim) on the four corners of the cloak (k'sut) that covers you."

When I first began attending a Messianic congregation, I noticed that the formal phase of the meetings always commenced with the donning of a particular garment. This custom was accompanied by the reading of a prayer that sparked my immediate interest. A portion of the prayer read:

"I have wrapped my body in tzitzits, so may my soul, my two hundred forty-eight organs and my three hundred sixty-five sinews be wrapped in the illumination of tzitzits which has the numerical value of six hundred and thirteen. Just as I cover myself with a tallis in this world, so may I be an heir in the white robe of the saints and a beautiful cloak in the world to come in the garden of YHWH."

After hearing this I became particularly interested in the tallit's symbolic relationship with the exterior cloud of glory exhibited in the pre-fallen Adamic pair and the Heavenly Host.

The tallit, meaning, "little tent," is a four cornered garment. The Hebrew word for its corners is "kanfot," which is translated as "wings," the same word that describes the wings of the seraphim. The four corners of these single seamless garments *(Leviticus 19:19)* end in long fringes called "tzitzits" and according to Strong's Exhaustive Concordance, are described as "a floral or winglike projection, i.e. a fore-lock of hair, a tassel, fringe, (or) lock." These fringes are dyed blue to represent the Hebrew word for "servant" and are wrapped and knotted in a particular sequence to represent the numerical value of the Hebrew words "unity" and "YHWH."

The purpose of these specifically woven fringes was to remind the wearer of YHWH's commandments. In biblical times Hebrews wore the tallit over their regular garments like a robe. They also served a practical purpose as well. If the wearer should lift up his garment to commit an act of fornication the tzitzits are supposed to get in the way and snap the wearer back into his right mind.

Several key events depicted within Scriptures clearly show that Yahushua wore one throughout his ministry right up to his execution *(John 19:24)*. It served as a vessel for healing in *Mathew 9:21* and its misuse as a symbol of works was also directly criticised by the Messiah in *Mathew 23:5*.

Apart from being a garment that carries physical reminders of YHWH's commands, it is also a symbol of his divine protection and a sample of a future gift that awaits all those who trust in his name. Could it be possible that the tallit is a precursor to the powerful mantle or white robe that will be given to those who inherit the New Kingdom?

Various Interpretations of the "Cloud of Glory" or "Glory Suit."

The term "Glory Suit" could be used by soldiers who wear such a garment because of its contribution to great victories on the battlefield.

Note the suit's external barbed appearance and the serpent-like shape of the helmet.

Adam in Glory Suit

An interpretation of Adam off to till the land before the fall.

Seraphim - Fiery Serpent

The Glory suit's limitations could have been endless and therefore, if appropriate, extended an apendage, similar to a tail to carry and enable the operation of an extremely maneuverable weapon.

Adam with Glory suit's hood withdrawn

The suit might have been much more than a mere garment in that it was the personal covering that co-existed in symbiosis with the individual.

Certainly if something that added so many capabilities to an individual was withdrawn, it would cause an occupant great shame.

The Serpent in the Garden of Eden

Though I support the stance that Satan and his minions were able assume the appearance of serpents, it is important to understand that by the time of man's entry onto the scene, they had willfully or otherwise subjected themselves to a disembodied state. While this may have served as the perfect camouflage, such a state was uncomfortable and would not assist with providing a consistent physical vehicle to attempt an effective strike on YHWH's newest creation.

The only way of achieving a successful persuasion was through possessing an already existing organic creature. In the instance of the serpent in the Garden of Eden, a breed of dinosaur was chosen because of its physical similarities to that of the warlike state of the Heavenly Host (Fiery Serpents / Seraphim).

The casual appearance of the serpent in the Garden of Eden is a curious element in the lead up to the original sin. The lack of any official introduction within the story suggests that it was a sentient cohabitant to the Adamic pair. The *Haggadah* describes the serpent as being as tall as a camel and possessing arms and legs that are later described as being "hacked off." The serpent's skin is also removed and prepared as clothing for Adam and Eve.

Shamans often insist that the same spirits who teach them knowledge also reveal that their initial manifestation on earth was an attempt to flee a greater foe. As stated earlier, the similarities with these reports of spirits encountered in hallucinogenic states are overwhelmingly similar to the biblical origin of fallen angels, even down to their subsequent unlawful interactions with men. Assimilating to a creature's "junk DNA" enabled the fallen angels to take full bodily possession of an organism. If a human ingests a specific plant extract under the guidance of a shaman they are invariably catapulted to this molecular level of consciousness, which then enables them to interact with these spirits.

Biological scientists are recognising that a potential exists to manufacture countless complex artificially intelligent nano-sized machine-like organisms that can drift and bond to another molecular structure. Once fuzzed to a subject they can set about overriding the existing molecular structure. Such a scenario, coupled with the knowledge of reducing one's conscience to this level, may reveal how such beings are able to become disembodied and assimilate occupancy to a foreign organism.

Spirits of the pre and post flood Nephilim and fallen angels prefer to inhabit bipeds or animals with a similar physical makeup as their former embodied states. For example, in The New Testament a human was favoured as a host over a herd of pigs. Yet even inhabiting swine was apparently preferable than being completely disembodied. In the Genesis account I believe the breed of dinosaur that was of similar proportions to humans was chosen for two reasons. The first is that it could interact and assist the new administrators of earth in a more affective way to build a level of trust. Secondly dinosaurs were fast, agile and very hardy creatures that dominated much of the animal kingdom at that time.

Spring Heeled Jack

The story of Spring Heeled Jack is one that very few people are familiar with. Possibly because it has managed to avoid any considerable notice from Hollywood, no doubt due to the lack of barbarity visited upon Jack's victims unlike those of the infamous Masonic slayings in Whitechapel. Yet this mysterious individual, who was said by witnesses to be able to effortlessly leap 20 to 30 feet into the air and spit blue and white flame beneath glowing red eyes, remains one of the most bizarre unsolved mysteries in England to this day. During the course of my research into the "mantle," or "robe" and the possible relationship of these biblical garments with nanotechnologies, I was already mildly familiar with the many strange encounters of Spring Heeled Jake that continued to terrorise people for nearly half a century and to this day remain unsolved. As I began to review some of the historical material from eyewitnesses my heart began to sink.

"Devil, or Stranded Deviant Time-Travelling Human in a Nanosuit?"

Late one September evening in 1837, a businessman was walking down a quiet street in London when Jack first struck. He was described as being tall, thin, having unusual facial protrusions, and wearing a black cloak. He leapt into the man's path and in the process managed to clear a 10-foot high cemetery railing. The businessman was badly shaken, but physically unharmed. A short time later the same evening, Jack sprang into the midst of a group of friends returning from a theatre. Again the witnesses' descriptions noted glowing eyes and facial protrusions. One member of the group, Polly Adams was sexually molested and later found unconscious by a policeman.

In October of that same year Jack attacked another woman by the name of Mary Stevens who was passing through Cut Throat Lane in Clapham Common. She was also molested, but managed to alert some locals whose efforts to track him down were unsuccessful. The following day, near Mary Stephens's abode, Jack bounded into the path of a carriage causing it to crash. Witnesses said that he escaped the scene by leaping over a 9-foot wall. Shortly afterward he then attacked another woman near Clapham church. Investigators at the scene of this second incident found two footprints that were both three inches deep, indicating the possibility of a type of spring mechanism in the heels of the assailant's boots.

In January of the following year, London's Lord Mayor, Sir John Cowen, declared Spring Heel Jack a "public menace." A group of men were especially assembled to track down the bouncing troublemaker who, in the months that followed, still managed to evade his would-be-captors.

The 20th of February yielded another noteworthy encounter, when Lucy Scales was blinded when Jack spat a fiery excretion into her face. Her sister, who was present during the attack observed Jack make his escape by jumping from the ground to the roof of a house.

Days later, Jane Aslop of Bearhind Lane, in the Bow district, answered the door to Jack who was posing as a policemen. She managed to escape a severe assault with the aid of her sister who pulled her out of his clutches and slammed the door. Jane later made the following statement (note the underlined observations):

"He wore a large helmet and a sort of tight-fitting costume that felt like oilskin. But the cape was just like the ones worn by the policemen. His hands were as cold as ice and like powerful claws.

But the most frightening thing about him was his eyes. They shone like balls of fire."

The appearances of Spring heeled Jack continued, several leading to subsequent deaths. One involved an encounter with a group of soldiers in August 1877. Residents of Lincolnshire also reported hearing their shotgun shells sounding as though they impacted on some sort of metallic object when they fired upon the fleeing menace.

In September 1904, over 70 years after his first appearance he was seen south of Liverpool atop the roof of a church. He launched himself off a steeple and was believed to have committed suicide. When onlookers arrived at the place where he fell (behind some houses) another helmeted man in a white uniform stood there waiting. He raised his arms and took off into the air over William Henry Street. Many theories exist as to the nature of these incidences. Some claim that he was simply a man in a specially designed suit. Some say he was the devil incarnate. Others say they were stories exaggerated by "Penny Dreadfuls" (pulp magazines) that added outlandish elements to existing true crime cases. Whatever the case, consistent eyewitness reports of a similarly attired individual displaying unusual abilities continued to come in from unrelated witnesses over a span of nearly 75 years. Theories on a suit have since been thrown into some doubt as Nazi's during WWII tried perfecting boots with a spring mechanism that had a pitiful 15% success rate as nearly all the test subjects fractured their ankles. However, there are now research programs in full swing that are utilising nanotechnology to enable the wearer of a specially designed tight-fitting suit to be endowed with many previously unattainable capabilities. These include an ability to climb walls like Spiderman, leap massive distances like the Incredible Hulk, move silently by deadening sound like a Ninja, emit chemical weaponry that disorients an opponent, and assume partial invisibility to the naked eye. All of which fit the profile of this 19th century sex offender.

Now up to this point, any self-respecting reader should be starting to notice a major flaw in my hypothesis. That is, what is someone with such an advanced piece of equipment doing in such a distant era? Before I launch into an explanation to support my view, I think it may be of some benefit to examine a concept that is usually relegated to the realms of science fiction. Believe it or not, scientists have been seriously investigating the principle of time travel for many decades and those in the know are now beginning to accept that it could one day become a reality.

Time Travel and the Myth of the Paradox

To explain the overall concept of time travel mathematically and its relationship to Einstein's theory of relativity, is a task best left to a single volume of work that has been penned by experts in the field. What I will try to do however is give a simple definition of time travel and cut to the main points that I wish to raise. To do this, it will be assumed that the reader has at least either read or viewed some small piece of serious material on the subject at some point.

Believe it or not we are all time travellers in that we all co-exist through the relentless unraveling of seconds that make up minutes, that make up hours, that make up days, that make up weeks and so on. But to be able to harness the ability to move through "time" in a completely isolated and accelerated backward or forward speed is difficult to comprehend.

There are many different types of this "abnormal" time travel. These include, time travel via mechanical apparatus that generates a necessary external field (popular with Hollywood), through an artificial or natural wormhole or gate, and mental backward or forward time and event awareness.

The biggest stumbling block to time travel is the ever-pervasive threat of the paradox. The concern is that if time travel where possible, what would stop a man from going back and killing a direct ancestor or even worse deliberately disrupting a Scriptural event such as severing the ancestral line of Adam or somehow keeping Yahushua from being executed. On the surface this seems like a very valid point and even some people, who do accept paradoxes and time travel, believe that if a paradox occurs it will spark an alternating sequence of historical events. The result of which is either the birth of a parallel universe or a collapse of the current one and a continuation from the new altered path. Both these options tend to generate major difficulties when trying to understand how YHWH or Satan could operate consistently within seemingly endless amounts of randomly and continually occurring alternating universes when the possibility of collapsing the one and only strand is entertained. As time travel becomes available, men might constantly try to leap frog one another until they achieve a desired goal or objective, the result of which might not be known for thousands of years. In short, the result is too chaotic to even comprehend. The two outcomes of either a continually altering single timeline or generating alternate ones bring forward two major theological problems. The first scenario means that following YHWH to the grave has no guarantee as an alternate path may be set at any time that might result in a follower being unmade or losing a blessing, such as children or being set on a path where their knowledge of YHWH is lessoned. In effect a whole series of ancestral lines might be obliterated or set on a completely different spiritual path within the blink of an eye. The second problem is that at any one time there may exist a countless amount of other versions of ourselves that co-exist in other universes that may or may not be saved and that YHWH Himself isn't one, but many.

Thankfully physicists have now discovered a fundamental law of nature, which prevents the time travel paradox and therefore can enable such a phenomenon to occur without fear of the above repercussions unraveling, multiplying or altering the overall fabric of reality. The principle is based on the same law that makes light travel in straight lines and this same concept underpins Richard Feynman's development of "quantum theory."

To the amazement of relativity scientists, Kip Thorn and his colleagues from the *Caltch Institute*, there is nothing in the laws of physics to forbid time travel. The predominant and most intensively studied method is the "wormhole." A wormhole is best described as a tunnel through space and time. The subject of wormholes being a viable form of transport from one location to another and one time-frame to another will be discussed later, but for now lets look at how time travel might be achieved without paradoxical repercussions. Igor Novikov, who holds joint posts at the P.N. Lebedev Institute, in Moscow, and at NORDITA (the Nordic Institute for Theoretical Physics), in Copenhagen, was the first to find the physical basis of what he called the "Principle of Self-Consistency." It is to do with an action of least or minimal consequence and describes the trajectories of things. Without getting too technical, this principle of "least action" equals the principle of "least time." It explains why light travels in a straight line and why a ball thrown (not dropped) out of a window no matter what the speed or trajectory will always follow a predetermined curved path on its way down. It is the unrelenting way that light or nature manages to find the cheapest or simplest path to its goal.

So ultimately if time travel were achieved with an objective to disrupt a time continuum, three scenarios might transpire. The first might be that for whatever reason, the objective is never realised. The second might be that the event's repercussions were always figured into the intervention. A good example of this is found in the plot of the first *Terminator* film where a cyborg's relentless pursuit of a future adversary, Sarah Conner, causes her to be equipped with the knowledge of her opponent's strengths and weaknesses. In effect by venturing back in time the super-computer is actually solely responsible for training a very effective enemy, whereas if Sarah were left alone, she would have possibly still remained a harmless waitress. Thirdly, a disruptive action might be righted by a subsequent event that overrides the potential for a paradox to take shape.

The big question is, 'will time travel be achieved by men before the events in Revelation take place and does Satan and his minions have an ability to time travel?' In light of **Genesis 11:6 ("And the Lord said, 'Indeed the _people are one_ and they all have one language, and this is what they begin to do; _now nothing that they propose to do will be withheld from them._")** the answer is possibly yes. I believe that time travel will become achievable to some degree in that a few missions may be attempted before YHWH comes in the clouds. In terms of Satan and his dark forces having the potential to time travel all the way through man's struggle, I think that they are limited to only mental observational accessibility and can therefore not physically interact with any locations outside the normal time continuum.

Now with my thoughts on the controversial topic of time travel revealed, let's get back to Spring Heeled Jack.

My theory, which is not new, is that he could have been the subject of a Top-Secret military experiment that experienced a complication not unlike the 1943 Philadelphia Experiment, in that he, for whatever reason had come from the near future and got himself stuck in 18th century England, and, when he wasn't assaulting beautiful women, was attempting to find a way home. Jane Aslop's description describes a helmet, a tight-fitting costume with a police cape (suggesting a uniform), clawed and cold hands (implying artificially powered nano-gloves that assist with climbing) and glowing eyes (possibly infrared goggles or the hue of visor digital data display). The flames coming from his mouth could have been a gas designed to disorientate and subdue close quarters opponents. The shots fired by Lincolnshire residence appeared to hit metallic armour that to Jane Aslop's recollection was like "oil skin," which suggests a defensive hardening "nano" based mechanism. Also supporting this are the accounts of slight variations in Jack's appearance and a noticeable progressive deterioration of his "tight-fitting" suit.

More Evidence of Time Travelling Nanosuit Clad Meddlers

An even less well-known documentation of the appearance of strange black men occurs in various historical records concerning plagues. Many sources, spanning from Asia to Europe, describe a heavy activity of comets trailing gas and other unexplained aerial phenomenon prior to the onset of some of the most famous plagues in history. Contrary to popular belief, few outbreaks of the Black Death were attributed to rat infestations and rather fit a pattern of UFO activity, the emergence of a green mist and the occasional sighting of blackened figures carrying scythes that emitted strange whooshing sounds. In the book, *Gods of Eden*, Author William Bramley puts forward some interesting observations in relation to these unusual sightings that preceded the occurrences of major epidemics. To support his hypothesis he draws upon a wealth of historical data from ancient Mesopotamian, Roman, and even Scriptural records that mention gaseous mists that kill vegetarians and cause victims to develop boils. *I Samuel 5:6* describes tumors or "emerods" (meaning painful swellings) that ravaged the people of

Ashdod. Bramley writes: "Strange men dressed in black, "demons," and other terrifying figures were observed in other European communities. The frightening creatures were often observed carrying long "brooms," "scythes," or "swords" that were used to "sweep" or "knock at" the doors of people's homes. The inhabitants of those homes fell ill with plague afterwards. It is from these reports that people created the popular image of "Death" as a skeleton or demon carrying a scythe." Could these have been planned operations acted out by individuals clad in a similar fashion to the stranded and unstable Spring Heeled Jack? Or as Scriptures points out, were they acts of YHWH?

Doorways to Other Worlds

An extremely interesting choice of words appears in Verse 32 of Chapter 13 in the Book of Numbers that enjoys a similar translation in all modern Bible translations. Aside from the astounding claim by those whom Moses had sent out to spy the outlaying land of Canaan that its inhabitants were giants, they also made the following claim: *Numbers 13:32; "And they spread among the Israelites a bad report about the land they had explored. They said, 'The land we explored devours those living in it.'"(NIV)* Many have speculated that this strange statement about a devouring countryside means that it was either barren or dangerous to those who chose to live in it that were not of giant stock. However both these explanations fall short when we examine the whole chapter in context. The land was in fact bountiful in produce as the scouts proved by bringing back evidence of its fruits. Yet how would these Israelite men have known that the land devoured inhabitants if they had not seen evidence of dwellers other than giants living there? Both these observations are contradictory with any minor application of commonsense. So what is the explanation for such an unusual description of a land that was supposed to flow with milk and honey and yet devour its occupants?

The solution is found again in the Bible's principle use of "phenomenological language," that is, the Israelites described what they saw from the point of view of their level of understanding. They saw something very unusual, something that they could only describe as a point in the land that, when entered by an inhabitant, caused them to disappear, as if swallowed up.

In the following verse there is a further clue as to what may have been witnessed as it states in *Numbers 13:33; "There we saw the giants (the descendants of Anak, who came from the giants; and we were like grasshoppers in our own sight, and so we were in their sight."* Ancient Sumerian texts clearly speak of a race of beings called the ANUNNAKI that first came to earth in gleaming discs that dropped from the sky and who later came by means of "glittering archways of fire." These Annunnaki are described in the Bible as "Anak," or in accompanying footnotes as "Anakim" which are also referred to as the "sons of God." Author, Zecharia Sitchen's claim that the Annunnaki were later called "nephilim" or "nefilim," by the Hebrews is incorrect. This is because Annunnaki means, "Those who from heaven to earth came," and the nephilim, their offspring, had no such origin as they were born on earth. Though the Annunnaki and the biblical "sons of God" were one and the same their nephilim children would have been delighted with people making this assumption.

Could these fiery archways have been traversable "wormholes" or "stargates?" Such cosmic occurrences have, until recently, only been confined to the realms of science-fiction, yet modern science is very close to discovering that such a mode of transport over vast distances may be possible.

"If space flight is like using stairs to reach a star, a wormhole is like a subway to the same location"

To the uninitiated the wormhole, also known as an *Einstein-Rosen bridge*, is essentially a shortcut from one point of the galaxy to another. The name "wormhole" comes from a simple analogy that was first used to explain its function. Imagine that the universe is the skin of an apple and a worm travels over its surface. To travel from one side to the other is equal to half the apple's circumference, yet if it travels straight through its core the distance is considerably lessened. In 1985, Professor Kip Thorn, of the California Institute of Technology found a mathematical solution that would allow interstellar passage using this logic. The solution displayed no adverse effects for physical travel, yet contained one major draw-back. In order for the throat of the wormhole to remain open, there has to be sufficient negative energy density involved. Though no known material exists, electro-magnetic vacuum fluctuations are occasionally measured by negative energy densities and are known as "exotic" or "dark matter." In order for the wormhole to function in the desired manner, it needs to be threaded with this substance to create enough tension to keep the walls of its throat apart. A column published in a 1994 issue of *Analog Science Fiction & Fact Magazine* reported on the findings of an Advanced Quantum/Relativity Theory Propulsion Workshop sponsored by NASA and stated the following in regard to acquiring this key ingredient:

"There are presently three groups conducting astronomical searches for non-luminous or dim Jupiter-size masses or MACHOs (Massive Cosmic Halo Objects) that if they occurred in sufficient numbers may provide a partial solution to the dark matter problem."

Scientists at the workshop unanimously agreed, given that the quest for dark matter may be accomplished, that both artificial and natural wormholes can be utilised for faster-than-light travel and are completely consistent with the standard gravity theory.

An article in *New Scientist* magazine entitled, "About Time," went a step further by claiming that wormholes may also function as time machines and that they are readily available throughout the Cosmos. The travelling process would work in a similar manner yet the travelling time would be considerably accelerated.

Wrestling for the title of "Creator"

The prospect of wormholes being a reality may be challenging enough, but what exactly do these ancient Sumerian texts reveal about these beings that utilised them? It is interesting to note that the Sumerian language is the oldest and most sophisticated writing for its time in existence, dating back to at least 3400 years BC. Its evolution cannot be traced, as there are no known sources to indicate that it had a process of development. It seems to have just materialised from nowhere in a wedge-shaped format called "cuneiform." In a similar vein to the language, the Sumerian's very culture appeared to exhibit all the attributes of a full blown civilised society that had everything from an established tax system to the manufacturing of beer. Many authors, including the most prolific on the subject, Zecharia Sitchen, who have delved deeply into the history of the Sumerians and Egyptians, have emerged with seemingly startling revelations. However, as much as I recommend reading Sitchen, he eventually comes to some truly disturbing conclusions that I am compelled to address regarding these beings and their ancestors. The claim is that certain Sumerian writings describe a god called, "Enki" that created humanity by mixing his DNA with that of an ape. While there is a definite indication in these ancient sources for such an event or series of events taking place, and indeed in the pre-first flood period some unusual unions between sons of God and animals did occur, all subsequent records of these times must be taken into consideration. We know that prior to the flood the sons of God set about increasing their numbers with the resources that were available on the earth after taking heavy loses in the battle for Heaven. We must also note that some time after this recuperation of their forces, their efforts were brought back to square one by a series of cataclysms that all culminated in a flood. According to Mesopotamian and Egyptian records the flood was instigated by Enki's rival half-brother "Enlil," because he was displeased with his siblings' callous use of humans to carry out a grueling excavation of precious stones.

At this point the assumption is often made that Enki is Lucifer and Enlil is YHWH. It is further surmised that YHWH Elohim is the name that the Hebrews later used for them, which is supported by the pluralism of the creation account in Genesis. But these assumptions fall flat when we examine the details of Enlil and Enki's origins and intentions. Through further analysis of these ancient Sumerian sources we find out that these two beings were in fact half-brothers, who both initially came to earth with a common goal and were the sons of a superior deity called "Anu."

The line of reasoning that puts forward a scenario that has Enlil cooperating with Enki and later initiating a disaster, disintegrates when a rift between them and a third foreign entity is evident from the outset of the two half-brother's occupation on Earth. At one point in the Sumerian account, Enlil departs Earth and returns, supposedly as an enemy of Enki's and as an ally his half-brother's human creations. It is my feeling that the purpose of the half-brothers' act of turning on each other assisted in aligning one of them to the acts of this displeased outside third party (YHWH). Enlil assumes the responsibility of initiating YHWH's actions of initiating the flood and over time this forms a premise that conveniently supplants YHWH's action and overlays a crucial truth about an actual historical event. Generations later, this version of the outcome sets like cement and absorbs into the psyche of the New Age Movement that develops near the end of the age. This in turn causes learned followers of this movement to conclude that Abraham and his descendants served Enlil while the ancient Egyptians served Enki. Thus removing YHWH from the equation and only leaving a good pagan god verses a bad pagan god as an option.

2 Samuel 1:18 makes reference to the *Book of Jasher*, a non-canonised text that has an interesting comment from Abram. It certainly suggests a false claim is made about man's origins by descendants of these beings when it states: *"And Abram said unto himself 'Surely these are not gods (Enki and Enlil) that made the earth and all mankind, but these are the servants of Yahweh. And Abram remained in the house of Noah and there knew Yahweh and His ways, and served Yahweh all the days of his life and all that generation forgot Yahweh and served other gods – Enki and Enlil" (Book of Jasher 4:19)*

Jeremiah 10:11 also states: **"Thus you shall say to them: 'The gods (Enki and Enlil) that have not made the heavens and the earth shall perish from the earth and from under the heavens.'"**

YHWH and the Heavenly Host persistently rendered assistance to these human creations that were continually under the oppressive rule of these Annunnaki descendants. This is made evident by drastic measures being utilised to quell such practices in the form of at least one global flood (Noah), a dismantling of a world economy (Babel), the bombing of the twin cities (Sodom and Gomorra) and rendering assistance to pure blooded humans in open warfare against these descendants (the striking down of the Amalek in The Book of Samuel). Not to mention other countless confrontations between these Annunnaki, their descendants and their human worshipers.

If these god-beings, Enlil and Enki are our makers and their immediate ancestral line, the Annunnaki are our forefathers, why were they wiped out and driven away by this successive series of catastrophes, which caused them such devastation while we, hardly god-like in contrast, remain in their stead relatively unscathed?

Points to remember against the Annunnaki creation hypothesis:

1) Someone else was continuingly displeased with their actions enough to focus disasters blatantly designed to erode their numbers, whilst protecting us.

2) Whoever that someone was, he rallied a special people together to call his own and brought them out of slavery and attempted to assist them in actions against these beings for many generations with devastating effect. So much so that these other so called creators could not match simple challenges like igniting an altar *(1 Kings 18:26)*.

3) They are not here in their former capacity, yet we are.

4) They have sent no spokesperson or messenger to comfort or direct the masses unlike their adversary who sent one made of a mortal biological consistency to do just that.

5) They are at war with this being that continues to help us.

6) If the Annunnaki were in fact the nephilim, which Sitchen claims, that are referred to in *Genesis 6:1-4*, then who is the other being or beings that came before them who created everything? There is a distinction made between God (YHWH) and his fallen "sons" and there is no indication that they were formally in union at the time of their occupation or visitations to Earth. Non-canonised writings, such as The Book of Enoch also support this notion.

Despite some pre-biblical Sumerian history claiming that YHWH was just one of many bnē Elohim (sons of God) subsequent history has shown us otherwise. It all comes down to comparing the track record of the Annunnaki and YHWH. Rather than making a decision based on the authenticity of a claim of a single act from records that predate Genesis, we should look at an Elohim's past interactive record. Where are these Sumerian deities today? They are nowhere. There is only one El, the El Shaddi (Master of all spirits) who is YHWH.

Chapter Eighteen

Finishing the
Jigsaw Puzzle

As I REFLECT ON some of the areas that I've pulled you, the avid reader through, I imagine areas where you've followed me without hesitation and elsewhere where I've had to tug on your arm and even at times no-doubt weather soft and on occasion strong objection. Yet here you are at the close of this work. For seeing it through, I thank you.

Unfortunately, I don't know who you are; in fact it is quite probable that I will never know who you are. But there is one who knows you better than yourself. He is ever watchful, so much so that He even watches the evil ones who watch you. He is all-powerful and above all, all merciful and waiting patiently for your company.

I encourage honest seekers of the truth to investigate not only Scripture, but also a broad range of material that deals with the evolution of the subject. Even books that question the very physical existence of Yahushua (Jesus), such as *The Jesus Mysteries*, *The Christ Conspiracy*, and *Children of the Matrix*, though written with a heavy bias, contain some well researched information that pro-Christian publications do not address. However, this doesn't mean that their overall conclusions and all the points they bring forward are correct or accurate. Indeed much of what Christianity is today is the result of decisions initiated by a Roman Emperor who had his wife suffocated, his son murdered, and deliberately avoided baptism (mikveh) until he was on his deathbed. Because a majority of practices Christians observe today is a recent amalgamation of pagan customs, the claim is often made that Christianity is completely fabricated from these practices. But even in the literature of those that make these claims, there is evidence of an original previously existing faith that had these foreign customs grafted to it.

Can the memory of such an influential Messiah figure be constructed and accepted overnight from a smorgasbord of pagan gods? The logistics of creating a physically tangible individual who exhibited supernatural abilities in factual localities before multitudes of onlookers would be impossible to orchestrate. Why would a group of men who were so viciously opposed to Judaism concoct a Messiah who said, "Salvation is of the Jews?" *(John 4:22)* And why do the Jews acknowledge this potential stumbling block of an individual and condemn his followers by their collective name (Notsarim) in their Talmud (Rabbinical commentaries on Torah)? Arguments that the name Yahushua could refer to someone else because it was a common name fall apart under closer scrutiny. Where Yahushua's name appears (in the Talmud) it is also accompanied with events that are specific to the New Testament, thereby breaking the backbone of coincidence.

What Should I Do?

This book has not been written to encourage you to join any particular religious denomination. However, if it has moved you to contemplate setting foot into a Christian environment, be warned, most churches are run by the enemy. These congregations teach (very subtly) that "The Judaic Remnant of Israel," was replaced by "Christianity." This doctrine is the key that lets Satan unlock the doors of the church and walk straight in.

The New Testament speaks of one true faith *(Ephesians 4:5)* that was given once and for all time *(Jude 1:3)*. There is ABSOLUTELY NO TEACHING that speaks of a *new religion* contained in either Testament. Even Paul identifies himself as a Jew in

Acts 21:39 and *Acts 22:3* as opposed to a Christian. In fact, he goes so far as to say that there is much advantage in being a circumcised Jew in *Romans 3:1-2*.

Yahushua observed the Torah and came to fulfill the already existing "old law." For him to start a completely new religion would have been in itself a Torah violation. "The New Covenant" that is often wheeled out, twisted and distorted to go against this teaching is merely a shift of the "old law" from tablets of stone onto the hearts and minds of the individual *(Jeremiah 31:33)*. There is NO CHANGE in the law (Torah) itself; there is only a change in its position.

YHWH sent His Son to teach us not only to obey the law, but also to love the law so that it becomes a part of our very being. The common theme pushed today by the majority of the religious community is grace, grace and more grace! The law is overlooked as the focus stays perpetually on forgiveness. As a consequence few Christians are able to rattle off all Ten Commandments, which is strange because the New Testament tells us that they are meant to be on their hearts. Which raises the question, how can they be on Christian's hearts if Christians don't even know what some of them are? The answer is we must learn and meditate on the Commandments as the Scriptures instruct. The fact that they don't magically manifest in a believer's heart is evident because the average Christian will not be able to successfully recite them off the top of their heads. Chances are most churches will have no in-depth teachings or studies scheduled for them either as this would be considered legalistic.

The Torah is foundational and must be studied and regarded for it to take hold in our lives. Instances of breaking the law (missing the mark) do inevitably occur, but through the act of repentance a believer can be redeemed through YHWH's favour. Repentance however, is not simply saying sorry. It is an act that is defined as a physical withdrawal of an action. For example if a sin resulted from being in a certain locality, an occupant must remove him or herself from that location or if it is an object, that occupant must dispose of it as soon as is humanly possible. If it is through contact with an undesirable person then the association must be severed. Circumstances may also occur where we might find ourselves unable to obey an aspect of the Torah, but it is our hearts that are discerned by YHWH, not physical adherence to it. For to obey the law and in the process knowingly commit evil, is to ultimately break the law anyway. For example if I had a sick relative that required round-the-clock care during which time a Sabbath fell, if I ceased providing for that person on the Sabbath and they subsequently became gravely ill or possibly died, I would be in violation of the law.

In-depth teaching on the Torah is predominantly available within the Jewish community. But rushing off to an Orthodox Synagogue with the light of Yahushua leading the way is not recommended. You will be shown the door as quickly as you arrived. The Jewish people are a very protective community and they have every reason in the world to be. I have a deep love for them and see them as my brothers and sisters. However the time has not yet come for the veil to be lifted and YHWH's watchmen remain blind *(Isaiah 56:10)*. So what's the alternative?

There are a growing number of Messianic Nazarene communities on the rise across the world. But, they are still few in number. I recommend trying to get in touch with a group that is closest to you via the Internet. If this is not possible the Internet itself is a good stand-alone resource for teaching.

The true faith of Scripture is best defined as having three major pillars. They are: Love of the Creator's name, Keeping the Sabbath(s), and holding fast to the covenants *(Isaiah 56:6)*. I know from personal experience that the Name was the key that opened a door to an avalanche of understanding. So I can honestly recommend investigating the name first and the desire to be obedient to Torah, YHWH willing, will hopefully come.

The Opposition of Legalism is Illegalism!

So what of grace? The following observation was noted when I was engaged in a debate on grace with a Christian gentleman. We were studying The Book of Romans when he read the following passage. *Romans 6:14; "For sin shall not have dominion over you, for you are not under the law but under grace."* There he ceased his reading and awaited my response. I looked down and noticed the Bible he and I had, had a break between verses 14 and 15. Between this break was the heading, "From Slaves of Sin to Slaves of God." This was unusual for two reasons. Firstly, the text broke in a section that wasn't the commencement of a new chapter as is painfully common in many modern translations. Second, the next verse *Romans 6:15* read: *What then? Shall we sin because we are not under law but under grace? Certainly not!* The layout appeared to give the impression that verse 14 was the conclusion of the topic, yet the teaching continues straight on through to 15 and beyond. I then proceeded to read verse 15 to my Christian friend's total dismay.

Sin can only be made known when one is conscious of the law. To be conscious of the law, one needs to be conscious of the need for grace, and to be conscience of the need for grace, one needs to be repentant. Where there is no knowledge of the law, there is no sin, and therefore no workable ground for grace to abound. Any mention of the "old law" within a church is often met with a conditioned rebuttal of "legalism," yet this type of thinking is actually "illegalism." Accusations of being legalistic oppose a stance in support of faith that is evident through obedience to the law. Active obedience to the law is evidence of faith in one's own salvation. To be in opposition to obedience of the law is to support a life of lawlessness and yet continually be under grace. The knights of the crusades virtually adopted this type of thinking and that is why they indulged in such despicable and sickening acts during this bloody campaign.

Many churches are simply breeding grounds for conditioning and ignorance that leads to stunted personal spiritual growth. Though they proclaim obedience to the Ten Commandments, further questioning will see them make excuses for several that are not observed. The bottom line is found in *John 14:15; "If you love Me, keep my commandments"* (End of story).

Mainstream churches (any church that receives a tax exemption and whose hierarchy reaches to the Vatican) are to be regarded with caution and though they may be beneficial as a stepping-stone, if no other choices of fellowship are available, can leave one worse off than before. People say churches are good because they promote positive values and provide opportunities for fellowship within a moralistic setting. My answer is, so do social clubs and that, in effect, is what the majority of churches have become. My suggestion is, find an "assembly" of people that know the truth and join them, for it is extremely bad to remain isolated with such knowledge. Stop looking for an A-frame building with a steeple and people wearing skivvies. On the flip side, Judaic groups that do not acknowledge Yahushua are just as bad as mainstream churches but at the other end of the spectrum. If possible find a group of people who are supporters of both Judaic law and the Messiah. Now with access to the Internet this should not be difficult, yet the locality of such a group may be.

Buy a good Bible. One that has the Hebrew and Greek concordance is best. Get a good dictionary, preferably an old one from a secondhand bookstore. The newer dictionaries are pointless, as you will find out if you look up the name "Jesus" in them. Continue to search the Scriptures when you have free time, and with discernment and discretion move to finding ways of going out and sharing this information with people.

Try putting away 10% of all your earnings and giving it to anyone that may be in need, (if required start with immediate family members first). Dropping a tithe (offering) mindlessly into a church plate invariably goes toward the upkeep of the place that is used to worship and not to the needy. Churches could do far more good by funneling congregational tithes into helping the poor if meetings were held in houses, or if churches were owned out-rightly by an individual or family. I personally save up an amount over a period of time so that I have a decent sum of money to give. Occasionally a portion of it goes to the group I meet with for special outreach functions, while the rest goes toward helping struggling family members or people that cross my path in need. Try to give money as you are led, not as the church leads you. If you are blessed enough to find a group, do not rely on any one member to solely feed Scripture to you or the rest of the group. Take turns in readings, sharing, and teaching. To have one member solely equipped to do so, weakens the group, as its strength becomes unequally distributed throughout its body.

Whether or not this book inspires any sort of action, remember that despite the fact that many foreign things may have confronted you, there is absolutely nothing new in what I have shared. It is simply a tour through a house that you've lived in all your life, only this time I've taken you on a tour of nearly all its upper rooms and flicked on every light as we've trodden through. Indeed some of the rooms you have been in before, but never as brightly lit, while others you've never known were there.

It is nearly time for me to end our tour and I have done little more than scratch the surface, but there is nothing stopping you from returning to explore these rooms more thoroughly without me. There is a better guide, a much better guide than me, who I'm sure will reveal areas of rooms I may have described poorly. I encourage you to seek Him yourself through a willingness to grow in knowledge, which leads inevitably to wisdom. *Proverbs 19:2; "Also it is not good for a soul to be without knowledge, And he sins who hastens with his feet."* However we must do this with the understanding that true wisdom is to know and fear YHWH. Any earthly wisdom, even earthly wisdom used to understand YHWH is doomed. *1 Corinthians 1:19; "I will destroy the wisdom of the wise, and bring to nothing the understanding of the prudent."* Do not set out for the sake of acquiring knowledge for knowledge's sake but set out to seek Him with love and the wisdom of YHWH will be added to you.

Whatever background you have – believer, non-believer, academic, unemployed, widow, musician, labourer, husband, homosexual, doctor, thief, priest, or just a person that picked this book up for something to read on holidays, know this – no matter what you have done or haven't done there is hope. We are the favoured and crowning creation of YHWH. The same parallel is clearly visible with Gandalf and his fondness of the simple Hobbit in *The Lord of the Rings* films. Sauron (representing a lieutenant of Satan) is baffled as to why Gandalf gives an ear to those harmless and simpleton halflings and appears to forget the principle that the meek shall inherit the earth. Furthermore consider this:

You may now stand as if having scratched away a piece of paint from a tired and poorly executed artwork to reveal a hint of an exceptional work of art. It is a work that radiates not just any truth, but the absolute truth and it shines brighter than the sun itself. Where you go from here is up to you. You can cover it over and pretend you never saw anything or keep scratching. But if you do desire to pull away this layer and pursue the truth, always remember: *"In My Father's house are many mansions; if it were not so, I would have told you. And I go to prepare a place for you. And if I go and prepare a place for you, I will come again and receive you to Myself; that where I am, there you may be also." (John 14:2-3)*

Terms of
Interest

Religion – According to the *Webster's Collegiate Dictionary* the term derives from an old Latin word, "religio" and means, "taboo." A more thorough study reveals that it is made up of the prefix "re," indicating a "return" to something. The Latin word "ligare," is where we get the word "ligament" and means, "to bond" or "bind." When the prefix "re" is put it with the word "bond" it brings about the literal meaning, "return to bondage." This meaning was never originally inferred in the three to five places where we find the word "religion" in modern Bibles today. According to *Strong's Exhaustive Concordance* it appears in ***Acts 26:5, Galatians 1:13, 1:14 and James 1:26, 1:27***. More accurate Restoration translations exhibit the following original translations in its place:

Acts 26:5 – This verse contains the word **"observance"** meaning, "the practice of adhering to a particular rule."

Galations 1:13,1:14 – Both verses contain the word, **"Yehudaism"** meaning, "Judaism."

James 1:26, 1:27 – The verse contains the word **"service,"** meaning, "an act of assistance."

As you can see none of these words mean, "return to bondage," yet when the New Testament refers to a "return to bondage" or "slavery," as in *Galatians 5:1*, the option to use the word religion is ignored. With this understanding, believers can confidently accept and sympathise with the phrase, "I don't like religion." However, on hearing this response from an ill-informed unbeliever, one should be quick to enlighten the occupant of the fact that the term doesn't even appear in modern translations of Scripture in its correct context. Furthermore its true meaning is not a concept that is endorsed from Scripture's pages anyway. Bondage is not associated with what YHWH offers or expects from His people.

Word choice in Bible translations can often set linguistic trends that negatively affect aspects of a belief system that the source manuscripts promote. This occurs when scribes of differing philosophical backgrounds copy manuscripts. If written language is the vehicle for ferrying truth to a reader, a scribe, over time, may successfully blend the vehicle with falsehood to cause linguistic misguidance. A translator can successfully misguide a reader providing that their will or ability to examine word origins and contextual meaning is withdrawn or discouraged. This can be done be revealing a Bible translation to foreign audience who is not familiar with its language of origin. Any curiosity of tracing a text's language of origin can be erased if its appearance in a former foreign language is denied (Greek New Testament Debate). Subtle changes in word meaning, reducing or increasing emphasis, rearranged sentence structure and inappropriate word use can also be utilised.

Could YHWH's plan, in letting this happen, be to have so-called mature believers expose the true shallowness of their commitment for the truth before a returning Messiah, when He hears them obliviously using a language that, to Him is littered with abominable obscenities? The Bible specifically states that believers are not to "make mention" (verbalisations) of the names of other pagan elohim (*Joshua 23:7*) and as we enter the end of this age many key biblical names and words which are unashamedly derived from the names of pagan gods abound within the Christian community. Some key terms include "God," "Lord," "Bible," "glory," "grace," "holy," "Easter," "Hallowed," "amen," and "church" to name a few.

Synagogue – From a Greek root meaning "assembly." The term gradually became more widely accepted as referring to a physical house of worship as in the present Jewish or Islamic *equivalent* of a church, mosque or temple. The use of the word "temple" may offend some traditional Jews, because biblically there was only ever one temple in Jerusalem. The correct, yet lesser-known meanings for synagogue can also be rendered "congregation" or "gathering," which appears most prominently in the New Testament.

Many Haredi Jews still have a regular place of worship that is not a synagogue by the usual definition of the term. Some Jews gather in rooms or little booths in private houses or places of business set aside for the express purpose of prayer. These "Shteibels," as they are called, do not offer the communal services of a congregation, and are for prayer services alone. Many non-Orthodox Jews conduct "chavurot" (prayer fellowships), which meet at a regular place and time usually in someone's house or apartment. "Synagogue" is a Greek translation of Beit K'nesset and also means "place of assembly" (related to "synod"). When the Jews came under Babylonian captivity, they commenced building small temporary structures to serve as little sanctuaries *(Ezekiel 11:16)*. These later became known as Synagogues.

Torah – Hebrew word meaning "teaching," "instruction," or "council," though Bible translators later appropriated the term to mean, "Law." Its Hebrew root means to "throw" or to "shoot an arrow." Therefore the phrase, "to miss the mark," is sometimes used when describing a transgression.

The word Torah primarily refers to the first section of the Tanakh, which consists of the first five books of the Hebrew Bible. Their names are Genesis (*Bereishit*), Exodus (*Shemot*), Leviticus (*Vayikra*), Numbers (*Bemidbar*) and Deuteronomy (*Devarim*). Collectively they are also known as the "Pentateuch" (Greek for "five containers," where containers presumably refers to the scroll cases in which books were being kept). Some scholars validly point out that Genesis is merely an introduction and the books of the Torah are essentially made up of the next four volumes. This certainly makes sense in terms of there being four gospels that mirror them. But the overwhelming consensus is that there are five books.

Books of the TORAH:

* Bereishith (In the beginning...) (Genesis)

* Shemoth (The names...) (Exodus)

* Vayiqra (And He called...) (Leviticus)

* Bamidbar (In the wilderness...) (Numbers)

* Devarim (The words...) (Deuteronomy)

Oral Torah – Some authorities refute claims from Jews who believe that Moses was given additional "Oral Torah." Their view is based on a verse in *Exodus 24:3-4; "So Moses came and told the people all the words of the Lord and all the judgments. And all the people answered with one voice and said, all the words which the Lord has said we will do."* The Torah was in existence long before the creation of the earth and with each progressive Revelation of the Adamic, Abrahamic, Noahide, Sinai and Renewed Covenant, more truth became revealed each time. This verse refers to all the teachings that were to be recorded as an example of YHWH's historic dealings with man since the creation of Adam to His appearance at Sinai. The books of the Torah are demonstrative accounts that vehicle all the oral teachings to a generation that had become dependant on writing.

Nephilim (plural); Nephil – Though this is indeed a Hebrew word and definitely appears in the Authorized King James version as "giants" in *Genesis 6:4*, it *does not* necessarily mean men who are of enormous physical stature. The true definition of Nephilim is listed in Strong's as follows: "5303. Nephiyl, nef-eel'; or nephil, nef-eel'; from H5307; prop., a feller[*], i.e. a 'bully' or 'tyrant:'--giant." Though giant is tacked onto the end of the Strong's definition it does not mean a measure of physical size. It is meant here to be used in the same context as the phrase, "he's a *giant* in his field," meaning someone who dominates. For the true translation of the Hebrew word for giant see *rephaim*. Another common misconception is that Nephilim means "fallen ones." Though this is commonly believed, (mainly through the efforts of Zecharia Sitchin) no such meaning can be traced. This has arisen because of the assumption that the Anunnaki, whose offspring are referred to as "sons of Anak" *(Numbers 3:33)*, are also called Nephilim or giants. The word giant that appears in this verse is actually derived from the Hebrew word "gibbor," which means "renowned" or "champion." The name, Anunnaki, comes from an ancient Sumerian word that refers to, "those who from heaven to earth came." The Anunnaki themselves are in fact referred to in Scripture as the "sons of God," who where the fathers of those tyrants that were *generally* of large physical proportion. So ultimately it is the "sons of God" who are associated with being fallen. But again this sense of fallen being contained within the root of this title is unfounded. See *sons of God.*

Rephaim (plural); Rapha – This is a Hebrew word that means "giant." Strong's Exhaustive Concordance renders it as: "raphah {raw-faw'}; from 'rapha' in the sense of invigorating; a giant:--giant, Rapha, Rephaim(-s). See also 'Beyth Rapha,' meaning house of (the) giant; Beth-Rapha, an Israelite:--Beth-rapha. Raphah {raw-faw'}; probably the same as "rapha;" giant; Rapha or Raphah, the name of two Israelites:--Rapha."

Sons of God – The *Oxford Companion to the Bible* says: "The sons of God (or children of God; *'benē elohim'* and variants) are divine members of God's heavenly host...The title 'sons/children of God' is familiar from Ugaritic mythology, in which the gods collectively are the 'children of El'...The sons/children of God are also found in Phoenician and Ammonite inscriptions, referring to the pantheon of sub-ordinate deities, indicating that the term was widespread in the West Semitic religions."

The title "benē ha-Elohim" is Hebrew for "sons" or "children of God." – *Genesis 6:2a* "...The sons of gods *(benē ha-elohim')* saw the daughters of men that they were fair..."

The three most prominent views on the identity of the "sons of God" are:

1) They were fallen angels.

2) They were powerful human rulers.

3) They were godly descendants of Seth intermarrying with wicked descendants of Cain.

As I will demonstrate, the first view holds the most water. It rests calmly on the strength of several simple observations. The first is to remember that the Old Testament phrase "sons of God" always refers to the angels in *Job 1:6; "Now there was a day when the sons of God came to present themselves before the Lord, and Satan also came among them."* The second is the inclusion of Satan's former title and a rejoicing of the angels at the creation of the earth in *Job 38:7; "When the morning stars sang together, and all the sons of God shouted for joy?" Jude 6* also describes angels who came to inhabit the earth, when it refers to *"angels who...abandoned their own home."* The biggest stumbling block is people's lack of knowledge about angels within Scripture. Arguments that angels cannot interact physically with humans quickly lose ground as *Hebrews 13:2* and *Genesis 19:1-3* clearly describes them as being able to take normal human form. It also must be made clear that if angels were not built with or able to utilise the correct anatomy to have sexual relations with human beings, then why were the people of Sodom so keen on having sex with the two guests in Lot's house *(Gen 19:1-5)*? Finally, early Hebrew scribes are in agreement that fallen angels are referred to as the "sons of God" mentioned in *Genesis 6:1-4*.

The biggest problem with the other two possibilities of "sons of God" is that if ordinary human males married ordinary human females there would be no reason why most of their offspring would exhibit massive physical abnormalities and have predispositions to exert dominance. Why would YHWH decide to wipe out all flesh on the earth *(Gen 6:5-7)* when He had not previously forbidden powerful human males, or descendants of Seth, to marry ordinary human females or descendants of Cain?

The many different titles given to the sons of God make them a difficult subject to discuss when pointing out their frequency in Scripture. There is a definite indication of a division of fallen and unfallen sons of God. Evidence suggests that one of their titles, that of "the watchers," has been deliberately suppressed in later Bible translations. See *watchers*.

Watchers – The term "watchers" refers to a specific race of divine beings known in Hebrew as resh 'ayin, *'irin'* (resh 'ayin, *'ir'* in singular), meaning "those who watch" or "those who are awake." The

Greek translation is rendered, "Grigori," and means "those who watch", or "those who are awake," or "the ones who never sleep." Strong's describes the name that appears in *Jeremiah 4:16* as: "nat-sar, naw-tsar'; a prim root; to guard, in a good sense (to protect, maintain, obey, etc.) or a bad one (to conceal, etc.):- besieged, hidden thing, keep (-er, -ing), monument, observe, preserve (-r), subtle, watcher (-man)."

The interesting parallel here is that the Hebrew root for Nazarene (meaning, "watchman") is also "natsar," which seems appropriate because those who proclaim themselves as followers after the Nazarene sect are described in the New Testament as being made like the angels at the resurrection of the dead.

The specific activities of the watchers are recorded in the pages of pseudepigraphal and apocryphal works. Despite much conjecture by Christian scholars, these books originated from Jewish sources. They include such works as the Book of Enoch and the Book of Jubilees.

The watchers were originally sent to earth to observe and render assistance to early man at various levels, which were determined by YHWH. Some of these sons of God exploited there positions, possibly at the coaxing of Satan and began interacting with men autonomously. They procreated with humans and relayed vast reservoirs of information concerning the finer points of civilisation at a rate and magnitude that was forbidden by YHWH. The initial numbers of watchers that partook in this dissension was between two to three hundred.

The evil watchers that taught men the following disciplines were:

1) Armaros – Enchantment

2) Araquiel – Signs of the earth

3) Azazel – Knife-making, swords, shields, ornaments and cosmetics.

4) Baraqijal – Astrology

5) Ezequeel – Knowledge of weather

6) Gadreel – Weapons of war

7) Kokabel – Constellations

8) Penemue – Writing

9) Sariel – Cycles of the Moon.

10) Semjaza – Enchantments, root-cutting etc.

11) Shamshiel – Signs of the sun.

Men of Renown / Gibborim – The records of the Hebrews often contain references to individuals that were called gibborim (the singular is gibbor). A *gibbor* is a "mighty man" or "hero." A mighty man or hero merely represents the greatest potential of an individual and does not necessarily describe someone who is fundamentally good or evil. Indeed a Nazi who fought in WWII could have performed a heroic deed that resulted in the lives of several German civilians being spared. Yet at the same time he may have also occupied a position of some authority inside a death camp and carried out such duties with ruthless intent.

In Greek and western thought a "hero" is defined as someone who exerts autonomy, that is to say someone who takes complete control or charge of a situation. In the Greek story of Gilgamesh, the hero struggles against one or more areas that he can't control, such as human mortality. Through the course of the story he attempts to change his circumstance by challenging the gods. In contrast the Hebrew view of human autonomy, that is to say someone who takes complete control over his or her actions, was negative and it was the opposite, that of relinquishing of one's control to a higher power, which was viewed as a positive.

Pagan / Paganism – Currently the word pagan invokes the notion of referring to any religion outside that of Christianity, Judaism or Mohammedanism. To this effect it has been used within this work.

It has evolved from the word "pagus," which means, "something stuck in the ground," or "landmark" and its root "pag" means "fixed," "stake" or "pole." Gradually metaphorical usage caused it to mean "rural district" or "country dweller." When the Roman Empire rose to the height of its power it carried a reference to the title of "civilian," as in a "local non-military inhabitant." As the gap between what rural dwellers believed and practiced and what city dwellers believed and practiced widened, it began to have negative connotations. In Chapter Five of this work I make the statement that "paganism held an essential role in a Roman citizen's life." Though this may appear contradictory to its root definitions, it is used in the context of describing an ordered observance to another faith that does not acknowledge the core attributes of Christianity or Messianic Judaism. The option of using the term "heathenism" was not appropriate because it describes "non-religious" and "uncivilised people," which the Romans were certainly not.

Pseudepigrapha – Literally means "secret" or "hidden" works that are written under a "pseudonym." The word itself was first coined to refer to a considerably large portion of books that have never been considered as canon by any formal council. The implication is the books were supposedly written for a learned few and that they were all written under a fake name. These two characteristics were not the case for the majority of pseudepigraphal works and has done little more than discredit such works down through the ages.

Canon – The dictionary describes the word canon as "a decree of the Church; a general rule or standard, criterion; a list of the books of the Bible accepted as genuine; the works of any author recognised as genuine." Canonicity was often applied to books that rang with the self-vindicating authority of YHWH. The Old Testament prophets often used the phrase, "The word of the YHWH came to me," which was used as proof of the inspired authenticity of the work. Because of this reasoning the Book of Esther was almost relegated to pseudepigraphy because it never mentions the name of YHWH.

The precedent of authorship was often sought, and based on the understanding that Moses claimed to be a spokesman for YHWH. He is commonly believed to be the author of the majority of the books of the Torah. However there is little evidence to show that any of the character driven books of the Old Testament were also written by them. Passages like, "Moses was a humble man before

God," and "Moses died," present a stumbling block for those who think he was the only author of the first five books of the Old Testament. This is not to say that the subject could not have relayed the story to a set of scribes.

To gain acceptance, a particular book had to either have a prophetic or apostolic feel. For example Paul's message in *Galatians 1:1* was considered authoritative because of the pounding nature in which it opens: *"...not sent from men, nor through the agency of man, but through Jesus Christ, and God the Father..."*

Another rule of canonicity is that a book had to be consistent with previous revelation. John 3 and the Book of Revelation itself nearly also became pseudepigraphal for this reason.

The historic reality is that the major rule of canonisation was driven by racism, interdenominational rivalry, and political gain. The orthodox Jews failed to recognise books because they were written in Greek, The Catholics disregarded books because they sounded too Jewish and the Protestants ignored books because the Vatican accepted them. Though taking council is often encouraged within Scripture, the requirement of an ordered assembly to sanction what is and what isn't the Word of YHWH is not found within any canon or non-canon source. The more correct road is for people to embark on a journey of learning who YHWH is through their own enquiry rather than receiving a pre-packaged rule of thumb view of Him. Understandably the question then arises, "how do we recognise what is the Word of YHWH?" How does anyone recognise the word of YHWH, whether it is spoken, written, or implanted in one's spirit? The answer is through prayer, fasting, the testing of the spirit, and the council of others who are in the spirit.

The painful legacy of canonisation has caused the conditioned mind of the Christian to throw up an immediate wall of disregard for any book that sits outside the accepted books of the Bible. This is despite the fact that the average Christian and even some ministers are either ill informed or blatantly oblivious to the processes that led to the formation of books that make up the Bible today. The Word of YHWH described within Scripture as being "sharper than any two edged sword," is often confused with the written fallible translated word of men. The very nature of a canon council was to decide what books among already existing Scripture was to be accepted as or excluded from Scripture in the future. It also added additional rules and regulations for the believer, and decided what already established doctrines should be relaxed. With that in mind let's examine the following verse. *2 Timothy 3:16* says, *"all Scripture is given by inspiration of God, and is profitable for doctrine."* This was written prior to the formation of any canon council. Furthermore the 1901 American Standard Bible exhibits the verse in its more accurate rendering as: *"Every Scripture inspired of God is also profitable for teaching."* As you can see the addition of the word, "is," gives a false sense that all Scripture was given in a formalised manner by an ordained council.

When man first walked the earth in harmony with YHWH there was no need to write anything down. Every word from an earth bound being created in the image of YHWH Elohim contained power, was considered sacred, and was always remembered. This is why we will be judged on every word that has come from our mouths, even words said in jest. It wasn't until one of the watchers introduced writing that a new precedent was set for the written word's reliance, which was later solidified in stone tablets scribed in YHWH's very own hand.

Apocryapha – The following text addresses a series of common misconceptions regarding the authority of the Apocrypha. This information has been arranged against nine statements that vary in validity from great to not so great and nonetheless deserve answers. I do not, for a moment, wish to proclaim that I have irrefutable proof that these books are Scripture, yet I hope to encourage sceptics to be less dismissive of them in future. Neither do I hold that familiarity with them is a necessity, yet to disregard them without any more than passing hearsay is completely irresponsible. To discourage the reading of them as a rule of thumb is unacceptable as without them there is a vast chasm of time[19] unaccounted for between Malachi and Matthew. They serve at the very least as "profitable and good to read" (Luther) and an "example of life and instruction of manners…" (Hierome).

Here are eight statements, accompanied by my responses that I have no doubt whatsoever was written with the best of intentions.

---

19   Bear in mind that not all books in Scripture fit chronologically.

But we should be vigilantly aware that labourers with the best of intentions also pave the road to hell.

1. None of the Apocryphal writers laid claim to Godly inspiration.

Response: When obvious factors, like references from other approved books, did not exist, or were not specifically mentioned by Yahushua, other indications of authenticity were used. A common rule of whether YHWH inspired a text was drawn on the premise that the author laid such a claim within the text itself. Many books within Scripture are written in different styles and tailored to different audiences. Some are written boldly and some are written in a more humble manner. Many books that did not make obvious statements like, "the word of the Lord came to me..." or "I was in the spirit on the Lord's day," still maintained canon approval. Therefore where specific statements of Godly inspiration were not found, books that possessed an unmistakably divine message retained their standing within Scripture. Therefore statement number 1 must be disqualified as it calls into question existing approved Scripture.

2. The Apocryphal books were never acknowledged as sacred Scriptures by the Jews, custodians of the Hebrew Scriptures (the Apocrypha was written prior to the New Testament). In fact, the Jewish people rejected and destroyed the Apocrypha after the overthrow of Jerusalem in 70 AD.

Response: No historical evidence exists to support the notion that the Jews initially rejected the Apocrypha. On the contrary evidence exists to indicate otherwise. While certain sects may have taken it upon themselves to form a council that reviewed the relevancy of some works, this does not necessarily mean that all Jews rejected it. An excerpt from the preface to the Apocrypha in *The Septuagint with Apocrypha: Greek and English*, by Sir Lancelot Charles Lee Brenton (1807-1862) certainly endorses this view:

"The Alexandrian Jews possessed a sacred literature in the Septuagint translation, and where other works of the same national character were either written in Greek or translated from Hebrew, these also were appended to the sacred books which they before possessed. The writers of the early church, however, while expressly declaring their preference for the Hebrew canon, quote the books of the Apocrypha as of equal authority with the Old Testament."

Denouncing books based on an estimated time that falls outside a period when the majority of recognised texts where written, has no Scriptural basis whatsoever. There is nothing within the Bible to indicate that a specific period in history was exclusive to an outpouring of Godly inspiration for selected authors. I also find it difficult to see a defeated Jewish people in 70AD, having just been banished from their city, putting the burning of a collection of a books high on their list of priorities at that time. This assumes they saw some credibility in removing these so-called apostate books to another location to be destroyed. In addition, this unlikely scenario should be considered with the fact that the destruction of Scripture was a vocation most enjoyed by the "First Reich" of the Holy Roman Empire.

To reason that certain books were not accepted by the (non-messianic) Jews would also call into question all the books of the New Testament. If this line of reasoning was extended we lose everything from Matthew through to Revelation in the blink of an eye. So due to the fair process of judging all Scripture with equal measure this line of reasoning must also be disqualified.

3. The Apocryphal books were not permitted among the sacred books during the first four centuries of the Christian church (prior to corruption from the Roman Empire).

Response: During this period Christianity was in a state of confusion. With so many competing sects it is very difficult to pinpoint any stable ground of orthodox majority that may or may not have recognised them. This statement says that Rome's "corruption" hadn't commenced until the start of the fourth century, which is not historically correct. Most churches recognised the Apocrypha including the Greek and Russian Orthodox Church and Church of England (1611 KJV). In fact most early Bibles, including The Bishop's Bible and the 1560 Geneva Bible all contained the Apocrypha. Initially there was no distinction between the Bible and the books of the Apocrypha. *Volume 10 of the Ante-Nicene Fathers Scripture Reference Index* reveals that there was no initial distinction between these books and the rest of "the sacred books." Therefore statement number 3 is provisional at best.

4. The Apocrypha contains fabulous statements, which not only contradict the "canonical" scriptures but also themselves. For example, in the two Books of Maccabees, Antiochus Epiphanes is made to die three different deaths in three different places.

Response: The entirety of the known Bible at first glance contains contradictions of such magnitude that they literally steam roll over the above example. The phrase "fabulous" could easily be attributed to any number of fantastic feats described anywhere within Scripture. There are fabulous accounts of the earth's rotation ceasing, a man surviving three days within the stomach of a great whale, another man becoming a beast, and a donkey that talks. Remember that all those found unrighteous at judgment are destined to die twice. Running with this premise that the Apocrypha should be rejected because it contains "fabulous statements" will, if we maintain a standard rule of measure to judge all Scripture, equally see statement number 4 utterly disqualified.

5. The Apocrypha includes doctrines in variance with the Bible, such as prayers for the dead and sinless perfection. The following verses are taken from the Apocrypha translation by Ronald Knox dated 1954:

Basis for the doctrine of purgatory: 2 Maccabees 12:43-45, 2.000 pieces of silver were sent to Jerusalem for a sin-offering... Whereupon he made reconciliation for the dead, that they might be delivered from sin.

Salvation by works: Ecclesiasticus 3:30, Water will quench a flaming fire, and alms maketh atonement for sin.

Tobit 12:8-9, 17, It is better to give alms than to lay up gold; for alms doth deliver from death, and shall purge away all sin.

Magic: Tobit 6:5-8, If the Devil, or an evil spirit troubles anyone, they can be driven away by making a smoke of the heart, liver, and gall of a fish...and the Devil will smell it, and flee away, and never come again anymore.

Mary was born sinless (immaculate conception): Wisdom 8:19-20, And I was a witty child and had received a good soul. And whereas I was more good, I came to a body undefiled.

General Response: A close analysis of these verses and comparing them with other more extreme examples of Old Testament Scripture render them tame in comparison. Pursuing these lines of reasoning, we can deduce that Yahushua condones self-mutilation as he suggests the amputation of hands and the plucking out of eyes if they cause us to sin.

Basis for the Doctrine of Purgatory Response: There are plenty of verses within existing canon approved Scripture that have been examined within the course of this work that can also be twisted to prove the false doctrine of purgatory. For example, Yahushua ministering to the dead spirits can be used with greater effect to prove this false doctrine.

Salvation by Works Response: This is in keeping with existing Old Testament dialogue that simply supports a giving heart as fruit of one's faith that leads to salvation.

Magic Response: Early Jews often practiced burning the heart, liver and gall of fish to ward of evil spirits as described in the Book of Tobit.

Mary was Born Sinless (Immaculate Conception) Response: From the following verse critics derived the notion that Mary was sinless. *Wisdom 8:19-20, And I was a witty child and had received a good soul. And whereas I was more good, I came to a body undefiled.* It is more likely that the use of the term "defiled" denotes an absence of any human male seed entering her body prior to Jesus' birth, rather than her never putting a foot wrong in anything she ever did.

6. It teaches immoral practices, such as lying, suicide, assassination and magical incantation.

Response: All the above elements are themes throughout the Bible, yet there is a vast difference between teaching them and showing these practices for what they really are. For example **Genesis 6:4** at first glance appears to have "son's of God," which sound like angels of the heavenly host, entering into sexual unions with human females.

Using the same rule of measure to judge accepted Scripture, which is usually given the benefit of the doubt, the following immoral practices are also evident:

1) Abraham lied to Abimelech and Pharaoh (Genesis)

2) Saul had priests of YHWH killed by Doeg the Edomite (1 Samuel)

3) Jephthah sacrifices his daughter to YHWH (Judges)

4) Levite has a concubine (Judges) as well as King David (1,2 Samuel and Chronicles)

5) Tamar becomes a harlot and is impregnated by Judah (Genesis)

6) Lot impregnates his daughter

7) Judas commits suicide two different ways (Matthew, Acts)

8) Paul mentions baptizing the dead (1 Corinthians)

Therefore statement number 6 must be disqualified.

7. No Apocryphal book is referred to in the New Testament whereas the Old Testament is referred to hundreds of times.

Response: This statement begs the question; does the New Testament refer to every single other book in the Old Testament? The answer is no. In addition the Bible contains over 18 references to other books apart from the Apocryphal books that were never included in Catholic canon law. The 1560 Geneva Bible, which has the Apocrypha, contains cross-references to these books in both the New and Old Testament. Prior to 315 AD, early church fathers referred to the Apocrypha over 352 times. (This can be checked in volume 10 of the Ante-Nicene Fathers Scripture Reference Index.) Paul refers to many verses that are contained throughout the Apocrypha and any claims that the New Testament never refers to it without thorough knowledge of both sources cannot be relied upon. A statement of the above nature must be qualified in terms of specific or general references. Certainly themes within the Apocryphal works are echoed elsewhere within the accepted canon of Scripture countless times.

8. Because of these and other reasons, the Apocryphal books are only valuable as ancient documents illustrative of the manners, language, opinions and history of the East.

Response: This final statement that sums up the guilty verdict gives the impression that this is another argument to the books when in fact it is a conclusion.

Anti-Semitic Comments by Prominent Church Fathers:

The following is a collection of quotations by prominent church fathers that blew my socks off. Where possible I have attempted to respond to them using Scripture.

"Many, I know, respect the Jews and think that their present way of life is a venerable one. This is why I hasten to uproot and tear out this deadly opinion. I said that the synagogue is no better than a theatre...the synagogue is not only a brothel and a theatre; it also is a den of robbers and a lodging for wild beasts..." – **St. John Chrysostom (344-407AD)**

Response: Nowhere in Scripture was there ever a teaching to cease meeting together in a synagogue and commence meeting in a pagan "Temple of Circe" (Church). Temple prostitution was a characteristic of pagan temple worship and was never tolerated within a synagogue whose male and female occupants were segregated anyway. Yahushua attended a synagogue, not a church! The word church was later added to the Scriptures over more appropriate terms such as "congregation," "assembly" and "gathering."

"For if we are still practicing Judaism, we admit that we have not received God's favour...it is wrong to talk about Jesus Christ and live like Jews. For Christianity did not believe in Judaism, but Judaism in Christianity." – **Ignatius, Bishop of Antioch (98-117AD)**

Response: The Scriptures say in *Romans 11:18; "do not boast against the branches. But if you do boast, remember that you do not support the root, but the root supports you."* This is why Yahushua says, *"salvation is of the Jews." (John 4:22)* NOWHERE, and I mean NOWHERE in Scripture do you find the phrase salvation is of the Gentiles!

"We too, would observe your circumcision of the flesh, your Sabbath days, and in a word, all your festivals, if we were not aware of the reason why they were imposed upon you, namely, because of your sins and the hardness of heart. The custom of circumcising the flesh, handed down from Abraham, was given to you as a distinguishing mark, to set you off from other nations and from us Christians. The

417

purpose of this was that you and only you might suffer the afflictions that are now justly yours..." – **Justin Martyr (135-161AD)**

Response: (Regarding circumcision of the flesh) The circumcision of the heart is a Torah teaching that originally appeared in *Deuteronomy 10:16; "Therefore circumcise the foreskin of your heart, and be stiff-necked no longer."* The circumcision of the heart is not a New Testament teaching that replaced flesh circumcision. Paul disputed the teaching of the flesh circumcision because it sent fear into the heart of the Gentiles and obscured the heart felt motive that should initiate it. Indeed circumcision, on its own, is worth nothing *(1 Corinthians 7:19)* without the circumcision of the heart that must precede it. Never is the act of circumcision described as an affliction, nor is it ever specifically required for Jews only. In fact circumcision is a seal of righteousness! *Romans 4:11; "And he (Abraham) received the sign of circumcision, a seal of righteousness of the faith..."* Paul also describes physical circumcision as profitable if the recipient keeps the law (Torah) and as unprofitable if the recipient abandons the law (Torah) *(Romans 2:25)*.

(Regarding Sabbaths) Nowhere in the Scriptures are any Sabbaths given as a burden. On the contrary, they were given as rehearsals and object lessons, which are to be a believer's delight *(Isaiah 58:13)*! The Commandment to keep the Sabbath throughout all generations *(Exodus 31:13)* was given to the Hebrews and the foreigners (Egyptians) who dwelt among them at Mount Sinai. *Leviticus 18:26; "You shall therefore keep My statutes and My judgments, and shall not commit any of these abominations, either any of your own nation or any stranger who dwells among you."* Watch a Sunday keeping Christian try and explain their way out of this one the next time you hear them say that the Commandments were just for the Jews. As a final note apply *Isaiah 56:3b,* which says, *"To the eunuchs who keep My Sabbaths and choose what pleases Me."* And then *Isaiah 56:6,* which says, *"Also the sons of the foreigner who join themselves to the Lord (YHWH), to serve Him, and...Everyone who keeps from defiling the Sabbath."*

"We may thus assert in utter confidence that the Jews will not return to their earlier situations for they have committed the most abominable of crimes, in forming this conspiracy against the Saviour of the human race...hence the city where Jesus suffered was necessarily destroyed, <u>the Jewish nation was driven from its country, and another people was called by God to the Blessed election.</u>" – **Origen of Alexandria (185-254AD)**

Romans 11:1-2a; "<u>I say then, has God (YHWH) cast away His people</u>? Certainly not! For I am also an Israelite, of the seed of Abraham, of the tribe of Benjamin. <u>God (YHWH) did not cast away His people whom he FOREKNEW.</u>" YHWH never once speaks of a newly chosen people that have replaced the former ones. Surely neither the Gentile nor the Samaritan could be these "other people" when we read statements from Yahushua like this one in *Matthew 10:5; "Do not go the way of the Gentiles, and do not enter a city of the Samaritans."* Any foreigners or strangers who follow YHWH (through the example of Yahushua) are "grafted in" or "joined" to Israel. *Isaiah 56:3; "Do not let the son of the foreigner who has joined himself to the Lord (YHWH) <u>speak saying, "The Lord (YHWH) has utterly separated me from his people</u>..."* Origen's statement is a perfect example of the emergence of "replacement" or "supersessionist" theology. Paul who was an Israelite *(Romans 11:1)* and a lover of the law (Torah) *(Romans 7:22)* only identifies with the Gentile for the purpose of provoking his own people to jealousy, because of their acceptance of Yahushua as Messiah *(Romans 11:13,14)*.

"How hateful to me are the enemies of your Scripture! How I wish that you would slay them (the Jews) with your two-edged sword, so that there should be none to oppose your word! Gladly would I have them die to themselves and live to you!" – **Saint Augustine (354-430AD)**

Response: As this above statement does not address anything biblical I am at a loss to apply the bandage of Scripture to it.

Let's sum this up with some memorable words from the great Protestant Reformer, **Martin Luther (1483-1536)**: "In sum, they (the Jews) are the devil's children, damned to hell...The Jews got what they deserved."

And then followed Hitler. Who will be next....Schwarzenegger?

Bibliography

Alnor, M. William (1998)	*UFO CULTS and the New Millennium*
Augustine	*Confessions Chapter XI*
Baigent, Michael / Leigh, Richard	*The Inquisition*
Barrar, Francis Edward (1999)	*In Defence of the King James Version*
Beachham & Bauder (2001)	*One Bible Only? Examining Exclusive Claims for the KJB*
Benner, A Jeff (2003)	*His name is One* (Virtual Bookworm.com)
Berliner, Don (1995)	*UFO Briefing Document*
Bivin, David / Blizzard Jr., Roy	*Understanding the Difficult Words of Jesus* (revise edition)
Boese, Alex (2002)	*The Museum of Hoaxes*
Bonwick, James	*The Highest Alter: The story of Human Sacrifice*
Boulay, R.A. (1999 Edition)	*Flying Serpents and Dragons*
Bramley, William (1989)	*Gods of Eden*
Canon Law Society (1983)	*Code of Canon Law, Latin/English edition*
Changeux, J.P. / Connes, A.	*Conversations on Mind, Matter and Mathematics,* Princeton University Press, 1995, p. 10
Childress, David Hatcher (2000)	*Technology of the Gods – The Incredible Sciences of the Ancients*
Cullmann, Oscar	*Christ and Time (London: SCM, 1962 3rd edition)*
Cook, Nick (2001)	*The Hunt For Zero Point*
Cook, Terry L. (1996)	*The Mark of the New World Order*
Cooke, Patrick	*The Greatest Deception*
Cornwell, John (2000)	*Hitler's Pope* (Penguin Books)
Cross, F.L. & Livingston E.A. ed.	*The Oxford Dictionary of the Christian Church*
Crossman, William (1999)	*Last Writes: Previewing the Reasons Why Written Language Will Become Obsolete by 2050*
Daniken, Erich von (1969)	*Chariots of the Gods*
Deyo, Stan (1982)	*The Cosmic Conspiracy*
Deyo, Stan (1989)	*The Vindicator Scrolls*
Elizabeth Clare Prophet (2000)	*Fallen Angels and the Origins of Evil*
Enrique, Florescano (1999)	*The Myth of Quetzalcoatl* (The John Hopkins University Press Baltimore and London)

Foxe, John (2001 edition)	*Foxe's Book of Martyrs*
Freke, Timothy & Gandy, Peter	*The Jesus Mysteries – Was the Original Jesus a pagan god?* (2000)
Gertoux, Gerard	*The Name of God Y.eH.oW.aH Which is Pronounced as it is Written I_Eh_oU_Ah – Its Story* (University Press of America)
Ginzberg, Louis (1956)	*Legends of the Bible* (Abridged edition of Legend of the Jews)
Graham, Billy (1975)	*Angels – God's Secret Agents*
Graham, Billy (1979)	*The Holy Spirit*
Graves, Kersey (1875)	*The World's Sixteen Crucified Saviours*
Hargis, David (1993)	*The Tallit: Garment of Glory* (Virginia Beach, VA: Star of David)
Harrison, Everett F. (1973 Edition)	*Baker's Dictionary of Theology*
Hill, Paul R. (1995)	*Unconventional Flying Objects – A Scientific Analysis*
Icke, David (2001)	*Children of the Matrix* (Bridge of Love)
JETP, vol 68 page 439	*Soviet Physics*
Jones, Ann Madden (1995)	*The Yahweh Encounters: Biblical Astronauts, Ark Radiation and Temple Electronics*
Jones, Rick (1995)	*Understanding Roman Catholicism* (Chick Publications)
Kaplan, Rabbi Aryeh (1979)	*In the Handbook of Jewish Thought*
Keel, John (1970)	*Operation Trojan Horse*
Keel, John (1975)	*The Mothman Prophecy*
Keith, Jim	*Mind Control, World Control*
Knight, Christopher / Lomas	*The Hiram Key* (1997)
Koster, C.J. (2004)	*Come Out Of Her My People*
Lancelyn Green, Roger (1965)	*Myths of the Norsemen*
Laurence, Richard (1883 Edition)	*The Book of Enoch The Prophet*
Little, Paul E. (1986 Edition)	*Know What You Believe*
Malcolm, South (1987) p.303.	*Mythical and Fabulous Creatures*
Marrs, Texe (1996)	*Circle of Intrigue*
McGrath, Alister (2001)	*In The Beginning (The story of the King James Bible)*
Michael J. Harner (1973)	*Hallucinogens and Shamanism*
Moortgat, Anton (1969)	*The Art of Ancient Mesopotamia* (New York: Phaidon)
Moseley, Dr.Ron (1996)	*Yeshua – A Guide to the Real Jesus and the Original Church*
Narby, Jeremy (1999)	*The Cosmic Serpent – DNA – And the Origins of Knowledge*
Natsis, Carol (1995)	*Reader's Digest / Almanac of the Uncanny*
Netzger & Coogan (1993 edition)	*The Oxford Companion to the Bible*

Oates, David & Joan (1976)   *The Rise of Civilization / Making of the Past Series*

Orr, James MA., D.D., (1978)   *The International Bible Encyclopaedia*

Pearsall, Judy – Editor (2001)   *Concise Oxford English Dictionary* (10th Edition Revised)

Quayle, Stephen (2002)   *Genesis 6 – Giants / Master Builders of Prehistoric and Ancient Civilizations*

Ratner, Dan & Mark (2003)   *Nanotechnology and Homeland Security: New Weapons for New Wars*

Ratzinger, Cardinal J. (1994)   *Catechism of the Catholic Church (Australian edition)*

S. Acharya (1999)   *The Christ Conspiracy – The Greatest Story Ever Sold*

S. Acharya   *Suns of God – Krishna Budda and Christ Unveiled*

Simpson, J. & Roud S. (2000)   *Dictionary of English Folklore* (Oxford)

Sitchen, Zecharia (1990)   *Genesis Revisited* – Is Modern Science Catching up with Ancient Knowledge?

Strassman, Dr. Rick   *DMT – The Spiritual Molecule*

Streiber, Whitley   *Communion*

Strong, James LL.D., S.T.D.   *The New Strong's Exhaustive Concordance of the Bible* (Nelson)

Smith, R. Barry (1996)   *Better than Nostradamus*

Swanson, Richard A. M.D. (1999)   *Hurtling Toward Oblivion*

Swartz, Tim   *The Secret Journals of Nikola Tesla HAARP – Chemtrails and the Secret of Alternative 4* (Global Comm.)

Temple, Robert (1998 edition)   *The Sirius Mystery*

Tesla, Nikola / Editor: Childress   *The Tesla Papers* (2000 Adventures Unlimited Press)

Tupper Saussy, F.   *Rulers of Evil – Useful Knowledge About Governing Bodies*

Vacca, Roberto / Whale, J.S.   *The Coming Dark Age* (1974) (Garden City NY: Anchor Books p.6)

Walker, Williston (1918)   *A History of the Christian Church*

White, Lew (2002 / 4th Edition)   *Fossilized Customs – The Pagan Sources of Popular Customs*

Wilson, Dr. Clifford   *Crash Goes the Exorcist...Where the Exorcist failed*

Wilson, Ian (1985)   *Jesus – The Evidence* (Pan Books)

Wilson, Marvin R. (1989)   *Our Father Abraham – Jewish Roots of the Christian Faith*

Woodrow, Ralph (1966)   *Babylon Mystery Religion*

Zangla, Dominick (1998)   *Jewish Roots – Part One Shofar & Prayer Shawl*

Bibles – The Authorized King James Bible (The complete multimedia Bible)
Compton's New Media
The New International Version
The New King James Bible
Cambridge University Press Bible
1611 King James Version (Hendrickson Publishers)
The Complete Jewish Bible – Translated by David H. Stern (JNTP)
The Scriptures – Institute of Scripture Research (1998)
Restoration Scriptures (True Name Edition) Study Bible
(Second Edition)
The Hebraic-Roots Version – James Scott Trimm
The New Covenant Paleo Signature Edition (PDF) –
Published by The Remnant of YHWH
The Emphatic Diaglott (Containing the Original Greek Text)
New Testament – Dr. J.J. Griesbach

Apocryphal Works – The Apocrypha of the Old Testament – Revised Standard
Edition (1957)
The Book of Enoch the Prophet – Translated by Richard Laurence
(1883 edition)
Prayer Book – ArtScroll Transliterated Linear Siddur (Weekday) –
Rabbi Nosson Scherman (1998)
The Daily Telegraph 13th Feb 2002 (pg33) Article – *"Technology that's ready to get under your skin"*
The Daily Telegraph 25th March 2002 (pg 32) Article – *"Future wars: the invisible soldier"*
The Daily Telegraph 18th January 2005 Article – *"Chipping in for Drinks"*
Jane's Defence Weekly July 24, 2002 Article – *Exotic Propulsion: Air Power Electric* – by Nick Cook
Dr. C. Truman Davis Article – *"A Physician Testifies About the Crucifixion"*
The Times of India – April 8, 1999 – *"The Vimanas" or Flying Machines of Ancient India* – by Mukul Sharma
Creation Magazine – June / August 1998 – *The Original 'unknown' god of China* – by Ethel Nelson
"Ceremony of Introduction and Extreme Oath of The Jesuits" excerpt –
The Engineer Corpse of Hell by Edwin A Sherman, page 118 as quoted by
Dr. Alberto Rivera Romero from the book, *Double Cross.*
Excerpt from the book, *"The Legends of the Jews,"* Volume 1, by Louis
Ginzberg.
"Surveillance Technology," 1976: policy and implications, an analysis and
compendium of materials: a staff report of the Subcommittee on
Constitutional Rights of the Committee of the Judiciary. United States
Senate, Ninety-fourth Congress, second session, p 1280, US GOV DOC Y
4.J 882:SU 7/6/76.

Internet Sites Sourced:
http://www.konnections.com/Kcundick/crucifix.html
http://s8int.com/dinolit1.html
http://www.angelfire.com/or/mctrl/
http://www.datafilter.com/mc/operational.html

"List of Giants in the Bible" acquired from "Bible Prophecy for the World Today," located at:
http://www3sympatico.ca/bibleprophecy/WebPage2/giants.htm

About the Author

Shabnam and Jason Jordan

Jason Jordan is an independent researcher, who after becoming disillusioned by the lack of biblical adherence by mainstream church practices, became motivated to embark on a journey back down the evolutionary timeline of Christianity and expose observances that are either surplus or a hindrance to salvation. Having no formal training or tertiary education in theology, ancient history, archaeology, languages, science, biology, or physics, Jason came to be fascinated with these subjects and began to note that all of them appeared to have areas of suppressed and misdirected information. In addition, his research began to note a common association with all these disciplines and the study of ufology.

He lives with his wife in New South Wales, Australia.

823333

Made in the USA